PRAISE FOR CREATING REGIONAL WEALTH

"Humanity needs places where people have a common vision and develop together creativity, modern innovation, quality of life, and humanism. This book will help."
— Pierre Laffitte
Senator, France

"Provides valuable insights and pragmatic advice for anyone interested in improving the economic well-being of a region and adopting an entrepreneurial mindset. Conveys the spirit, knowledge, and courage of leaders in all sectors of the economy."
— Henry C. Manayan, Esq.
Mayor, City of Milpitas, California

"A comprehensive/commendable compilation of the experiences of the entrepreneurial spirit across cultures."
— Pradeep Kar
Microland Group, India

"A must-read for anyone interested in building ecosystems of excellence and economic advancement in any region or country. Truly invaluable."
— Kailash C. Joshi, Ph.D.
President, TiE Silicon Valley

"A most important and stimulating contribution to the new leadership agenda for further development of intellectual capital of regions as the driver for future regional wealth and prosperity."
— Leif Edvinsson, Professor
*Associate, of Intellectual Capital, University of Lund, Sweden
and CEO of Universal Networking Intellectual Capital, Sweden*

"Which regions will prosper and how are they positioning themselves today for tomorrow's opportunities? A thoroughly researched and stimulating work, a sort of strategic manual for companies, scientists, and regional politicians."
— Dr. Hans Christoph von Rohr
Chairman, Industrial Investment Council, Berlin, Germany

"This is a great book for those who want to find out what powers regional developments. A good read for anybody interested in this subject."
— Hermann Hauser, Ph.D.
Founder and Director, Amadeus Capital Partners, Cambridge, United Kingdom

"An important contribution to the field with clear and practical findings for investors, business leaders, and policymakers."
— David J. Blumberg
Managing Partner, Blumberg Capital, San Francisco, CA

"The successful transformation of the Irish economy over the last decade has surprised even those within the social partnership process who contributed to its delivery. This is a well-researched account of how it happened."
— David Begg
General Secretary, Irish Congress of Trade Unions

"Well researched and engagingly presented. An excellent work on a timely topic."
— Cheryl Fragiadakis
*Technology Transfer Department Head,
Lawrence Berkeley National Laboratory (U.S. Department of Energy)*

"An insightful inquiry into the sources of innovation and entrepreneurship that determine global and regional leadership in today's knowledge-based economy."
— R. Sean Randolph
President, Bay Area Economic Forum

"Presents a jointly optimizing global perspective. Should be valuable for people in all regions to understand how to succeed in the high-tech Innovation Economy."
— George Lin
President, SEMI Asia-Pacific

"This book balances the varied but complementary perspectives of management and research issues. The Israeli chapters are especially important since they enable the readers to learn about one of the fastest-growing high-tech regions."
— Dr. Avi Fiegenbaum
Director of the MBA Program, Technion University, Israel

"Excellent lessons for knitting the core strengths of a region into a compelling and saleable value proposition. Filled with entrepreneurial insights."   — Shirley Horn
Senior Director, Brand Management, Agilent Technologies, Inc.

"I strongly recommend this book to everyone involved in creating, developing, and sustaining a dynamic entrepreneurial marketplace, be it in an emerging market or an industrialized country. Based on research and interviews with top experts around the world, the book provides a real 'tour de force' of the key success factors."
— Jyoti Gupta
Professor of Finance at ESCP-EAP University, Paris

"This book very succinctly brings out the challenges that the Internet age poses and the tremendous response of the industry, particularly of the Indians in Silicon Valley."
— Rajendra Abhyankar
former Consul General of India, San Francisco

"A superbly lucid analysis of the world's information technology hot spots. This book is a veritable traveller's guide to the global Information Economy."
— Dr. Shyam R. Chidamber
Director, Center for Information Technology and the Global Economy,
Kogod School of Business, American University, Washington D.C.

"For anyone responsible or interested in regional development, this is a gold mine!"
— Jerome S. Engel
Executive Director, Lester Center for Entrepreneurship and Innovation,
University of California at Berkeley

"This thoughtful book goes a long way to explaining the Silicon Valley mystique and how other parts of the world are following the model with varying degrees of success and localization. This will be a textbook for some, a reference for many, and a fun read for all of us working in the high-tech industries."   — George Koo
Director, Chinese Services Group, Deloitte & Touche

"Valuable insight for both practitioners and researchers in emerging IT markets."
— Shyam Sethi
Consultant, Technical Services & Visiting Faculty, IIT Delhi

"An excellent piece of research work reflecting the essence of globalization based on convergence of new ideas, thoughts, knowledge base, and innovativeness on an international plain."   — Abhijit Halder
Consul of Community Affairs of the Indian Consulate, San Francisco

"An excellent book about the regional high-tech clusters that have emerged around the globe. The book is very insightful and stimulating. It is a must read for anyone who wants to understand emergence of a place like Bangalore."
— Kanwal Rekhi
Founder of Excelan, Co-Founder of TiE (The IndUS Entrepreneurs)

CREATING
Models,
REGIONAL WEALTH
Perspectives,
IN THE
and
INNOVATION
Best Practices
ECONOMY

ISBN 0-13-065415-9

90000

9 790130 654150

FINANCIAL TIMES PRENTICE HALL BOOKS

For more information, please go to www.ft-ph.com

Dr. Judith M. Bardwick, PhD
Seeking the Calm in the Storm: Managing Chaos in Your Business Life

Thomas L. Barton, William G. Shenkir, and Paul L. Walker
Making Enterprise Risk Management Pay Off:
How Leading Companies Implement Risk Management

Michael Basch
CustomerCulture: How FedEx and Other Great Companies Put the
Customer First Every Day

J. Stewart Black and Hal B. Gregersen
Leading Strategic Change: Breaking Through the Brain Barrier

Deirdre Breakenridge
Cyberbranding: Brand Building in the Digital Economy

William C. Byham, Audrey B. Smith, and Matthew J. Paese
Grow Your Own Leaders: How to Identify, Develop, and Retain
Leadership Talent

Jonathan Cagan and Craig M. Vogel
Creating Breakthrough Products: Innovation from Product Planning
to Program Approval

Subir Chowdhury
The Talent Era: Achieving a High Return on Talent

Sherry Cooper
Ride the Wave: Taking Control in a Turbulent Financial Age

James W. Cortada
21st Century Business: Managing and Working
in the New Digital Economy

James W. Cortada
Making the Information Society: Experience, Consequences,
and Possibilities

Aswath Damodaran
The Dark Side of Valuation: Valuing Old Tech, New Tech,
and New Economy Companies

Henry A. Davis and William W. Sihler
Financial Turnarounds: Preserving Enterprise Value

John R. Nofsinger
*Investment Madness: How Psychology Affects Your Investing…
And What to Do About It*

Tom Osenton
*Customer Share Marketing: How the World's Great Marketers Unlock
Profits from Customer Loyalty*

W. Alan Randolph and Barry Z. Posner
*Checkered Flag Projects: 10 Rules for Creating and Managing Projects
that Win, Second Edition*

Stephen P. Robbins
The Truth About Managing People…And Nothing but the Truth

Jeff Saperstein and Daniel Rouach
*Creating Regional Wealth in the Innovation Economy: Models,
Perspectives, and Best Practices*

Eric G. Stephan and Wayne R. Pace
*Powerful Leadership: How to Unleash the Potential in Others
and Simplify Your Own Life*

Jonathan Wight
Saving Adam Smith: A Tale of Wealth, Transformation, and Virtue

Yoram J. Wind and Vijay Mahajan, with Robert Gunther
*Convergence Marketing: Strategies for Reaching
the New Hybrid Consumer*

FINANCIAL TIMES

Prentice Hall

In an increasingly competitive world, it is quality
of thinking that gives an edge—an idea that opens new
doors, a technique that solves a problem, or an insight
that simply helps make sense of it all.

We work with leading authors in the various arenas
of business and finance to bring cutting-edge thinking
and best learning practice to a global market.

It is our goal to create world-class print publications
and electronic products that give readers
knowledge and understanding which can then be
applied, whether studying or at work.

To find out more about our business
products, you can visit us at www.ft-ph.com

Pearson
Education

CREATING
Models,
REGIONAL WEALTH
Perspectives,
IN THE
and
INNOVATION
Best Practices
ECONOMY

Jeff Saperstein | *Dr. Daniel Rouach*

FINANCIAL TIMES
Prentice Hall

An Imprint of PEARSON EDUCATION

Upper Saddle River, NJ • New York • London • San Francisco • Toronto • Sydney
Tokyo • Singapore • Hong Kong • Cape Town • Madrid
Paris • Milan • Munich • Amsterdam

www.ft-ph.com

A CIP catalogue record for this book can be obtained from the Library of Congress.

Production editor and compositor: *Vanessa Moore*
Cover design director: *Jerry Votta*
Cover design: *Nina Scuderi*
Interior series design: *Gail Cocker-Bogusz*
Manufacturing buyer: *Maura Zaldivar*
Executive editor: *Tim Moore*
Editorial assistant: *Allyson Kloss*
Marketing manager: *Bryan Gambrel*
Full-service production manager: *Anne R. Garcia*

 © 2002 Pearson Education, Inc.
Publishing as Financial Times Prentice Hall
Upper Saddle River, New Jersey 07458

Prentice Hall books are widely used by corporations and government agencies for training, marketing, and resale.

For information regarding corporate and government bulk discounts please contact:
Corporate and Government Sales (800) 382-3419 or corpsales@pearsontechgroup.com

Other company and product names mentioned herein are the trademarks or registered trademarks of their respective owners.

Printed in the United States of America
10 9 8 7 6 5 4 3 2 1

ISBN 0-13-065415-9

Pearson Education LTD.
Pearson Education Australia PTY, Limited
Pearson Education Singapore, Pte. Ltd.
Pearson Education North Asia Ltd.
Pearson Education Canada, Ltd.
Pearson Educación de Mexico, S.A. de C.V.
Pearson Education—Japan
Pearson Education Malaysia, Pte. Ltd.

To our wives and children

Chantal, David, and Michael
Elisheva, Jonathon, Yael, and Yuval

CONTENTS

LIST OF TABLES

FOREWORD

By Mary Harney TD
Deputy Prime Minister and Minister for Enterprise,
Trade and Employment of Ireland

Despite the recent economic downturn, there is little doubt that the "New Economy" in the form of knowledge-based enterprises competing in a global marketplace will continue to be the mainspring of economic growth and the opportunity for increasing living standards into the future. Therefore, a rigorous examination of the factors that enable regions to create wealth and compete in the global economy through successful adaptation to the New Economy is to be welcomed.

We in Ireland are very conscious of the fact that our recent economic growth has been largely driven by the high-technology sector, which has provided both a significant increase in employment and very high productivity growth rates. The U.S. has been the source of much of our investment in these sectors and, indeed, Silicon Valley has provided the model and inspiration for many of our successful indigenous high-tech companies.

The major lesson that we in Ireland have learned, as a small open economy, is that the only constant is change and that the flexibility to respond to it is the key to achieving and maintaining success. I believe that such flexibility is best fostered through:

- Policies that promote openness not just to trade and investment but above all to ideas
- Investment in education
- The promotion of a research, technology, and innovation ecosystem that is the basis for developing high value added goods and services
- A fiscal regime that encourages enterprise and innovation

While it is clearly not possible for a region to just replicate a standard model of successful high-tech regions it is possible to learn from the underlying factors in their success and consider how they can be adapted to meet the needs of regions with different histories and stages of development. This publication therefore raises many important questions for policymakers in both developed and developing countries and regions to ponder.

PREFACE

By 2003 there are expected to be 650 million worldwide users of the Internet. Yet, in this same world it is estimated that two billion people have never made a phone call.

The digital divide between wealthy and poor regions of the world is astounding. Yet, there may be hope that rapid adoption of the Internet and what we call the Innovation Economy (IE) in an expanding number of regions in the world may be able to change this daunting divide.

Creating Regional Wealth in the Innovation Economy: Models, Perspectives, and Best Practices is a guide to understanding how regions and businesses are successfully profiting from this dynamic change through the perspectives of those "entrepreneurial champions," who are improvising new strategies, organizations, and programs.

There is an Innovation Economy, based on the entrepreneurial application of innovative technology, linking regions, and creating great wealth. These regions are successful because individual champions in business, venture capital, universities, government, and nonprofit organizations are collaboratively working and adapting to this Innovation Economy. This book provides their perspectives to help others to better understand and succeed.

This book written is for anyone concerned with these kinds of questions:

- *"Where is the right place to be?"(For companies and individuals.)*
- *"What are some of the most important principles and practices that have enabled regions to make successful adaptations in the IE?"*
- *"How can regions with different geographic, socioeconomic and political/institutional structures succeed in 'plugging in' to the IE, utilizing their own particular strengths?"*
- *"What lessons can be learned that can help develop new regions for economic development by those who are involved directly with regional and business development?"*

- *"Why are some regions attracting much greater foreign direct investment (FDI) and how can businesses ranging from start-ups to multinationals best plug into a successful region?"*

Departing from the hundreds of recent business books documenting the successes of the California region Silicon Valley, *Creating Regional Wealth in the Innovation Economy* examines and illustrates successful principles and examples from several world-class regions. You get the benefit of in-depth perspectives of people who are leading the way in government, business, universities, and NGOs (non-government organizations). This is truly a global book — with expert perspectives and focus on success factors from nine regions, which represent a breadth of geographic and circumstantial diversity.

As important, the regions and organizations we've modeled have discovered ways to adapt to the IE, illustrating varying approaches to success. We have also included resources and Web sites the reader can access for more detailed information on subjects of specific interest. For Web site links go to *www.creatingregionalwealth.com* or *www.creatingregionalwealth.net.*

There are obvious omissions of great dynamic markets that are major players in the IE such as Boston, Seattle, and Austin in the U.S.; Finland; Japan; and Singapore to name just a few. The authors selected the markets we and our colleagues knew with the hope that these would provide sufficient examples to assist other regions in the world. So, the selected regions do not indicate a ranking of importance relative to other world-class high-tech regions. The regions are:

- Silicon Valley, California
- Ireland
- Cambridge, England
- Munich, Germany
- Sophia Antipolis, France
- Sweden
- Israel
- Taiwan
- Bangalore, India

The authors define and illustrate some of the principles that have enabled each of these regions to succeed, by focusing on several key factors in each region.

We wrote this book with several principles in mind:

- There is an IE (Innovative Economy — linked regions based on an entrepreneurial application of innovative technology), which despite great market upheaval and temporary market contractions, will continue to grow and rapidly evolve.

- Successful regions and companies have discovered ways to create great wealth and competitive advantage. These lessons can be learned and adopted by other regions.
- This growth, which is inexorable, will create opportunities for new regional wealth based on technology, globalization, and deregulation.
- There are new business and job-sharing work models emerging in the IE. Countries/regions are competing both for investment from multinational companies and the development of home-grown, niche-small businesses, and market opportunities which are worldwide focused.
- Rather than one model for what was called the New Economy, such as is commonly referred to in Silicon Valley, California, there are multiple models that are based on unique local advantages and utilize different competitive strengths from regions. Different regions can provide different offerings in the IE. For example, India provides engineers and programmers for the world; Israel provides new technology product and service ideas in communications; while Ireland excels in attracting foreign direct investment for use of its knowledge industry work force.
- You can both better understand and apply the knowledge gained of how different regions, through the perspectives of highly successful people in those regions, have developed ways to successfully adapt to the IE. Their insights and practices, based on their own socioeconomic and market environments, provide the great value of this book. While each market model may differ from the other, they work in combination to create an integrated global economy that is more inclusive than exclusive.

We highlight significant changes in the dynamics of the following fields and disciplines, through selected focus on examples in each of the markets:

- Technology and knowledge transfer
- Human resources management and flexible labor relations
- Marketing and positioning of companies and regions
- Venture capital, risk management, and investment
- Government role (national, state, and local)
- Formal networking/linking organizations, business associations, and philanthropies
- The role of educational institutions as sources of knowledge workers, new business ideas, and as incubators for start-ups

We also highlight the cultural factors directly affecting the success of these disciplines and approaches:

- The openness of a society for change and receptivity to new ideas and integration of different peoples

- Free and open social and business networks
- The role of "knowledge worker immigrants" in certain regions such as Silicon Valley and Israel
- Proximity of like-minded individuals and complementary businesses and institutions which create the right habitat for innovative technology
- A regional capacity for speed and flexibility for change, which is consistent with the nature of the technology-driven marketplace

We illustrate through excerpts of conversations with those who are on the front lines of change in business, education, and government how to create regional wealth. We also provide case studies to illustrate some of the success stories in these regions. We have tried to transmit the wisdom of these different individuals in their own words, using their own idioms and examples. Hopefully, we have captured their exuberance and passion as well as their insights. Each gave freely of their wisdom in the hope that their experience could help others. In that respect they are all our true collaborators in this endeavor.

For every region, we enlisted the assistance of professors and colleagues who were native to that country in the hope that we would provide a truer "flavor" and veracity for the dynamics of the region profiled.

Rather than replicate Silicon Valley, California, each of the regions and companies we profile here have utilized Silicon Valley principles and created their own models to leverage their particular competitive advantage. Through their examples, others can learn how to develop their own methods to define a technology strategy that works for them.

This book should help the reader to better understand how the dynamics of the IE have been harnessed for making regional wealth. Our hope is that through the wisdom and insight of remarkable people, across a broad array of cultures and economic circumstances, who are discovering, innovating, and creating the success stories of our era, this regional wealth creation will be shared.

The authors invite you to visit their Web site at *www.creatingregionalwealth.com* and *www.creatingregionalwealth.net* for more information and links to the many organizations' Web sites mentioned in this book.

ACKNOWLEDGMENTS

We would like to thank Russ Hall, who read through the manuscript in its many stages and always improved it; Corinne Gregory, who made several useful suggestions that we incorporated into the book; and Tim Moore, who sped this book through the publication process and always encouraged us.

There are many people who contributed their time, talents, and energy to this project, whom we wish to acknowledge.

The group of experts, who contributed their written work:

- Thierry Picq, prof. of human resources management, E.M. LYON, France
- Leslie Shaw, prof. of negotiation, ESCP-EAP Paris, France
- Li Chun, vice president of Otto Capital based in Singapore and Taiwan

We are grateful to Mary Harney, deputy prime minister of Ireland, for her gracious contribution of the foreword and the example she sets for entrepreneurial government leaders everywhere.

Special thanks also to Shirley Horn, Kailash Joshi, Davidi Gilo, Lester Thurow, and Jacques Attali for their continuous support, time, and energy.

We would like to acknowledge Ruth Croke in New York, and give special thanks to Ted Kahn, Satyendra Dhingra, and Steve Ellinghuysen.

Our thanks to our assistants Philip Heimann and Arti Kuthiala, who devoted so much to the project. Also special thanks to Lara Sao Pedro for her diligent work and Patrice Santi for all his efforts.

Thanks to our teams in San Francisco and Paris, to whom we owe much.

- San Francisco: Aurora Hadijat, Ramneeta Kochar, Jocelyn Miller, Kim Sakaue, Maggie Sattosanti, Roxanne Schwartz, Sandy Yao.
- Paris: Birte-Janine Fehse, Celine Nelen, Biljana Maksimovic, Faustino Obeso, Robert Specterman, Nicola Campbell, Solenn Caradec, Ilka Gischewski, Julia Townsend, Pascal Rosenfeld, Florence Brière, Anouck Chazelas, Roopam Le Berrigaud, Jeremy Benamara.

Daniel Rouach would like to thank ESCP-EAP, and especially Jean-Louis Scaringella, dean and general director of ESCP-EAP, Jérôme Bon, deputy director of ESCP-EAP, Alain Chevalier, dean of faculty at ESCP-EAP, and Elisabeth Tissier-Débordes, associate dean for research, for authorizing a sabbatical year that enabled him to invest the time and energy for this book.

Special thanks also to Jyoti Gupta, for the valuable contributions to the India chapters of this book.

For their special contributions, Daniel would like to thank his students from the Kellogg Recanati University International Executive MBA program in Tel Aviv; those from the High Tech Management School, Ecole Leven; and those from Technion - Israel Institute of Tecnhology.

Jeff Saperstein, Mill Valley, California   •   *Daniel Rouach*, Paris, France

INTRODUCTION

We developed the idea for this book based on our collaboration to educate ESCP-EAP (European School of Management sponsored by the Paris Chamber of Commerce) MBA students about the New Economy. Together, we launched a program combining a seminar with transporting the students from Paris to Silicon Valley to hear the perspectives of what we are calling "entrepreneurial champions," who were actively working in the high-tech economy.

We were very impressed by the speakers' insight and candor. The participants were gratified by both the presentations and the "give and take" question and answer periods with the speakers.

Ironically, the speakers, who were all very busy and only committed to half-hour presentations, would inevitably stay much longer because the opportunity *to tell the story* of how their organizations were part of the New Economy that was transforming business practices was gratifying for them as well. So, we learned that highly placed and active players in a region would be enthusiastic to speak about transformations in their market, and to share their insights in how to be successful.

This book is our attempt to replicate and expand that process by providing the reader with some of the principles and changed practices, through the perspectives of worldwide entrepreneurial champions, to help understand the dynamics of the Innovation Economy (IE).

We have selected regions that are varied in size, success, geography, and focus in the IE. These are markets we knew best and for which we had access to highly placed individuals. So this effort is not an attempt to be either comprehensive or evaluative of regions for inclusion. However, when taken together, these nine markets, are representative of the trends, and important areas of focus about which regions, companies, and individuals who wish to successfully plug into the IE should become knowledgeable. We do not evaluate or rank one region over another. Our thesis is that they are all linked and create value and wealth together in a way never before possible. While some of these regions have been more successful than others in generating wealth and opportunity for their people, the people we have selected each have important lessons to teach. In conversations with these regional champions, we have been impressed and humbled by the way these individuals demonstrated initiative, intelligence, and a "can-do" attitude that is quite extraordinary. Collectively, they are a vanguard in utilizing technologies to create wealth for themselves, their industries, and their regions.

This begs a question that is implicit in all of our study. There are regions of the world which to date have been left out of this extraordinary economic transformation. Much of Africa, the Middle East, Eastern Europe, Latin America, and Asia are not major players in the IE. In the global struggle subsequent to the events of September 11, 2001, the issue of making regional wealth becomes even more critical to world stability. The overarching regional characteristics that we heard over and over again are that attitude, culture, and societal structure are major factors that determine success in the IE. We hope that these factors will continue to spread throughout the world so the wealth creation will be more equitable.

Here is a personal story to illustrate how that process can happen. It is written in a style that we will replicate throughout the book with the dozens of profiles we have documented. Each person will be named and their comments will be excerpted and edited so they tell their story or insights with their own style and idioms.

AUTHOR'S PERSPECTIVE

The power of globalization to change the world: extending the classroom

Each semester I teach marketing courses at San Francisco State University's Graduate School of Business. Most of the students are foreign nationals who come to learn American business practices, so they can apply them in their home countries.

The case study method of free and open exploration of problems and opportunities in specific business situations is a proven way to bring marketing and management principles to life. I frequently gain insights from the discussion of case studies with my students. Their insights sometimes reveal greater significance than just the solutions to a business issue. Living and studying in a free-spirited, ever-changing, and cosmopolitan region such as the San Francisco Bay Area frequently helps to transform these students. Many want to go back to their home countries and change their world. These lessons then extend the classroom to many regions and societies.

Here is an example of one of them . . .

Competition can set you free

I introduced a video case study and a *Wall Street Journal* article on the MTV phe-nomena and how it had swept the globe, capturing the attention and discretionary funds of teens everywhere. The students' attention perked up as we discussed the worldwide appeal to teens of MTV and their emergent demand for products such as Levi's jeans and Nike athletic shoes. I posed the question as to whether this was creating a universal solidarity based on music and teen identity or whether it was American cultural imperialism. Was this a good thing for Chinese and Thai teens and their societies?

The discussion was lively. A young mainland Chinese woman named Szeyuan spoke up for the first time in my class. She said it was a good thing that Chinese young peo-ple could now buy Levi's and Nike in China. She explained that the Chinese govern-ment has never had to compete for anything in China. Maybe if they compete with Levi's for jeans, then they will have to compete for other things as well.

After two or three years of graduate business school, Szeyuan and thousands of other foreign students who attend our universities will go back and demand funda-mental changes in the way their countries and economies are managed. In some small but significant way, through the globalization of business education, we are bringing the world closer together. This is not so everyone feels the need to wear Nike or Levi's, or to use American technology. Rather, because the creation of regional wealth, at its best, helps to initiate the successful businesses and organiza-tions that provide people with the opportunity to make choices about how they wish to pursue happiness and enhance their lives. ■

— *Jeff Saperstein*

In the academic year ending in June 2001, there were almost 550,000 foreign students attending U.S. colleges and universities, with nearly 11% coming from China alone. These students were trained and acculturated in American attitudes and practices. Most will return to their native countries and many will become a powerful influence in the creation of regional wealth. This cross-cultural transfer of knowledge and best practices is driven by both universities and multilocation corporations.

Through the perspectives of successful entrepreneurial champions, who have actively helped to create wealth in their regions, we profile multinational and start-up companies, regional and local governments, venture capital sources, educational institutions, and incubators to illustrate these principles in action across a broad array of cultures and economic circumstances.

We will synthesize their management wisdom and experience through extensive interviews focusing on the success factors that have leveraged their regional competitiveness in the IE. Our hope is that their wisdom and exam-ples will provide a deeper understanding of the changes this economy is bringing and the opportunity for other regions of the world and businesses to profit from what they have learned and done.

ABOUT THE AUTHORS

JEFF SAPERSTEIN is a well-respected marketing instructor, writer, and consultant to government, product, and service companies and NGOs. He has extensive contacts with Silicon Valley companies and business associations, and hosts tours for MBA students to meet with Silicon Valley entrepreneurs, venture capitalists, and multinational company executives.

He is the coauthor of *How to Be a More Effective Account Manager* (with Len Gross and John Stirling, Kentwood Publications, 1989), and *Practical Approaches to Impromptu Speaking* (with Frederick Isaacson, Kendall-Hunt, 1988). Jeff has written marketing columns for the *San Francisco Business Times* and the *San Jose Business Journal*.

Jeff has conducted marketing workshops for *ADWEEK* (trade publication for the advertising industry) throughout the U.S. He has taught marketing courses to business professionals throughout Latin America, France, and Israel. He is an instructor at San Francisco State University Graduate School of Business where he teaches marketing. He is also an instructor at the University of California at Berkeley Extension and the Stanford University Professional Development Program. He teaches a course in marketing and high technology at ESCP-EAP European School of Management in Paris.

DR. DANIEL ROUACH is strategy professor at the ESCP-EAP European School of Management based in Paris, Oxford, Berlin, and Madrid, and previously dean of the full-time MBA of the school. He is an international expert lecturer in the fields of international technology transfer, innovation, and competitive intelligence management. In addition, Daniel manages the ESCP-EAP GTI lab, the ESCP-EAP research center specializing in technology transfer and competitive intelligence. He also has managed corporate education programs, participated in executive training programs, and has been a consultant on projects for many high-technology organizations.

Daniel has actively researched and published in his expertise fields for several years. He has also created and edited numerous case studies in the context of his Ph.D. thesis on the management of international technology transfers with application in Eastern Europe. Daniel also specializes in Israeli-related topics and has written various books and articles on the Israeli economy.

His educational background includes a Doctorate de Gestion (equivalent to a Ph.D. in management) from Université de Lyon III, an MA from Université des Sciences Sociales Grenoble, an MBA from E.M. LYON, and an International MBA from York University Toronto. He has served on the faculty of the E.M. LYON as a senior research fellow in international business and international technology transfer.

DR. LESLIE J. SHAW, an Irish citizen resident in France, is an economist by training and holds a Ph.D. from the University of Dublin, Trinity College. A former supplier account manager at the Irish Electricity Supply Board, he now designs and runs workshops in intercultural negotiation at ESCP-EAP European School of Management in Paris.

DR. THIERRY PICQ, professor of human resources management at E.M. LYON, a leading French business school, teaches both students (master's in management and MBA) and executives in the fields of organizational behavior, team management, and project management.

Thierry was previously a consultant in the largest French consultancy company, Bossard/Gemini Consulting (for five years in Paris, and one year in Geneva), where he carried out many projects in organizational change and management development for large French and international companies.

In 1999, Thierry spent a year in Silicon Valley, as a visiting professor at San Francisco State University, doing research on human resource evolution trends. He published a book and several articles in both professional and academic reviews about high-tech firms management practices. Thierry has a Ph.D. from the Université of Grenoble.

LI CHUN has more than nine years of working experience, including heading a European private equity investment firm in Asia, management consulting with Gemini Consulting, and project management with Mobil Asia Pacific. He has an MBA from INSEAD, and a BEng (Electrical Engineering, Honors) from the National University of Singapore.

PHILIP HEIMANN studied management at ESCP-EAP European School of Management in Paris, Oxford, and Berlin. He has worked for the consulting firm A.T. Kearney and is currently preparing his doctoral thesis on linking corporate and regional innovation systems. Philip currently resides in Berlin, Germany.

ARTI KUTHIALA holds a bachelor's degree in applied psychology from Delhi University in India. She has worked for the United States Chamber of Commerce and the San Francisco Global Trade Council. Arti is currently pursuing a master's degree in business administration at San Francisco State University, where she is also collaborating on numerous projects with the Ohrenschall Center for Entrepreneurship.

PATRICE SANTI is consultant and research associate at ESCP-EAP. He has collaborated on a wide variety of research projects in the fields of competitive intelligence and technology transfer, resulting in the production of case studies and articles. In addition to his academic activities, he has undertaken numerous field projects in marketing and competitive intelligence. He has also managed binational studies, notably including a study on France-Israel key complementary technologies. Patrice is a graduate of ESCP-EAP, where he received his European Master's in management in 1995.

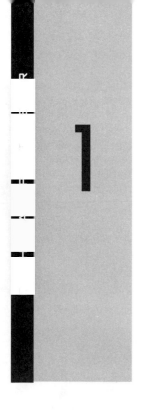

THE INNOVATION ECONOMY

T ake a look around you. Most of us live our everyday existence in routines that acquire a familiar rhythm. Our homes, transportation, work, and activities with friends and family seem to continue much as they always have. Sure, we might own a hand-held device and find it more useful than a paper pocket calendar. Many of us check in with e-mail and find both the expanded access to people and the quickened speed of communication convenient. These technologies that we as individuals see and experience do not appear to be either radical or life-changing. *Yet, the convergence of innovative technologies, being introduced and integrated in certain world regions with a rapidity never seen before, will dramatically change the way we live, work, and relate to one another. It will also provide opportunities for generating regional wealth in new ways that we are just beginning to understand.*

Think about the advances in medicine and healthcare, based on the integration of technology with international research and development in the life sciences that may extend the typical human life span over the next several generations to biblical ranges of 100 to 120 years.

Consider product and service development that operates 24 hours a day, 365 days a year, and relies on integrated teams who defy the accepted workday routine and have groups in San Jose, California; Bangalore, India; Herzliya, Israel; and Dublin, Ireland, all working to accelerate innovation to spawn new industries, products, services, and business opportunities.

One of the long-term significant changes at the turn of this millennium is the rapid expansion of a phenomenon called the "New Economy." We prefer to call it the Innovation Economy, because at the core of the new wealth being created is the rapid acceleration of change through innovation. This Innovation Economy is being developed with the combination of financial capital and what the Swedish theorist Leif Edvinsson calls "intellectual capital": the ever-expanding knowledge resource that lies at the core of producing new wealth.

This Innovation Economy is largely driven by the intersection of technological innovation, globalization, and deregulation.

Technological innovation is identified most closely with the Internet, but is not exclusively defined by it. Satellites, telecommunications, biotechnology, advances in microchip technology and applications embedded in products, digital technology, optics, and major breakthroughs in renewable and portable energy are all integrating elements of this rapidly changing environment. In this Innovation Economy, rapid innovations in these categories have begun to create wealth and economic advantage for businesses and regions, which have adapted to the principles of this rapidly changing marketplace. This phenomenon may have revolutionary implications in the shifting of economic advantage and power among regions. Those who "plug in" (that is, invest in the education and skills of their people as the greatest resource for wealth) will thrive. Those regions not developing the intellectual capital of their people, and whose institutions of government, industry, universities, and non-government organizations are dysfunctional, as in much of Latin America, the Arab Middle East, and Africa, will continue to decline.

Sir Peter Hall, author of *Cities in Civilization*, provides a useful perspective on the transition from an industrial to an informational era.

PETER HALL

There are four elements, all technologically driven. The first is the development of a new infrastructure of communication, commonly called the Internet, and its probable successor, the information superhighway. The second is the increasing interconnectivity of different electronic machines — telephones, computers, faxes, modems — both in terms of numbers of connections, and the bandwidth of connections. The third is perhaps the most fundamental: the fact that almost all information is becoming digital. The fourth is the development on this basis of new applications — the so called killer applications that will constitute the new basic industries of the information age.[1] ■

The fast-growing Innovation Economy is not a fantasy. It is largely driven by massive amounts of investments in innovative information technology. The United States has been the primary driver of this investment, enabling U.S. financial markets, governments, and corporations to cut costs and increase flexibility and efficiency. The result is long-term faster growth and lower inflation.

Table 1-1 illustrates the dramatic difference in cumulative annual growth rates (CAGR) between the total and the Internet segment of the U.S. economy.

TABLE 1-1   The New Internet Economy

	1995	1999	CAGR GROWTH
U.S. GDP	$6,762 b	$7,801 b	3.6%
Internet Economy	$5 b	$507 b	213%

Source: Center for Research in Electronic Commerce, University of Texas.

This dynamic is even more dramatic in smaller countries such as Ireland, which has seen 9% to 10% growth in GNP from 1995–2000. The Irish have figured out how to adapt to the new economy and are emulated by small regions throughout the world. Smaller nations, such as Ireland, Israel, and Taiwan, tend to have the most global orientation because these countries acquire goods, services, and capital not easily generated domestically.

But just throwing money at technology is not enough. To translate technology into faster productivity growth, financial markets have to be able to fund innovation, provide more flexibility in corporations and labor markets, create a faster pace of deregulation, and increase competition. In addition, the roles of national and local government, industry associations, higher-education institutions, and emergent linking/networking organizations will make a critical difference in the ability of a region to accomplish these needed changes to effectively integrate into the worldwide Innovation Economy.

KNOWLEDGE WITHOUT BORDERS

Globalization of the work process happens through technology. This is key to understanding how swiftly the world is changing. New industries and companies are being created based on international operations linked by technology. Alongside this, a new class of knowledge entrepreneurs who are international in background and business perspective is emerging.

One such example is Davidi Gilo, CEO of DSP Communications. Headquartered in Cupertino, California, DSPC's engineers are in Israel and its customer base is in Japan. In October 1999, DSPC was acquired by Intel Corp. to be run as a subsidiary. DSPC signal processing technology originated through the Israeli military and is useful in answering and dictation machines.

DAVIDI GILO

The high-tech revolution is significantly different from the industrial revolution. When you talk about the global economy or technology, the model may involve, for example, product definition and innovation from the United States, engineering and development efforts could be done in Europe, and manufacturing could be performed in the Far East perhaps. So in that sense, it's very, very different, because a certain level of knowledge is moving from here to Israel, enabling the engineer to design the product, and then on to Japan, enabling them to make the product.

Now you have multinational companies opening offices in Israel and other places. They move people from location to location, who then return to Israel. And while they're here, they learn a lot of the discipline and the technology that they later on employ back in Israel. We live in a very mobile world today and you can see this phenomenon; it's very good, because that's how knowledge, product development, and marketing ideas get transferred between people and help young companies become more successful.

People in Israel who work on a major project at Intel get the same training as they would in Santa Clara. So basically a company like Intel, Texas Instruments, or IBM that has research centers in Israel operates on a global basis. Every multinational company doing business in different countries and using the same standard that made them successful in those countries helps bring the professionalism from engineering, management, and marketing, which is very significant.

When you have American companies setting up in other countries, then they are tapping human resources, which can be very good. It can be cheaper. The Internet, networking, and optic technology enable you to transfer files in a few minutes. Technological innovation enables all these things to happen. This is huge! ∎

DEREGULATION AND GREATER RISK ARE REQUISITES TO REGIONAL PARTICIPATION

Investment in innovation is risky, which creates great anxiety and doubt. Certainly, the recession of 2000–2001, the meltdown of the dot-com industry, and the economic roller-coaster ride in core industries such as telecommunications and semiconductors are just a few of the major calamities that have shaken world confidence in the "New Economy" model. Deregulation by nations to open up their markets and industries to international competition is a necessary condition for participation in the global economy. But as evidenced by the recent default on its huge national debt by Argentina, and the bankruptcies of leading large multinational corporations such as Enron and Global Crossing, deregulation sometimes leads to much greater instability. When fraud, corruption, and mismanagement go unchecked, companies that expand too quickly are also more prone to spectacular failures. But the price of the quest for regional riches seems to be to accept the risks of a U.S.-style freewheeling economy with its huge uncertainty and gyrations of boom and bust built into the high-tech–driven economy.

This globalization, deregulation, and attendant risk is not always enthusiastically received. Many see this as Americanization and a new form of economic imperialism. Indeed, it is quite threatening to the established order. François Mitterand, the late President of France, said, "France does not know it, but we are at war with America. Yes, a permanent war, a vital war, a war without death. Yes, they are very hard, the Americans — they are voracious, they want undivided power over the world."[2]

Speed: A Most Valuable Currency

Speed to product development and market is driving the Innovation Economy and changes the way we work and evaluate success. This is one of the reasons the role of federal, state, and municipal government becomes far more critical to regional success for wealth creation. Government can either slow down or speed up the process of business. It can provide the necessary infrastructure and resources, so technological innovation can thrive. Government investment in educational institutions, technology parks, and transportation, combined with enlightened regulatory policies, can enable regions to respond strategically to a fast-changing marketplace, attract multinational corporate investment, and nurture start-up businesses.

Regionalization of the Innovation Economy

Hot spots for innovation all over the world present an historic opportunity for new career paths for individuals and strategic directions for companies, regions, and countries to participate in a global economic revolution, which is now just at its inception.

Peter Hall suggests that throughout history, technological innovation has always been developed in regions that share very similar characteristics. His observations are reinforced through the perspectives of the "entrepreneur champions" in the regions we profile.

PETER HALL

These regions are characterized not by an abundance of fixed resources, but rather by a set of developed social and cultural structures that are favorable to conceptual advances. They may be old, established, cosmopolitan, liberal, metropolitan cities, but are often emerging city regions that serve as entrepots (intermediary centers) between the already-developed world and a frontier beyond it. Their economies are expanding rapidly through imports of goods from that developed world; and they have a high rate of immigration, predominantly of young people, who are highly experimental and untraditional in their outlook. They have strong but often very informal structures for exchange of technical knowledge and conceptual ideas. There is a constant search for the novel. Levels of synergy, not only between like-minded individuals but also between quite disparate socio-economic-cultural groups, are very high; this is the archetype of an open society.[3] ■

UNIVERSAL ADOPTION OF ENGLISH AND FREE ACCESS TO INFORMATION IS TRANSFORMING THE WORLD

A major issue for the creation of regional wealth at this stage of the Innovation Economy is the use of English as the universal language for knowledge workers everywhere. Israeli-born Davidi Gilo suggests that English is the international language of engineers; there is now a mobile world of business in which there is work being conducted 24 hours per day, seven days a week, by programmers and engineers in Silicon Valley, Israel, India, Taiwan, etc. Peter Hall observes that even in Continental Europe, the common language of young Europeans is now English. English-speaking regions, workers, and enterprises have an enormous advantage of being able to access the largest pool of knowledge workers worldwide.

At the same time, freedom of information and perspectives, and the promise of commercial egalitarianism threatens established regional and cultural ways of thinking. During this period of tension arising from the struggle with Islamic fundamentalist terrorism, this aspect of the Innovation Economy takes on even greater significance.

Consider what effect this has on India. Kailash Joshi, President of the Silicon Valley chapter of TiE (The IndUS Entrepreneurs), suggests that one of the reasons the Indian government has been moving to open its markets and eliminate, or at least diminish, the bureaucracy and corruption that have so impeded India's economic development, is that Indians now have access to international broadcasts such as CNN and BBC, as well as a host of indigenous private TV channels. At last, they know how others live and are governed. Joshi believes the popular movement to cut Indian bureaucracy and corruption is inexorable, because the "genie of information is out of the bottle." The government can not hide its own ineptitude and must meet the rising expectations of the people.

Global business and entrepreneurial opportunity accelerate the removal of regulatory barriers between countries and regions. The threat is a great expectation for change that is difficult to implement.

But we are just at the beginning of this change. The implications for the regions of the world to not only catch up, but to adapt, change, and apply these technologies in their own way as part of a greater whole worldwide experience is one of the most exciting parts of the Innovation Economy promise. Every country need not develop its own wine industry, but can import from Europe, California, Chile, Australia, or other regions better suited for wine cultivation. In the same way, *every region does not have to graduate all its own programmers and engineers (India can best do that), nor develop from scratch its own mobile telecommunications industry (Finland and Sweden can best do that), nor develop all its own high-tech R&D (Silicon Valley, Germany, and Israel can best do that), nor set up manufacturing foundries and fabs for the semiconductor industry (Taiwan can best do that).*

The Innovation Economy dynamics of rapid technological innovation combined with globalization and deregulation will continue to grow, despite the fits and starts of market capitalization bubbles bursting and whole sectors of the Innovation Economy being disrupted.

While beginning as a primarily American experience that seems exported, we believe the Innovation Economy will become even more multifaceted, diverse, and integrated. The hope and promise of this Innovation Economy is that countries and regions of the world, both developed and developing, will all benefit from the application of technologies to increase wealth and improve the quality of life for people everywhere.

ENDNOTES

1. Peter Hall, *Cities and Civilzation*, Fromm International: New York, NY, 2001, p. 945.

2. Conrad Black, "Britain's Atlantic Option—and America's Stake," *National Interest* 55 (Spring 1999), pp. 21–22

3. Peter Hall, *Cities and Civilzation*, Fromm International: New York, NY, 2001, p. 302.

SILICON VALLEY
THE MAGNETIC FORCE

Perhaps no region has captured the imagination of the world quite like Silicon Valley, California, has. Just as the '49er gold miners stampeded to San Francisco 150 years ago to pan for gold, hundreds of thousands of young, ambitious people flocked to Silicon Valley in the mid to late 1990s to become part of what seemed the modern-day Silicon Valley gold rush. But the hype of quick wealth has receded now. The triple hammer blows of the meltdown of the Nasdaq stock market and the dot-com industry, the electrical energy crisis in 2001, and the aftereffects of the September 11, 2001, tragedy have brought hard financial reality back to the region.

However, Silicon Valley was not a flash in the pan success story. It has weathered several such economic meltdowns before, and the resilience of the high-tech industry in "the Valley" will continue as long as there is a demand for innovation through the applications of technology. Silicon Valley has shown the most extraordinary resilience to bounce from wave to wave of continuous innovation. It continues to be a magnet for bright, entrepreneurial people from everywhere.

Sir Peter Hall, professor of planning at University College in London and author of *Cities in Civilization*, is no foreigner to California and Silicon Valley. He is also professor emeritus of city and regional planning at University of California at Berkeley. He shared the following observations with us about America and how Silicon Valley is a quintessentially American phenomenon, yet also notes how similar the Valley's development is to other innovative regions throughout history.

PETER HALL

America still remains unlike any other country in that the culture is based on immigration, and the U.S. continues to keep it's doors open. One result is the mix of people in Silicon Valley — people who have gone where the action is. American culture — California culture — is special. This incredible openness of California culture allows people to enter, especially if they speak English. Even if they don't speak English, they somehow still integrate fairly quickly.

What we have seen throughout history is that city-regions proved to be extraordinarily innovative and thus productive. The striking parallel I found is between Lancashire in the 1770s, at the time of the first industrial revolution, and Silicon Valley since the 1950s. The two regions are about the same size, intensely networked, with innovations taking place everywhere, and cooperative, competitive relationships among these different people. Similarly, Glasgow in the 1800s grew on the strength of steamships as part of the then globalization of the world. So, I found this principle of intense networked innovation to be true of all periods in history. ■

So, Silicon Valley is entering a new phase of its regional development, functioning much as a great incubator for research and development and the hub of a network of technological innovation linked to every other high-tech region of the world.

2 GLOBAL ENTREPRENEURS AND MARKETING OF MULTINATIONAL COMPANIES

Silicon Valley has become a geographic metaphor for the Innovation Economy. Yet, it is a relatively small geographic area comprising Santa Clara County and adjacent parts of San Mateo, Alameda, and Santa Cruz counties, with a population of more than 2.5 million people. While the city of San Francisco, located 20 miles north of Silicon Valley, is a worldwide cosmopolitan attraction, Silicon Valley actually has triple the population of San Francisco, with average population growth rates of between 10% to 15% in its counties over the 10 years between 1990 and 2000. San Jose, the largest city in Silicon Valley, increased its population by over 14% during the 1990s, passing San Francisco in size, and is a far more dynamic market than its better-known neighboring city. The term "Silicon Valley" has become generic for worldwide regional technology environments or habitats, all plugging into the global high-tech economy.

Silicon Valley combines all of the elements we have discussed as emblematic of the emerging regional networks, with a world-class educational institution (Stanford University), a high concentration of venture capital and risk management, an entrepreneurial spirit, highly skilled immigrants, and companies and linking associations that support each other in a regional network.

TABLE 2-1 Facts at a Glance — Silicon Valley

Population	2.5 million
Number of jobs	1.35 million
Exports	$35.2 billion, accounting for 34% of California's non-agricultural exports
Number of technology-based companies	7,000
Amount invested by venture capitalists in Silicon Valley companies in 2000	Almost $17 billion
Average investment	$17.7 million, almost double the average investment in 1999 ($9.6 million)
Average wage in 1999	$66,400 (+9% vs. +2% in U.S. overall)
Software	The fastest-growing category of new jobs, with an average wage of $125,000
Earnings of highest paid 20% of households	An average $149,000
Adult education attainment	88% at least high school graduate, 42% at least bachelor's degree
Foreign born	35% of residents compared with 10% foreign born in the total U.S. population
Ethnic composition	48% white, 24% Hispanic, 24% Asian/Pacific islander, 4% African American
Annual growth of jobs	3% to 5% over the last seven years
Percentage of work force in high-tech industries in Silicon Valley	40% (double the norm of the same industry clusters in the greater San Francisco Bay Area)
Commuters going into Santa Clara County to work	20% of work force

Sources: Joint Venture's 2001 Index of Silicon Valley (www.jointventure.org/resources/2001Index/2001home.html); United States Census 2000 (www.census.gov).

A PLAYGROUND FOR SKILLED KNOWLEDGE WORKERS

One of the reasons Silicon Valley continues to be a "magnetic field" for highly skilled technology workers is that it has industry clusters of interdependent firms that can cross-pollinate projects, people, and ideas. This enables workers to move from project to project, company to company, or venture to venture with great ease, while continuing to earn large salaries.

Another very important indicator for regional wealth creation is value added, or productivity per employee. In the year 2000 individual productivity increased by 7% to $127,100 on average per employee, compared with the U.S. average of $60,800. This extraordinary productivity is attributed to the integration of technology into the workplace as well as the long hours employees tend to work in Silicon Valley. Cisco exemplifies this integration by incorporating the Internet into nearly every facet of its operations. The company claims that its productivity per worker in 1999 was a staggering $688,000. By integrating the Web into its operations, Cisco saved an aggregate $825 million for the whole company through increased efficiency.

Figures 2-1 through 2-3 illustrate the extraordinary premium paid to knowledge workers in Silicon Valley relative to salaries in the rest of the U.S. (see Figure 2-1). This salary premium is accompanied by a corollary differential in increased productivity (value added) per worker in Silicon Valley relative to the U.S as a whole. The historic productivity differential will probably ensure continued premium salaries in Silicon Valley into the near future.

Growth of the average annual wage in inflation-adjusted terms indicates job quality. From 1999 to 2000, the estimated average wage in Silicon Valley grew 9.2% while the national average increased 2%. The Valley's average wage is 84% above the nation's average.

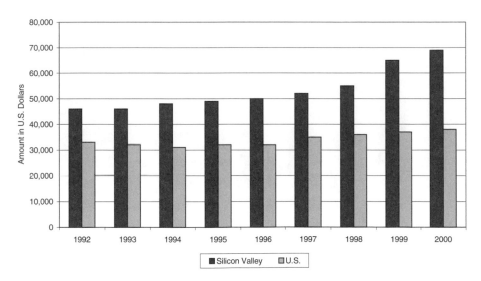

FIGURE 2-1 Average wage per employee, 1992–2000.
Source: *Joint Venture's 2001 Index of Silicon Valley.*

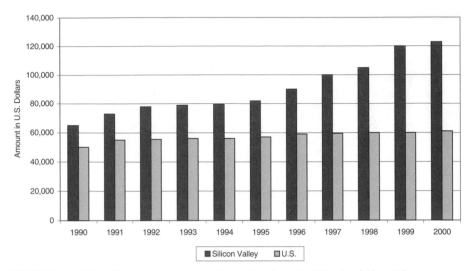

FIGURE 2-2   Value added per employee overall. Source: *Joint Venture's 2001 Index of Silicon Valley.*

As shown in Figure 2-2, the value added per employee overall has increased over the 1990s, and the differential between Silicon Valley and the rest of the U.S. has been increasing.

As shown in Figure 2-3, the value added by Silicon Valley clusters is higher than that of their national counterparts. This is especially pronounced in computers, semiconductors, software, and innovation services.

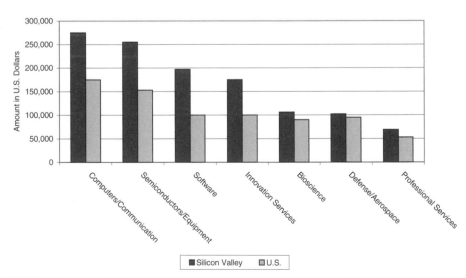

FIGURE 2-3   Value added per employee by cluster, 2000. Source: *Joint Venture's 2001 Index of Silicon Valley.*

Given this widening differential compared with the rest of the U.S. in productivity, in these key sectors Silicon Valley will probably continue to attract highly skilled workers from many countries.

EDUCATIONAL INSTITUTIONS ARE PARTNERS IN CREATING INTELLECTUAL CAPITAL FOR THE REGION

In many other regions of the world, universities may perceive their role as bastions of knowledge divorced from economic applications, with little responsibility for their graduates entering the knowledge-based work force. Here, as in other emergent regions in India, Taiwan, and Ireland, higher education institutions are more likely to see themselves as active partners in the creation of regional wealth and in preparing their students for good employment opportunities. The role of higher educational institutions has been critical to the success of Silicon Valley. Stanford University and the University of California at Berkeley are well known as research incubators and generate many of the skilled scientists, engineers, and entrepreneurs who founded the leading high-tech companies that Silicon Valley was built on, such as Hewlett-Packard, Cisco, Intel, Yahoo and many more.

If you want to buy tickets for any Stanford athletic event just dial 1-800-BEAT-CAL. That tells you where the Stanford community's priorities are relative to Berkeley in their intense, but amicable relationship. The football rivalry of the red and white uniformed Stanford Cardinals and blue and gold uniformed Berkeley Bears on the athletic field is long-standing. Far less appreciated is the high level of cooperation between the two educational behemoths in the laboratory and in scientific endeavors. This cooperation combined with the multilevel coordination (informal, but still regionally complementary) with the State University schools of San Francisco, San Jose, and Hayward; other local universities such as the University of Santa Clara and UC Santa Cruz; and the community colleges such as De Anza and Foothill, all enable Silicon Valley to have one of the most comprehensive and vertically integrated educational systems of any region in the world. This higher educational consortium produces the continuing supply of knowledge workers of all levels of talent and skill sets necessary to keep the Silicon Valley's regional advantage.

INDUSTRY EVOLUTION, JOB HOPPING, AND MOBILITY

Silicon Valley remains a hub of technology innovation and cutting-edge entrepreneurial business because it is not dependent upon any single industry or sector of technology. So, the region evolves in an unplanned way to take advantage of emergent disruptive technologies, rather than be saddled to one industry or technology and find its fortunes sunsetting with that particular sector or technology.

These are the major industry clusters for Silicon Valley:

- Computers/communications
- Semiconductors/semiconductor equipment
- Software
- Bioscience
- Defense/space
- Innovation services
- Professional services

Together these clusters represent 40% of all jobs in Silicon Valley.[1]

The region evolved from a focus on defense in the 1950s to integrated circuits in the 1960–70s to personal computers in the 1980–90s to the Internet in the 1990–2000s.[2] This ability to evolve technology emphasis is what may account for the region's success in staying ahead of the curve in innovative technology. Along with this continuing evolution of industries is a culture of independent contractors and project teams, who frequently move from employer to employer. The average tenure of employment in Silicon Valley is two years compared with almost seven years job tenure in the U.S.

HIGHLY SKILLED IMMIGRANTS

During the 1960s, Rheingold beer ran a series of TV commercials linking the ethnic mix of New York with the popularity of Rheingold. The ad campaign proudly announced that New York had more Greeks than there were in Athens, more Jews than in Tel Aviv, more Puerto Ricans than in San Juan, etc. The advertising idea was that a greater variety of people in New York drank Rheingold beer over any other beer. Today, Rheingold beer may be gone from the shelves, but the concept of diversity in a small region lives on in Silicon Valley. Indians play more cricket in Silicon Valley than anywhere else in the United States; and Chinese, Hebrew, and other foreign languages are commonly heard spoken.

Meanwhile, the influx of highly skilled technology workers has continued to increase. There are 200,000 foreign-born technology workers in Silicon Valley. A well-known Silicon Valley joke is that IC has been responsible for Silicon Valley success. IC is an acronym for both the integrated circuit and Indians and Chinese (including both mainland China and Taiwan), who comprise two-thirds of foreign-born workers and make up an estimated 40% of all skilled technology workers in Silicon Valley. Bay Area Indian immigrants have been one of America's most successful ethnic groups. Collectively, they've created companies estimated to account for $235 billion of market value. In an interesting twist of history, 500 years ago Columbus discovered the New World because he was looking for a quick route to the riches of India. In the beginning of this millennium, Indians have discovered that the trade route for riches to America is through Silicon Valley.

The influx of immigrants has also increased entrepreneurial activity in Silicon Valley. Chinese and Indians are estimated to be running 29% of the region's high-technology companies. It is interesting to note the frustration of other regions attempting to attract these workers, such as Germany. After much debate, the German government approved 30,000 visas for high-tech workers from India and other Asian countries. Yet, few came to take up the offer.[3] Foreign workers feel free and at home in Silicon Valley where so many of their highly skilled compatriots live in a very exciting and open society. This region's capability to easily absorb and integrate people from other cultures and ethnic groups is an important strength that is based on attitude, not just high compensation.

In a recent discussion with the authors of this book, Peter Hall observed this immigrant Diaspora phenomenon as being significant for many innovation regions throughout history: "The main discovery I made was the role of Diaspora in creativity. That creativity overwhelmingly came from the groups that had come from someplace else. They were self-made, feeling like they were not quite belonging."

TRANSNATIONAL AND MULTILOCATION JOB SHARING ENABLES THE REGION TO EXTEND ITS POWER AND WEALTH

Many believe that Silicon Valley has reached its limit for the numbers of people the region can sustain. The regional infrastructure for transportation, housing, and education is being strained there as well as in other successful regions in the knowledge-based economy. Many companies choose to move all but necessary functions out of Silicon Valley. It is just too expensive and too much of a hassle to live and work there, owing to the high costs of housing and the congested transportation infrastructure. While population growth in Silicon Valley may have reached its limit, there are other dynamics that extend the power and wealth of this region exponentially. Two of these factors are as follows:

1. Transnational ethnic groups such as Indians, Chinese, Israelis, and others are able to work between their native countries, Silicon Valley, and other regions of the world.
2. The use of job-sharing in multilocation teams enables companies to work around the clock every day through technology linkage, and to train many people in the culture and best practices of U.S. technology firms.

What is fascinating about this phenomenon is that wealth is being created in the home country and Silicon Valley simultaneously. Knowledge is flowing back and forth, and people in both locations are benefiting. This helps in the development of other regions and foreign countries, whose knowledge workers can still work with Silicon Valley but do not need to live there.

Job-sharing work teams, who operate in different regions linked by technology have been a boon for the world in disseminating best practices across many regions. The West Coast work methods of Intel, Hewlett-Packard, Microsoft, and many others have been effectively transmitted to many knowledge workers in places such as Ireland and Israel. So, knowledge workers in these smaller markets can have the same level of experience and know-how in technology development, management, and marketing as anyone in Silicon Valley. This both extends the reach of the U.S. companies and enhances the level of expertise in these multilocations. The result is a win-win situation. Silicon Valley companies get the best and brightest people working with them as employees or suppliers, manufacturers, distributors, etc., without adding to the expense and congestion of Silicon Valley itself. The home countries get foreign direct investment and world-class employment for their best knowledge workers, and those talents can be used to build business and wealth in the local region. This dynamic is playing itself out all over the world. It does not just emanate from Silicon Valley, but also regions such as Boston, Seattle, Austin, San Diego, and other large high-tech network centers.

WHAT'S NEXT FOR SILICON VALLEY?

Despite regional economic slowdowns and the recent evisceration of the dot-com sector, the huge technology economic base of this region continues to expand and thrive. Silicon Valley is well positioned to continue to lead the global technology economy because of the diversity of its business sectors, its linkage to the high-tech world regions, and the ability of its economy to be flexible and adapt to the ever-changing technology trends. Silicon Valley today functions more like a technology research and development laboratory than a manufacturing region, even though many of its most powerful corporate entities such as Cisco, Intel, and Solectron are manufacturing companies. The actual manufacturing is produced with vendors and suppliers in far-flung regions of the world. This enables Silicon Valley to be the knowledge headquarters for much of the original thinking for whatever the next waves of the innovative technology global economy will be. It is in the hands of global entrepreneurs that many of the new businesses and industries will arrive. To understand how global entrepreneurs work from Silicon Valley, we now focus on the story of DSPC and its founder, Davidi Gilo.

GLOBAL ENTREPRENEURS: LEADERS IN CREATING IE ENTERPRISES

Intellectual capital is the fastest-growing source of wealth in the digitally linked innovative technology economy. Silicon Valley is the nexus for the capitalization of knowledge. The emergence of high-tech global businesses emanating and linked through Silicon Valley to other regions is an important success factor making it the "magnetic force."

A new global entrepreneurial class of industry executives drives this multiregional digital knowledge economy. Davidi Gilo, founder of DSPC who sold his business to Intel for $1.6 billion in 1999, is such an example.

Davidi Gilo, born and raised in Israel, served in the Israel Defense Forces, and like many of his compatriots came of age through his experience with innovative technology in the army. In 1986 Gilo took $500,000 of his own seed capital and built DSPC based on products using digital signal processing, a technology originated by the Israeli military that is a key component in products such as answering machines, global positioning systems, and laptop computers.

Headquartered in Cupertino, California, DSPC based its organizational model on engineering in Israel, manufacturing in Japan, and focused the management and marketing base in Silicon Valley. Gilo originally sought to buy a company in Israel; he found that Israeli businesses had very good basic technology capabilities, but unfortunately, very poor marketing and business understanding. So his strategy became to start a company in which the R&D was in Israel, but the headquarters were in Silicon Valley. This approach has been successfully applied by many multinational global businesses.

ISRAELI MILITARY BRAIN CULTIVATION BECOMES A SILICON VALLEY HARVEST

Gilo offers an insider's view of the reason for the Israeli engineering advantage in the global economy, and most significantly in Silicon Valley. Many of these top engineers either utilize their skills for U.S. multinational companies, become entrepreneurs who base their companies in Silicon Valley, or join Israeli companies who then sell their technology worldwide.

Israel is particularly prone to having its innovators base their companies outside of Israel because of punitive tax and arcane regulatory laws. Most successful start-ups in Israel eventually leave the country.

In his remarks Gilo illustrates some of the challenges of working globally in technology and how high-tech professionals in smaller regions, such as Israel, come to succeed by plugging into the larger Innovation Economy through their linkage to Silicon Valley.

DAVIDI GILO

The chosen people for intellectual capital in Israel

Most of the people innovating new products and ideas in technology came from two or three units in the Israeli army. So, what is unique about Israel is that they identify and utilize their very, very talented engineers. By the time they graduate from the army, the top ones go into a special program called Talpiot. The government scans the high schools and picks the top 1% of students in math and related subjects. Instead of serving in the regular army at age 18 like anybody else, these students go through an intensive undergraduate engineering program, and then they serve in the army in some kind of engineering capacity. In return, these select few must commit to sign on for a few extra years. By the time they finish five or six years of working in the army in very advanced technology projects, mainly in the area of communications, they are highly accomplished engineers. Israel is very strong in communications, networking, and software because of this program.

Product testing needs a big market

Israel, unlike Japan or the United States, is a very small, local market. So you can't really develop a product for the local Israeli economy or test acceptance of the product for worldwide distribution, based on how it is accepted in Israel. In fact, I was an investor in a company that made a simple, interactive keyboard for kids. The product was very successful in Israel, but a complete failure when we tried to sell it in the U.S. I learned that because of the distance from the market, especially 15 years ago before the Internet, you had to use "legwork" to analyze the market. To do all that from Israel is very hard. So for me it was very clear that in order to be successful I had to run a company from here (Santa Clara, California) if I wanted to have a market-driven company rather than a technology-driven one.

DSPC took advantage of tax incentives put in place by the Israeli government to lure high-tech companies into Israel. The tax breaks as well as grants available from the Bird Foundation[4] and the Israeli Chief Scientists are very positive actions the government has taken to encourage high tech in Israel. Many companies, such as Intel, Motorola, and Microsoft, established research centers in Israel that were benefiting from both the talent in Israel and the government incentives.

Working globally with Israel is not all milk and honey

There are a lot of very appealing things in Israel. People are very talented, very resourceful, and come up with very creative ideas to solve problems. They are very dedicated because they are results-oriented and pride themselves on being able to overcome obstacles. That is part of the culture. They are also, overall, very loyal. People will stay and work at a place for many years. Israeli companies have a turnover rate of about 2% a year, which is unheard of at U.S. companies. Even a successful company like Intel has a turnover of at least 10% to 15% every year. That's a very big asset because we have people that stay in the company. They learn the product and the technology.

One downside to the DSPC business model has been navigating through the Israeli bureaucracy. When it comes to corporate governance and stock options and trying to merge an Israeli company with another company or change the bylaws of an Israeli company, all of this is very arcane and anti-business. There has been an attempt over the years to change this, and some laws have been in front of the Israeli Knesset, but because political coalitions seek other benefits, it never gets done. This makes Israel not the easiest place to do business. If you want to merge two American companies, it's no problem. If you want to merge two Israeli companies or an American company with an Israeli company, you have so many tax, accounting, and corporate governance issues that you need to go through because of arcane Israeli corporate laws, that it makes it very challenging.

Another challenge is the work stoppages due to religious holidays, the one month of reserve duty required of men until age 45 in Israel, and normal vacation schedules. Engineers work long hours — six days a week in Israel. But the long periods of absence make it more difficult to coordinate with other regions. There are also cultural differences between U.S. managers, the Israeli engineers, and the Japanese manufacturers.

"First convince me, then I'll see if I want to do it"

There are different management assumptions between American managers and Israeli engineers. It starts with basic things like communication styles. Israelis are very direct and say what they think. They are usually very good at improvisation. Usually, American managers have been trained in large company systems. If you worked for years at Intel, Cisco, Nortel, or Lucent, you were taught to think in a certain way. You do not see many Israeli companies that have achieved a size to develop those systems. So, you have a completely different approach to how you look at business, how you make decisions, and very different personal dynamics.

Most American managers cannot manage Israelis. In Israel there is a camaraderie or bonding that you build fighting in the same unit of the army; this sets them apart. They look down on people that try to manage with a tie and suit. Trusting other people is something that Israelis are not good at in general. So when an American manager walks into an Israeli company that is doing the product engineering, and that manager has to get product specifications from the engineers, there has to be some trust; it's very hard to build this trust. In the past, the engineering group was usually very strong and the headquarters group was usually very weak because they were always dependent on the Israelis. And the engineers were always in Israel.

In the early days of DSPC it was a challenge to convince the Israelis to listen. PhoneMate was our customer. We worked with them to develop a model of one of the first digital answering machines, and they specified the features. And when we took this to Israel, the engineers started arguing with the features specified by the customer. And I said, "Who cares what you, Mr. Engineer in Tel Aviv, think about what features they need in Los Angeles. They pay us and we have to do what they want." And we had to argue with them, because unless they understood why they needed the features, which was a marketing issue, they couldn't quite do it.

All these notions of strategic thinking, planning ahead, and corporate market analysis . . . they are very naive in their approach to these. ■

Despite all these challenges, however, in the five years from 1994 to 1999 DSP grew from a $16-million business to a publicly traded, global company with 230 employees and $175 million in revenue before its sale to Intel for $1.6 billion.

One reason bright people like Davidi Gilo come to Silicon Valley is that this is the Innovation Economy marketing headquarters as well as a center for technology innovation. To understand how marketing is a Silicon Valley competitive advantage we now turn to the story of the Agilent spin-off from HP as a lesson in high-tech branding and advertising.

SILICON VALLEY: BRANDING HEADQUARTERS FOR THE INNOVATION ECONOMY

One of the greatest success factors for the U.S. in general and Silicon Valley in particular is the significance placed upon marketing and positioning by its leading businesses and institutions. The high-tech industry in the U.S. has taken the lead in marketing and positioning by companies such as Dell, Microsoft, Intel, Cisco, HP, and many others. Regional wealth creation can be greatly enhanced through skilled use of marketing which can be adapted for successful enterprises — companies, regions, and organizations.

One example of successful branding and marketing is the Agilent Technologies spin-off from Hewlett-Packard (now officially renamed HP) which at the time was the largest new company introduction in the history of Silicon Valley. This section addresses lessons learned in branding. We will explore the dynamics of positioning a region to attract foreign direct investment in Chapter 7, "The Branding of Ireland."

WHAT IS POSITIONING AND WHY IS IT SO IMPORTANT IN THE INNOVATION ECONOMY?

Positioning may be defined as the purposeful creation of value in a consumer's mind. Usually, positioning will differentiate one brand over others in a category so the consumer will have a more positive inclination to purchase and use that brand. Successful positioning must answer a marketing problem. That problem may be defined in terms of:

- Justifying a premium price (as in the semiconductor industry "Intel Inside" campaign)
- Differentiating a product or service (as in the hand-held personal assistant devices "Simply Palm" campaign)
- Changing an attitude about a brand we may already know (as in the business solutions Internet category, changing the perception of Cisco from introducing the "Internet — Are You Ready?" campaign to providing product specific solutions for business in their subsequent "Empowering the Internet Generation" campaign)
- Establishing an identity for either a new category or a brand that requires credibility (as the establishment of Agilent in the "Dreams Made Real" campaign)

Technology-intensive companies have products and services based on continuing advances in science and technical know-how. Managing marketing for these companies is complex because they require speed to market with continual innovation and change. These markets are characterized by great risk:

- A particular product can be surpassed in function (such as cell phones superceding pagers).
- The product can be substituted by another whole category (such as 3½-inch disks replacing 5-inch floppy disks for personal computers).
- The product can be bundled in some other category package (such as when word processing software was included in office suites' software packages, which then became bundled as part of the software in personal computer packages).

Another major challenge is to be able to differentiate the role one brand plays in the context of others, since factors such as partnering, mergers, and outsourcing are much more common in the technology industry than in traditional market categories.

Regions of the world are also complex environments, defying simplification and jingoism. Do conventional marketing disciplines apply to companies who seek brand leadership in innovative technology or to regions of the world seeking to establish credibility in the global marketplace? If so, then what is similar and different about technology and regional marketing from traditional commercial products and services such as fast food?

Most people acknowledge that, for brands such as McDonald's and Coca-Cola, marketing and advertising play a critical role in establishing a successful business franchise that dominates their respective categories. Can marketing and advertising be utilized successfully in the same way in innovative technology industries and in regions as they are in selling hamburgers and soft drinks? Silicon Valley companies and institutions have pioneered successful adaptations of traditional marketing for the Innovative Economy.

THE DIFFERENCE BETWEEN COMMERCIAL PRODUCT POSITIONING AND TECHNOLOGY/ REGIONAL POSITIONING

The principles of positioning in marketing and advertising apply to technology companies and regions just as surely as they do to commercial packaged goods products.

The key difference is that technology innovation moves so quickly relative to commercial products that the emphasis on branding and positioning in technology must focus on *the needs of the market to be fulfilled and positioning ahead of actual product availability*. Thus the umbrella positioning of Agilent goes beyond any particular testing solutions or products they sell today. This is not true of traditional product companies such as Coca-Cola or McDonald's, whose products are widely familiar and where the challenge is to create a brand awareness and positive perception that helps to differentiate what is essentially a commodity product.

Regional advertising and positioning also follows the principles of commercial advertising and marketing. The challenge in regional positioning is that it must integrate with government, societal institutions, organized labor, and regional policy that may be more difficult to coordinate than in commercial sector private company decision making.

AGILENT TECHNOLOGIES AS THE POSTER CHILD OF THE INNOVATION ECONOMY

The Agilent introduction illustrates one of the great commercial phenomena of the Innovation Economy — the emergence of positioning and advertising as the builder of brand identity and value in the world market.

Agilent Technologies, Inc. is a global technologies company headquartered in Palo Alto, California. With approximately 39,000 employees, Agilent operates in more than 120 countries with R&D and manufacturing in multiple locations worldwide. First listed on the New York Stock Exchange on November 18, 1999, Agilent's net revenue that year was $8.3 billion. Currently, over half of Agilent's net revenue is derived from outside of the U.S.[5] Since its spin-off from HP in March of 1999, Agilent has focused its business in four core areas: communication, electronics, healthcare, and life sciences.

ESTABLISHING A NEW BRAND WITH A SEPARATE, YET FAMILIAR IDENTITY

In the fall of 1999, Agilent, the non-computer systems spin-off from HP, launched their positioning statement, shown in Figure 2-4.

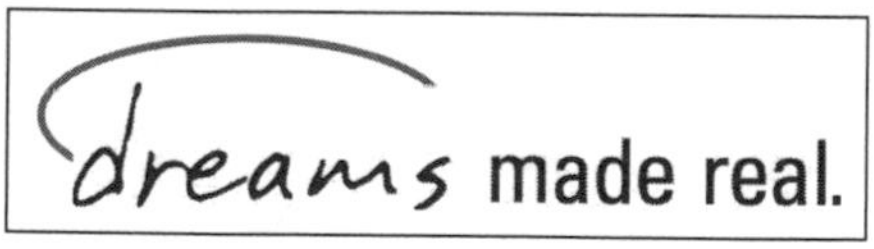

FIGURE 2-4   Agilent's positioning statement.
Source: Reprinted with permission of Agilent Technologies, Inc.

DEFINING THE PROBLEM

One of Agilent's first challenges as a company had been finding a way to keep the history and strength of its parent company, HP, which is known for being a quality innovator, while creating a new and vibrant business. "Dreams Made Real" evolved from this initial focus and was shaped through a desire to be seen as a forward-looking company, innovating and positioned to grow in communications, electronics, healthcare, and life sciences.

When Agilent was spun off from HP, the company gained a whole new focus, as seen below. The immediate challenge Agilent faced was how to build a corporate brand for an $8 billion "start-up" that was losing one of the most highly respected names in the business. The marketing effort was one of the most ambitious new brand introductions in history, with a $150 million budget spent in 27 countries and four major geographic regions. All 40,000 pages of the Agilent Web site rolled over to the new brand identity on the day of the launch.

The criteria set for building this new brand positioning was quite daunting. The objectives included:

- Finding ways to create an emotional connection with multiple target audiences
- Differentiating Agilent from the competition
- Distinguishing Agilent from HP
- Creating a flexible brand image
- Implementing the new brand consistently throughout the world.[6]

The positioning needed to communicate Agilent's core values of speed, agility, focus, accountability, and the ability to "create like a start-up and deliver like a Fortune 100 company."

The following three ads from the continuing Agilent campaign illustrate how with simple visual and copy, the company has successfully positioned itself to meet these campaign objectives (see Figures 2-5 through 2-7).

FIGURE 2-5   The Agilent campaign.

Source: Reprinted with permission of Agilent Technologies, Inc.

FIGURE 2-6 The Agilent campaign.
Source: Reprinted with permission of Agilent Technologies, Inc.

FIGURE 2-7   The Agilent campaign.

Source: Reprinted with permission of Agilent Technologies, Inc.

Shirley Horn is the senior director of global brand management at Agilent. She managed the Agilent brand naming process and the marketing introduction of the brand simultaneously in 27 countries. Here is her insider perspective of the challenge of branding and marketing a worldwide technology company. We have summarized the lessons learned after each of her excerpted comments.

SHIRLEY HORN

Setting the right objectives for communications

We focused the objective on getting the name Agilent recognized and creating the simple knowledge that we compete in the communications and life sciences categories. It wasn't that critical in the early days for a broad audience to understand exactly what we did in life sciences.

Now we have accomplished that. Agilent has the name recognition. Some of our people are champing at the bit to do the next wave. Many people want to do ingredient branding — say, "Agilent Enabled" as Intel did with "Intel Inside" — and get our corporate signature on everybody else's products and boxes. There's tremendous enthusiasm for building the power of this brand, but you've got to take it in the right steps. What use is building an "Agilent Enabled" type ingredient brand if you don't build the role that you play first?

Lesson: Build awareness and recognition of the role you play in the technology field so people can understand the function and value you bring to the process. Just positioning the brand as having a role in the process may be useful if you introduce early in the category development (such as Cisco accomplished in positioning the brand as driving the Internet revolution in the "Are You Ready?" campaign in 1997–2000). This method is less effective when the field is crowded with business enterprise enabling companies that all seem to provide business solutions without a clear difference in their area of expertise.

Does technology really change the basic rules of positioning?

Our positioning challenge at Agilent is to communicate what we do and to say it in broad enough terms that our role can be understood by nontechnical audiences and at the same time doesn't patronize the technical audiences.

There is a dichotomy. Some technology companies feel compelled to explain everything about their engineering, so their audiences miss the point completely. Others are trying to get a message across that they are players in such major markets, like communications, that they don't explain enough about their role, and therefore they fall into the trap of sounding like everybody else. So the marketing challenge becomes: How do you bring the two together? Of course, the more direct your message is to your technical customer, the more specific you need to be about the technology.

Lesson: Technology companies have to balance specificity of what they do with an interesting, but relevant way to present the product and the category. This combines communication about the product benefit with the intuitive emotional insight of people and their relationship to this category.

The balance of being an American headquartered company, yet a global multilocation rnterprise

The American card plays much better when you create the premise of how we partner with the countries and the communities that we're in. Going back to the very basic corporate positioning outside the U.S., the messaging is weighted more toward the global Fortune 100-sized company compared with the entrepreneurial start-up. So the unique positioning is, "creates like a start-up, delivers like a Fortune 100." In the U.S., the "create like a start-up" played much better during the first two years of our brand program, when all start-ups were hot. Outside the U.S., and now in the U.S. following the dot-com demise, we want to dial up the "global Fortune 100 world-class company." But even when you say Fortune 100, you automatically attach an American label. The way we handle it outside the U.S. is by a combination of all of our corporate functions: public relations, internal communications, university relations, philanthropy, and public affairs. We talk about the contribution of the company to the local economy. We speak about our R&D manufacturing facilities there. What are we contributing? How many jobs do we provide? We can't do this in every country because, of course, we can't put manufacturing and R&D in every country. But it tends to work where we do. We're getting 90% of our sales from the places where we have most of our employees and manufacturing and R&D facilities, or we have R&D and manufacturing facilities there because that's where our customers are.

Lesson: Global companies can be perceived as good citizens if they utilize local managers and personnel, contribute to community life, and are perceived as part of the regional strength that enhances the quality of life and the economy. Be sensitive to what aspects of the company identity are most valued by the region.

The demise of the dot-coms is a lesson in the basics

Advertising has a role to play, but it is only a small part of the whole picture. During our launch phase, it helped to position Agilent as a powerful and professional contender in its market categories. It did an awful lot in terms of getting the employees excited and making them feel proud. It got the name out there, and got people familiar with the name. The advertising was the top of the duck swimming in the pond and everything else was paddling like hell underneath. Had we been a dot-com and spent $100 million on a brilliant campaign, but not brought in revenues, profits, or delivered on our promise, it would not have succeeded. Then we might have been featured on the most memorable ads on the Super Bowl (the most-viewed televised event each year in the U.S.) three years from now, but that's all we'd have to show for it, if, indeed, we were still in business.

If you do not have substance behind your brand, or you can't deliver on your promise, brilliant advertising will not save you. While part of HP, the future Agilent business divisions had been delivering on market leadership, technology innovation, and world-class manufacturing and service and expertise for 60 years. We didn't lose any of that.

What was risky from an advertising perspective was the promise of what would be different. What would change? What are the benefits of being a separate company that are relevant to the audiences? And that's where we came up with these attributes of speed, and focused commitment to these particular industries, being able to accelerate the revolution. Now that we're Agilent the shackles are off; we can move faster but have the same great, or even better levels of performance.

Lesson: Focus on benefits that your target market can easily understand and value, and on benefits that you have confidence you can deliver. ■

Positioning in technology categories is complex. As these insights from Shirley Horn demonstrate, the challenge for a brand is to create an identity across many target audiences that not only describes the category of technology, but also the value of that branded company within the category.

Positioning must be for market need and not merely for the product or service that is here today. Agilent is positioned as the toolmaker that enables researchers to "make dreams real." The challenge is to establish a world brand, not just be perceived as a Silicon Valley company. Marketing is the vehicle to accomplish this.

Marketing and positioning will continue to play key roles as institutions such as technology parks, governments, universities, global businesses, and start-ups vie for the human and capital resources that drive the Innovation Economy. The lessons learned from Agilent, one of the most significant branding stories of the Innovation Economy, provide best practices direction in the challenging discipline of marketing.

ENDNOTES

1. Anna Lee Saxenian, *Regional Advantage: Culture and Competition in Silicon Valley and Route 128*, Fourth edition, Harvard University Press: Cambridge, MA, 1996.
2. Doug Henton, "A Profile of the Valley's Evolving Structure," *Silicon Valley Edge*, Stanford University Press: Palo Alto, CA, 2000.
3. Anna Lee Saxenian, *Regional Advantage: Culture and Competition in Silicon Valley and Route 128*, Fourth edition, Harvard University Press: Cambridge, MA, 1996.
4. For more information on the Bird Foundation see *www.birdf.com*.
5. Agilent Technologies, *www.agilent.com/about/index.html*.
6. Agilent Technologies, *www.agilent.com/about/index.html*.

LINKING ORGANIZATIONS

NON-GOVERNMENT ORGANIZATIONS, STRONG REGIONAL BUSINESS ASSOCIATIONS, AND PHILANTHROPIES

☐ ne important factor contributing to the strength of Silicon Valley as a region is the emergence of interconnected formal and informal organizations that are part of the vibrant nonprofit sector. While governments may have a commanding role in providing organizational linkages in many other regions of the world, the dynamic nonprofit or non-government organization (NGO) sector in the United States, and particularly in Silicon Valley, provides support to connect people and businesses in a vibrant network, having great flexibility to adapt to innovation and changing economic trends.

BUSINESS LINKING ORGANIZATIONS FOR NETWORKING: FOCUS ON TiE

Personal networking, formal and informal, drives innovative technology development. While traditional networking and business assistance organizations such as Chambers of Commerce, Rotary Clubs, and the Small Business Administration have long been in existence, new networking models are breaking the mold. TiE (The IndUS Entrepreneurs) is one of the most successful of these entrepreneurial NGOs.

TiE is a nonprofit mentoring and networking organization chartered by a group of successful expatriate Indian and other South Asian entrepreneurs and business executives in Silicon Valley. It has since rapidly expanded to 30 chapters, with 10,000 members predominantly in the U.S., India, and seven other countries. TiE's mission is threefold:

1. To foster entrepreneurship and nurture entrepreneurs
2. To facilitate networking among its members
3. To help members integrate with the mainstream communities

Kailash Joshi is the Silicon Valley president and co-founder of TiE. He started his career on the research faculty of Cornell University in New York and had a distinguished 23-year career with IBM. He was the general manager of IBM, Lexington, which is now Lexmark. Now retired, he devotes his time to TiE and other charitable organizations.

These are Dr. Joshi's insights into how TiE is rooted in the Indian tradition, why the model works so well in Silicon Valley, and why it has been so scalable and exportable for international wealth creation.

KAILASH JOSHI

In Indian culture, the knowledge roots run deep

TiE is a blend of Silicon Valley culture of wealth creation through entrepreneurship and the ancient Indian tradition of knowledge transfer from generation to generation. In the over 6,000-year history of Indian culture, knowledge has been revered. The tradition of the guru-chela, or teacher-student, was mostly responsible for the generational transfer of the knowledge of scriptures and the arts. Some of this tradition was disrupted in the aftermath of the Mogul and the British rules of India. However, in the knowledge economy, the Indian knowledge tradition is once again emerging with full force, and I anticipate that India will gain significant benefits from this trend.

It is my view that knowledge and ideas cannot be passed on from one generation to another by way of tradition alone. Such transfer requires valid knowledge and substance or it will be rejected. One hundred years from now, the world will be inhabited by people unborn today and only knowledge seen valid by them will stay alive. Therefore, the evolution of mankind also means a parallel evolution of knowledge.

Guru-chela for a high-tech age

The guru-chela (teacher-student, mentor-protégé) tradition of India was the primary means of knowledge transfer for centuries. In this process persons renowned in the knowledge (gurus) took the budding knowledge seekers (chelas) under their wings and imparted their knowledge in a very disciplined and personalized fashion. This was usually done in a modest setting where a one-on-one relationship was developed over time. The guru took pride in the success of the chela as much as the chela enjoyed the association with a well-known guru.

At TiE we have created a mentoring and networking process that blends the entrepreneurial ambitions of the Silicon Valley culture and the ancient Indian tradition of guru-chela relationships. Within such a framework, in Silicon Valley we have hundreds of accomplished entrepreneurs who become gurus and thousands of budding entrepreneurs who are the chelas. Most of this group shares the background of South Asia, where they received their education and developed a strong competitive spirit. They come from middle-class backgrounds and find the Silicon Valley setting ideal for sharing new business ideas. In this process, the mentors impart knowledge and experience to the protégés, who in turn bring currency of knowledge in their fields to the mentor. It is this two-way nature of the relationship that keeps this mentoring and networking process energized.

Mentoring is a face-to-face process requiring intellectual honesty. Typically, the mentoring session is arranged ahead of time and the open and frank discussion lasts about an hour. It is not uncommon for a mentor to suggest that the protégé drop a business idea for specific reasons or suggest a meeting with an expert in the field. In some cases the mentor may agree to join the board of the protégé's company or introduce potential investors to the company.

The mentors are mostly the charter members who are invited to join TiE on the basis of significant past accomplishments as entrepreneurs, business executives, or partners in professional services organizations. Collectively they form a large pool of intellectual capital from which the members can draw. TiE membership is open to all with the payment of a nominal fee. The TiE activities are sustained through membership dues, sponsorship contributions, and the efforts of a large group of volunteers. TiE sponsors include established venture, law, and accounting firms, as well as some of the blue-chip corporations. Both sponsors and volunteers are able to network with the entrepreneurs and participate in their areas of interest.

Starting in Silicon Valley, TiE has become one of the most respected networking organizations in the world, as evidenced by the growing number of chapters and the large attendance at its monthly events and the flagship annual TiEcon conference in Silicon Valley. TiE events are always open to the public and take place at each of the TiE chapters around the world. The participants at these events come from various ethnic and national backgrounds. TiE Silicon Valley also supports economic policy analysis at Stanford University in regard to India and engages in relevant discussions with the policy makers in South Asian countries. It is one of TiE's explicit goals to spread the fervor of entrepreneurship and free markets in all countries of South Asia. In summary, TiE sees itself as an organization that unites people and nations for economic value creation in the emerging borderless world. ■

TiE is one of the most respected organizations in Silicon Valley, as evidenced by the large attendance at its events by the whole spectrum of venture capital and start-up firms beyond just the Indian community. It has effectively become a consultant to the Indian government, helping to make changes directly in India to help create regional wealth. In addition, the emergence of 30 TiE chapters throughout the world is great confirmation that its wisdom and effectiveness in harnessing capital to ideas is a global phenomenon.

BUSINESS ASSOCIATIONS CAN HELP ADDRESS REGIONAL ISSUES

TRANSPORTATION, HOUSING, EDUCATION, AND ENERGY — FOCUS ON THE SILICON VALLEY MANUFACTURERS GROUP

Silicon Valley was never envisioned as a major industrial center, and its transportation infrastructure was not developed to handle the level of traffic that now commonly chokes the region. Unlike urban centers such as New York, Chicago, London, and Paris, Silicon Valley does not have a well-established metro and bus system to transport its hundreds of thousands of workers around each day. Public rail (Cal Trans and Light Rail) and bus transportation (SamTrans and VTA) transport about 85 million riders a year. This represents only 4% of total commuters. Only 15% car pool, while 78% of people drive alone to work. Most of these people use the two highways that form the twin spines of transportation through the Valley. This causes massive congestion and is a limiting factor to how many people can actually physically work in Silicon Valley.

There is a chronic housing shortage for the professionals who work in Silicon Valley. While a large number of permits were issued for commercial building space during the 1990s Internet boom, little residential housing was built to accommodate the massive influx of highly skilled workers. This was exacerbated by the fact that there is very low density in California housing; Californians love their single detached homes. So, many people commute long distances because home ownership is hard to come by.

Perhaps the great lesson here is that the creation of jobs should be accompanied by the creation of housing and transportation. Between 1992 and 2000, Silicon Valley produced 329,000 new jobs but only 60,500 new housing units (1 home for every 5.5 jobs). One reason why housing was not increased relative to commercial space is because commercial real estate produced large tax revenues for the municipalities, while residential housing produced far less revenue for the same amount of space. This, coupled with restrictive environmental regulations, has made the housing shortage in Silicon Valley a major crisis. So, many people live and commute farther away from their work, which further exacerbates the transportation problem.

BUSINESS ASSOCIATIONS IN PARTNERSHIP WITH GOVERNMENT ATTEMPT TO ADDRESS REGIONAL ISSUES

Strong, highly effective business associations and linking organizations can provide business communities access to work in partnership with government on a regional basis. We illustrate this through our focus on the association of the Silicon Valley Manufacturers Group (SVMG) and the following interview with its president, Carl Guardino.

SVMG was founded on the belief that local employers should be actively involved in working with their governments to find innovative solutions to issues such as transportation, housing, education, and energy resources consistent with a positive environmental balance. It believes the best way to address these challenges is to unite the broader community, government officials, and business leaders. This model came to life in 1977 thanks to David Packard, co-founder of Hewlett-Packard.

SVMG represents 190 of Silicon Valley's employers, who provide nearly 275,000 local jobs. Membership is open to high-tech firms and supporting industries such as software, systems, manufacturing, finance, accounting, transportation, healthcare, defense, communications, education, and utilities.

Carl Guardino is the president and CEO of SVMG. He discusses how this association is so successful in making a difference in the Silicon Valley region. Mr. Guardino identifies success factors such as the fundamental philosophy upon which the association was built; the organizational structure of the group; the communication between, focus on, and influence of its member companies; and its mutually respectful relationship with the media. This is a truly unique and effective organization, harnessing the power of business to work cooperatively on crucial regional infrastructure issues such as transportation, housing, education, and energy resources for industry. SVMG continues with David Packard's vision to nurture and create a positive environment that is conducive to the region's continued economic success.

CARL GUARDINO

The core purpose of SVMG is for Silicon Valley executives to problem solve proactively. We can engage top executives because our operating philosophy is minimum time, maximum impact. Our founder, David Packard, co-founder of Hewlett-Packard, established the model. As with many things he did, he was quite visionary. His idea in forming this association was to engage senior executives directly working with each other and working with the broader community as private sector leaders to proactively solve the region's challenges. Structurally, he made that successful in several ways.

David Packard's four principles for a successful business association

First, the organization needs positive peer-to-peer pressure by electing a board of directors solely consisting of CEOs and top executives who drive each other as well as their organizations. This keeps the companies focused at different managerial and executive levels because their CEOs are involved. That is why it is important to have a board of CEOs and principal officers that are truly engaged and not just a letterhead board.

Second, make sure their time is well used. That is our mantra: minimum time, maximum impact. We have only a set number of board meetings per year that they are required to attend. So when we have them, we have them fully engaged. We are able to do that by having a tremendous message strength in terms of managers and directors and issue leads from their companies and our other member companies who comprise committees and task forces. With that we have probably 500 member company volunteers from our 185 member companies.

Third, SVMG always has a very small budget, because that forces us to have a very small staff. David Packard's position was to keep the staff small, so it could not dominate the organization. This forces it to be owned and driven by its members. Our budget is less than $1 million a year with a staff of less than 10 people because we have the strength of those 500 volunteers doing so much work.

Fourth, we have a series of executive champions for our different issues. So on the 1999 Measure A Transportation initiative (increase local taxes for increased transportation expenditures), for instance, there were literally thousands of hours of work leading up to and then running a voter initiative campaign. We will have a champion from our board, who plays a key role and who is very visible, and we can maximize her or his time.

Carefully select initiatives for broad executive support

One of our region's most serious problems is a shortage of affordable rental and first-time home-buyer housing. So SVMG joined with other community organizations to help create a housing trust, which serves as a revolving loan fund for first-time home purchases, affordable rentals, and outright grants for homeless shelters.

The fund leverages dollars on a ten-to-one ratio by combining with other housing funding sources, so the fund provides the deal-making dollars. This is an innovative way to begin to address the housing crisis here in Silicon Valley. There are about 150 housing trust funds in different communities in the United States, and our $20 million raised in 2001 is the biggest initial housing trust fund effort in the country and the largest nonprofit fund raising campaign we've ever done in the Valley.

Good public relations are essential

People have the right to know what we're doing. Even though we are a private organization of private citizens, we want to help our community, so we think we have the responsibility to inform the public. We know the press can disseminate information that helps us advance our core issues, and so it becomes a strategic part of our game plan to have them understand what we are doing.

The main way you work well with the media, besides reaching out, being accessible, and being honest with them at all times, is to actually have a story to tell — that you're accomplishing something. So I think to whatever extent we have success in working with the media is hopefully because we are doing things that are media worthy — like quantifiable successes and return on investment.

Even journalists who, by profession or by experience, are occasionally cynical are often surprised at the very proactive, positive work that our members do through this organization. They have acknowledged and treated us well through that. We try to stay very sensitive to their deadlines and what they are trying to accomplish. When we can't help them we, at least, refer them elsewhere. So we try to provide a resource even when we're not the direct resource for a particular piece. Over time that serves us, and therefore our issues, members, and the Valley, well.

Proactive voices on regional issues

The concern David Packard had in forming the group was that business could not be effective speaking with separate voices on important regional issues. In the summer of 1977, he sent a lunch invitation to about 35 of the top CEOs in the Valley because he didn't feel they had a united, proactive, positive voice in the issues that were impacting the economic health of the region and their individual companies. Equally critically important to Mr. Packard was the quality of life of their employees. So he wanted to form a group that brought together those top employers to address again, not only issues that impacted the economic health, but the quality of life of the region — and the Manufacturing Group was born.

So would they have that voice united without the Manufacturing Group? Well, hopefully someone else would have created it, but I think it took someone as well respected within the industry and around the community as David Packard to create this type of model. The model, which we hope can be emulated in other regions, is simple, but difficult:

- Find someone who is a well-respected business voice to pull together other business leaders.
- Make sure that person is also respected across the entire community, beyond business circles, for credibility's sake.
- Ensure that the agenda engages CEOs, so that there really is a reason to come together.
- Ensure that the projects selected have quantifiable outcomes and are driven by successes, rather than just studies.

We have a three-year rolling business plan that our members update annually with quantifiable accomplishments to reach each year so that we know at the end of the year whether they received the return on investments that they expected through their dues and their participation. ■

GIVING FOR THE PUBLIC GOOD, SILICON VALLEY STYLE: FOCUS ON THE ENTREPRENEURS FOUNDATION

One of the measures of regional health in the United States is the level of philanthropic giving. This sector helps to build the institutions and to support and enhance a community's arts, education, social service, environmental, and religious needs. In many countries these services are funded by the government and the nonprofit sector has a very limited role. In the U.S., $203 billion is donated every year to nonprofit organizations by individuals, charitable foundations, bequests, and corporations.[1] Many regions of the world seek to develop philanthropy in their communities. Perhaps the insights from the high-tech professionals we next profile, who have dedicated themselves to making a difference in their societies, can be helpful in strengthening philanthropy for other regions.

Compared with many other U.S. geographic areas and industries, Silicon Valley companies and individuals have had a reputation for low levels of philanthropic giving. High-tech money was perceived as fast and easy, made by young multimillionaires who did not care about the communities they lived in and did not share the values of previous generations of business leaders to give back. To a large extent, this perception is rooted in reality and, with a few notable exceptions in companies with great philanthropic corporate cultures such as Hewlett-Packard and Cisco, the new high-tech wealth has generally been less forthcoming for charities.

However, this bad reputation may be a bit exaggerated. From 1992 to 2000, Silicon Valley donors have contributed $1 billion to community foundations such as the Community Foundation Silicon Valley and the Peninsula Community Foundation.[2] This comes largely in the form of asset giving of appreciated stock, and wealthy individuals donating through planned giving instruments such as charitable remainder trusts that have positive tax benefits. Founders of successful high-tech companies seem to focus their giving to issues of personal concern or to institutions of learning. In 2001, retired Intel Chairman Gordon Moore and his wife Betty, through their combined foundation and personal giving, donated $600 million to the California Institute of Technology, which is the largest single donation to any educational institution in the U.S. Traditional community charities such as the United Way, which raise cash annually for "umbrella giving" to local NGOs, have not fared nearly as well.

New approaches to community-building philanthropy based on problem solving and asset-based giving are evolving. The Entrepreneurs Foundation is a good example of community building through the venture capital community. Through interviews with Gib Myers, chairman of the Entrepreneurs Foundation, and Emil Wang, recipient of the Foundation's Entrepreneur of the Year award in 2000, we will profile this organization as an example of Silicon Valley style experimentation with philanthropy.

VENTURE PHILANTHROPY — WHAT A CONCEPT!

Entrepreneurial innovation is a highly rated value in Silicon Valley. Just as with technology breakthroughs and new products, people here want to break new ground in approaches to community building and problem solving. Major community foundations, such as the Silicon Valley Community Foundation and the Peninsula Community Foundation, primarily work with wealthy individuals to channel some of their fortunes into designated giving based on donor choice in the community. There are also new approaches to community-building philanthropy based on problem solving and asset giving by newly created businesses. Venture philanthropy is one of those approaches in which the venture funding organization becomes actively involved between the donor and the recipient in the matching of donor interest and creation of innovative programs by the nonprofit agency.

While these approaches are still embryonic and do not account for great sums of money, they do begin to address a major issue in Silicon Valley: how to initiate newly created businesses into giving something back to the community in a way that can be systemic and ongoing in their corporate culture. The high-tech start-up culture that is so prevalent in Silicon Valley seems resistant to traditional appeals for community-based philanthropy, such as the United Way annual giving campaigns based on payroll deductions.

We sought the people who are beginning to address this issue, who are creating new approaches from within the venture capital and start-up business community. Through understanding their motivations and desires to link the high-tech business world with the regional needs in order to improve the quality of life in their communities, we gain an understanding of how individuals take initiative to solve problems. This characteristic of individuals defining a problem then initiating approaches to find and implement solutions is an important key to comprehending how things get done in the Valley.

Gib Myers, a partner in the Mayfield Group, a blue-chip venture capital firm, founded the Entrepreneurs Foundation in 1998. The mission of this foundation is both to change Silicon Valley corporate culture by bringing community involvement into the core of start-up companies, and to strengthen local nonprofits by providing access to capital resources and best business practices to aid their growth. The foundation has $10 million in assets from over 66 start-up companies that gave a one-time gift of at least $100,000 or a small percentage of their future stock (¼% to ½%). Contributors to the Entrepreneurs Foundation also include Credite Suisse First Boston, Hambrect & Quist Group, Silicon Valley Bank, Cisco Systems, Inc., SGI, and Intuit, Inc. Myers' goal for the foundation is to attract 500 companies to participate and accumulate $200 million of appreciated stock to invest in about 15 community ventures.[3]

These efforts led Myers to be the first recipient of the American Spirit Award from the National Venture Capital Association in 1999.[4] In addition to his work with the Entrepreneurs Foundation, Myers has been a partner in the Mayfield Group since 1969, has worked in computer systems and divisional sales for Hewlett-Packard, and holds an MBA from Stanford, where he was the co-founder of the Center for Social Innovation.

His words illustrate both the challenge and response of the Entrepreneurs Foundation. He has also emphasized that it takes more work over a longer period of time than most people realize to create and sustain these innovative efforts.

GIB MYERS

The entrepreneurial high-tech sector is not contributing to the community

It seems obvious that if we are going to sustain the San Francisco Bay Area as a great place to live, there are lots of issues that need to be addressed on a regional basis, not just a particular nonprofit agency or area of philanthropic interest such as education. The entrepreneur sector is a huge part of the economy. By and large the high-tech economy has become a dominant force in the increase of wealth here. However, most of these companies do not support the community in any way.

We have an enormous concentration of leadership, money, and talent, but traditional ways of giving were not attracting the major groups of companies. If you drop below the billion-dollar annual revenue level, you see many companies not doing anything.

Another dynamic is individual wealth creation. There is a very long cycle of education of how to give back; 10 years before they start doing something. Can we cut the time lag to five years? Our philosophy is to make a fundamental difference to start early and make giving part of the culture.

The innovative approach of the Entrepreneurs Foundation

We proposed to take stock and stock options from a private company before IPO. We wanted $100,000 or about ¼% to ½% of available stock. It would be given to us, we would hold the stock option; when the company went public, we would realize the gains. The company gets a deduction for the full value of stock from federal taxes. We have signed on 73 companies in two years.

Companies are more ready to give stock than cash. The gift comes from the corporate treasury. It is a CEO and board of directors' decision and stock is readily convertible. EF also gives back a portion of the stock proceeds, so the organization can start its own foundation; this is because companies felt better having some funds back for their control.

The other innovation EF has made is venture philanthropy. When we use this money to give back to the community, we use venture capital principles. We seek leaders in the nonprofit sector who will scale up and address problems for the whole Bay Area region. So our focus is to scale up seed projects to become major players in solving the problems they are addressing. These are venture principles applied to the nonprofit sector.

The truth about entrepreneurs, venture capitalists, and philanthropy

By and large it is true that entrepreneurs and venture capitalists don't donate to their community. I have a lot of venture capitalist friends who do contribute, but quietly. The traditional ways of giving, such as the United Way, do not interest these people. People who made money in high tech are proud of how they made their money. They want to be smart about how they invest time and money in whatever they do.

Not everything you can give to makes a difference. Entrepreneurs typically want to wait until they know the best route to take in their giving, so they often end up doing nothing. It is hard to get the money flowing; these people are so busy, and, unfortunately, often do not get around to making it happen.

We do not work with the individuals as the community foundations do. We leverage through the companies, grow philanthropy with the companies. But, we will direct individuals for donor-advised funds and send them to community foundations.

Diminished growth shrinks philanthropy during harder economic times

This is a problem. Our kitty is much smaller right now and the economy is having an impact on what we can do. The Mayfield Fund has really underwritten much of this. A key lesson for other regions is that the driving force of a venture firm is needed to make this work.

The Mayfield Fund has set up their own foundation, a matching program, so partners' efforts can be matched. The philanthropic heritage must be there in a venture firm or forget it. Where we are now is getting companies on line to get behind what we are doing. The public stock got up to $12–13 million and then, with the market retreat, it went down considerably. This is one of the difficulties of pre-IPO stock as the giving currency.

The exportability of venture philanthropy

The Entrepreneurs Foundation has gone national. Austin started independently; now they have joined us. They had 60–70 firms join in nine months. They have a much tighter, more responsive philanthropic community than Silicon Valley. In the Bay Area it is harder to get people's attention. We are also working with Dallas, Atlanta, and Boston.

You have to have a venture firm and people, venture attorneys, and receptive entrepreneurs to get the idea going. Good capital markets make this work. ∎

Gib Myers and the other venture philanthropists who are successful, well established, and older represent one view of this phenomenon. To better understand the appeal of philanthropy in start-up cultures, we sought the viewpoint of the younger participants who are being recruited. It is their outlook that defines the future for the success of these entrepreneurial philanthropic efforts.

THE YOUNG VENTURE PHILANTHROPY ENTREPRENEURS

Emil Wang is president of Latitude Communications, which provides enterprise solutions for voice and Web-based conferencing to Fortune 1000 companies through products such as its Meeting Place Conference Server and services integrated with Microsoft Outlook, Lotus Notes, and wireless technologies. Headquartered in Santa Clara, California, Latitude Communications' customers include Oracle, Merrill Lynch, NBC, Union Pacific Rail Road, NASA, and the Federal Reserve. The company was named one of Silicon Valley's top five fastest growing companies by Deloitte and Touche LLP in 1999 and 2000, based on revenue and overall market momentum.

With 250 employees, it is one of thousands of small- to medium-sized companies in Silicon Valley that have developed niche technologies to serve businesses. What is atypical is their commitment to build philanthropy into the corporate culture right from the start, providing employees with up to 40 hours per year of paid leave, in addition to their vacation time, to pursue their community service interests.

Mr. Wang's background is in engineering and business, having worked at Bain & Co., ROLM, and most recently for seven years at Aspect Telecommunications. He was awarded Entrepreneur of the Year by the Entrepreneurs Foundation in 2000.

EMIL WANG

Community-oriented corporate culture is smart business

Many start-ups in the Valley look at a financial play. Create a buzz — then sell out. In our case, we really wanted to build a company. We incubated from our venture capital firm the Mayfield Fund. We actually spent considerable amounts of time specifying a company cultural environment.

In start-ups you normally build a sustainable market and business strategy; less typical is to also build a sustainable corporate environment. The big issue here in the Valley has been recruiting and retaining good employees (especially during the boom of 1998–2000). We did not offer extravagant salaries. Rather, we opted to create a company environment with flexible work hours. In addition, our employees could take time off for nonprofit activities. We were not going to be the kind of start-up that made people work until they dropped. Balance of life was built into the business model. Our top performers have personal family lives and lives in their community.

Here in the U.S., even our kids are thinking more about community service and it is part of the lifestyle. Company exercise rooms are now standard because business leaders realize that physically fit employees are more productive and happier employees. Companies should recognize that many individuals engage in community service to balance their lives; like exercise, this should be embraced as part of the corporate culture.

This provides an opportunity to distinguish ourselves for recruiting good employees. We created a policy where we offered, in addition to vacation time, one week of paid community service that every employee can take advantage of. One example of how this is used is for an employee to participate in the AIDS bicycle ride from Silicon Valley to Los Angeles; this raises money for AIDS research.

Companies are looking for ways to entertain their employee base. We also try to organize community service events that attract our employees' interest. We have supported Habitat for Humanity, an organization of volunteers who help to build homes for poor people; sponsored a triathalon; established a corporate charity challenge; and raised money for charitable organizations.

**We need help to get smart about how we
can make a difference in the way we want to do it**

A person who is attracted to a start-up might want to make an individual contribution or find an innovative way to give, but few of us are in the business of knowing which organizations will be good for us. The Entrepreneurs Foundation brokers and filters what is best for us given our interests. For example, we wanted to do something with Ronald McDonald House, which hosts children with serious illnesses. We were able to donate our software so the kids could video-conference with their relatives. This was a unique contribution that we could make with our product and a volunteer effort.

In the same way that venture capitalists help to set up a company, the Entrepreneurs Foundation asks you what your idea is. If it makes sense, then they will help you find a group to work with.

Start-ups have been laggards in giving back to their communities

There is a recognition that start-ups need to look at their participation in the community, but by no means is it widespread. The vast majority of companies are just trying to survive. But, many more people have set up their own private giving foundations. Still, the leap from individuals to small companies has not yet arrived. The larger companies like Hewlett-Packard and Cisco are set up for community service. It is embryonic for start-ups. That is where EF has made a dent. They market to pre-IPO companies for serious corporate philanthropy.

**For many foreign-born entrepreneurs and workers,
philanthropy is an alien concept**

The individuals we hire are exposed to it. By being exposed to it in the corporate culture, they get it. Even with the Internet bubble burst, a lot of people still give money and time. People want to be in a start-up because they want to be more involved in the business. That same ethos carries to community involvement. We made a conscious effort to build this into the company structure. And we made the commitment to designate an employee to coordinate the company's volunteerism and community service.

Being part of the community is a quality of life decision, just as are healthy lifestyles and creating family time. ■

This focus on linking organizations illustrates the vibrancy of Silicon Valley and the initiative people here have to continually innovate — in community development just as in high-tech business. These organizations are all part of the vibrant community fabric helping to make Silicon Valley such a dynamic place to live.

ENDNOTES

1. Giving USA 2001: *The Annual Report on Philanthropy*. The Center of Philanthropy at Indiana University.

2. *Joint Venture's 2001 Index of Silicon Valley*, *www.jointventure.org*.

3. Janet Zich, "Cultivating a Culture: Venture Capitalist Gib Myers is Leveraging Silicon Valley's Most Valuable Assets — Money, People, and Talent — to Grow a Better Community," *Stanford Business*, March 1999.

4. "Gib Myers Receives American Spirit Award." *Philanthropy Journal Alert*, Vol. 3, No. 64, April 21, 1999.

4

LOCAL GOVERNMENT WORKING IN PARTNERSHIP WITH BUSINESS

The city of Milpitas, California, provides a prime example of a local government that not only uses today's technologies to work more effectively and efficiently, but one that truly supports the continued growth of the high-technology industry. While it is true that cities in close proximity to Silicon Valley have a greater opportunity than municipalities in most other regions to be considered by high-tech companies, the 15 cities in Santa Clara County actually compete for those businesses among themselves. They simultaneously cooperate across jurisdictions to provide regional advantage, such as with the online Smart permit system, which we will profile in this chapter.

Dubbed the Gateway to Silicon Valley, Milpitas is located 45 minutes south of San Francisco, and serves as the crossroads of the Valley. Milpitas continues to draw high-tech expansion and support services into its 14 square miles. With a population of 65,000 people, Milpitas might be viewed as just one of the many small cities in California. Yet, the city has become a government entrepreneur in its aggressive pursuit of high-tech businesses. Milpitas hosts 350 high-tech companies, facilities, and offices, counting world-class Quantum, Solectron, and Cisco among them.

The following are comments by Henry Manayan, mayor of Milpitas, who discusses how local government can play an integral role in the economic success of a region.

HENRY MANAYAN

On the spirit of cooperation

Silicon Valley started with a spirit of cooperation that has continued and amplified in recent years. Local government is intertwined with the private industries, and the businesses here are also connected through the spin-offs that are at the roots of the Valley. All these technologies need each other; they interact with each other, and their technologies feed upon each other. That's why our region has valued cooperation rather than competitiveness.

The high-tech industry here understands that it needs to have a good relationship with the city in order to get its physical goals accomplished. For example, building a plant in a certain place, making sure the zoning is appropriate, or that health and safety codes are enforced. Most CEOs and facilities managers realize this is a very important part of doing well. In addition to being mayor of Milpitas, I am also the president of the Santa Clara County City Association, which comprises all 15 cities here in Silicon Valley. We are cognizant of the rule that three entities have to interact — the three entities being government, private industry, and education. It's like a triangle where we all interact very closely with each other and we try to cooperate in a manner that I have really never seen happen anywhere else in this country.

Government in partnership with business creates regional wealth

Your healthiest cities, and the cities that offer the best services to its citizens, are cities that have a sound economic base. Without this economic base you cannot offer services to your residents, such as parks and recreation, police and fire protection, and the other amenities that come with being a city resident. So it's very important that we here in government focus on the high-technology industry, since this is Silicon Valley.

Milpitas has one of the highest concentrations of high-tech companies of any Silicon Valley city. If you look around, within the 14 square miles of Milpitas, there are more than 350 high-tech firms among the thousands of businesses.

Speed, flexibility, and service

When a high-tech firm needs to move and establish a plant here, it needs to move very quickly. And if we as a government can't respond quickly enough, we will lose out also. First, we are going to lose the company because it will find another place that can meet its timing. But more importantly, from the company's perspective, two things can happen if it can't move fast enough. Number one, its technology will become obsolete; or number two, its competition will overtake them.

Here is an analogy to help better understand how speed, flexibility, and good service can be compared with normal expectations.

In this country the biggest hardware manufacturer of retail products is Sears, Roebuck and Co. When you order your refrigerator from Sears, they'll tell you what day they're going to come and deliver your refrigerator. But you won't know what time. You have to wait around all day just for a delivery truck to come by and bring you your refrigerator. When Pacific Bell, our largest phone supplier for Northern California, delivers your phone they'll tell you maybe morning or afternoon, so they'll narrow it down to a half-day difference, but you still have to wait around. That's a tremendous waste of time. If you're not there, you don't get your telephone. In the city of Milpitas we can schedule our building inspections in 15-minute increments. No other city in this Valley has ever been able to do that. Not only can we schedule our building inspections in 15-minute increments, we can schedule them seven days a week. You want it done on a Saturday or Sunday? Fine, we're there. We can do that. Not only can we do it seven days a week, we can do it 24 hours a day.

Government can be customer focused and use the same improvement techniques as the private sector

We went back and asked our own people in building and planning, what would it take for us to succeed beyond anyone else. Our own people came up with the ideas for being more responsive in partnership with their counterparts in the private sector. Of course, for the companies it isn't free. They'll pay a little extra for it. Our employees benefit; they will get overtime pay. The city benefits; we get more revenue. The company benefits, because they get their projects completed on time. The best example I have is that we had our city engineers on a national holiday, December 24, 1999 — Christmas Eve — doing building inspections at Quantum Corporation, the largest hard drive manufacturer in the world.

We can offer a dedicated planner for a company, if they really have to move. We can expedite the permitting system for companies that are willing to pay the extra fees and where the urgency is very apparent.

Regional wealth helps the city of Milpitas

Milpitas has continued to grow despite other cities cutting back and that's because we're well diversified. In high technology we weren't dependent on the dot-coms like a lot of other places. We have a strong manufacturing base, we have telecommunications, some dot-coms, and a strong retail base. As a result of that, the city has continued to grow. We have added more staff members, more managers, and more departments. We have expanded departments of public safety. Crime has decreased every year for six consecutive years. We are building the most technologically advanced city hall in the nation. It will cost $35 million. We don't have to raise taxes or issue bonds to pay for this — the money is in the bank.

Work with your business partners to simplify the process

The only thing that we continue to be a model for, and have people from all over the country studying and touring our systems almost monthly for, is that we have been able to cut through the layers of bureaucracy, cut through the paperwork and look to the bottom line. If a city wants to do this, it must reengineer its process by first asking its own people how they can improve upon what they are doing and then implement their suggestions. This works very much like the method of total quality control as implemented in places like Japan, where they have teams of workers putting their heads together to improve and become better. That's what makes us stand out. ∎

Of course, government in partnership with business sounds good, but it is never as smooth and easy in practice as it sounds in theory. Next are the opinions of the president and facilities manager of one of the large businesses attracted to Milpitas in 1999. Their comments support the contention that government can be responsive.

David Ferrari is the president of One Workplace, which focuses on improving efficiency, controlling costs, and increasing productivity through all the stages of office design and works with over 200 suppliers of furniture, fabric, lighting, carpet, and accessories to attain this goal.

One Workplace's services include managing moves, performing feasibility studies to help find the optimal design for your workplace, project management, asset management, furniture liquidation, warehousing and storage services, installation of new products and reconfiguration of existing products as necessary, and providing both custom product and product repairs.

The business generates $250 million a year in revenue and provides a good tax base for the city of Milpitas.

Ferrari and his facilities manager, Dave Martinez, comment on how the Milpitas planning department and the Smart Permit program facilitated the process of relocation of One Workplace.

DAVID FERRARI AND DAVE MARTINEZ

We found the city of Milpitas flexible to deal with when we decided to move from San Jose. They streamlined the process and gave good incentives. In our case, we wanted to combine front offices with a warehouse. The Smart Permit system made it easier to get the job done and faster to get through the city process. The city is responsible with services and inspections, and the buildings are safe. In other cities, the permit process is a royal pain in the butt. Trying to get improvements is tough and time is money.

Responsiveness is more important than just tax incentives. They value the people who are here; they want them to stay here. We have direct access to anyone in city government.

When we moved to Milpitas, I met with the building department, and they were open to any issues. The facilities we moved into were already built. For the most part, Milpitas city government staff members were helping me to find a solution and were on my side. They were willing to spend time with me. This contrasts with other city experiences we have had where they put up obstacles.

For city government to become a partner in the whole process, you need to work with them to try and develop whatever needs to be done quickly. They provided concessions in moving fees, making it affordable to move. What Milpitas is doing is the exception. My advice to facilities managers is to get in early so you can understand the city process and get them on your side. ■

REGIONAL COOPERATION TO STREAMLINE GOVERNMENT USING AN ONLINE PERMITTING SYSTEM

Government in collaboration with business can accelerate regional wealth in the knowledge-based regional economies. One critical element to understanding the importance of local municipal government is that it can contribute to business competitiveness through reducing the time it takes to get facilities built, permits approved, and inspections scheduled and completed. In high tech, time is money because being the first to market is an advantage for business.

Because high-tech companies have offices and plants across municipal jurisdictions, it is also important that these government innovations happen on a regional basis. It would be far less useful if it were being implemented in only one town.

In Silicon Valley the story of how local jurisdictions have collaborated to upgrade, standardize, and link new Internet-based solutions for building permits is both unique and exemplary for illustrating how government can be part of the solution for creating regional wealth and advantage.

The permitting process should lead to new collaborations in land use and infrastructure planning; this is critical to Silicon Valley continuing as a competitive regional magnet for high-tech businesses. The adaptation of computerized geographic information systems (GIS) will enable this regional analysis and information sharing to progress in regional planning development.

JUMPING THROUGH HOOPS

One of the lesser-known factors in the success of Silicon Valley is the degree to which local government works in partnership with industry for regional advantage.

Ask any business person about his or her opinion of local government; your replies will usually be neutral at best and antagonistic at worst. Complexity, inefficiency, inertia, and just plain inability to move quickly and be flexible seem to be the norm. Of course corruption, cronyism, and worse are always suspect. The authors have frequently polled graduate business students in the U.S. and Europe about what factors are necessary for regional advantage in high technology, and local government working in concert with business is almost never identified as a significant factor.

Yet, when government partners in a vibrant collaboration with industry, a region can create amazing innovation and competitive advantage in areas many people consider a weak link. A good example of this is the development of the Smart Permit process.

The Smart Permit's roots are in streamlining of government processes. In 1993 the cities in Silicon Valley started out to reengineer government, and focused on transforming the architectural, engineering, and construction (AEC) industry and the delivery of public services. Government can be an enabler or a roadblock to transforming the AEC industry because its communications infrastructure and systems must be in place for the users to complete the transformation and actually use these streamlined services. Permits and inspections are normally a point of contention. Because permit applications and inspections delay construction, this process is usually an annoying bottleneck for rapidly expanding businesses. Facilities managers liken this process to jumping through hoops, which compares what they are required to do to get municipal approvals with what animals do in a circus performance to entertain audiences. The facilities managers responsible for the process on the company side are usually in conflict with city managers and planning departments for approvals of complex construction projects.

GOVERNMENT COLLABORATING WITH BUSINESS TO WORK IN A MUTUALLY BENEFICIAL PARTNERSHIP

The Smart Permit process that has been created and adopted in Silicon Valley is a great example of such collaboration.

Several important developments influenced the creation and enabled Smart Permit's progression in Silicon Valley:

- Exponential growth in the acceptance and use of the Internet
- Technology advancements in networking, software, and desktop tools
- Successful completion of several permit process improvement projects by Joint Venture's Regulatory Streamlining Council, the Silicon Valley Manufacturing Group, and Silicon Valley cities
- Publishing of a series of *Permitting Best Practices* by the Silicon Valley Manufacturing Group
- Creation of the Silicon Valley Uniform Building Code Program and adoption of Uniform Local Amendments and Interpretations by building officials from 29 Silicon Valley jurisdictions[1]

WHAT IS SMART PERMIT?

The mission of the Joint Venture's Smart Permit project is to "bring together the public and private sectors, civic entrepreneurs, and community resources to electronically optimize building permit and community development processes within Silicon Valley."

Smart Permit is a free, standard, online application form for filing simple permits and, just as importantly, getting changes approved quickly along the course of a project. It is available to users 24 hours a day. Besides filing for permits, the system allows people to track their permit applications and to submit drawings electronically along with digital signatures. In Silicon Valley the cities of Sunnyvale, Mountain View, San Carlos, Fremont, Santa Clara, Palo Alto, San Jose, and Milpitas participate in the project. The project receives corporate support from well-known companies such as Autodesk, Carta, Microsoft, Open Data Systems, and Tidemark Systems.

Silicon Valley businesses highly value time-to-market. Product life cycles have shortened, and are reduced to times as little as six to nine months in some instances. Facility managers feel that the Smart Permit, along with other streamlining processes, will enable them to obtain permits faster and thus let them contribute directly to the company's competitive advantage.

With the traditional permit process, it could cost a manufacturer hundreds of thousands of dollars per day to wait for the approval of the building permit. Smart Permit has enabled cities in Silicon Valley to better serve the needs of high-tech companies and thus make the area a very attractive place to do business. In turn, it benefits the region, as it ensures the growth of the local economy. The automated permit process enables the issuing offices to dramatically increase their productivity, while becoming much more cost effective. It used to take an average of $10,000 in company employee time to process the paperwork for a traditional permit application for a new commercial building. Now the time is sharply reduced, leaving time and money for other issues.

The widespread use of the electronic permitting system is not instantaneous or guaranteed, since it changes the way an entire industry, including government, does business. And everybody resists change. One of the lessons learned from this process was that you have to market, train, demonstrate, and service this system in order for each of the parties involved in permitting to adopt it as standard procedure. It also takes time for the private sector to drive demand for usage of the system. Since it is not off-the-shelf software, there is also a great amount of time needed to adapt this software for individual use.

Here is the story from three people who were involved in this effort from its inception. Bob Kraiss, director of facilities management at Adaptec in Milpitas; Mike Garvey, San Carlos city manager; and Brian Moura, San Carlos assistant city manager. These excerpts from their discussion provide insight into the dynamics of how initiatives can work and the role individuals, who often sit across the table from each other in contention, have in making the extraordinary happen.

BOB KRAISS, MIKE GARVEY, AND BRIAN MOURA

Bob Kraiss: There was a reason to do this back in 1993. Milpitas had a lousy inter-action with the industry. Permits took three months and if you don't like it, tough! I supervised the construction of a campus for Solectron, a two time Mal-colm Baldridge winner (international business excellence award). We used great productivity techniques with ISO 2000 and Malcolm Baldrige principles, and the city just kept doing what it had been doing, with no improvement. So I invited the top 15 facilities managers whose companies represent about 85% of the jobs in Milpitas to lunch and we talked. We talked about the stuff the city did wrong, but also the stuff that we did wrong that made it tough on the city. We used to be forced to get serial permits (one process approval at a time). We needed to institute parallel processing, so multiple aspects could be applied for at one time and with ongoing changes you could apply for approval in real time.

So that was the beginning. Milpitas became cooperative. It was a partnership of mutual benefits as opposed to us screaming about how bad they were. And I took that concept to the Silicon Valley Manufacturing Group.

Simultaneously, Joint Venture Silicon Valley was setting up a regulatory stream-lining effort. So, Joint Venture and Silicon Valley Manufacturing Group began the relationship-building efforts that took place, which I think is a key.

Brian Moura: Right, so that was the original issue. And the first question that we heard from a gentleman from I believe IBM, was, "Why don't you just put it on the Internet?" I said, "Well, that could be done, but what is it that would happen if it was on the Internet? If we don't change anything else, what have we achieved?" And so we began talking and people started to conceive of what this project could be and what it would cost. And there was a person from one of the chambers of commerce who said, "All of this should be done by the cities for business and it shouldn't cost any more than it already does." And one of the high-tech folk interrupted this person and said, "Excuse me, you are not from my city, and who cares what it costs? I will pay more for a permit in a city that has its act together, that is streamlined, and is on the Web. That is a value-added service. Frankly, in the scheme of things, the difference of paying $300 and $325 for some permit is trivial compared with the fact that if my plant gets up a month sooner, I stand to make a $1 million! So let's not argue over $25 or $50!"

Why the collaboration for Smart Permit worked in Silicon Valley

Bob Kraiss: The top four or five guys in city government and industry liked each other. The first time we got together at the Silicon Valley Manufacturing Group, we tried to identify best practices, which is a management process to improve quality. Within that one-month time frame, they took the best ideas from the ideas presented, implemented them, and presented them to us. By the time we went through a series of these best practices questions and answers, every city that was involved became significantly better in the way it conducted business. They were talking to each other and figuring out ways to do things in a cooper-ative manner as opposed to operating in isolation.

If the city and government officials got together on their own and asked, "How can we do things better for our customers?," it might work, but it's doubtful. We, the customers, were in the room. We had 20 industries sitting there, listening to 11 cities present and that made a difference. They would ask, "By the way, if I do this, will it help you?" So, we created a relationship between industry and city, between industry and industry, between city and city. Suddenly, as opposed to looking out for our own interests, all of us were saying, "How can we, collectively, do it better?" And we no longer used the term "the city," we didn't say those words anymore; they were immaterial. It was, "How is Ron going to solve this problem? How is Ron going to help? I see, Ron's IS department isn't strong enough to figure this one out, let's go to San Carlos or Sunnyvale, because they have got a really strong IS department and they will be able to put this into words that technologists can understand."

Brian Moura: In the beginning, the driving force behind Joint Venture was the concern about the economy being down (during a recession in California during 1990–1994). Our economy was down because the federal government was downsizing the defense industry, we were transitioning to a new economy, and there was a high cost of living in Silicon Valley. So both the industry and the local government had an incentive to fix that. And that was the reason that they thought, "Well, gee, if we streamlined things or if we made it better, our business can expand faster and we will get those jobs back and the economy will wrap up sooner, so it is in everybody's interest to do that." At the first meetings, there was some finger pointing going on, but people began to roll up their sleeves and ask, "How are we going to fix this?" We put all the issues on the table. Now let's talk about how it actually might happen.

And I think what is interesting about this is that when we began talking about improving the process, improving software, and outing it on the Internet, originally there were a lot of cities competing to be first. They thought, "We will get better businesses coming into town, we will have our name in lights." But once we actually started spelling out what it all actually meant, there was a bit of a pullback. Everybody said, "We want to be involved and see where it is going, but I'm not sure that we are necessarily ready to put our toe in the water."

In some cities, as Bob suggested, we had some enlightened building officials. The reason we were able to reduce the number of amendments (procedures) from 400 to 11 for all the cities and regions is because we had three building officials get together and they came up with something. They took everybody's amendments and spread them out and went back to all the building officials in the region and negotiated and basically said, "Look, a lot of this could be reduced."

Collaboration is driven by personalities and enlightened businesses

Bob Kraiss: I give Becky Morgan (former executive director of Joint Venture Silicon Valley) credit for being the queen of collaboration. She taught people what collaboration really means and she promoted it in every instance. She is a former state senator and understood government; she was well regarded, the wife of the CEO of Applied Materials (John Morgan), so she had a good industry link. People listened to her. The second element was that we have in this region access to companies that virtually no other region has access to. One of the most important facts to make this thing work was that Autodesk, who owns the CAD (computer-assisted design) market and whose software all the architectural drawings are developed with, created some software to allow us to do online checking. It had never been made before. It had to be user friendly and they offered to give it away free. Where else in the world could we build a project based on an attitude of cooperation and generosity like this?

You need that entrepreneurial and collaborative spirit in your community to make this work. If you don't, it doesn't work. If you have this collaborative spirit, then you are going to do smart programming whether we assist you or not.

It is true we had access to technology at this location that the others would not get. But in terms of the spirit that businesses are ready to pitch in, that potential exists in all areas, mostly in metropolitan areas, but even in rural areas if the local businesses want to go to work on it, it can happen.

Mike Garvey: We simply didn't have the software to mark up the CAD drawings electronically. Also, with the slow modems we had back then (this was five or six years ago), it would have taken four weeks to upload a drawing. But with the current paper process, we required six sets of drawings, so that we could hand them in to different departments at the same time to speed up the process. But if changes needed to be made, the revised six sets had to be handed in again. And it was especially complicated if different departments required different changes to be made on the same project. So, some of this old process was really hard to coordinate. I had to get sign-off from five different departments.

We formed a committee of 12 employees who had several department heads. And they worked for 18 months with one of the TQM (total quality management) consultants provided by Joint Venture and were provided with lots of donated time from private industry professionals. The rule was that they could do whatever they wanted to, but there was confidentiality. They wouldn't even report back to me. They would just clean up the system. Later, some of the stories drifted out and it was embarrassing to think I was the chief executive of a city like that. It doesn't take just high-powered experts. It also takes people at the street level to get them thinking.

Early interest in the Smart Permit process . . . marketing is essential

Bob Kraiss: We used one of the meetings of the SV chapter of the Facilities Managers Association to create a venue called Smart Permit Presentation. We had 500 people show up both from the industry and from the cities. Then we hosted a second presentation and had 800 people attend. So it was a great momentum builder. Many people were now hearing about it. We had people from all over the country attending these meetings. The third one we did, two years later, we did at the San Jose Tech Museum. We had little booths for all our partners, such as Autodesk, to let them show how they participated and to demonstrate their products. So there was a lot of marketing going on.

Mike Garvey: Marketing was a good lesson, too. I think some of the cities thought they just needed to put the Smart Permit system up on their Web sites and expected people would discover it somehow. One of the things we did in San Carlos, was that every time we had a major piece of this to unveil, we went to the city council, we had press releases, and really made it a big deal. You have to market this system to the users of the permitting system.

Brian Moura: There needs to be a warning for governments that want to move to Web-enabled capabilities. You may introduce new services, new ways of doing things. But you are not necessarily streamlining government, because there is an expectation by your customers that the old way, the legacy systems, are still in place. So, even though there are changes that we are seeing, such as that 60% of our routine permits are coming in over fax, and once we go to the Web, we see similar numbers. So we free up time. But we also are going to have to have the old way as well for those who don't have a computer. Even if we change the way that government works, some people may not notice or it may not be the format they want. ∎

SUMMARY

The people we have profiled in this chapter combine an unusual blend of personal openness, collaborative spirit, and willingness to take risks and try new approaches to solving problems. They are action oriented, and like to "get things done." Each has contributed to the vibrancy of the region and their examples demonstrate how Silicon Valley has been able to continually innovate and lead through an unusual combination of government, NGOs, and business working together.

ENDNOTES

1. "Smart Permit: A Blueprint for Success," Joint Venture: Silicon Valley Network, *www.jointventure.org/initiatives/smartpermit/history.html*, March 2001.

IRELAND

THE ENTERPRISE ISLE

Ireland was long considered a backwater of Europe and an economic appendage to the United Kingdom. Its greatest export over the past two centuries has been its people. George Bernard Shaw, the great early 20th century playwright, bespoke the Irish predicament when he said, "I showed my appreciation of my native land in the usual Irish way by getting out of it as soon as I possibly could."[1]

Ireland has turned itself into an exemplary model of economic strength through linkage to the Innovation Economy. Its story is a great inspiration for those regions seeking to elevate themselves through economic development.

Moving up the value chain to adapt to economic and technological change is built into Ireland's development strategy. Competitive advantage is dynamic, not static. In the 1980s, low wage costs and tax incentives attracted mainly assembly and manufacturing activity. As cost pressures in the 1990s began to reduce the attractiveness of Ireland as a location for mobile investment, the focus moved to software development. In the late 1990s, Ireland vigorously sought to ride the wave of the Internet and e-business

---

1. Jon Winokur, *The Portable Curmudgeon*. New York: New American Library Trade, 1987.

explosion by highlighting its competitive edge in state-of-the-art facilities such as broadband connectivity. Today Ireland is set to become one of the foremost knowledge-based societies in Europe.

Throughout this remarkable "Innovation Revolution" one fact remains certain: Ireland has a pro-business political culture that has built a regulatory, service, and fiscal environment that few countries can match.

5

ENTERPRISE SPIRIT AND TRADE UNION SOCIAL CONTRACT

IRELAND: EUROPE'S HIGH-TECH HUB

Ireland, a small island at the edge of the continental shelf, attracts a quarter of the U.S.'s high-tech investment into Europe, although it accounts for a mere 1% of Europe's population. It provides the highest rate of return on that investment, a whopping 24% according to the U.S. Department of Commerce. With phenomenal growth rates (11% in 2000) in real GDP over the past decade, and the highest proportion of exports (90%) of GDP, Ireland has turned itself around from being the poor man of Europe into one of the shining lights of the global economy, earning the epithet of Celtic Tiger and attracting policymakers and planners from all over the world seeking to learn the secrets of her economic success.

TABLE 5-1 Facts at a Glance — Ireland

Population	3.6 million
Population under age 25	40%
Work force	1.5 million
Estimated work force under 25 in 2010	36%
GDP per capita in 2000	$24,000
Real GDP growth in 2000	11%
Unemployment rate in 2000	3.6%
Number of foreign multinational corporations (MNCs)	1,212
Employment in foreign MNCs	140,000
Computer equipment as percentage of exports in 2000	23%
Total number of software companies	840
Total employment in software companies	30,000
Foreign software companies	140
Employment in foreign software companies	15,000
U.S. corporations as percentage of MNCs	41%

Source: IDA Ireland, www.idaireland.com.

ECONOMICS: COMMON SENSE AND CASH FROM EUROPE

The success of the 1990s is in stark contrast to the Irish economic situation during the preceding decade. A potential foreign investor contemplating the financial position of the Republic of Ireland in the early 1980s would have had serious reservations about the economic viability of the state, and in particular the colossal national debt that by 1987 had soared to $25 billion, or 129% of GNP.

Servicing that debt swallowed up 35% of tax revenues and accounted for 25% of government spending. The free state that had broken the link with the United Kingdom in 1922 and declared itself a republic in 1949 was on the verge of bankruptcy. Ireland was an economic disaster!

Selling Ireland as an investment location to foreign corporations was, to put it mildly, a Herculean task, made possible by the consistently positive approach of successive Irish governments to business development in general, and foreign direct investment in particular, since the mid 1980s.

The turning point in Ireland's economic fortunes came when the government adopted the tough supply-side economic policy recommended in the National Economic and Social Council's (NESC) *Strategy for Development 1986–1990*. The central message in this report was that Ireland could only survive as a viable economic entity if the national debt was stabilized through cuts in public spending. Ray McSharry, then minister for finance, gives a gripping account of the radical policy turnaround in *The Making of the Celtic Tiger*. The success of the government's management of the economy that made the boom possible is reflected in some key indicators:

TABLE 5-2   Comparison of Ireland's Economic Benchmarks, 1986 and 2000

	1986*	2000*
Budget (deficit)/surplus	($1.6 billion)	$2.25 billion
Growth in GNP	-0.7%	10.4%
Unemployment	17%	3.6%

* Actual GNP in 1986 at 1995 constant prices = 23,037.
  Actual GNP in 2000 at 1995 constant prices = 55,772.
Source: Central Statistics Office, Ireland, www.eirestat.cso.ie.

As the government initiated drastic cuts in public spending to stabilize and then reduce the debt, Ireland benefited from a huge injection of aid from the European Union — $11 billion in financial transfers between 1989 and 1999. This cash was deployed wisely to upgrade transportation infrastructure, raise the skills base of the work force, and support local urban and rural development.

SOCIAL PARTNERSHIP, IRISH STYLE

The government knew that one of the underlying causes of the country's economic ills was the wage inflation that had resulted from free pay bargaining (unrestricted requests for wage increases). The unions needed to be convinced that accepting tough measures, such as spending cuts, was in their members' interests, because increases from short-term pay claims were being eroded by tax and inflation. The government proposed tax cuts in return for pay restraint, a deal the unions bought. The new style of social partnership that emerged was a response to the national crisis in employment and public finances. The radical change in union thinking and behavior laid the groundwork for what was to become the Irish economic miracle. Pay restraint increased Ireland's competitiveness for investors, gave employers a degree of certainty on payroll costs, and resulted in increases in employment and growth together with a drop in inflation.

Between 1987 and 2000, there was an 80% increase in real take-home pay and a 12% drop in income tax rates. The improvement in industrial relations is evidenced by the drop in the number of days lost due to strikes, from over a million in 1979 to less than 35,000 in 2000.

The key to the Irish system of centralized bargaining (originally outlined in the NESC report mentioned above) is the linking of pay and non-pay items such as tax, welfare benefits, social insurance and provision of services, and the inclusion of unions in the medium- and long-term macroeconomic management process.

THE U.S. CONNECTION

Because the majority of target corporations were located in the U.S., the close historical and emotional links between America and Ireland (sometimes referred to as the 51st state) also played a part. Ireland has always been extremely receptive to American ways (the first MBA program to be set up outside the U.S. was at University College Dublin in the 1960s). The Irish are flexible and adaptable and had no problem operating under the supervision of U.S. managers. Local Irish managers could also be appointed with confidence that corporate procedures and methods would be applied and respected to the letter. So it's not surprising that a quarter of Europe-bound investment from the U.S. lands in Ireland.

Brendan Halpin is international media and marketing manager for IDA Ireland (The Investment and Development Agency). He discusses the advantage that Ireland offers to U.S. companies, the new European economic reality that the public need not be served exclusively by their own nationals, and the emphasis on value-added services that has given Ireland a competitive edge over its European counterparts.

BRENDAN HALPIN

In terms of access, networking, and getting to the starting line, the links between Ireland and the United States are extremely important. Ireland has a very good reputation worldwide as a high-skilled, forward-looking, technological society, with a lot of young, exciting people. And we're English speaking; for Americans that's a particular attraction. Americans prefer to recruit management locally, managers who understand how business operates in Europe. We have enormous experience, over a long time of being true international businesses, compared with the U.K. where they are more inward-looking because of the huge internal market. The managers of these plants in Ireland have virtually no internal market. So they have developed vast experience and know what it means to manufacture or to have a service product in Ireland that is traded throughout Europe. They also know all the difficulties, cultural differences, and other aspects that go along with doing that business.

The information, communications, and technology (ICT) industry is dominated by the U.S., which will continue to provide our main source of investment.

The proof is that Microsoft has its European operations based here; Intel is putting its European manufacturing in Ireland; Dell has its European headquarters in Ireland. You don't have to be in all these countries to sell into all these markets. It is becoming less nationalistic. For example, we have continued to get a lot of German investment in Ireland. Companies may be headquartered in Germany, but operations need not be based in Germany. A German customer today is different from a German customer 20 years ago; they are beginning to demand more quality and more service than in the past. Service in a lot of companies in Europe was nonexistent. Many on the Continent would say, "There is the product, there is the price. It is high quality. If you want it, buy it; if not, fine." But the Japanese and the U.S. companies coming in focused a lot more on service.

Ireland was more service oriented because of the American influence. Most of the businesses in Ireland were run by Irish people. They learned a huge amount about international business, especially in Europe, and they learned pretty quickly. Their American counterparts did not have this experience. So U.S. companies were recruiting Irish people who did have it. They became expert, especially in really sophisticated services like freight. In Europe, you sent it to your local railway station, and just put it on the train. In Ireland, there were all sorts of value-added services to compete. And there are very sophisticated and creative ways to do this. ■

THE IRISH ENLIGHTENMENT: DOVETAILING TECHNOLOGICAL PROGRESS AND GOVERNMENT POLICY

Having fully deregulated the telecommunications market (with over 20 companies competing), the government set about positioning Ireland as a hub for Internet business. It adapted a proactive approach to e-commerce, which was translated into legislation giving validity to electronic signatures and contracts (in the E-Commerce Act, July 2000). The taoiseach (prime minister), Mr. Bertie Ahern, was presented with the Cyber Champion Award by the Business Software Alliance in October 2000 in recognition of his efforts to support the software industry.

In terms of infrastructure, over 98% of national telecommunications is carried on fiber optics. A high-capacity cable capable of handling 30 million calls simultaneously now connects Dublin to the U.S. and 36 European cities. This broadband capacity is being extended to all the counties in Ireland, making it one of the best-connected countries in the world and providing firms with a platform upon which to build their e-business.

This enlightened approach has made Ireland the preferred European location for software companies, and is likely to make her a global leader in knowledge-based industry and services.

In Ireland, politics has always had more to do with pragmatism, vision, and adapting to change than ideology. Cooperation between the public and private sectors has never been problematic. Albert Reynolds, who held numerous cabinet posts (posts and telegraphs, industry and commerce, finance) before becoming taoiseach in 1992, was a millionaire who made his fortune from meat products and ballrooms. He is typical of a breed of Irish politicians with a keen sense of business. Ireland is a small country where networking is a way of life. This facilitates the flow of information and points of view among politicians, businessmen, civil servants, academics, and union leaders. So it is relatively easy to make things happen.

Major investment decisions are taken quickly both at a local and a national level. Whether it is getting a bridge built in a provincial town because a Korean investor complained of traffic congestion, or investing $5 billion to build that state-of-the-art digital telecom system, Ireland is a place where civil servants and politicians get things done in double-quick time when local or national interests are at stake. Brendan Halpin continues his discussion of IDA responsiveness.

BRENDAN HALPIN

The lines of communication between the IDA and the taoiseach, and the ministers for industry and education are very short. The responsiveness of government, irrespective of the party in power, was a key factor. That would be impossible in a lot of countries. The people who set up the IDA devised this view that an independent, professional organization with wide-reaching powers should be established to sell Ireland as a product. That it should get fundamental support through legislation to enable that to happen was quite far-reaching. The IDA was the largest property developer in the country, competing with private developers and even subsidizing potential clients and selling or leasing property below market prices. In other countries that would have been terribly difficult. Even in Ireland, you probably couldn't do that today. ∎

EDUCATION: THE KEY TO SUSTAINED COMPETITIVE ADVANTAGE

The quality of the Irish secondary educational system is a tribute to the high standards and dedication of the religious orders that have provided education for the vast majority of Irish youth for decades. Respect for knowledge and wisdom is ingrained in the Celtic cultural tradition. Access to secondary education for all is relatively recent; until 1966, quality secondary schools were tuition-based and reserved for children from the middle class. The system remains highly competitive and only those students gaining excellent scores in the Leaving Certificate may enter university. The Irish university system is primarily focused upon developing a large pool of workers for the Innovation Economy: 60% of university graduates major in science, engineering, or business studies. The *IMD World Competitiveness Report* ranks Ireland number one in Europe for quality of education.

The government has made technological literacy a priority at every level of the educational system, from introduction of multimedia PCs in every school and provision of Internet access to every child and teacher, to the $35 million funding of MediaLab Europe, which is modeled on the MIT MediaLab and specializes in multimedia, digital content, and Internet technologies. Bill Riley, public affairs manager at Intel described to us the great advantage the Irish education system provides for Intel Ireland and how the focus of the education system has shifted to support a technological knowledge-based economy.

BILL RILEY

The general education is very good; the quality of the technical graduates we get is very, very good. There just aren't enough of them. When we first came to Ireland 10 years ago, we had two sources for knowledge workers. Ireland had been exporting graduate engineers for the previous 25 years, so we immediately had a worldwide population of qualified semiconductor engineers willing to return to Ireland. We also had a large stream coming out of the universities; 50% of them would have gone to the U.S. or the U.K., or maybe to Germany or Holland. When we arrived on the scene it was a major factor in choosing Ireland versus going to England or Scotland, where there already was a semiconductor industry.

This is historically the island of saints and scholars. While Ireland has produced a sizeable number of Nobel Prize winners in literature, we haven't produced many Nobel Prize winners in science. So, we're clearly trying to shift the system in a direction more focused on hard science. ■

The Irish government continues to show the same foresight it did in the 1980s, when its strategy was to attract corporations in the information technology field to drive economic growth. Now that Ireland is no longer a low-wage economy, the next step is to move up the value chain, which means fostering research and innovation. With this objective in mind, the government is making over $2 billion available for education and research in biotechnology and ICT, a budget to be administered by the newly created Science Foundation Ireland.

The turnaround in Ireland's economic fortunes over the past 15 years is a striking example of how a region can generate wealth by creating a macroeconomic environment favorable to foreign direct investment. The Irish have attracted corporations from high-tech industries to build an economic fabric of high added value manufacturing and service industries that will eventually drive innovation among indigenous companies. This induces not only massive increases in real living standards for the population of the region, but also radical cultural change.

However, this significant change could not have happened without a major commitment by the organized labor unions to make a fundamental shift in their part of the social contract. This process has not been easy and it entails significant risk by the unions in the future role they will play in Ireland's economic development. It is to that story that we now turn.

IRISH TRADE UNIONS AND THE SOCIAL CONTRACT

Partnership is a cornerstone concept in attracting multinational corporate investment projects to Ireland. While partnership with government and indigenous business is to be expected, partnership with labor is a uniquely Irish strength.

The IDA's objective is to maintain Ireland's position as a prime location for investment, to attract new companies, as well as to win repeat investment from established ones, all the while moving up the value chain as a corporate site. This multifaceted goal requires a synthesized presentation of Ireland's competitive advantages over other Western European countries.

Ireland's well-educated labor force offers the advantage of skill availability at a competitive cost. The competitive cost factor is due largely to a strong labor union organization (which has taken an active, positive role in Ireland's social partnership), a coalition of employers, government, and trade unions. This partnership brought an awareness to the trade unions of the long-term necessity of flexibility in relation to the multinational corporations' labor force conditions.

For example, until the mid-1980s the IDA had been encouraging the investing corporations to talk to unions. This approach changed to accommodate companies like Intel and Dell, who had clear no-union policies. Generally, Ireland's relationship with multinationals has been a rocky one. As we will show, the government encouraged a laissez-faire attitude on this issue.

TRADE UNIONS

The Irish Congress of Trade Unions (ICTU) functions as an umbrella trade association for Ireland's trade unions. Approximately 50 trade unions are affiliated with the ICTU, representing around 550,000 workers in the Republic of Ireland, of which half work in the private sector. The main objectives of the ICTU, as outlined in its constitution, are to protect workers' rights to join a union, negotiate pay and working conditions, and participate in decisions affecting their work. In addition, the ICTU negotiates with employers and government to promote macroeconomic and social policies reflecting the interests of the labor force.

Until 1987, relations between unions and employers were adversarial; free pay bargaining was the norm, contributing to the high level of inflation and frequent strikes. From 1987, a more realistic attitude on the part of the unions, led by progressive, visionary leadership, ushered in a period of wage stability, with pay restraint being traded for tax cuts.

Tom Wall is assistant general secretary of the ICTU. He spoke with us about the "social contract" and the challenges of labor relations in a high-tech economy. We have also provided the comments of Bill Riley, who illustrates the difference of opinion on the management/labor relationships.

TOM WALL

Reasons for labor changing its approach

Two aspects were the stimulus for action. One was the depth of the economic crisis; it forced a rethink. And, linked to that, the fact that real earnings had been decreasing. Clearly, enterprise-level bargaining wasn't working and there was a move back to the centralized agreements we had in the 1970s. The second factor was a generation change that occurs in the leadership of all organizations. Around 1987 Peter Cassells was acting general secretary, but there were also some trade union leaders, Phil Flynn and Billy Attley, who developed a new strategy that proposed a clear statement of what our objectives were in the social and economic fields, moving away from the narrow bargaining arena. They saw there was no way they could achieve anything on this unless they sat down with government and considered the possibility of tradeoffs.

Social partnership 1987–2000

The union delegations were not optimistic that they would get a deal because we had a significant agenda; we were willing to trade off moderate pay, but we didn't just want aspirations about employment creation, we wanted targets. To our side's surprise the taoiseach was prepared to put figures on it and stick his neck out. The trade-off between pay moderation and tax cuts was key, there was no way we could get an agreement without that. Although inflation had been dropping, it was still around 4% to 5%, so to move to 2.5% for the average earner, we couldn't have done that without significant tax cuts. ■

Securing wage moderation contributed to lowering inflation and public spending, and consequently boosted the competitiveness of Irish-based corporations. Employment and growth improved, and the foundations for the remarkable takeoff of the Irish economy were laid. The payoff for the Irish work force was an across-the-board increase in real take-home pay.

The three-year social partnership format was repeated in the 1991 Programme for Economic and Social Progress, the 1994 Programme for Competitiveness and Work, and the 1997 Partnership 2000.

By abandoning the hard-nosed approach to pay bargaining, union leaders were able to increase their input into, and influence on, economic management. Union representatives are positioned to play a more proactive role through participating with employers and government.

RELATIONS BETWEEN LABOR AND HIGH-TECH MULTINATIONALS

The arrival of multinationals in Ireland in the 1960s met with some resistance. Major and sometimes violent disputes arose. The labor movement, however, soon came to recognize that foreign direct investment was the motor of growth and employment. Tom Wall described it this way: "By the 1980s the view had emerged that if there's anything worse than multinationals, it's no multinationals."

In the late 1970s and early 1980s, the IDA had a policy of encouraging companies to talk to unions. That changed with the shift toward a high-tech industrial base. Companies such as Intel would not have come to Ireland if they had been encouraged in that direction. So as a consequence, foreign direct investment did not tend to lead to any growth in union membership.

TOM WALL

So we had this divide, with companies like Apple, who were there before and who were unionized, and with the newer computer companies who weren't. The crossover point was DEC; there was actually an agreement with DEC, which said that if anybody wanted to join a union they could be a member of the ITGWU. But then they did their damnedest to make sure nobody would actually apply. A few were members but they never recognized a union. After that, international companies had the confidence to forego that exercise.

ICT companies are not renowned for their positive attitude toward unions

The problem for us is that American multinationals see unions as what they experienced in the past in America — this slight taint of crime, these highly rigid and conflict-ridden contractual arrangements. We've tried to convince them that's not what we're about. ■

Intel prides itself on what it considers an enlightened style of manager-employee relations. It sees little role for unions. Next, Bill Riley provides Intel's perspective.

BILL RILEY

Our work force is not unionized. There is no legal requirement for us to do that in Ireland, although EU labor legislation is gradually encroaching on the freedom of Irish business to manage its employees. Going back 20 years or so, the IDA were certainly encouraging people to do sweetheart deals with unions, a practice which they have sensibly ceased because it was counterproductive. If you look at the investments that have come to Ireland in the past 15 years, the vast majority have been by companies who do not use third parties as part of their relationship with their employees.

Intel would not be in Ireland or any country that obliged us to work with a third party. It's counter-intuitive. The knowledge and engagement of our employees is the critical success factor. If we are not free to work with those employees in an open and transparent fashion to win that commitment, then we fail. You don't get commitment from people by pushing them around or treating them badly.

Intel managers are held very accountable for the people who work for them. We wouldn't even allow our HR people to get between a manager and the employee, so why would we put anybody else inside that relationship? Therefore we spend enormous amounts of time and energy with managers and supervisors whose job it is to bring out the energy and commitment of every single employee, particularly in a very competitive job environment. If you have the wrong approach to people, they're just going to get up and walk out and say, "Hey, I can go and make my living elsewhere." That wouldn't have been true ten years ago when Intel came to Ireland, but Intel's culture has always been egalitarian and a meritocracy, valuing knowledge above hierarchy. ■

Irish labor leaders rebut this argument and maintain that they make positive contributions to the employee management process.

TOM WALL

Intel has had its problems. The fact that a company is non-union doesn't mean it doesn't have labor problems. Intel was threatened with a strike over a shift system; it wanted to introduce a 24-hour shift over the Christmas period and people stopped working. So they brought in an ombudsman, Kevin Heffernan; now he's essentially the union. If people have a grievance, they go to Kevin Heffernan. It's the same thing. We reckon that we could probably add value to that company. I think there is a value in having an independent forum for people to express their grievances in confidence, without the fear of their promotion or employment prospects being affected. People have the courage, through a union, to actually say what they think instead of what they think the managers want them to say. But that's an ideological question; we're not likely to convince most employers of it. ■

LABOR RELATIONS IN THE INNOVATION ECONOMY

Some workers in the knowledge economy do not see a need for trade unions. They are better educated and better able to represent themselves. They are in high-quality employment, working for companies with enlightened management where workplace relations may be excellent.

The Irish unions have accepted this view. The type of seemingly ideal situation they had in the 1970s, when members were delivered to unions by their employers through rigid agreements, is gone.

The cultural revolution in the Irish trade union movement is such that the leadership believes they have a role to play. The key elements of speed and risk that underpin the global Innovation Economy have been taken on board by progressive elements in the labor movement. In certain cases, unions have taken initiatives in promoting new modes of workplace organization.

TOM WALL

Analog Devices was a unionized company. They decided to build a major extension, called the unions in, and said the extension would be non-union, no hard feelings. The union pointed out that they've never had a strike and asked why. The company replied that the consultation process was too slow. So the union did a deal, fast tracked all procedures so no dispute would hold anything up, and everyone was satisfied with that.

There's been a lot of that. There are places where, at the union's insistence, we went from a highly centralized autocratic type of management structure toward autonomous team working systems, which have really worked well. The unions were proactive in putting that in place.

Workers have become highly aware of the threats to their employment, mostly from other subsidiaries of the same corporation. I've listened to shop stewards talking about Puerto Rico, where the next investment might go, saying we've got to make sure that we get it. ■

While labor clearly does not share all of the assumptions of the multinationals and IDA Ireland regarding the needs of the guest multinationals, it has taken a progressive and practical position.

THE FUTURE OF IRISH SOCIAL PARTNERSHIP

The abandonment of militancy in favor of consensus and the recognition that the interests of employers and workers needed to be accommodated in the national economic interest not only marked a turning point in labor relations but also constituted a social and political watershed.

The strategic macroeconomic objectives of low inflation, increased competitiveness, job creation, control of taxation, and healthy public finances were achieved and maintained in a remarkably short time frame. Thanks to the setting up of an institutional framework, the social partners are committed and communication is frank, open, and positive, notwithstanding great strains between the demands of MNCs and the responsibility of the union to protect the rights and job stability of their members. This is much harder to accomplish during recessions than it is during boom economic growth periods.

TOM WALL

There has been a significant change. I remember shop steward training courses where the attitude was very hostile to employers on a personal as well as an intellectual and collective level. That has fundamentally changed. People are more confident, and class divisions aren't as apparent as they used to be; a lot less than in Britain, I suspect. The guy in the maintenance department or on the shop floor is as likely to play on or even be a member of the golf club as the manager.

It will inevitably run into problems, some believe it already has. I think we'll probably find a way around that. But we still have a relatively democratic process. Every agreement goes back to the unions who ask their members to vote. So there's no doubt at some stage they'll say no. Now maybe we'll go back and renegotiate but we've always wondered about that. I think the institutions surrounding the partnership are so much a part of our society and our political arrangements now that that will continue. ■

The lesson to be learned from the Irish experience is that sound institutions, a high degree of realism, and rational behavior are necessary ingredients for the attainment of social objectives. The hatchet of overt industrial conflict has been buried in the land of the Celtic Tiger.

THE FUTURE AND THE CHALLENGES AHEAD

One major problem remains for the leadership of Irish labor, and this is the paradox and apparent injustice of the social partnership. To some extent the union leadership feels that they have been short-changed by what has happened over the past 15 years. First they agreed to pay restraint, flexibility, and a more cooperative approach, which enabled the economy to take off. Then, all these high-tech multinationals came in, but the unions are still excluded from participation in the labor management process in these companies, which are, and will continue to be, the engine of Irish prosperity.

Labor issues in Ireland, as in most of the world, are clearly not neatly settled. Ireland is a new and positive model of a cooperative, non-adversarial approach in labor relations. The quick change of attitude on the part of the labor unions only points out the core flexibility of the Irish economic personality.

The negotiation process continues to calibrate the balance of power. Indeed, this continually practiced negotiation process is a valuable step up on the value chain and a clear competitive advantage. A truly vibrant national economy would be expected to encounter ongoing labor involvement as the first global, knowledge-based work force evolves.

▶ *About the Author*

This chapter was written by **Dr. Leslie Shaw**. Shaw, an Irish citizen resident in France, is an economist by training and holds a Ph.D. from the University of Dublin, Trinity College. A former supplier account manager at the Irish Electricity Supply Board, he now designs and runs workshops in intercultural negotiation at ESCP-EAP European School of Management in Paris.

6 NATIONAL GOVERNMENT DIRECTING THE GROWTH OF IRELAND

For the past 150 years, since the advent of the Great Famine, Ireland's major export was its people, who fled the country for their own survival and for a better future for their children. The continuing emigration threatened Ireland's economic and political independence. This pattern of heavy emigration persisted until the 1970s. Ireland has since transformed itself from a predominantly agricultural society to a high-tech, high-income society with more than 50% of its GDP in the service sector, 56% in 1998.[1] Agriculture now makes up a mere 5% of GDP, and industry comprises the remaining 39%.

Since 1994, Ireland has experienced a stunning economic performance, growing at the rate of 9% to 10% annually, compared to the European average of 2.5%, making it the fastest-growing economy among OECD (Organization for Economic Cooperation and Development) countries.

TABLE 6-1   Ireland GDP Growth Rate

	IRELAND	U.K.	FRANCE	GERMANY	NETHERLANDS	U.S.	JAPAN
Real GDP growth 2000	9.8%	3.0%	3.2%	3.0%	3.9%	5.0%	1.7%
Real GDP growth 2001 (forecasted)	7.8%	2.5%	2.6%	2.2%	3.0%	1.7%	1.0%

Sources: OECD Economic Outlook, May 2001; Stephane Garelli, The IMD World Competitiveness Yearbook 2001, IMD, 2001.

The Irish government has been exemplary in its aggressive economic policies to attract foreign direct investment, which resulted in the miracle of the Irish economic success. The steps they took were:

- Abolishment of protectionism in favor of free trade
- Efforts by IDA Ireland to attract foreign direct investment (FDI)
- Provision of capital grants and tax concessions
- Increased investment in the educational system
- Successful application for Ireland's membership in the European Economic Community (EEC) in 1973, which enabled it to reap the benefits of major EEC capital investment in Ireland

While riding the economic peaks and valleys of boom times and recessions, the Irish people have greatly benefited from the government commitment to make Ireland the "Enterprise Isle" in Europe.

Unemployment has dropped dramatically since its peak of almost 20% just a decade ago, and the migration flows have reversed. During a 12-month period in 1999–2000, the Central Statistics Office recorded 42,300 immigrants arriving in Ireland, the highest increase in population since 1881. Forty-three percent of those were returning Irish nationals.[2]

To coordinate the efforts from various agencies and attain its economic goals, the Irish government has set up Forfás as The National Policy and Advisory Board for Enterprise, Trade, Science, Technology and Innovation. Forfás was given broad legal powers for industrial promotion and technology development. It, in turn, delegates powers to Enterprise Ireland for the promotion of home-based industry and foreign trade and to IDA Ireland for the promotion of inward investment. Its functions are to[3]:

- Advise ministers on industrial development
- Advise and coordinate policies for Enterprise Ireland and IDA Ireland and other associated bodies under the statute
- Encourage development in industry, technology, marketing, and human resources
- Encourage the establishment and development in the state of industrial undertakings from outside the state
- Advise and coordinate Enterprise Ireland and IDA Ireland in relation to their functions

DEPARTMENT OF ENTERPRISE, TRADE, AND EMPLOYMENT

Established by the government in July 1998, Enterprise Ireland is one of the bodies developing a national position on Irish trade, sales, and marketing issues; exports; and employment of Irish companies. Its primary clients are Irish manufacturing and internationally traded services with 10 or more employees, and overseas food and natural resources companies operating in Ireland. Enterprise Ireland also administers national and EU supports for developing technological innovation capability and cooperation between industry and higher education institutions.

In association with industry and state agencies, Enterprise Ireland supports Irish companies in building capability, innovating, and growing, whether by creating new partnerships or reaching international customers. It also supports international businesses in matching them with world-class suppliers and partners in Ireland.

Mary Harney is the tánaiste (deputy prime minister) and minister for enterprise, trade, and employment of the Republic of Ireland. A member of the Progressive Democrats, she is the first woman to hold these posts, and to have led her party in an election campaign and into negotiations to form a government. Educated at Trinity College in Dublin, she began her political career as a senator, and was first elected to Parliament in 1981. She provides us with her perspectives in the economic success in Ireland.

MARY HARNEY

The Irish miracle combines high growth rates, high employment in better-paying jobs, low unemployment, and net immigration. We have now got a very healthy budget situation, and a very healthy economy.

Technical education and joining the EU made the difference

Undoubtedly the economic recovery in Ireland was facilitated in part by the introduction of free second-level (secondary) education in the late 1960s. The education reform resulted in a substantial increase in enrollments and shifted its focus away from the traditional humanities coursework to technology-oriented curricula in the third-level (colleges and universities) education. Close links were established between the industry and educational institutions, especially with the Institutes of Technology (formerly known as Regional Technical Colleges, RTC). The increased investment by the government in education created a skilled base of human capital that would eventually become one of Ireland's competitive advantage factors as a nation.

For the past three years, spending on education has increased by 40% to account for 28% of all government spending. It shows a strong commitment of the Irish government to ensure the future in the information age. Today, the Republic of Ireland boasts four universities and 11 Institutes of Technology located throughout the country, with a student population of 53,400 and 35,500, respectively. Ireland has since emerged as the most favored industrial location for foreign investment, particularly in the high-tech sectors.

When we joined the EU in the early 1970s, it was a big step for us, because until then we were very insular, and very protectionist. Our only trading experience was with the U.K. We exported agriculture and imported manufactured products. Because of our history with our nearest neighbor, we had a huge inferiority complex and a chip on the shoulder.

Joining the EU was making a big statement. Now Ireland was going to be outward looking. It was going to look at the opportunities, instead of trying to protect ourselves in the world — protectionist policies don't work anyway — we are going to become part of something much bigger. And that opened up our minds and attitudes.

At the same time, we began to invest very heavily in education. Until the late 1960s, the only people who really could get a full second-level education right to the age of 18, were the people who were reasonably well-off, or people who were educated by the religious. And for a long number of years, the religious filled a vacuum not filled by the state. They educated young people free of charge. And indeed there are many examples of people joining the nuns, the priests, and the brothers — to be educated, and subsequently maybe leaving the church.

So, the introduction of free second-level education was the beginning of the focus on education. At the same time, we started to reorient our education system away from being humanities-oriented to a much more science and technology and engineering focus. Many used to argue that we were educating for foreign countries. We had massive brain drain, particularly to Germany, Japan, the U.K., and the U.S. These were among the debates we were having at the time.

Technology provides leverage in other economic sectors

It would be wrong to think that all our eggs are in one basket. Yes, we've become very technology-focused, but we've become so across the board. For example, consider an Irish company called Kerry Ingredients, which was started on the southwest coast of Ireland in a very small town in county Kerry. It is now the second-largest food ingredients company in the world. From a very peripheral base, it started in 1973. The two big reasons they've grown are technology and people. Every year they've been able to hire, through a graduate placement program we run, highly talented people. So they've acquired companies all over the world, and they've been able to surpass their competitors in places like Malaysia and Australia.

This is the filtering effect of embracing technology even in a very traditional sector like food. Nobody would have said, a few years ago, that Ireland could become a world leader in food. It's so competitive, and so labor-intensive. And yet, through the use of technology and young people, it's happened. And that's what we're trying to do, to instill that culture across the sectors.

But equally, we have our eggs in a few baskets. We're very successful in financial services. Half of all the large insurance companies in the world have a facility here. A very high percentage of the biggest banks in the world are here. We concentrated software to where we have become the world's largest exporters.

Social partnership

In the wake of serious economic downturns in 1980s — large budget deficit, high taxes, unemployment, and mass emigration — Ireland had developed a system of social partnership among government, employers, unions, and voluntary groups. Under this framework, they strived to agree on the priorities for economic and social development, which gained strong public support, thus creating national cohesion toward common goals.

Recently, e-business has been seen as the new end of the business. Ireland seeks to provide infrastructure and competition and to get players into the market. In order to encourage Global Crossing to provide the broadband, the Irish government went 50/50 on a PPP (Public Private Partnership), because it would not have been economically viable for Global Crossing to take the risk of supplying broadband to a small country.

Ireland strongly believes that, in order to promote competition and free trade that result in economic efficiency and consumer choice, the government should only regulate where necessary. The Electronic Commerce Act, 2000 is the subsequent effort of partnership between government and the private sector. It formulates a legal framework for e-business activities in terms of business, private law, and public administration.

If you ask foreign companies why they are here, they will tell you it is because Ireland is a very pro-business environment; unlike many mainland European countries, Ireland is very loosely regulated. We are not over-bureaucratized; not big into red tape. Because we're small, businesses find they can have easy access to government, both locally and nationally. They can get decisions made quickly; they can get speed-to-market. So, you've got to continue to remain competitive.

Moving up the value chain

With a tight labor market now, here as it is worldwide, we're moving up the value chain. We are not attractive to basic manufacturing. Neither is anywhere else in Western Europe. We've seen several examples in the textile industry, for example, in basic, low-scale employment, where it's moving offshore to Morocco, or to Asia, or to some African countries. That is why we have moved to providing both the infrastructure for e-commerce and e-business, and also the skills. And for the first time in our history, we're now establishing a foundation in science. We're going to spend a considerable amount of money, for us, on basic research in both ICT (information communications technology) and biotechnology. These are two sectors where we believe we need to go, which is the seedbed of serious researchers. Ireland never had money before to go into basic research.

Attitude contributes to competitiveness

In the era of globalization and the rise of the knowledge economy, competitiveness is key to the nation's economic success. What makes Ireland competitive are its multifaceted skills, education, taxes, regulations, innovation, and flexibility. It takes more than simply a good educational system and infrastructure. Flexibility and adaptability also play major roles in attracting inward investment in a country that is not overly regulated or heavily prescribed. As such, with the education, administrative, and physical infrastructures in place, Ireland is able to take advantage of the opportunities presented at each corner of the challenges in the environment.

Taxation will now be standard for all companies

In Ireland we are going to have a standard rate of corporate tax of 12.5%. We used to have 10% on manufacturing and international trade services. The EU objected that is a subsidy for those sectors, so it must be up to their standard rate. So we decided to bring our standard rate for all corporate taxes down to 12.5%. We take the view that it's better to take 12.5% of something big, rather than 40% of nothing. Lower taxes and certainly education, particularly for small countries that don't have a big market internally, are factors that will give you a competitive advantage. The industry of the future is all about people, really. ■

OFFICE OF SCIENCE AND TECHNOLOGY

In its National Development Plan 2000–2006, the Irish government has identified research, technology development, and innovation as important keys to sustained economic growth and maintaining Ireland's competitiveness in the knowledge economy. The Office of Science and Technology in the Department of Enterprise, Trade and Employment is responsible for providing advice on research, technology, and innovation (RTI) issues to create an awareness of the significance of RTI in economic and social development.

Ireland is well along in the process of building an advanced knowledge-based and high-wage economy. Irish people now want more than just to be employed; they expect a higher standard of living. With a tight labor market, Ireland is not attractive to basic manufacturing companies. It needs to build its RTI capability to strengthen Irish industrial performance. Unprecedented advances in science and technology are becoming the bedrock of economic growth, and Ireland's economy is increasingly based more and more on information and knowledge.

The Higher Education Authority is responsible for research infrastructure in the universities. The amount of resources now available for research, technological development, and innovation (RTDI), in the context of the National Development Plan, is vastly superior to what was allocated to these areas in the past.

In 2000, the Irish government has earmarked almost £2 billion Irish pounds (U.S.$2.3 billion) for RTI. One example, Science Foundation Ireland (SFI), was recently launched to establish Ireland as a world-class center of research excellence in the strategic niche areas of biotechnology and information and communications technologies (ICT). This center will support the future enterprise environment in Ireland. SFI, in turn, oversees the management, evaluation, and allocation of the Technology Foresight Fund of over $550 million for investment in research areas. This fund represents the largest single investment ever in the history of the state in research and development.

SFI has set up advisory panels that are composed of two bodies of high-level experts, industrialists and academics, from both inside Ireland and the international arena. They provide advice on key areas, niches that are internationally recognized and of strategic importance to Ireland.

SFI will fund world-class research teams in universities and technical colleges in Ireland, led by outstanding, world-renowned researchers (SFI principal investigators). Using these research capabilities, Ireland is projecting into the future with policies that are geared toward creating world-class research companies that develop new and innovative ideas, companies that will compete in the global, knowledge-based economy.

As director of the Office of Science and Technology, Mattie McCabe is responsible for compiling and advising Ireland's overall science and technology innovation policy, particularly as it affects industry and competitiveness. He speaks about the huge investment in basic research the Irish government has committed toward making Ireland an even more competitive site for innovation. The expectation is that Ireland will become a cradle of innovation for future commercial technologies.

MATTIE MCCABE

The dream of the Science Foundation Ireland and the criteria for success

Our primary investment focus is in life sciences, particularly in biotechnology. To create a cadre of world-class basic researchers, we need to establish an international reputation and a location for carrying out such basic research. What we need to do, in five years' time, in the biotech area, has not even been developed yet. We would want to see the IDA bringing in companies that can apply the results of the scientific endeavors that we are making now to create new products, and to become stronger companies. The economic benefits for us would be that we have the top-drawer technology companies setting up research operations here and developing viable products in the biotech and ICT areas, which are being derived and collaborated upon by the efforts of Science Foundation Ireland. That then meets the IDA's requirement of creating jobs, which are higher up the value chain.

So we're moving away from manufacturing jobs, creating higher value-added jobs here as a result of the infrastructure, both physical and human. If we are successful, we will see that Ireland will have many more multinational companies here with their research operations embedded, building around the basic science infrastructure that we are investing in.

Now, eventually, the benefits for Ireland will be that these people will move out to become better teachers in universities or they will move out into companies, or collaborate with companies to do new research. The basic research will attract those who will apply the basic research and by applying it in Ireland, presumably that will lend more credibility to Ireland as a place for not just where you extend your operations, but for the place where you actually initiate your operations.

The Irish research model is based on MIT

The best model for this is the National Science Foundation (NSF) in the U.S. and the people who are senior management in Science Foundation Ireland have built up extensive contacts with the NSF. We also looked at the EMBL, the European Molecular Biology Laboratory, on the bio side. In setting up the structures, and setting up the assessment processes, our people spent a lot of time at the NSF. The people who are running Science Foundation Ireland adopted the best practices based on the U.S. model. ∎

THE INVESTMENT AND DEVELOPMENT AGENCY OF IRELAND (IDA)

One of the great driving forces for the Irish success story is IDA Ireland. First established in 1949, and originally named the Industrial Development Authority, it was given the authority to attract new industrial investment in Ireland in the capacity of a civil service body. Under the statute, the IDA had a dual function to advise the minister on industrial development and to promote greater investment in Irish industry.

In 1969 the IDA transitioned from being limited to having full autonomy. The IDA became a non-civil-service, state-sponsored agency and was renamed Industrial Development Agency. Legislative measures covered IDA promotion, capital grants, the development of industrial estates, and advance factories. This gave the IDA greater license to become entrepreneurial in its mission.

Through IDA's efforts, Ireland is promoted as the ideal location for foreign companies to undertake global expansion to the EU market and beyond. And indeed, international companies play an important role in the growth of the economy in Ireland, which has become the ideal export base to penetrate the European market. Its earlier objective of job creation was met with considerable success. But the globalization of business means that, in order to respond to the global trends, the features of Ireland's competitive advantage must also change to meet the needs and challenges of the international companies operating in Ireland. In 2001, IDA became the Investment and Development Agency of Ireland.

TAX INCENTIVES

The core IDA tax incentive principle has always been that Ireland should offer any foreign investor the longest possible time horizon. To attract foreign direct investment, the Irish government has committed to a 20-year tax benefit package. For many years, Ireland had a maximum of 10% corporate tax rate for manufacturing and data processing companies that are allowed to keep that benefit until 2010. However, beginning in 2003, a new tax rate of 12.5% will be introduced for all companies. Despite the low tax rate, corporations in Ireland contribute about 12% of the tax take, as compared with 5% in other European countries that have higher corporate tax structures.

With a longer time horizon, the investors can forecast their tax liability with confidence and can estimate net return on their Irish investment some 10 or 20 years into the future. Furthermore, reinvestment and expansion can be planned with greater assurance. The productive base of the economy has been transformed by long-term investments. This is part of the reason that about 23% of all new mobile investment into Europe locates in Ireland, which has only 1% of the EU population.

TRANSFORMING THE ECONOMY IN IRELAND

About 75% of total exports comes from the foreign sector, creating a huge percentage of wealth in the region. Today, the FDI comprises more than 1,200 companies, employing more than 140,000 workers. To a large extent, it is the foundation of the whole economy.

TABLE 6-2   IDA Highlights, 1998–2000

	1998	1999	2000
Total new jobs filled	15,996	18,079	24,717
First-time jobs out of total new jobs	14,436	16,277	20,257
Total full-time employment	115,981	124,664	141,258
Change in full-time employment	8,810	8,687	16,415
Total number of IDA-supported companies	1,140	1,279	1,278
Projects fully agreed	243	186	96

Source: IDA Annual Reports, 1998, 1999, 2000.

But the benefits extend far beyond the numbers. One of the huge advantages derived from the FDI sector is in developing the expertise of the indigenous population. Many people in Ireland have gained enormous experience either working directly in some of these world-class companies or by supplying these companies domestically. It has, in a very unique way, helped to grow a new indigenous Irish high-tech sector.

GOVERNMENT COLLABORATIONS WITH INDUSTRY

Ireland has adopted a pro-business attitude and her businesses are loosely regulated. The IDA makes a policy of going to great lengths to ensure that the needs of every new foreign company locating in Ireland are met, and understands that interceding with local and national authorities might be necessary to facilitate the process and achieve its economic objectives.

Because of the nature of the electronics industry, change is very rapid, particularly in the ICT sector. Although companies often are unable to foresee the changes, they want to be assured that whatever problem they may face in the future, the Irish government will be there for them. It is the willingness of the governmental system to "go the extra mile" to help companies solve these unexpected problems that tips the scale for Ireland as a favorite destination to do business.

Dr. David Hanna has held several key positions with the IDA, including manager of the Financial Services Division. He now is director of information and communications technologies, focusing on development in the south of Ireland.

DAVID HANNA

MIDAS is an example of structural innovation in government relations to industry sectors

We are trying to build up, in Ireland, a very strong industry in integrated circuit design. And one of the things that became clear was that we had a shortage of integrated design engineers. The industry and the IDA got together and we decided jointly to create an industry-representative group called MIDAS (Microelectronics Industry Design Association), a lobbying group. We did our level best to facilitate the creation of MIDAS. And MIDAS is now in existence, and its members are drawn from 16 or 17 companies involved in integrated design in Ireland.

Its functions are similar to those of the Silicon Valley Manufacturers Group, but just for this sector. And its secretariat is in the National Microelectronics Research Centre in Cork. So here you have a group of both the industry and government, one of whose major functions is to put pressure on government. So in fact, the system is open. In other words, one bit of government is quite content to join with the private sector and pressure the other bits of government to get things done. That's because a group of people and a group of companies have decided that integrated circuit design is strategically very important for the future of the electronics industry.

Access is key to the Irish success story — Microsoft

Because the lines of communication are so short, we can get an issue on the table of the deputy prime minister (Mary Harney) by our chief executive. The relationship is such that our chief executive can phone the deputy prime minister and say, "Look, we really do have a problem here."

Assuming that he convinces her that there is an issue, she can actually get the system working immediately. That's a unique thing. Several years ago, Microsoft was looking to put a big server farm into Europe. We thought we had it because Microsoft had made major investments in Ireland. I was the first person in our group to meet with Bill Gates of Microsoft. I just walked up to him at a PC conference in Phoenix in 1985, and quickly put the proposition to him about setting up in Ireland. They did in 1986, a year later.

And we were close with Microsoft. It was a big operation and we expected to get the server farm. But they looked at Ireland and said, "No, we are not going to do this." That really caused a shock in the system. Microsoft took a look and said, "There's a deficit in bandwidth." You've no idea how quickly the Irish system worked to sort that out. A task force was put together involving the IDA. And the Irish government actually bought increased bandwidth and brought it into Ireland with a company called Global Crossing.

We persuaded the government to buy massive bandwidth from Global Crossing. GC brought it, and then we said, "Okay, we will be responsible. If no one wants to buy it, don't worry, we will pay for it. We then helped to sell it, and of course, it's all sold. Microsoft has recently set up its major software distribution system, so that anybody in Europe who wants to download Microsoft software, comes in to the server right here.

This involved tens of millions, maybe even a hundred million dollars. It was big money for a small country. Essentially, the government took the risk. As I say, it worked out fine, because, the government is, of course, not completely powerless. We then, in IDA, started peddling Ireland as a major center for server farms and e-business, confident in the knowledge that there was reasonably priced bandwidth because we owned the system . . . Come along for this ride! Come to Ireland!

A model for development agencies

During periods of high unemployment, IDA's main focus had traditionally been on job creation. IDA continues to play an important role in promoting economic development. However, one of IDA's main objective functions is to raise the quality of both new and existing overseas companies and to strengthen their sustainability and strategic value in Ireland. IDA has seen impressive results for taking proactive steps in establishing Ireland as a significant e-business platform in Europe and for its capacity to quickly respond to international trends as well as indigenous needs. As such, IDA has become a model for development agencies all over the world.

IDA acts as a link between academic institutions and industries to ensure the necessary skills needs of the international companies.

The strength of the educational infrastructure

One of the ingredients of the success of Silicon Valley came from Fred Terman, the visionary dean of engineering of Stanford University. He saw the contribution that educational institutions could make as being broader than just producing 500 computer scientists. Ireland's educational infrastructure is equally visionary. We are driven by the fact that Ireland is a relatively poor country, and that we have only had about five or six years of prosperity in the last 200.

The educational institutions in Ireland feel they have a duty to capitalize on the economic development and well-being of the country. Not just producing engineers per se. But producing them with an entrepreneurial bent; encouraging them to set up new businesses in incubator units; sharing faculty with companies who want to get a step up on the ladder of R&D; or taking scientists from companies into faculty, to help them in some way. All of that is part of a process of economic well being, very similar to the California model.

Universities changed their purpose to the public good

We had a traditional university sector, very much along the lines of Oxford and Cambridge, where there really was very little social responsibility as far as the broader economy was concerned. They were regarded as engines, producing well-educated, in the broadest sense, well-rounded people, people who could speak Latin — excellent philosophers. All of that is great. But a country that is sinking economically has to be a bit tougher and demand more. We set up a network of 11 regional technical colleges around the country. They were to produce the first generation of technicians. People with two-year certificates and three-year diplomas could find employment in the big electronic companies, which were coming to Ireland at the time. They are now called Institutes of Technology and they produce thousands of well-qualified young people each year.

And then we decided to set up two more advanced educational institutions, the National Institute for Higher Education in Dublin and the National Institute for Higher Education in Limerick. We looked at Stanford and MIT as the models. We said, keep your academic respectability even though you are much closer to the commercial world than the traditional universities. You are happy to work with companies, share staff, share faculty, have your Masters Degree students in companies rather than the academic world.

They developed and became very successful. One of them is now Limerick University and the other is Dublin City University. So we did things like that to force the system to change, because, from an evolutionary point of view, it wasn't changing fast enough.

Ireland can move quickly and cooperatively across sectors — Analog Devices

The system, when it has to, marches in step much more easily than in most countries. The reason for that is that everyone in the country, from a government minister to a university president to someone sweeping the streets, was affected by the same plague, which is that their kids had to emigrate. To let the kids stay at home, so they don't have to emigrate, was one of the reasons that we marched in step.

Just to get back to universities. I brought in Ray Stafford, president of a company called Analog Devices, about 23 years ago. He was thinking of setting up an operation in Europe. He chose Limerick and Analog Devices has been there for 23 years. He was very impressed by The University of Limerick and by the fact that Ed Walsh had come back from Michigan to run it. He knew that with that U.S. philosophy, that if he needed help, in a master's program, a course, or a consultancy, he would get it. So he chose Limerick. He set up an IC (integrated circuit) design group — this is 22 years ago — which has now flourished, and employs around 500 people.

That was a tangible outcome. The university has an openness and a willingness to change to work with companies and that is why AD is in Limerick, because Ed Walsh had a philosophy, which was to cooperate with industry and to help them in any way possible.

Walsh's concept was that he could do far more than just provide industry with graduates. He could help them with their R&D, and with their design. That fit, if you like, between the education and industry is actually incredibly important, probably one of the most important things that we offer — highly skilled people. Tax is the other one. That's why the system works well in Ireland, driven by people with a U.S. economic and political philosophy.

Ireland, in terms of its economic and political philosophy, is somewhere between Europe and the U.S. The model is not the German-French model. It's not even the Silicon Valley model; it is somewhere in the middle, which actually makes U.S. companies comfortable. ■

The Irish government has been outstanding in its initiatives and commitment to attract, retain, and grow foreign direct investment — not only for job and wealth creation — but also to continuously work up the value chain. Ireland's most talented people now have an incentive to stay in Ireland and make their contribution at home.

Their efforts at home have been matched by their efforts abroad to attract business through their outstanding marketing and advertising campaigns that are the marvel of regional development agencies throughout the world. In the next chapter we will profile these efforts along with the perspectives of two of the large MNCs that have European operations based in Ireland: Intel and EMC Corporation.

ENDNOTES

1. *The World Factbook 2000*, Central Intelligence Agency (ed.), 2000.
2. Central Statistics Office, Ireland, *www.eirestat.cso.ie*.
3. Forfás, *www.forfas.ie/flash_main.html*.

7

THE BRANDING OF IRELAND

INTERNATIONAL CORPORATIONS CHOOSING IRELAND FOR MULTIFUNCTIONAL OPERATIONS

THE BRANDING OF IRELAND

The positioning of Ireland as the most favorable region for multinational companies to situate their European operations is one of the great marketing success stories of the Innovation Economy. Indeed, the Irish have shown that with clear, consistent, and compelling communications, in combination with diligent face-to-face contact with the targeted companies it seeks to attract, small regions can succeed in the Innovation Economy.

The Irish advertising story is remarkable for several reasons. Ireland was positioned as an attractive, profitable place to do business despite significant prejudices and handicaps the country faced in the 1970s and 1980s as an economically and politically troubled region. Just as significant has been the determined effort of Ireland to move up the value chain to attract high-tech jobs and operations, not just manufacturing from foreign direct investors.

Ireland's efforts very much parallel Taiwan's in this respect. They moved from a reputation for cheap labor and low taxes to respect as a world-class region for the full spectrum of multinational operations.

Advertising Ireland's business environment was designed to both position Ireland as a good industrial base to enter the European market and as a great place to make a high profit. The advertising set the stage for a sales call from IDA Ireland representatives, who would target specific companies that had been designated desirable for Ireland economic development.

The goal of advertising Ireland over the past four decades was to establish Ireland as a stable, secure, and profitable location for investment, with an especially pro-business operating environment. This progression may be tracked through the decades of Ireland's ad campaigns.

1960s–1970s: Establishing Ireland as a Location for Investment

Location was the main theme of the advertising message in the 1960s — "If you're considering Europe, consider Ireland" was one such campaign slogan. In this decade, IDA Ireland first started advertising Ireland as a place for overseas investment in the U.S. and Europe. The ads encouraged U.S. businesses to see Ireland as the ideal location from which to join the emerging and newly unified European market.

In the 1970s this theme changed to profitability. The advertising message strongly concentrated on the high returns on investment. Profit and tax were the main focuses — "The highest return on investment in the Common Market" was one such ad slogan (see Figure 7-1). At this time, the Irish tax legislation allowed tax-free export profit, which was an appealing incentive to many U.S. companies looking to set up a European base.

Ads were placed in *Business Week*, *Fortune*, *Dun's Review*, and other leading publications targeting the decision-makers, CEOs, and CFOs in North America.

In the 1970s Ireland was in the grips of a modern industrial revolution with dramatic increases in industrial output and exports. Ireland had the highest economic growth in Europe in the late 1970s. Since 1973, the year of membership in the European Common Market, Ireland experienced a major change in the rate of exports to continental Europe. The average rate of return on capital employed by U.S. corporations in 1975 and 1976 was 29.5%, almost 250% the European average. Inflation was on a steep downward spiral. Also during this time, emigration had slowed down considerably.

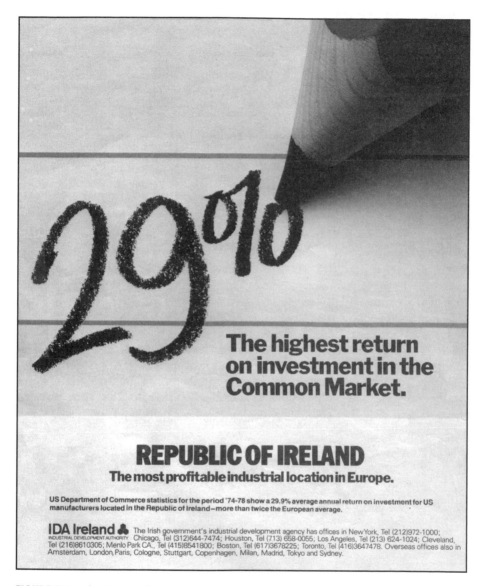

FIGURE 7-1 The "29% — The highest return on investment in the Common Market" advertisement touted Ireland's protit-making potential. Reprinted with permission of IDA Ireland.

1980s: COMBATING UNEMPLOYMENT

The location theme had achieved its success by the 1980s. Other locations in Europe began to compete in the market, offering generous incentive packages. Ireland was now offering export profits for 15 years, non-repayable cash grants toward fixed assets, and total paid training of an already English-speaking work force. The advertising message was sector focused. Specific ads were designed for each industrial technology sector and referred to the major U.S. corporate names that were already operating in Ireland. An educated, highly adaptable, and skilled labor force was now an additional theme running through the advertising, along with profitability and location. U.S. corporations were being told that a committed, educated work force was ultimately more important than any amount of introductory incentive packages.

The 1980s were also the toughest years for Ireland's economy; unemployment reached a record high. At this time, 50% of the population was under the age of 25. The Irish government took some dramatic steps in reversing the poor economic situation. IDA Ireland sponsored the successful advertising campaign "We're the Young Europeans" in 1984 (see Figure 7-2). This advertising campaign ran in the leading newspapers in North America, showing Ireland as a hotbed of talented, flexible, innovative youth. Taglines such as "People are to Ireland as oil is to Texas," "People are to Ireland as champagne is to France," and "The young Europeans — Hire them before they hire you" focused upon Ireland's ample supply of highly skilled people for any corporation wishing to locate there. This focus on education, particularly on staff training, rounded out the previous campaign by emphasizing people, as well as tax incentives and infrastructure.

The ad shown in Figure 7-2 was placed in specific industry and trade journals as well as the leading business publications such as *Electronic Business, Electronic News, Industry Week, Business Week,* and the *New York Times.*

PEOPLE ARE TO IRELAND AS OIL IS TO TEXAS.

The Irish.
Europe's youngest and fastest-growing population. Educated, talented, flexible, innovative.
   Ireland.
A member of the European Common Market. Noted for its favorable government attitudes towards business. The most profitable industrial location in Europe for U.S. Manufacturers.
Ireland. Home of the Irish. The young Europeans.

IDA Ireland ⬡
INDUSTRIAL DEVELOPMENT AUTHORITY

IDA Ireland has offices in New York (212) 972 1000; Chicago (312) 644 7474; Cleveland (216) 861 0305/6; Los Angeles (213) 829 0081; Menlo Park, Calif. (415) 854 1800; Houston (713) 965 0292; Boston (617) 367 8225; Fort Lauderdale (305) 785 9430; Atlanta (404) 351 8474.
   This announcement is published by IDA Ireland, 200 Park Avenue, New York 10017, which is registered under the Foreign Agents Registration Act, as amended, as an agent of the Government of Ireland. This material is filed with the Department of Justice where the required registration statement is available for public inspection. Registration does not indicate approval of the contents by the United States Government.

REPUBLIC OF IRELAND

"WE'RE THE YOUNG EUROPEANS."

FIGURE 7-2   The "We're the Young Europeans" ad campaign aimed at selling Ireland's young work force as another valuable asset. Reprinted with permission of IDA Ireland.

IRELAND

The average rate of return on U.S. manufacturing investment in Ireland from 1982-1991 was 25.3%—almost four times the European average.
Source: U.S. Department of Commerce

The Place.   The People.   The Profits.

American teleservice operators are reaching Europe in a big way—from Ireland. By locating in Ireland, companies like Best Western, Dell and Gateway 2000 enjoy the best of all worlds: lower costs, higher productivity, access to all those European markets and, of course, superior telecommunications. What's more, they benefit from a well-educated, multi-lingual young Irish workforce. For lots of good reasons, Ireland is the place for profitable American teleservice operators. You can profit too, by joining them.

Profit by us.

◆ IDA®
IRELAND
INDUSTRIAL DEVELOPMENT AGENCY

ATLANTA (404) 351-8474 · BOSTON (617) 367-8225 · CHICAGO (312) 236-0222 · LOS ANGELES (310) 829-0081 · NEW YORK (212) 750-4300 · SAN JOSE (408) 294-9903

FIGURE 7-3   The "Profit by Us: The Place, The People, The Profits" ad campaign.
Reprinted with permission of IDA Ireland.

1990s: HIGH TECHNOLOGY

In the 1990s, the concepts of the previous two campaigns were synthesized into "The Place, The People, The Profits" campaign (see Figure 7-3). Profitability and high technology were the main messages throughout the ads. There was a strong industry focus highlighting medical devices, tele-services, electronics, engineering, financial services, and software. As a measure of the effectiveness of the campaign, customer services centers were situated in Ireland, especially for the financial services sector. By the mid-1990s, Ireland became known as the "Call Center of Europe."

The advertising campaigns of the 1990s were run in tandem with appropriate government initiatives, promotional trips abroad by government ministers, and the day-to-day work of the IDA's marketing executives. IDA's advertising was a potent factor in developing a much more positive, well-rounded image of Ireland among IDA's target companies.

The advertising budget was mainly targeted at the U.S., where 75% of foreign direct investment originated. It was particularly used to promote the new services sector in specialist publications such as *Electronic Business*. While the advertising was limited by financial constraints, it was an important part of the drive to win investment in the new sectors, and it reaffirmed that Ireland was still a serious contender for inward investment.

THE ADVERTISING CHALLENGE

Rick St. Vincent, president and executive creative director of St. Vincent/ Milone & O'Sullivan, Inc., has been working on the IDA account since 1971. He created much of the advertising that has successfully attracted U.S. businesses. This advertising worked in combination with sales efforts from regional IDA offices throughout the U.S. and especially in Silicon Valley. He speaks of the special marketing positioning challenges Ireland faced and how they overcame them.

The experience of Ireland in advertising demonstrates that regions can be positioned and advertised successfully. The major factors leading to the Irish success are:

- Consistent advertising support over decades
- A simple, clear message relevant to the business community that is both credible and effective
- Integration to support aggressive sales representation efforts in specific markets directed toward targeted industries and companies
- Leveraging the effectiveness of the budget through smart media placement

RICK ST. VINCENT

Ireland was a tough sell

It was hard a real challenge convincing Americans to seriously consider doing business in Ireland. Our campaign set out to redress images of Ireland held at that time that Ireland was industrially backward. And potential investors were unable to differentiate between the troubles in Northern Ireland and the Republic of Ireland.

The "Young Europeans" campaign was a breakthrough

In the early 1980s, Ireland faced a "brain drain." Young people needed jobs and were leaving the country to find them. The campaign showed a young, well-educated, vibrant work force. No country featured its own people in its advertising.

We had been running the "29% Return on Investment" campaign for years. We now had to talk about talent. Ireland has its human resources to sell as well. This is a very powerful message.

How did IDA measure or evaluate its success? When we started to run local, all-news radio and outdoor billboards, we were contacted by the KSTS cable TV station in San Jose, California. They wanted to do a story on Irish development. It became a half-hour documentary entitled "The Greening of Ireland." That kind of value is hard to come by. The IDA knew how to leverage their stories.

Advertising supports direct sales efforts

IDA representatives needed support. We also used 60-second commercials on local Sunday morning TV programs such as *Face the Nation* and *Meet the Press*. These can be purchased at a very reasonable cost and beamed locally. In the process, we stretched the advertising funding by concentrating on New York, San Francisco, Chicago, Boston, and Los Angeles. It made a difference for sales calls. Periodically we sent direct mail. Ireland's advertising activity stimulated competitive regions to also conduct advertising and this raised awareness for the whole category of regional advertising for foreign direct investment and location.

The great challenge for regional development agencies marketing in the U.S.

In the beginning, IDA identified its primary goal as bringing home more jobs for the local Irish population. With that in mind, they wisely chose McConnells Ltd., a Dublin-based agency, for the initial efforts. They did a great job, too. But when the emphasis switched to reaching American manufacturers, IDA came to our New York agency for planning and creativity. I think the biggest point of all is this:

The solution is not to direct the advertising strategy from overseas, but from the region you are advertising in. For example, we had to be sensitive to advertising messages soliciting American business to locate in Ireland when there was high unemployment in the U.S. in the late 1970s and 1980s, as well as be highly selective and creative in our media selections.

We put IDA people on the radio and televised interview shows so they could handle questions about the perception of "stealing American jobs." They were able to direct the attention to the job creation in Europe that did not take away from U.S. employment markets. ■

FIGURE 7-4   The "Catch the eBuzz in Ireland — And Profit" ad campaign was geared at showing a modern, technically developed Ireland. Reproduced by permission of IDA Ireland.

Ruth Croke, vice president of IDA Ireland in New York, is responsible for IDA's public relations and advertising in North America. She suggests that the "Catch the eBuzz" campaign presents Ireland in a different way than in previous ad campaigns.

RUTH CROKE

Through our advertising and public relations campaign, IDA Ireland has succeeded in taking on the stereotypical images of Ireland so regularly portrayed in media and preserved in the minds of the Irish American community.

The Internet took precedence in our advertising campaign for 1999. Within a short period of time, corporations and countries were revamping and modernizing their image and direction. This raised new objectives for IDA's campaign. Our aim was to reposition Ireland's brand and capitalize on the excellent national initiatives taken by the government to establish Ireland as a pro-business environment with technology developments in hand to support e-commerce activities.

The "Catch the eBuzz In Ireland — And Profit" advertisement had a short and simple message with eye-catching creativity. The "Buzz" reflected excitement. What we were offering was fresh and different. We were projecting an image of a modern Ireland. The kids in the ad mirrored city streets in Ireland. They were sophisticated, highly educated, Web-savvy kids with dominance over demographics and tech knowledge!

We advertised in technology journals such as *Upside*, *Red Herring*, *eCompany Now*, *Business 2.0*, and *Industry Standard*. We tried some online advertising on the *Wall Street Journal*'s interactive Web site, and we took sponsorship of *Business Week*'s e.biz conferences.

While the ad raised a few eyebrows, it also raised the bar of our creativity in advertising. We were trying something totally different and going out on a limb, but essentially, that is what IDA has consistently done, resulting in the Ireland we know today. ■

Ireland has demonstrated that marketing can work in combination with the other factors to create regional wealth by attracting MNCs. To see how well the Irish can cultivate and retain MNCs once they come to Ireland is our next focus.

INTERNATIONAL CORPORATIONS CHOOSING IRELAND FOR MULTIFUNCTIONAL OPERATIONS

Foreign direct investment is the driving force of the Irish economic miracle. To help understand this dynamic economy better from an MNC perspective, we investigated two major international high-tech corporations: Intel and EMC Corporation. Each has made a major commitment for multioperational functions in Ireland. Importantly, both of these leading companies began with simple manufacturing operations in their industries and each expanded up the value chain in Ireland, demonstrating their confidence in the abilities of the Irish managers and work force to be partners in company growth.

Compared with other European countries, Ireland has the youngest population, and it should remain that way for the near future. About 40% of today's population of 3.8 million are under the age of 25. Given the demands for highly skilled, flexible knowledge workers in an Innovation Economy, Ireland is well positioned to compete for European-based MNC operations owing to the relative youth and highly developed skills of its work force.

TABLE 7-1   Future Availability of Work Force

	IRELAND	U.K.	FRANCE	NETHERLANDS	GERMANY	U.S.	JAPAN
Work force under 25 by year 2010	35.5%	31.0%	30.1%	28.7%	24.4%	34.2%	25.3%

Source: *United Nations Statistical Division, www.uneve.org/stats.*

INTEL IRELAND

Ireland, strategically located on major air and sea routes between North America and Northern Europe, has become Intel's gateway to the EU countries, with a collective market of 370 million people.

Intel Ireland opened its chip-manufacturing facilities in 1990 in Collinstown Industrial Park, Leixlip, County Kildare. By the end of 2000, Intel had invested over $2.5 billion and directly employed about 3,300 Irish people. Another 1,200 people work on site for companies that have supplier or service contracts with Intel. It is Intel's largest manufacturing site outside the United States. Intel's European division comprises seven countries, including Ireland, and represented 24% of Intel's $33.7 billion revenue in 2000.

Intel has chosen Ireland as a major base of worldwide operations for these reasons:

- The numbers and quality of educated people
- The government and the Industrial Development Agency offer competitive financial and tax incentives
- Ireland is a member of the EU
- Ireland has an appropriate cost structure
- The necessary infrastructure is available — zoned industrial land, transportation, electricity, and water

Anyone who visits Leixlip would be impressed with the growth of prosperity in this Dublin suburb brought by the Intel complex. Since 1995, housing prices have increased 300% in the area, a source of both pride and concern of the locals.

Bill Riley is public affairs manager for Intel Ireland. He provides a perspective on the reasons for the match between Intel and Ireland and the components that contribute to Ireland's success: cultural congruence and the government's activist role.

BILL RILEY

Cultural congruence between Intel and Ireland

Culture does make a real difference in the new knowledge-based society. If you look at any society, you have high priests — the people who control knowledge — and the people who are controlled. And in some societies, the controllers could be paternally benevolent, or they could be absolute despots, but that was almost an arbitrary factor. The reality was that there was a knowledge-based elite and a knowledge-disenfranchised mass. And I do believe that the cultures that still have this centralist, knowledge-based elite are the ones who are in fact, the most resistant to a culture that drives for the knowledge of every individual.

The most important key factor for Intel to select Ireland over seven other European countries as a location for its business expansion in Europe was the availability of skilled young people, their enthusiasm, and can-do attitudes. This has proven vital to the success of Intel Ireland.

While Intel culture puts emphasis on teamwork and openness and promotes egalitarianism, its business values foster risk-taking, maintaining innovation, and increasing productivity. Both individual freedom and self-discipline are integrated from the very beginning, which create a challenging and rewarding work environment at Intel.

In the new knowledge-based society, people are respected for their knowledge and contribution to the society. And at Intel, a person who has knowledge that makes the difference between the company being successful or not, is a great asset to the organization. Thus, the knowledge must be able to be translated into action, with potentially positive outcome. Knowledge that is solely academic in nature and inwardly focused has no standing within Intel's business environment.

As a colonized country prior to 1948, Ireland has an enduring heritage that is traditionally entrenched in the society. Irish people, due to their suspicion of the authorities, tended not to rely on government to solve their individual problems or community issues. Instead they built a strong solidarity among their own countrymen to take on causes for the good at large. Even today, Irish people do not expect government to shape their lives. Individuals take charge to drive their own lives and be responsible for the outcomes. As such, the Irish mentality matches well with Intel's philosophy that people own their own employability. Intel management believes that while working at the company, people become more effective and are able to raise the level of their knowledge and capability to create more independence for themselves. The knowledge-based industries encourage the work ethic for people to act on their own, thereby generating the excitement and energy that are characteristic of this innovative work environment.

The U.S. is a very diverse country, not just in the context of ethnicity, but in other aspects as well. In business, each corporation has its own unique culture, a behavioral culture. At Intel, business objectives are communicated at the very beginning and clearly expressed at every level of the organization. The cultural overlay enables them to pull diverging individual behaviors together across diverse communities. Whether Intel people work at one of the U.S. locations, Ireland, or other parts of the world, they perform their duties and complete their tasks within Intel's cultural framework. In essence, geographical locations are unimportant to Intel. With 86,000 employees worldwide, spanning over 45 countries, Intel continually promotes diversity and believes that, as a multinational company, its success hinges on a wide range of perspectives, ideas, and experiences from its varied work force. Thus, in a knowledge-based society, knowledge in action is what shapes the world.

To put knowledge into action requires a cultural context. You have to be engaged in something. You have to want to do something, to deliver something, to achieve a goal. And, therefore, what pulls people together is something that they can see. If it is in business, does this company have a goal? Is it going to drive things? And therefore can I get excited about bringing my knowledge to bear, knowing that it's something much bigger and more fundamental than that which I am trying to shape? This is really what the business culture of the knowledge-based industry is trying to do. It is trying to create the excitement and the energy for people who do have many, many choices. Because it is global it is exciting and many people want to be a part of it.

Recently, an increasing number of Irish people, especially college students, have chosen the U.S. as their destination for summer work. Many have contacts and family relatives in the U.S., making them familiar with the American culture. The fact that Irish people also speak English contributes to the congruence of the cultural fit between Intel and the Irish work force.

Government's activist role

The deepening recession in the early 1980s prompted the IDA to shift its policies from attracting labor-intensive industries to those with high-output growth using the most advanced technologies. At first glance, it may seem inconsistent with the IDA's traditional approach in securing foreign investment to create jobs with the highest possible number, since Ireland had an abundant supply of human capital. Nonetheless, the most technologically advanced firms were generally perceived to be the most successful in their industries. As a result, the domino effect of economic gains would have great downstream impact throughout the region, most notably in services, materials, and indirect job creation.

Against this backdrop, the IDA exercised its autonomous authority and leverage to work with various local and regional officials to secure the Intel project, from infrastructure to fast-track planning process, from overcoming politics to financial grants. Intel, on its part, was impressed with Ireland's pro-business attitude, its flexibility, and the ability to quickly change and adapt to the business environment.

The Irish government had shown a willingness to learn and understand Intel's business needs, especially in the initial stage of establishing its operation in Ireland. Intel Ireland took almost two-and-a-half years to build and made over $2 billion in initial investment. There was almost a certainty of missed opportunities in the market, especially in the rapidly changing technology industry. Thus, speed, certainty, and the government's flexibility were critical in getting Intel Ireland off the ground. And the IDA has been instrumental in its commitment to assisting multinational companies like Intel in move up the value chain.

Intel also enjoys a very transparent relationship with the Irish government, one that is mutually beneficial. Multinationals, regarded as wealth generators to the economy, are also major tax contributors. As revenue grows, so does the tax burden. And to ensure a continual growth for Intel, the government has an open door policy to discuss issues with Intel, such as tax savings. The commissioners are generally forthcoming with advice on tax planning, a prudent step that would eventually be taken by Intel. It is this type of mind-set sympathetic to business that is critical to the success of Intel Ireland.

There is a degree of negotiation with the IDA that is usually very positive in trying to understand the nature of the problems that corporations need to overcome, and the things that they can do for you will make a difference. They are a partner as well as someone with whom you can negotiate. The IDA is there to help you become successful, so an arm-wrestling type of negotiation would be counterproductive. ■

EMC CORK

EMC was founded in 1979 and is now considered the leader in the data storage market."[1] The Massachusetts-based company ranks first in various categories in one of the fastest-growing industries in the world:

- #1 in revenue share of the worldwide disk storage systems market in 2000
- #1 storage management software supplier
- #1 in overall customer satisfaction by 400 IT professionals polled by *InformationWeek*
- Revenue in 2000 was $8.8 billion
- Net income was $1.89 billion
- Market capitalization is $146 billion
- Market share was 31% in 2000

EMC's systems are manufactured in the U.S. in Massachusetts and North Carolina, and in Cork, Ireland. Ireland also supports EMC research and development and customer service. Other research and development facilities are located in Israel, Japan, and France, while other customer support centers are located in Australia and Massachusetts.[2]

EMC Ireland was established in Cork in 1988, employing 22 people solely for manufacturing purposes and utilizing 47,000 square feet of space. Today, it has grown to about 1,650 employees working in 17 separate departments, occupying 560,000 square feet of space in a 24-acre estate, known as Cork Campus.

EMC Cork has been instrumental in elevating the company as a whole to become a major player in the worldwide information storage market. Within 13 years of its initial operation, EMC Cork has evolved from a small company creating traditional manufacturing jobs to a much higher value-added company, based increasingly on information and knowledge. It plays an increasingly vital role in the value chain of its parent company.

As with Intel and other MNCs, the success of EMC Cork has been partly based on the Irish government's positive approach toward business development. Ireland offers international companies a stable, profitable, English-speaking base to serve the European market and beyond. EMC Cork also finds a favorable tax environment, generous financial grants, low operating costs, and a productive and flexible work force.

Veronica Perdisatt is Vice President of the EMC Cork manufacturing division. She explains the growth of the Irish EMC Corporation, its commitments, and the challenges for a multinational high-technology business.

VERONICA PERDISATT

The challenge of working globally for ever-expanding operations of a multilocation company

When EMC went global in 1988 they were a smaller company. The lines of communication were small; everyone knew the goals and the challenges were different. We went from pure manufacturing to 17 separate functions for EMC in Ireland.

The challenge is in understanding explicitly the goals of the corporation. In this campus environment, we need to commit to the overall company goals. We cannot tolerate campus conflict. We also became a reserve for other regions, if needed. The days of not working in a collaborative are no longer viable.

Functional expansion is easier for EMC in Ireland

We have talented labor and do not have to replicate everything. We can expand to additional functional areas quickly because we already know EMC culture. Ireland has also been a great location to minimize corporate tax. We have a friendly character, which makes the Irish easy to work with, particularly for Americans. We are neutral and do not have the antagonisms that some Europeans have with Americans. The IDA has been very supportive for development grants and training. A lot of other regions may not have had the national mechanisms like the IDA. Ireland is less bureaucratic than other regions and the government approach has been consistent across political parties. That stability is a strength for Ireland. The Irish attitude for flexibility to address and solve problems can be communicated in the phrase, "Let's not create pneumonia, if it is just a cold."

The Irish fit with a high-tech culture

In Ireland, we have always been willing to accept change. An environment of constant change such as in the high-tech industry is an advantage for the Irish. We are not a very structured, formal, hierarchical people, which may characterize the business cultures in Europe. Our culture is approachable. We are also used to getting help or support from external sources. So, multinational companies coming in do not upset us; we welcome them.

Advice to other multinationals seeking to do business in Ireland

There is a great representation of multinationals here. Multinationals bring their experience with them to Ireland and tend to have local Irish managers. We are learning best practices from each company who comes. The amount of knowledge and cross-fertilization within Ireland has grown phenomenally as a result of this. We have built regional capital with knowledge. But, to succeed, it's important to learn to work the system. ■

The success story in a region such as Ireland lies in its willingness to be flexible and to work in collaboration with government, education, and industry. The IDA strikes a balance between government structure and entrepreneurial mindset to achieve economic development. From the multinationals' perspective, they learn to work the system and bring experiences with them to Ireland. As a result, there is a phenomenal growth of cross-fertilization of knowledge that moves the region up the value chain. It is evident in a higher proportion of skilled workers and graduates employed, who benefit from experiencing the most advanced technologies that these companies have to offer.

SUMMARY

Intel and EMC Corporation are good examples of international companies that have made a great commitment to establish major operations in Ireland. The challenge facing Ireland with multinational companies such as Intel and EMC is that Ireland may have reached the limits of its physical infrastructure of housing and transportation to support more people, just as in Silicon Valley.

Another challenge is that growth may not be sustainable. The Irish dependency is on multinational companies. The downturn in the U.S. economy can be quite severe for Ireland. As local Irish companies have grown, they tend to become absorbed by larger multinationals. Ireland is not big enough to recreate Silicon Valley. The era of cheap labor and cheap land is now gone. The Irish labor market has tightened, wage costs are climbing, and the impact of a weak Euro currency is threatening economic growth.

A third concern is that, with consolidation in the European Union, new labor laws may inhibit the Irish. The Irish also worry that the tax advantages they now have will be eliminated with a uniform corporate tax in the EU.

The Irish have succeeded in technology, food production, and tourism. Whether these industries will be able to sustain the Irish miracle is yet to be determined. If the task can be done, the Irish government can do it. They have proven themselves to successfully recruit, retain, and cultivate foreign direct investment to provide high quality jobs for Ireland's people.

ENDNOTES

1. MSN Money Central, *moneycentral.msn.com/home.asp*, July 6, 2001.

2. EMC Corporation, *www.emc.com*.

P A R T

STOCKHOLM, SWEDEN

"THE HIGH-SPEED GLOBILE[1] INNOVATIONS COMMUNITY"

Few countries in the world have mastered the transition from an industrial society to an information society as quickly and as successfully as Sweden.[2] At the heart of the Swedish information and communications technology revolution lie Stockholm[3] and the Stockholm suburb of Kista,[4] which over the past two decades have become home to the world's most important center for mobile information and communications technologies (ICT).

The Swedish high-tech phenomenon developed in the early 1990s, when Sweden was fighting an economic and ideological crisis. The social democratic "Swedish Model" was considered to have failed, resulting in unprecedented levels of unemployment and budget deficit. To bring new life to the economy and new perspectives to the Swedish people, the government decided to focus on emerging information and communications technologies.[5] This proved to be a brilliant recipe for success that leveraged Sweden's traditional set of commercial skills and existing communications infrastructures while positioning the nation for the information age.

1. "Globile": Global and Mobile. Source: Welcome to eSweden, Invest in Sweden Agency, *www.isa.ie*.
2. Virtual Sweden, *www.virtualsweden.net*.
3. The City of Stockholm Development Agency, *www.stockholm.se/english*.
4. Kista — Sweden's Leading Industrial Park, *www.kista.com*.
5. The Swedish ICT Commission, *www.itkommissionen.se*.

International Comparisons

	SWEDEN	U.S.	GERMANY	U.K.	FRANCE	IRELAND
Large companies per million inhabitants[a]	3.3	N/A	1	2.8	1.1	1.7
Corporate income tax, 2000 (%)[b]	28	40	43	30	37	24
Average annual venture capital growth 1995–1999 (%)[c]	210	40	42	39	N/A	N/A
Total expenditure on R&D (percent of GDP)[d]	3.7	3.1	2.3	1.8	2.2	1.4
Investment in knowledge (percent of GDP)[e]	6.5	6	4.2	3.9	4.1	3.1
Percentage of population at highest literary skills[f]	36	19	19	19	N/A	12
Nobel Prizes per capita[g]	1.1	0.7	0.3	0.8	N/A	0.3
Country ranking microeconomic climate[h]	4	1	6	10	9	N/A
Future readiness in Europe (index)[i]	93.2	N/A	81.3	84.9	84.0	88.8

a. Ranked according to sales 1998. Source: *EuroBusiness*, December 1999.
b. Source: KPMG, April 2000.
c. Average annual growth of private equity and venture capital investments. Source: PriceWaterhouseCoopers and 3i, 2000.
d. Sweden, UK, Ireland are 1997 figures, US, Germany are 1998 figures. Source: OECD.
e. Public spending on education plus spending on R&D and Ssoftware in 1998. Source: OECD.
f. Population aged 16 to 65, literacy levels 4/5. Source: OECD, *Education at a Glance 1998*.
g. As of 1998. Source: *World Competitiveness Yearbook 1999*, IMD, 1999.
h. 1999 MICI index rank. Source: M.E. Porter, "Micro-economic competitiveness: Findings from the 1999 Executive Survey," 1999.
i. The index measures the availability of Internet hosts and access to telecommunications lines, R&D and the existence of well-educated people. Source: A.T. Kearney, "Global Leaders of Tomorrow," 1999.

8 INDUSTRY SPECIALIZATION AND LEVERAGING INTELLECTUAL CAPITAL

N ames such as "Mobile Valley" and "Wireless Valley" have been given to Sweden's seven large mobile ICT clusters, which together comprise a regional network unsurpassed in the world. The largest and most important one is the Stockholm-Kista cluster. Sweden has become a "high-speed globile innovations community,"[1] centered around cutting-edge innovation for global applications in mobile computing technologies, while preserving the traditional Swedish small community character.

Sweden's high-tech success has in part been enabled by the Swedish people's natural acceptance and thorough utilization of information and communication technologies. During the past 10 years, these technologies have become well integrated into professional and personal life.

TABLE 8-1 Facts at a Glance — Sweden

SWEDISH DEMOGRAPHICS	
Population	8.9 million
Population density	19.7 per square kilometer
Area	450,000 square kilometers (roughly the size of California)
GDP per capita 1999	$26,616
Exports 2000	$11,711 (44% of GDP)
Unemployment rate 2001	Less than 4%

THE STOCKHOLM-KISTA ICT CLUSTER	
Stockholm (capital city) population 1999	1,783,000
Number of IT and telecom jobs	90,000 (45% of Sweden's IT employees)
Location of Kista	15 minutes from Stockholm Arlanda International Airport, north of city center
Foundation of Kista Science Park	1976 by Ericsson, IBM, et al.
Number of IT companies in Kista	700, with 29,000 employees
Gross salary of a network engineer 1999	Low: $33,000; High: $41,000; for total cost add 33%
Largest company in Kista	Ericsson (founded 1880; 13,000 employees in Kista today)
University in Kista	Royal Institute of Technology IT University (3,500 students)
Cross-fertilization in Kista	Electrum Foundation (cooperation of state, city, and industry)

ICT PEOPLE EXCELLING IN AN ICT WORLD — AN INFORMATION SOCIETY FOR ALL!

Sweden describes itself as an ICT nation. ICT has fully penetrated Swedish society, including individuals, businesses, and the public sector. Swedish consumers are known as demanding early adopters, while Swedish corporations are among the world's leaders at employing ICT for competitive advantage. Since the first half of the 1990s, the Swedish government and even the labor unions have embraced new technologies as "wings to human ability,"[2] and since have been propagating an "Information Society for All."[3]

As Figure 8-1 illustrates, Sweden leads Europe and the U.S. in mobile phone, PC, and Internet penetration. The high levels of penetration were in part achieved by a government initiative during the early 1990s, when all Swedish employees were given the opportunity to purchase home PCs through their employers from their pre-tax income. This discounted 50 percent off retail prices. The employers benefited from reduced employee social payments, and the home PC industry enjoyed a substantial boost.

The labor unions played an important role in this process. Very early on, they recognized it was crucial that they also be engaged in the ICT development to increase the competitiveness of the labor force. The unions saw the risk that PCs could become a white-collar tool only, leaving blue-collar workers behind. Modern production required workers to have an intuitive understanding of ICT. So the goal to provide every single home with a personal computer was actually a long-term social democratic ambition rather than a mere industry subsidy.

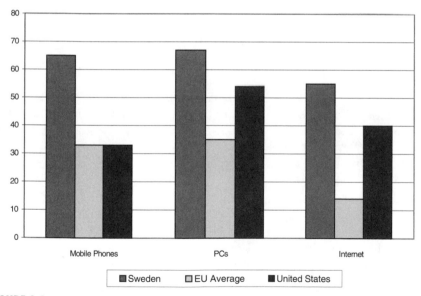

FIGURE 8-1
Penetration of mobile phones, PCs, and Internet in Sweden, based on 1999 population percentages.
Sources: EITO; Global Mobile; ITU; *World Competitiveness Report, 2000*, IMD, 2000.

Since the turnaround of its economy, Sweden invests more into the knowledge of its people than the other large nations profiled in this book (see the International Comparisons table on page 110). Consequently, the Swedish ICT environment has earned international acclaim. Sweden increasingly attracts research and development investments from leading global high-tech companies that see Sweden as a leading global test market for mobile and computing technologies.

DEVELOPING MOBILE COMPUTING SOLUTIONS IN A KEY GLOBAL TEST MARKET

Global high-tech companies are attracted by Sweden's high penetration rates, having made the Stockholm region a key test market for innovative global computing solutions. The development of this test market environment was enabled by Sweden's highly demanding consumers, who are known to be early adopters of commercial technologies, and a strong national communications infrastructure, a priority to the government for many decades. In large parts of Sweden, especially to the north of the country, the population density drops to about three inhabitants per square kilometer, as approximately 25% of the Swedish population lives around the city of Stockholm. Communication has thus always been a prime concern to the Swedish people. As early as 1909, the city of Stockholm had 60 telephones per 1,000 inhabitants, while Berlin had 18, Paris had 10, and London merely had only two.

Today, more than 70% of the Swedish population uses mobile telephones and more than 50% of the population aged 16 years and older use the Internet. However, the fastest-growing segment of surfers on the Web at 80% growth in 1999, were the 50 to 79 year olds, driven in part by SeniorNet,[4] a national nonprofit organization set up in 1997 to promote ICT usage by everyone over 55 years of age.

Information and communications technologies are regarded by the Swedish government as key to the development of the remote regions of the country, which include hundreds of marginally inhabited islands that scatter the Swedish coastline. With the development of wireless hyper-LAN technologies capable of several kilometers of transmission range, Sweden plans to connect all of its inhabitants to the information age and is already preparing to do so by laying far-reaching loops of fiber optic cables across the distant regions of the country.

As illustrated by our next market highlight, since the economic crisis in 1992, Sweden's high penetration rates, demanding customers, regionally dispersed demographics, and supportive government have caused foreign direct high-tech investment to the region to boom.

A GLOBAL MAGNET FOR HIGH-TECH R&D FACILITIES

Sweden's test market reputation has helped it to attract a large number of corporate R&D facilities. The ICT cluster in and around Kista Science Park[5] began to develop when Ericsson and IBM decided in the late 1970s to move their Swedish operations to a deserted military training ground just outside of the city of Stockholm, 15 minutes by car from Stockholm Arlanda International Airport, where land was cheap and the municipal government decided to set up a technology park. A few years later, Ericsson's closest rival, Nokia, placed an R&D center in Kista. The magnetic force exerted by the presence of Ericsson, IBM, and Nokia in Kista quickly attracted more technology-driven companies to the area from different fields of communications and computing. As it became apparent that Sweden and the Stockholm-Kista area had developed as a prime breeding ground for emerging mobile computing markets, many other global high-tech companies decided set up R&D facilities in the region and the Kista phenomenon became a self-fulfilling prophecy.

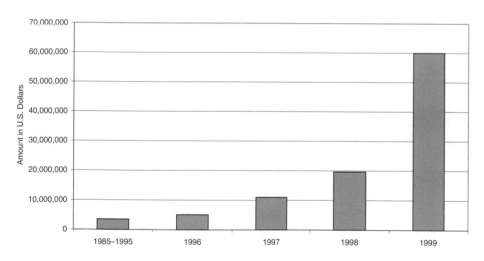

FIGURE 8-2

Total inward FDI in Sweden, 1985–1999, in U.S. billions.

Source: *World Investment Report 2000*, UNCTAD.

Between 1990 and 1999, the number of foreign-owned companies in Sweden increased by 65% from 2,600 to 4,300, accounting for nearly 20% of the private sector R&D expenditure in Sweden, and nearly half of the country's exports.[6] Today, every sixth employee in Swedish private business has a foreign-owned company employer (see Table 8-2).

TABLE 8-2   Recent Investments in Wireless Communication in Sweden

COMPANY	INVESTMENT
Andersen Consulting (U.S.)	Global center for WAP applications and services
Motorola (U.S.)	Development centers for wireless applications and services
Cambridge Technology Partners (U.S.)	Global wireless competence center
Nokia (Finland)	R&D in mobile communication infrastructure
Cap Gemini Ernst and Young (France/U.S.)	Joint competence center for 3G mobile systems
Nortel Networks (Canada)	R&D center for datacom, telecoms and wireless communications
Compaq (U.S.)	Wireless competence center and e-commerce knowledge center
Hewlett Packard (U.S.)	Wireless research and a joint project with Ericsson and Telia
Oracle (U.S.)	Center of excellence for wireless product development. Joint-company established with Telia of wireless services, Halebop
Intel (U.S.)	Wireless competence center and e-business solution center
RSA Security (U.S.)	Development of secure wireless communications
IBM (U.S.)	Wireless Internet center
Siemens (Germany)	R&D center for mobile applications
Microsoft (U.S.)	Acquired Swedish Sendit, a leading provider of mobile Internet solutions and formed a strategic partnership with Ericsson to develop and market end-to-end solutions for the wireless Internet
Sun Microsystems (U.S.)	Wireless center of excellence
Sybase (U.S.)	Test center for mobile business applications and a strategic alliance with Ericsson around mobile banking solutions

Source: Invest in Sweden Agency, 2001, www.isa.se.

Based on the strong culture of early technology adoption in Sweden and the government's rigorous policies aimed at moving the whole of Swedish society to the information age, it appears that Sweden will remain an attractive test market for emerging ICT applications, and will cause many more high-tech companies to locate their R&D facilities within the region in the coming years.

CASE STUDY:
CISCO SYSTEMS SWEDEN —
A MARKET OF FOCUS FOR ACQUISITIONS

Acquisitions constitute an important part of Cisco's growth strategy. Even though 70% of its growth is internal, core company strategy is to aggressively acquire new talent and ideas. During the past decade, a breeding ground for high-tech companies has developed in and around Stockholm, which has attracted Cisco, like so many other global technology firms, to the area. When it comes to scouting the world for the best companies to acquire, two areas have gained the company's special focus: Israel and Sweden. We spoke with Peter Kopelman, managing director of Cisco Systems Sweden, who explained why Cisco has selected Sweden as a key global focus area for the acquisition of companies.

He believes that a local focus and a deep understanding of the company's requirements are equally important in order to be able to identify potential acquisition candidates.

In order to address the Swedish shortage of networking professionals, Cisco collaborates actively with governmental and educational institutions by installing equipment in schools and households and by teaching teachers how to use it. The first contract for the Cisco "Net Academic Program" in Europe was signed with Mr. Carl Cederschiöld, the mayor of Stockholm. According to Mr. Kopelman, "Stockholm officials are not scared of technology." The shortage of highly skilled personnel in Sweden was recognized by industry and government many years ago. Consequently, the government has come up with a concept that intends to link science parks and university education.

PETER KOPELMAN

A breeding ground for acquisition targets

There was always an entrepreneurial spirit in Swedish firms. As soon as sufficient capital became accessible in the region, people started to jump ship from large corporations like Ericsson to start their own companies. Releasing the Swedish potential that lay subdued for a long time has created a surge of innovation and the spawning of many new companies. Hence the new concept of a breeding ground. The Swedish government has been very pro-ICT, which has helped the process a lot. They made sure that all infrastructure-related questions were properly taken care of so that things could really get going.

Cisco came to Sweden to identify and acquire innovative companies that it believes will have an impact on its future markets. One of the reasons Cisco is so interested in Sweden is that at the same time, there is a flavor of the U.S. culture, a flavor of the European culture, and a flavor of our own company culture around here. Due to the country's widely dispersed demographics and the excellent information infrastructure, there has been a lot of experimentation with new forms of "virtual" company organization that interest us very much.

Cultural fit

When searching for companies to acquire, we primarily look for a cultural fit with the potential candidate. Since Sweden has traditionally been so dependent on exports, the Swedish business culture is open to foreign practices and can be easily integrated within a larger corporate structure. The Swedish cultural flexibility works well with Cisco's business culture: We adapt our products to the rest of the world, not the other way around.

The crisis benefits the breeding ground

Through its acquisitions in Sweden, Cisco aims to stay at the forefront of technological development, enabling it to catch on to new growth cycles faster than through internal development. The technology crisis, which I consider a necessary cleansing of the market, has struck Sweden especially hard. When companies die, there is new "soil" for the breeding ground, enabling the emergence of new kinds of companies. This kind of development can be seen with the Swedish Internet consulting companies that shot up like rockets and then crashed faster than anyone else. The Swedish entrepreneurs who have founded and run these companies are true pioneers. Even if their companies may not survive the crisis in the market, they have learned a lot in the process. Today, Swedish entrepreneurs know better than most other people at least what doesn't work. This is a competitive advantage enabling innovative Swedish companies to be faster at producing new and improved value propositions. ∎

Linking Science Parks and University Education — A Governmental Prerequisite

Kista Science Park did not originally develop around a leading university. Already in the 1980s, large corporations in Kista needed more competent people and more quality research than the region could offer. Discussions were held between Sweden's leading technical university KTH (Royal Institute of Technology),[7] the state government, the Swedish Board of Technical Development, Ericsson, Asea, and the city of Stockholm. The consortium decided to set up the Electrum Foundation[8] to enable a greater proximity between people from industry, research, and education. Based on the concept of networks of people rather than networks of organizations, local industry, research, and education professionals were all given the opportunity to work and meet in the same building, to get to know the others' problems and thus to build a basis for cooperation. Since 2000, Electrum has been regularly publishing a competence newspaper. It is working to install non-scientific education subjects in Kista, convinced that the region also needs people using the right, not only the left, part of the brain.

Even though Sweden has one of the most literate and well-educated populations in the world (see the International Comparisons table on page 110), the country's shortage of skills increased as more and more innovative companies moved to the region.[9] Today, the Swedish government demands that each science park, in order to be acknowledged as one, needs to include a university or at least part of a university with its own campus to produce new generations of qualified graduates.

In 1999, KTH founded IT University Kista,[10] which in 2000 employed 30 full-time professors, 300 researchers, and educated 3,500 students. A new campus is planned for 2003, enabling the university to double its student body to 7,000 by 2005. IT University Kista is a tenant on the premises of the Electrum Foundation and has become a part of the Electrum competence network. Its curriculum is coauthored by educational and industrial individuals. The university aims to be problem focused, rather than theoretical, interacting with the issues facing Kista's high-tech companies.

The competencies built by such government initiatives complement the Swedish people's traditional skills at operating in global markets, based on a business culture of "global compatibility" and a far-ranging know-how of how to set up and operate global businesses.

A HISTORIC IMPERATIVE OF GLOBAL COMPATIBILITY

Swedish companies have traditionally been dependent on exports due to its small domestic market size of 8.9 million inhabitants. Most Swedish multinationals generate between 80% and 90% of their revenues abroad. Sweden has been in favor of free trade since a comprehensive political debate in 1867. The government realized that in the long run, it could not restrict the entry of foreign goods to the Swedish market if it wanted to create wealth by selling Swedish goods abroad.

Sweden's early dependency on exports forced Swedish companies to develop an understanding of how to gain access to foreign markets and how to develop products for global distribution. Hence, Swedish companies exposed themselves to global competition, heterogeneous markets, and foreign technologies early on, enabling them to bring home and instill within Sweden a global business mindset.

THE ENGLISH LANGUAGE — A BASIS OF GLOBAL INTEROPERABILITY

Understanding the importance of an international "interoperability" of the Swedish people, the Swedish educational policy has succeeded at making Sweden's entire work force practically fluent in English. Television programs are rarely translated from English to Swedish. Instead, they have Swedish subtitles, which amounts to free English classes for all of Swedish society. Furthermore, the Swedish educational system allows tax money to "follow the pupil" to the parents' choice of educational institution, enabling a broader and more diverse range of private schools. In a private school in Stockholm, 50% of classes are taught in English. The system attracts foreign families such as expatriates, knowing that they will find a spirit of international openness, will be "understood," and can easily integrate into Swedish life.

Even though Sweden today has the highest number of large multinational corporations per capita in the world, not many medium-sized companies have had access to the capital, the networks, and the skills required for successful global expansion. The political system in Sweden is not built around the needs of medium-sized companies, typically causing small enterprises to select niche markets and to stay small, waiting to be bought up. Hardly any medium-sized companies exist in Sweden today, as the work force is active either in very small companies or very large companies with over 5,000 employees.

AN ECONOMY BASED ON
LARGE MULTINATIONAL COMPANIES

Although Sweden's welfare to a large extent depends on its exports, the exports of only a handful of its giant multinationals are the true determinants of Swedish prosperity. In 2000, 44% of Sweden's GDP derived from exports, of which 15% alone was generated by Ericsson. The automotive manufacturers Saab (General Motors), Volvo-Passenger (Ford), and Volvo Scania, together contributed another 13%. There is a general awareness of the fact that when things go well for Ericsson, things go well for Sweden, and vice versa.

NETWORKING AND COLLABORATION —
VIRTUE, NOT NECESSITY!

In Sweden, leading businesspeople, academics, and politicians traditionally keep tight networks, since most of them have attended the country's top three schools — the Royal Institute of Technology, Stockholm School of Economics,[11] and University of Göteborg.[12] In addition to the educational networks in Sweden, business networks play a significant role. Before the boom of entrepreneurship in the late 1990s, top university graduates were generally recruited by large Swedish companies such as ABB and Ericsson. They provided exciting international career opportunities, enabling Swedish managers to build strong international business networks.

CASE STUDY:
ERICSSON — A FOUNTAIN OF
NETWORKING AND INNOVATION

At the center of the Swedish ICT personal networking phenomenon is the omnipresent Ericsson; try speaking to high-tech executives in Sweden about their past, and almost everyone has worked at Ericsson or Ericsson is their main customer or their technology partner. The opportunities to gather practical experience and build networks within Ericsson have been a strong source of leverage to entrepreneurs all over Sweden. These personal networks unfolded their potential when the climate for start-ups developed and entrepreneurship became fashionable in the second half of the 1990s. Large innovative companies such as Ericsson eventually proved a good basis for individuals to "jump ship" and start their own companies.

Sweden's tight networks are generally complemented by a strong culture of teamwork, collaboration, and the sharing of information. Collaboration, even with competitors, is becoming increasingly important in nascent markets, where different technologies are necessary to develop innovative solutions. Collaboration is a paradigm of Swedish economic reality: "Collaborate in order to survive." An example for this traditional Swedish characteristic within a modern context, is the coexistence of Ericsson and Nokia in Kista.

Jesper Ejdling Martell, director of Comintell,[13] a Stockholm-based company providing solutions and software for enterprise knowledge management, is a former employee of Ericsson, where he was manager of corporate business intelligence. He describes Ericsson and Nokia as having an almost brotherly relationship. Finland was once part of Sweden and the two countries have a history of military alliances. There have always been special sports competitions between the two countries, underlining a relationship of friendly competition. This historic tradition has materialized in the Ericsson/Nokia relationship.

Supporting innovation in Sweden are flat organizational structures and employee empowerment levels considered to surpass those of other European countries as well as those of the United States. Hierarchy and elitism are seen very negatively in Sweden, the roots of which lie in the country's socialist history.

Within this context, most of the information that is available to the management in Swedish companies is shared with the employees. Rather than top-down management directives for product development, it is usually the engineers who may have five or ten different projects going on at the same time, who drive product development. They compete internally for which project will eventually go to market. Unlike a typical American company, that will develop a project only if it recognizes a market demand, Ericsson engineers are free to "sit down and play" in the hope that something will emerge for which there will be a market.

Foreign companies entering the Swedish market, attempting to lure individuals away from Swedish companies by offering higher pay, have had to deal with this Swedish cultural specificity. These companies were initially successful at attracting Swedish employees. However, they have had to watch many of these Swedes return to their original employers, accepting lower pay in return for the freedom of the Swedish culture, which is characterized marked by more of a sense of community than internal competition.

The spirit of collaboration in a wider sense has become of central importance for companies such as Intel, increasingly building open architectures that build on cross-company and cross-industry collaboration in order to develop groundbreaking new solutions.

JESPER EJDLING

Ericsson and Nokia — Collaborative competition in Kista

The collaboration between the two companies started soon after Ericsson moved to Kista, when in 1984 its closest rival Nokia moved there as well in order to be close to the technological developments that were going on in the region. Since then, the proximity of the other has proven beneficial to both companies, an acute sense of competition constantly driving both of them to get better all the time.

Regardless of their competitive relationship, Ericsson and Nokia often work in symbiosis, sharing information that would be considered highly confidential in other regions of the world. Neither of the two are out to make large amounts of money in their local markets, aiming rather to quickly develop solutions and standards and gain access to larger markets all over the globe that offer both of them vast opportunities at once.

The Swedish concept for information sharing is, "if you feed information into the system, you become part of this system and you will probably get something out in return." Ericsson and Nokia have offices very close to each other and one can often see Ericsson and Nokia employees having lunch together discussing how to solve certain problems. There is a lot of personal interaction between the two companies, which is being actively encouraged by management. The relationship between the two companies can almost be described as a love/hate relationship: You share what you know and you hope the product gets developed. In the end it might not even matter who develops it, as long as it gets developed and new markets are created.

Naturally, competitors can pick up internal information more easily in Sweden than in other countries. However at the pace of development in today's high-tech markets, it is not the information itself but what you do with it that matters. Things are happening so quickly that if Motorola got hold of Ericsson's strategy documents, they wouldn't be able to do much with them. They wouldn't have time to act on the information. ■

INTEL SWEDEN — COLLABORATING TO ESTABLISH TOMORROW'S STANDARDS

When Intel reformulated its corporate focus from building microprocessors for PCs to becoming the preeminent building block supplier for the worldwide Internet economy several years ago, the company needed to move into previously unexplored fields of communications technology. Lars Östmarck, Nordic regional manager at Intel Sweden, describes that the company decided to invest in Kista to become competitive in emerging mobile computing markets. In addition to the wireless competency center in Stockholm,

Intel Sweden operates a wireless communications center and full-scale customer testing center. Of its large sales force specifically selling components to Nokia and Ericsson, 50% is involved with communication, and 50% is involved with traditional microprocessing.

LARS ÖSTMARCK

An ideal environment to build co-opetition–based communications architectures

At Intel, the new "green business" in communications was organized so that the "big mother" would not kill all of the little initiatives. At this time, a lot of companies were acquired in the communications field, especially in the Nordic regions. At the beginning of 2001, there were about 500 employees working on R&D in these acquired companies in the Nordic region, adding needed complementary capabilities to Intel's core competencies.

The Intel wireless center in Kista works as a satellite of central R&D in the U.S., together with two other wireless competency centers in China and in Japan. China was selected due to the large market potential, while Japan was chosen in order to create new services. Their role is to drive the evolution of wireless computing, to watch, and to report on the latest happenings and players in the mobile ecosystem. Furthermore, these centers work on achieving higher acceptance of new architectures that are replacing today's microprocessor architectures. The combination of many manufacturers, service providers, and the high ICT penetration has attracted Intel to use the Swedish market as a test bed.

The Swedish business community is quite used to working with remote management. It is very convenient, for example, to place an R&D center in Sweden and to connect it to other centers in the U.S. The spirit of leadership is, of course, local. Whereas in Finland the culture is very masculine, Sweden, Norway, and Denmark are very consensus driven. Nonetheless, Sweden and the U.S. are quite close in the area of how people behave and manage. The clashes are much larger with Germany, where, for example, it is often not possible to send promotional material in English.

The Swedish business culture has been an ideal environment for the development of open communications architectures that are conceived for collaborative development between companies and industries. Collaboration initiatives have for instance aimed at the establishment of industry standards, new services, and the understanding of customer usage patterns.

Intel's mission in Kista is to develop standard building blocks on the basis of which other players can build new products. This strategy contrasts with the proprietary stand-alone solution stacks offered by other infrastructure providers. Intel does not believe in these proprietary solutions, since all members within the business ecosystem share an interest in the creation of open standards. Enabling two industries such as the communications and the computing industries to cooperate and eventually merge requires a sense for collaboration. Sweden is a good test ground for such an emerging business logic. Co-opetition is a characteristic inherent to the area because it is small, people know each other and it is easy to gather and work together on developments.

An Intel success story within this context was when the Finnish company Sonera, which wanted to develop new services for its networks, utilized Intel's horizontal building block approach to construct its architecture. It was a beautiful way of getting operators and customers to endorse Intel's products at the same time. Sonera was the first operator in the world to do this. Its pioneering initiative influenced the entire ecosystem. Intel now wants to work increasingly with operators as well as service providers to develop open architectures. ■

Sweden's collaborative spirit is complemented by a far-ranging understanding of intellectual capital (IC) and the implications of IC for businesses. IC is considered by leading Swedish academics and business people to be at the basis of economic success and has prompted Swedish companies to adapt IC-oriented management tools centered around the intellectual capacities of their employees.

Leveraging Intellectual Capital — Building the "Club Med" of the Global Innovation Economy

Sweden has made historic efforts to achieve an egalitarian society in wealth distribution, high levels of general education, and full employment within a democratic system. An individual's capabilities have traditionally been highly valued, respected, and cared for by the state and the country's employers. Even though the Swedish welfare state model did collapse in the beginning of the 1990s, followed by comprehensive waves of deregulation and other free-market reforms, the "new" Sweden nonetheless inherited a "human" approach to doing business, viewing the value of employees rather than their cost. Given the central importance of intellectual capital in a global Innovation Economy, the Swedish today find themselves further along the learning curve than some other nations, having for many decades propagated collaboration, flat hierarchies, and consensus-driven decision making. Today, as entrepreneurship, personal wealth creation, and other personal success stories have become accepted phenomena in Swedish society, the Swedish model has shifted from "protecting the individual" to "enabling the individual." The country has become a breeding ground for innovative management techniques and solutions focusing on making the most of a company's intellectual capital.

According to the Swedish company Comintell, companies need to build "Intelligent Communities" to leverage the full potential of their employees by maximizing the collective experience.[14] Intelligent Communities combine the management of people and of information, balancing between the creativity of people and the structure of information. Comintell defines Intelligent Communities as "a network of trained knowledge workers who systematically work together to maximize the value of their combined knowledge." The management of Intelligent Communities differs from regular line management or project management in that it involves the management of people over whom the executive has no line authority over an indefinite period of time.

Whereas Comintell has been successful in the Nordic countries, the company recently decided to close its London office, claiming that the U.K. market was not mature enough for its knowledge management solutions. U.K. executives were generally hesitant to accept the benefits of information sharing and the prevention of information overload, benefits that are widely acknowledged in Sweden.

Leif Edvinsson, former director of the Skandia Future Center[15] and the world's first director of intellectual capital, was named 1998 Brain of the Year by the Brain Trust Foundation in England for his pioneering work in the field of IC. Mr. Edvinsson, who has recently founded the IC consultancy company Universal Networking Intellectual Capital (UNIC),[16] has developed tools to measure the intellectual capital of regions.

LEIF EDVINSSON

Measuring and cultivating the intellectual capital of regions

The world has a certain amount of intellectual capital. However, there are different levels of efficiency with which the regions are accessing and utilizing their intellectual capital. Traditionally neglected but highly relevant when "regarding the future as an asset,"[17] are the opportunity costs that are incurred when intellectual capital is left underutilized.

Innovation hot spots around the world can be identified by using the measurement "value added per capita." This measurement highlights how well the employees are utilizing the structural capital and the infrastructure of the region to create value. Based on this value added, they are paid incomes, while generating dividends for shareholders and tax revenues for the government, which in turn forms the basis for future research and development. The big question is: what exactly drives this value added? In search of the answers to his questions, I have developed a tool to measure the IC of regions, which we are currently testing on Kista.[18] Maximizing the leverage of intellectual capital in a society is a complex endeavor, involving several dimensions that include a leadership dimension, a political dimension, and a technology dimension. The political dimension is of central importance.

Key to the Swedish success story within this context were two points in time that enabled the region to set out on its path to become what it is today. The more obvious of the two points was when it became apparent to the outside world that there is a "wireless valley" in Sweden, which was the "attention point" in the media. This attention point was an article in *Newsweek* and just before that a conference at which Cisco and Microsoft announced that they would be investing in the region. When working with intangibles like intellectual capital, an effective attention point and subsequent media communication are important to build a brand around what is inside the "intangible region." Behind the scenes, the second key moment occurred when the political aspiration of turning the region into "something" materialized. This was the actual beginning of everything. Once the aspiration of a region is clearly defined, leadership or more specifically regional political cultivation is required in order to turn this aspiration into reality.

The most important element of regional cultivation is to enable networking, and Kista still does not have enough of it, even though the Electrum Foundation in Kista has been playing the role of the regional cultivator. This might be astounding since networking is a societal paradigm in Sweden, but the existing networks in Stockholm and Kista are still too ad hoc and task oriented. They are not nourished in the same way as in Silicon Valley, where numerous institutions like First Tuesday provide a conceptual and physical arena for networking and a master of ceremony moderating each event. How long is the life cycle of a network? It is very short if it is merely task oriented. It is the ongoing interplay between people that nourishes innovation. Someone has to bring on this interplay, and Club Med with its concept of the "gentil organisateur" is a good example. In other words, for a region to become successful, network facilitation requires two elements: a "producer" in charge of providing the platform or infrastructure for interaction, as well as a "director" in charge of placing the right people in the right positions on this platform. In this way, value added can be derived from the interaction between the network's members.

Landscaping is critical in order to enable the cultivation of innovation. Whereas most plans for science parks are based on industrial work plans, experience has shown that knowledge workers dislike this kind of environment. They need open space, nature, and water in order to create a collective experience. Research at Skandia Future Center has revealed that the water dimension is indeed critical. In this context, the concepts of traditional harbors and knowledge harbors are linked. In most places, the harbor is the ugliest area in the city, except for San Francisco, where it was turned into a beautiful area starting 20 years ago. If you were going to describe a leading harbor for the flow of intangibles, what kind of a landscape would you locate it in? How do you design knowledge harbors? While these questions remain to be answered, they indicate that many existing industrial infrastructures might well be unsuited for the leveraging of intellectual capital in the globally linked innovative digital economy.

Now suppose you have beautiful landscape, you have the tech infrastructure, you have people, you have the brand — who is going to connect all of these factors in order to generate higher value added per capita? That is where I think we should focus in terms of creating what I call "political entrepreneurship." It seems to be lacking in most regions. Most political leadership today is maintenance rather than entrepreneurship. We train business entrepreneurs but where do we shape political entrepreneurs? Singapore has renamed the Ministry of Labor to the Ministry of Manpower. The value added per capita in Singapore is very high. Think about that. ■

SUMMARY

In summary, the Swedish culture is characterized by collaboration and flat hierarchies. Its small domestic market size and thin population density have enabled Swedish businesses to become communication technology leaders at a global level. The penetration of communications technologies in Swedish society have enabled the region to become a global test market. A traditional focus on intellectual capital has caused Sweden to use pioneering concepts to link high technology and university education in order to prepare the knowledge workers it will require in the future.

The Swedish market overview indicates that the region's high-tech success in part resulted from a natural evolution. Many argue that Sweden just happened to be at the right place at the right time. They claim that Sweden happens to have a tradition of telecommunication industries and that Ericsson just happened to move to Kista when suddenly global wireless telecom markets started booming, and the entire region found itself in a strong position to cater to these emerging global markets. Within such a context, foreign regions may conclude that the creation of regional wealth through high-tech clusters is not merely a matter of short- or mid-term policies. Rather, the Swedish example shows that traditional skills and capabilities that lay unexposed for generations enabled Sweden to become what it is today. The exposure of these skills was aided by global economic developments and a national economic crisis; these made it apparent that the Swedish government needed to initiate wide-ranging reforms and to introduce small business-friendly policies to leverage existing Swedish skills and position the country for the global Innovation Economy.

However, the determined action recently taken by Swedish government, as well as research and industry organizations, indicate that tradition and good fortune alone do not suffice in order to develop successful high-tech clusters. In this sense, three areas of specific importance for Sweden have been:

- Political entrepreneurship
- Successfully attracting and leveraging human resources
- Enabling an entrepreneurship revival

Next, we will take an in-depth look at each of these focus areas. They describe in greater detail how short- and mid-term projects and policies have enabled the application of traditional skills and capabilities to new contexts within the Innovation Economy.

ENDNOTES

1. "Globile": Global and Mobile. Welcome to eSweden, Invest in Sweden Agency, *www.isa.ie*.

2. Former Prime Minister Carl Bildt aimed to revitalize the country based on his 1994 paper "Wings to Human Ability" by promoting the utilization of information technology.

3. Ministry of Industry, Employment, and Communications, *www.naring.regeringen.se*.

4. SeniorNet Sweden, *www.seniornet.se*.

5. Kista Science Park, *www.kistasciencepark.org*.

6. Invest in Sweden Agency, *www.isa.se*.

7. Kungl Tekniska Högskolan — Royal Institute of Technology, *www.kth.se*.

8. Electrum, *www.electrum.se*.

9. *ISA Council of Economic Advisors Report*, Swedish Open, 2001.

10. IT — Universitetet/KTH, *www.it-universitetet.kth.se*.

11. Handelshögskolan I Stockholm — Stockholm School of Economics, *www.hhs.se*.

12. Göteborg University, *www.gu.se/english*.

13. Comintell, *www.comintell.com*.

14. Comintell, Intelligent Community, *www.comintell.com/solutions/overview.htm*.

15. Skandia Future Center, *www.skandiafuturecenter.com*.

16. Universal Networking Intellectual Capital, *www.unic.net/about/leifedvinsson.html*.

17. Gottfried Grafström and Leif Edvinsson, *Accounting for Minds — An Inspirational Guide to Intellectual Capital*.

18. Intellectual Capital Sweden AB, *www.intellectualcapital.se*.

▶ *About the Author*

This chapter was co-authored by **Philip Heimann**. He studied management at ESCP-EAP European School of Management in Paris, Oxford, and Berlin, has worked for the consulting firm A.T. Kearney and is currently preparing his doctoral thesis on linking corporate and regional innovation systems. Philip currently resides in Berlin, Germany.

9

ENTREPRENEURSHIP INFUSION

POLITICAL AND SOCIETAL CHANGE FOR THE INNOVATION ECONOMY

POLITICAL ENTREPRENEURSHIP

Picking up on Leif Edvinsson's concepts of political entrepreneurship and regional cultivation, this chapter identifies and describes some Swedish initiatives that exemplify how government involvement has helped Sweden to develop as a high-tech region and is continuing to do so today. The government has traditionally played a central role throughout Sweden's business environment, contrasting it to the UK and the U.S. for example. The Swedish government's efforts aim to intervene where free market dynamics are unable to supply the elements required for a high-tech–friendly environment. Accepting a new reality and the consequences implied by the global innovation economy, government policies are geared to promote change rather that to preserve the status quo. High tech is not viewed as a threat to Sweden's social democratic aspirations; rather the government seeks to continue to establish itself as a leader in the Innovation Economy as a prerequisite for the long-term accomplishment of these aspirations.

The following focus on maximizing the effectiveness of deregulation describes the concept of AB Stokab,[1] a company that was founded by the city of Stockholm and Stockholm County to capitalize on the deregulation of the Swedish telecommunications market. It shows how a government initiative can at the same time improve the efficiency of competition; serve the interests of a city, a county, and the entire nation; and turn profitable practically overnight.

AN ALTERNATIVE INFORMATION INFRASTRUCTURE — MAXIMIZING THE BENEFITS OF DEREGULATION

Sweden was the first country in Europe to fully deregulate its telecom markets; this happened in 1993. The results were practically free-falling prices and the rise of a multitude of new telecom and service providers. More than 60 international telecom providers operate in Sweden today. During the liberalization process, the city of Stockholm (91% holding) and Stockholm County (9% holding) founded the company AB Stokab with a special mission: In competition with the incumbent network provider and former state monopoly Telia, Stokab began renting out capacity on its newly constructed fiber-optic network to telecom operators, allowing them to save the enormous fixed costs connected with setting up proprietary networks. The Stokab business concept was an immediate success, expressed not only by the company's financial performance, which proved immediately profitable, but also by the degree of competition it has created in the telecom provider and services sectors in Sweden, making it a financial success to its owners practically overnight.

Anders Comstedt, president of AB Stokab, considers his company to be one of the main enablers of the Swedish "ICT Society." He explains that soon, everyone in Sweden will have several megabits of transmission speed per second, made possible to a large extent by the Stokab alternative information infrastructure and its look-alikes. In fostering a dependable broadband infrastructure that spans the entire greater Stockholm area, Stokab sees itself as an important cost-sharing mechanism for the entire industry.

ANDERS COMSTEDT

A catalyst for competition in telecommunications

The AB Stokab business model is based on the concept that it is cheaper for telecom operators to rent network capacity than it is to lay out a proprietary infrastructure. The concept was designed to enable as many telecom operators as possible to enter the market soon after it was deregulated, and save them the tremendous fixed costs associated with constructing such networks. The concept was seen as a win-win situation since the city of Stockholm was trying to avoid competition based on how fast operators could get their cables down. After already having been through the roll-out of the cable TV networks overbuilding side by side in the 1980s, the city and county had an interest in reducing the street digging. Competition was supposed to occur in telecom services, not in how fast one or two new individual operators could get their cables down. Constructing and maintaining a dependable, high-capacity information infrastructure capable of satisfying the needs of a large number of providers and consumers was considered a prerequisite for a flourishing telecom services market with continuous innovation.

In practice, Stokab made sure it could cater to all operators' immediate needs at once by taking their network requirement plans, laying them over each other, and then just looking right through them. Even though the operators' network plans all had different shapes and sizes, they could all be embedded within the Stokab structure. The aggregated approach also meant that individual shifts in competitiveness between operators was evened out at the fiber level.

When the concept was introduced, operators feared they would be too dependent on Stokab for network capacity. Their worries were that the Stokab infrastructure would not be rolled out at a convenient pace, or that Stokab would be influenced by the interests of their competitors. Stokab responded that if the new infrastructure roll-out happened in an uncoordinated manner, it would take too much time and would be too costly for all of them collectively. Stokab also reminded the operators that the city owns the streets anyway and would balance telecom interest with other use. A coordinated telecom build-out would gain more leverage versus other interests.

At the same time, Telia, the incumbent telecom operator, claimed that Stokab's plan would never work. Just providing an infrastructure was nothing that could be found in the textbooks, and it was not considered possible to run a profitable business based on this model. According to common knowledge, money was made by selling services at a premium price. The concept was truly innovative and nobody else had ever tried anything like it; if for no other reason, in most countries of the world at the time, it was simply illegal.

Even though Stokab's fixed costs represented a heavy up-front investment, the lower prices resulting from deregulation implied such savings for Stockholm, the largest user of telecommunications services in the area, that the investment was immediately justified. Also, the networks that were rolled out to the hospitals outside of the city enabled Stockholm County to quickly save far more than it had invested. In addition to the savings realized by its shareholders, Stokab achieved its first positive result in 1998, and since then has been a profitable business.

Lessons learned

There is an evolution of government officials' attitudes toward a liberalized tele-communications sector, its benefits to society, and the role that the government should play within the context. The "mentality gap" between officials at different levels of understanding of what liberalized telecommunications markets mean for a region can make it impossible for them to communicate. This evolution can be described in four phases:

1. Regarding operators merely as a source of income to the state/local government and thus granting them rights of way against a fee. In this phase, the motivation for authorities to increase the number of providers in the region is given only if it will increase the fee income they receive in the process.

2. Focusing on the government's own telecom costs. The realization that the government can make more money by savings generated through increased competition than by charging fees. In this phase, authorities will aim to maximize the level of competition between operators in order to maximize their savings.

3. Understanding that not only the city and the municipal governments have a problem with high telephone bills, but that a lack of diversity of service providers presents an inward investment problem for entire industries in the region.

4. Aiming to improve the quality of life of the whole region by enabling the spawning of new industries through an efficient process of deregulation. This implies ensuring that quality network infrastructures are available for large and small players to find fast access to the market.

Originally, Stokab saw its concept as something that would work primarily in developed economies, primarily metro areas, to create competition and spawn new markets. Lately, however, the company has been approached by officials from developing countries as well, claiming that they wish to "leapfrog the industrial age" and enter directly into the information age. These regions have an even greater incentive to create a single infrastructure capable of supporting multiple operators, since their economies might not allow them to duplicate communications infrastructures in the way that they were duplicated in Sweden and in other developed countries around the globe. ■

The insight provided by Mr. Comstedt indicates that deregulation alone is not enough to derive the maximum benefit from competition in the tele-communications sector. This Swedish model describes a coordinated deregulation, ensuring a large diversity of service providers that operate in a competitive environment. However, the right mindset is required of government officials in order to implement such a concept. As Mr. Comstedt describes, officials need to "speak the same language" to reap the full benefits of deregulation, knowing when and how to take part in the process and when to stay away.

Regardless of the Swedish government's progressive stance toward information infrastructure, Joe Armstrong, co-founder of the Swedish software company Bluetail (which was acquired by Alteon), believes that politicians are still not doing enough to optimize this infrastructure. Creating an analogy with water works, Mr. Armstrong says that if a company wants to deliver a life-critical product such as information via its infrastructure, it needs to guarantee that the delivery will take place at a high quality level and a high rate of consistency. If the company fails, it should have to pay a fine until the service is back to the required level. Mr. Armstrong believes that once the authorities realize that information will be as important to the functioning of society as water and electricity, they will understand that it is not appropriate to allow private enterprises to supply information infrastructure at inconsistent quality levels. "The state should say: If the data transfer rate drops below one megabit per second, the operator has to pay a fine until they fix it. Just like they don't allow any old cowboy to build the roads. This is a sign that the market has matured."

Our next focus on educational institutions and technology transfer shows how the Swedish government devised the "third task," a national policy aimed in part at the creation of new high-tech businesses. This policy has proved instrumental in creating a paradigm shift in Sweden's universities, and is considered a key ingredient to spawn a multitude of new companies into the telecommunications environment created by deregulation and Stokab's alternative information infrastructure concept.

LEADERSHIP AT ALL LEVELS — HOW A TRADITIONAL EDUCATIONAL INSTITUTION LEARNED TECHNOLOGY TRANSFER

During the second half of the 1990s, the Swedish national government defined the third task for their universities in addition to their two original tasks, which were to conduct research and to educate students for the good of society. The third task expanded the role of the higher educational institutions to include activities such as technology transfer. The potential to create new wealth in society by transferring university research to commercial solutions had traditionally gone largely unexploited in Sweden. Academics showed little interest in the commercial application of their work. In order to successfully implement this new national policy, political leadership became committed and incentives for entrepreneurship were introduced on national, regional, and local levels, as well as inside the universities.

Peter Holmstedt, who was appointed president of the Electrum Foundation in 2001, is the former president of Teknikhöjden[2] (Stockholm Technology Park). This business incubation infrastructure is owned by the Royal
Institute of Technology (50%), Stockholm University[3] (20%), and the public
KTH Foundation (30%). Over the past two years, Mr. Holmstedt has set up
the Teknikhöjden incubator and integrated it within the structures of KTH
and Stockholm University in an effort to create the optimal environment for
the implementation of the third task. Given the considerable tradition and
prestige of KHT, this proved quite a challenge.

PETER HOLMSTEDT

Dramatically improving entrepreneurship at university

While a small number of start-ups originate from KTH every year, historically the
university has been more oriented toward the interests of large corporations.
When KTH changed its management three years ago, I was assigned to build a system that could radically improve entrepreneurship at the university. Rather than
focusing on commercialization through company projects or technology licensing,
KTH decided to focus on creating start-ups.

Over the past two years, I have worked together with the university's management
to set up two units to improve commercialization at campus: Teknikhöjden Innovation and the Teknikhöjden Incubator. Teknikhöjden Innovation, a service center
for KTH students planning to start up their own companies, was located on the
university campus, while the incubator was located off campus, just outside the
center of Stockholm. Two managers were recruited from outside KTH to lead the
two units under my supervision. Teknikhöjden's aim is that 10% of KTH students
should be active in their own companies.

Good professors are also good at commercialization

The ambitious goal of commercialization of research on campus implied confront-
ing a traditional culture with entirely new concepts. Appropriate leadership
needed to be installed on different levels within the university environment. Given
the university's traditional emphasis on research and education, its best professors
would typically pursue their careers in these fields. However, since the third task
became national policy, this type of career would only be supported if society
came to benefit from the commercialization of research. The best professors all
over the world are typically also very good at commercialization. KTH management simply took the very best professors it had and put them in charge of realiz-
ing the third task for the university. This top-down, role-model–based approach
proved successful at generating acceptance and internal support for the institution's new mission.

The third task was also built into the university's merit system. Each of the 34 KTH divisions today has a person responsible for the collaboration with Teknikhöjden. They are selected based on their personal affinity and experience with technology transfer and new business creation. All professors at KTH are required to report to Anders Flodström, the university's president, on their commercialization results. When professors request an academic appointment, they need to prove that they are promoting the third task. KTH is measured by the government on the number of start-ups it creates, and on how it enhances the start-ups' performance.

The four-step technology transfer program

The Teknikhöjden model for technology transfer is based on a four-step program, beginning with the innovation park on campus. There is an office that acts as a one-stop shop for questions and answers. If someone has a good idea, free advice is given by patent lawyers at a very early stage.

The next step is the "start-house" a pre-incubator. A space on campus provides a process advisor and a work environment free of charge for six to 12 months. In return, the preliminary business plan has to be ready after six months, and a mature version must be available after 12 months.

The third step is the incubator. There is a screening process and the incubatees have to pay rent. The rent is fixed during the first three years at 80% of market prices. The last two years are at market level. For the 20% in savings, the business plan must be continually improved, monitored by the incubator's management. Incubation time is usually five years for biotech companies and one to two years for IT companies.

The fourth and final step is the fully commercial Technology Park. The only thing special about the park is the proximity to the university and the services that entrepreneurs can buy, which are also available to the pre-incubatee and the incubatee companies.

The Teknikhöjden strategy is "seed, network, and trademark." Even though KTH, the holding organization, takes small equity stakes in the start-up companies in return for seed financing, Teknikhöjden prefers to see itself as an initiator. The main value added comes from the comprehensive network and the strong brand name of KTH. Many of the big company leaders in Sweden have been to KTH and when Teknikhöjden believes in a company, the venture capital people come. If we want to help companies become commercially competitive, we must act commercially. We cannot be university people. We must be business people. ■

These examples show how the political entrepreneurship of the Swedish government has helped to create a high-tech environment in favor of competition, diversity, and new business creation. In order to further complete the picture of Sweden's ICT environment, the Stockholm city government's efforts to reform itself and become an "e-government" are of interest. The general openness toward new technologies in Sweden has enabled Stockholm's government to become a pioneer in e-government initiatives.

DEMOCRACY AND MUNICIPAL LIFE IN THE INFORMATION AGE — STOCKHOLM'S E-GOVERNMENT

The Stockholm municipal government believes that the world is shrinking and that a new Europe is growing according to a totally new game plan in which regions and cities will play an increasingly instrumental role. Stockholm officials believe that the increasing competition between economic regions will affect the preconditions for the political activities and the operational development of cities.

In 1999, Stockholm's IT Advisory Committee proposed an e-strategy to make IT a central, executive-level issue for the city's administrations and enterprises. The strategy aims to facilitate reaching the objective to become a "municipality of the future." The most important areas of application in the proposed e-strategy are e-democracy, control and management, e-structure, competence development/supply, a more attractive Stockholm, procurement, and municipal services. These points are discussed below.

- Democracy and political activities — The city of Stockholm e-strategy intends to use IT in order to contribute to the strengthening and deepening of democracy through improved information and discussion. The city's inhabitants must be assured of integrity, self-determination, and participatory rights. IT can create increased opportunities for human contact with municipal organizations for city users and inhabitants alike.

- Control and management — Analytical and processing opportunities presented by IT shall be increasingly utilized in Stockholm to provide support for management and control through improved information on which to base decisions. Using IT, control and monitoring can be more rapidly achieved through immediate access to reports and analyses.

- E-structure — The development opportunities for trade and industries and the establishment of new companies in the region will depend on the preconditions provided by the available IT infrastructure. The city's data and telecommunications services should be continuously developed, while extending these services into the home environment will enable the creation of new functions and services.

- Competence development/supply — The increasing use of IT is furthermore seen as important for educational activities to develop and supply competence, and enable lifelong learning for both citizens and employees.

■ A more attractive Stockholm — IT will help to streamline transportation activities, improve the utilization of street space, and decrease the pressure on the environment, making Stockholm an even more attractive place to work and live in the future.

■ Procurement — Electronic commerce will be used to streamline the city's commercial processes. Transparency created by the Internet will enable increased choice for city inhabitants, the quality of purchased goods will improve, costs will go down, and the establishment of new companies will be encouraged.

■ Municipal services and the citizens — Integrating IT into the city's administration is seen as a tool to better afford citizens a central role in its operations. IT will more easily provide citizens with benefits, contact, and service-oriented municipal operations. Information technology is furthermore seen as a tool to enable the citizens' right to transparency of operations, while facilitating access to municipal services.

Carl Cederschiöld, mayor of Stockholm, sees the city's e-strategy as a systematic way to use new technologies to make municipal government more effective and efficient. It will make it possible for the city to give the population better, faster answers, for instance when applying for building or restaurant permits. At the same time, the democratic process will be improved, by allowing citizens to post opinions and vote online. In Kista, the EU project Cybervote[4] intends to make online voting feasible.

CARL CEDERSCHIÖLD

It's not just about throwing information on the Net

Constructing an e-government has far-reaching implications for individuals inside and outside of the administration, as well as for private business in the area. The city is currently involving many private businesses in trying to find solutions for its e-government project. Stockholm sees itself as a large and hopefully competent buyer of technologies that will make e-government possible. In the long run, these government efforts are expected to create important prerequisites for research and development in the field of creating e-governments.

Finding support for the city's e-strategy has been fairly simple both politically and privately, since Stockholm's citizens in general have a positive view of new technology. The challenge in implementing this e-strategy has been to ask the right questions of the people with the right competence. There needs to be a lot of interaction between the technical systems competence and the city's politicians, civil servants, and others who are going to formulate the right criteria for the technicians to construct.

Everything starts with the homepage. The key is to be receptive to the feedback from users. Experience shows that there is a lot of feedback, which initiates a trial-and-error process that will eventually lead to the right angle from which to approach political issues using new technologies. It's not just about throwing information on the Net. Building the Stockholm e-government has been an iterative process implying frequent site adaptations and responding to the requests of users.

Getting people to accept the new technologies in the government realm requires dependably functioning services. In principle, all official documents can be made available though the Internet. For citizens who frequently use the system, the present intranet, which is in place for the exchange of official documents, must also be made accessible to the population. For instance, access needs to be given to citizens through computers at local district offices, while the Web-based access needs to be continually improved. The next step for the city of Stockholm will be to start implementing interactive services such as permit issuing.

Citizens will not accept walls between different levels of government

In the future, citizens will no longer accept walls between the systems of municipal, regional, and national government systems. In order to unleash the full potential of e-government, these systems will eventually need to be seamlessly linked.

Old rules encumber new processes such as citizen contact by e-mail

However, constructing and running an e-government comes with many hurdles and difficulties. I regularly receive e-mails from citizens with questions, including e-mail campaigns, for instance, against high taxes. Recently, 60 e-mails arrived in one day with the same question: "Why do I only get to keep 39% of my income?" According to the law, the mayor must answer all of these e-mails. The citizens have a right to have access to their elected officials, and the mayor should indeed be in touch with citizens, answering their e-mails and maintaining a dialog with them. However, within this context, the Swedish Law of Transparency poses a problem: According to this law, each piece of correspondence has to be registered and subsequently filed away and kept in storage, which is not yet possible electronically. This means that each e-mail needs to be printed out, given a number and filed away. When the citizens' questions are answered, every answer has to be printed out, given a number and filed away. The law requires this procedure in order to guarantee accountability of government officials.

Ensuring the manageability of the newly increased flows of correspondence may well necessitate some changes in the national law. This is where the feasibility of implementing the e-government becomes an issue. When these laws were being written by the Royal Commission, starting in 1980, e-mail did not yet exist. Ensuring the implementation of an e-strategy thus requires a strong belief in the possibilities of new technologies. Officials need to understand that if they are really determined to offer this service to their citizens, they must be willing to go through the existing rules and regulations and to rewrite the law in numerous aspects.

If officials are not ready to do this, they will soon find out that the entire vision of what could be achieved with these fascinating technologies will be destroyed by some old rule that was written before computers even existed. It will be inevitable to run into political conflicts. In order to enable an e-government, officials will have to change rules that may infringe on a right that has been existent for over 100 years. ∎

We have shown some examples of how high-tech–related government initiatives can effectively support the development of regions. However, for these initiatives to become successful, the different levels of government must be fully convinced of the potential benefits offered by new technologies and must be willing to act against existing barriers in order to reap this benefit. On an economic level, the Stokab example implies that market deregulation can be aided by market-focused government intervention, and in turn can benefit the long-term social democratic aspirations of a nation. In Sweden, the social democratic aspirations of an "ICT Nation" could not have been possible without an appropriate information infrastructure. The Teknikhöjden case demonstrates that incentives and leadership need to be present at different levels throughout a country's government and educational system in order to develop a successful technology transfer program. Integrating new technologies into government policies has the potential to improve the efficiency a government's operations and empowers the citizen to increasingly take place in the democratic process. However, our discussion with Carl Cederschiöld indicates that that transfer to an e-government involves many potential hurdles, such as rewriting existing legislation, and thus requires strong government commitment in order to be feasible.

We will now focus on how human resources are attracted and leveraged in Sweden. We will examine how Sweden uses its international "cultural fit" in order to create an international business environment, which is regarded as critical for success in global high-tech markets.

THE ENTREPRENEURSHIP REVIVAL: REAPPLYING TRADITIONAL SOCIETY AND CULTURAL PARADIGMS TO CREATE CHANGE

European countries have marveled at the enormous entrepreneurial spirit of Silicon Valley. In an effort to "plug into" the Innovation Economy, they have tried and are currently trying to copy or import certain elements of this culture to the "old world." Sweden is a best practice example in this context, having turned its business environment into one of Europe's most entrepreneurial in just a few years. As this chapter indicates, creating entrepreneurship in Sweden has been a question of removing barriers and establishing role models. Its first focus describes how Swedish society paradigms were transformed in an unplanned manner, turning an environment that despised individual entrepreneurial initiative to one that honors it, practically overnight. This entrepreneurship revival was not a political initiative. It happened because entrepreneurship was a character trait of the Swedish people that lay suppressed for generations, revived by the imperatives of the global Innovation Economy. Entrepreneurship in Sweden has a different face than in the U.S. We will describe a Swedish-American cultural divergence, indicating that entrepreneurial cultures are global, but with regionally differing characteristics. We will also show how a pioneering Swedish company established a European presence based on the newly acquired entrepreneurship culture, and how it approached the heterogeneous European markets, benefiting from hype and booming venture capital markets.

TRANSFORMING A SOCIETY FROM "DON'T STAND OUT" TO "IF SHE CAN DO IT, SO CAN I"

Swedish companies are generally considered to be poor at marketing, which is explained by the fact that the venture capital scene historically had all its focus on technical evolution. In Sweden, entrepreneurs traditionally had a hard time acquiring money for marketing concepts, unlike in the U.S.

Until a few years ago, Sweden seemed a hostile environment for entrepreneurs. The egalitarian approach to wealth distribution inhibited any one person from making much more money than anyone else. High personal taxation discouraged individuals from taking on initiative, while corporate taxation was low, since corporate profits could be redistributed to society through their shareholders. Privately owned companies were regarded as personal enrichment at the cost of everyone else. As a result, innovation occurred mostly in large corporate structures.

So strong was the egalitarian culture in Swedish society, that a traditional code of conduct called the "Jante-Lo" taught Swedish citizens that they should not see themselves as better than others. Self-aggrandizement was frowned upon, even if someone was very good at something.

When the "Swedish Model" collapsed in the early 1990s, Sweden's far-reaching economic reforms indicated a path to a "New Sweden," driven by a social market economy built on structural renewal, personal initiative, and entrepreneurship. Jane Walerud is director of advanced products of Alteon Sweden. The Swedish software company Bluetail, which she co-founded in 1999 and headed as CEO, was purchased by Alteon of the U.S. for U.S.$152 million in 2000. Ms. Walerud believes that the entrepreneurship revival in Sweden has been successful because of the character traits inherent to the Swedish people, qualities that merely lay suppressed under societal norms for many decades, waiting to emerge. Today, she says Sweden leads other high-tech clusters such as Munich, Germany, which does not have the same degree of individualism and self-sufficiency and does not show the same degree of acceptance of entrepreneurship.

JANE WALERUD

Allowing nails to stick up — Unfolding the potential of the Swedish entrepreneur

There used to be a saying in Sweden that you should not believe you are anything because any nail that would stand up would get hammered down to the level of the others. This attitude was a clear regional disadvantage for a long time. During the last decade, the societal paradigm has been transformed to, "If she can do it, so can I!," which has proven a much healthier attitude toward creating personal initiative and innovation. Instead of treating success with jealousy, the Swedish norm is now to say, "How did you do that? Because I have an idea and want to start something similar." Even though personal wealth creation has become an accepted phenomenon in Swedish society, it is still much less the wealth that Swedish entrepreneurs aspire to, when comparing them with their American counterparts. Rather, it is the ability to realize their own technical idea, to have fun, to have an impact on the world, and of course also to make money. There is a certain arrogance in believing one can impact the world. This arrogance is required to become a successful entrepreneur, and Swedes have always been prone to this kind of arrogance.

The paradigm change that occurred around personal initiative can be illustrated by Sweden's interpretation of national taxation: "The social democrats have traditionally played the role of milking the cows of capitalism. If you want a lot of milk you must take good care of your cow." For this reason, company taxes were fairly reasonable, causing the locking-in of money and innovation into the companies. However, even though the taxation system has not fundamentally changed over time, the message gained by its interpretation has changed completely since the entrepreneurship revival: "If regular salaried work is taxed very highly, then don't work at a regular salary. Instead, start and own your own company." The new values that have emerged in society are enabling people to take advantage of this logic and are starting them on their way to independence.

There weren't any key events that initialized this metamorphosis. It seemed that suddenly, it was okay to be an entrepreneur. Before, people with their own companies were seen as being dishonest, failing to contribute to society. Today, starting a company has become very trendy in Sweden. There has always been a fear of being wrong and a fear of being different in Sweden, driven by the Swedish consensus-driven culture. Starting a company today is something to be considered simply because others are doing it. Swedes will always have a haircut that is reasonable because a lot of other people have it. This is also why Sweden went quickly from nobody owning shares to everybody owning shares and from nobody having a cellular phone to everybody having one. Trends catch on very quickly in Sweden. Swedish society is being driven by the feeling of trends and the following of trends. For this reason, the New Economy hype may have been stronger, and the crash more devastating than in other countries.

Successful entrepreneurs act as important role models for future generations of entrepreneurs in Sweden, who say to themselves, "If she can do it, so can I." Icon Medialab founder Johan von Holstein is one such entrepreneur role model. He publicly criticized Swedes for not being proud of what they do, claiming instead that Swedish entrepreneurs could successfully expand throughout Europe and the rest of the world. The fact that three Ericsson spin-offs alone were sold for more than U.S.$120 million each in 2000 has had an incredibly supportive effect in this context. ■

Our discussion with Ms. Walerud showed that entrepreneurship in Sweden was promoted by an emerging trend of rebellion against traditional society paradigms, and by Sweden's consensus-driven culture that allowed it to catch on faster than in other European countries. The future sustainability of this trend will rely on an ongoing supply of success stories, embodied by entrepreneurial role models. Whereas political initiatives were not the driver behind this revival, the business environment created by political entrepreneurship and the presence of high-level intellectual capital will aid the entrepreneurship culture to become more deeply rooted in Swedish society. Much of the entrepreneurial impetus in Sweden today comes from global high-tech corporations that have set up R&D centers in the region. However, we next explore the question of how regional culture plays an important role when trying to efficiently leverage entrepreneurial skills in a global company.

VENTURE FUNDING, OWNERSHIP, AND INNOVATION

It is important to see the Swedish entrepreneurship revival within the context of the uniquely Swedish characteristics that survived the transformation to the "New Sweden." They constitute the reality that Swedes are, after all, still Swedes and not Silicon Valley entrepreneurs.

In certain aspects, the Swedish business environment has become more like that of the U.S. For example, Sweden is developing the type of cross-functional personnel rotation inherent to Silicon Valley. One of Bluetail's founders worked as a university professor before he went to work for Ericsson. There he stayed for 18 months before founding Bluetail. Today he works for Alteon in the U.S. However, Joe Armstrong, co-founder of Bluetail, believes there are nonetheless fundamental differences between Swedes and Americans.

JOE ARMSTRONG

Quiet, collaborative, and disobedient — Swedish engineers differ from their U.S. counterparts

While American patent law is fixed on finding who had the idea, in Sweden, when they ask who had the idea, nobody knows, because nobody can remember. When Bluetail was founded, there were discussions on how the shares were going to be divided up and it just seemed natural that everyone was going to have one-twelfth each. The more senior members did not ask for more equity. Then, some of the international press asked the founders, "Hey what are you, a load of communists?" But it turned out that this partition of shares helped avoid many problems in building the company. It was also the fastest way to do it. The founding engineers wanted to build a company quickly so they said, "There, that's it." This type of pragmatic mindset has been a competitive advantage to the company since its founding.

As Bluetail grew, its managers considered whether to get funded in the U.S. or in Sweden. In the U.S. they would have been able to raise more money for the company, but would also have had to deal with much greater control exerted by their shareholders. The traditional way of founding a company in Sweden had been to take a bank loan out on the house and to finance growth through profits. The risks involved were personal. IKEA, a privately owned furniture company that doesn't even publish its books, fueled its expansion through its own profits. The owners are speculated to be some of the richest people in the world. This is a very Swedish way of going about doing things, so U.S. venture capitalists need to understand that by nature, Swedes are skeptical of giving up control.

Communicating on the job furthermore demonstrates a slight difference between Swedes and their American colleagues: The Americans will send e-mails with a colossal amount of people in CC to demonstrate how hard they work, and how clever they are. As an example, an e-mail was recently put in our system saying that we had a problem with a customer. Now from the U.S. side, there would immediately be a flood of e-mails: "We're working on it, we're doing it, we're on the job, Bill," and then they would be writing progress reports every day. At the same time, there was this stunning silence coming from Sweden, since the Swedes were actually working on the problem rather than writing e-mails to each other! And then the Americans criticized the Swedes: "Hey, we are not seeing much visible evidence that you are working over there." "But we are! We're not talking about it, but we *are* working!"

The Americans have a habit of overstating everything, they market themselves and everything they do, while the Swedes understate everything. A lot of people aren't aware of this difference. Whereas Americans will say they are the world's best at something, a Swede may say he knows a little bit about something, which may actually mean he is really good at it! This can lead to grave misunderstandings in business.

A funny story to illustrate this is when the American side set up an e-mail discussion list for the technicians. The measure of performance was how many mails were sent by each team to this mailing list. The Swedish team was once again criticized by its U.S. colleagues: "You guys are not very active, can't you mail a little more to this list?" In fact, I admit I never even read the list. Nonetheless, the Swedish side finally decided to mail around a bit . . . and the U.S. side got really angry. Deciding that this sort of miscommunication could not go on, the Swedish team sent one of their technicians to the U.S. for a meeting. After about half-an-hour the Americans realized that the guy knew what he was talking about. And after about two hours, the meeting had turned into a straight question and answer session, the Americans just sitting there dreaming up any possible question, and he had definitive answers to them all. From that point onward, the Swedish team received no more criticism.

Company survival through disobedience

In general, Swedish technicians get a lot more trust than U.S. technicians. Swedish engineers won't ask their boss for permission, they will just do it. Quite a few claim that Ericsson has survived so well because of the disobedience of its technical staff. The mobile phone was created even though the Ericsson board decided not to put any development money into it. The technicians believed so strongly that they managed to hide the development behind some other projects. This was true with the electronic switch as well. This atmosphere at Ericsson has created a lot of spin-offs, which initially was seen very negatively, until it was understood that letting employees outside the corporate structures actually increased product development speed as they started to buy back the spin-off companies.

The way Swedish companies arrive at decisions is also very different from what I have experienced in other countries. Once, I asked the head of Ericsson strategy how decisions were made in his company. The reply was: "I don't know." One day, a senior executive managed to explain: "Imagine a big cocktail party in a room with a lot of doors. All the doors open, the big bosses come in and begin talking in groups of twos and threes. They frequently change the group they are talking with and this goes on for a while. At the same time a gang of workmen come in and start painting the floor. The management doesn't notice the workmen because they are so busy talking. So the workmen are painting, saying 'would you mind moving this way a little bit,' and finally they have painted everything including the doors and there is one door left and then everyone goes out to dinner through the one unpainted door. And when you ask them afterwards, nobody remembers the painters or why they went out through that one door." And that is the way decisions are made in Swedish companies. This is interesting. ■

Our focus shows that transnational high-tech companies need to be aware that knowledge workers innovate differently in different regions. When operating with worldwide networks, such considerations may require extensive training of personnel and the formation of multinational groups to promote the efficiency of cross-cultural team-working. The next focus shows how one Swedish company approaches cultural differences in general and how the hype of the New Economy influenced its expansion in Europe.

NEW SWEDISH ENTREPRENEURS' APPROACHES TO EUROPEAN EXPANSION

When expanding throughout Europe, the cultural heterogeneity that companies encounter is a central challenge. One of the most important factors for successful expansion in the European environment is sufficient capital. Whereas the venture capital market in Sweden in the second quarter of 2001 was probably in worse condition than that of other European countries, two years ago the situation was excellent, and was considered by some to be the best in Europe. From 1995 to 1999, the average annual growth of private equity and venture capital investments in Sweden exceeded 200% per annum. Today, there are approximately 250 venture capital companies in Sweden. Due to the generally risk-averse Swedish culture, the largest VC investments in Sweden are typically not taken by Swedish VCs, whereas Swedish VCs are seen as very good for seed and start-up financing. In the case of the online fashion retailer Boo.com, for example, which expanded into several European countries simultaneously before being shut down shortly after in 2000, it was mainly non-Swedish capital that was lost.

The Swedish Internet ventures that expanded throughout Europe in the second half of the 1990s were true pioneers, and they consumed more capital and rose faster and higher than other companies, thanks in part to the hype surrounding the growing e-commerce bubble. As a consequence, they also had a longer way to fall, and when the bubble burst they fell faster and farther than most of their European counterparts. In this respect, Sweden experienced wider extremes than did the other countries.

The strong drive of Swedish ventures such as Boo.com, Boxman, Framfab, or Icon Medialab to internationalize during the second half of the 1990s indicates that Swedes may well "have it in their blood" to expand across borders. Niklas Flisberg is co-founder of Result Knowledge Venture Management, a Swedish firm that specializes in internationalizing Internet-related start-up companies. Mr. Flisberg tells the stories of Result and Boxman, the online retailer that was eventually bought by Bertelsmann and then closed down to stop its towering losses.

NIKLAS FLISBERG

Networking enabled expansion —
A truly european e-commerce site? Well, almost.

Boxman was one of the first European companies to sell compact discs over the Internet. The initial success of Boxman outside of Sweden was achieved through extensive public relations and personal networking. Personal networks are considered to have been a key success factor in the short but exciting life of Boxman. The founders' international networks were complemented by the local networks. These were brought into the company by locally hired country managers. These local networks enabled the company to transfer what had already worked in Sweden to foreign markets. Boxman failed shortly after one of its co-founders left to start Result. His previous experience with Boxman provided Result with a great set of contacts to expand into Europe, so Result could grow while it was internationalizing its clients, setting up its own international operations in the process.

Today, Result has offices in numerous European countries, employing 100% local management. I believe that customers in France will buy from a French company more readily than from a Swedish company. Result's satellites throughout Europe thus need to be "truly local" companies. Within this context, the challenge has not been to recruit the local managers. Rather, the challenge surfaced when cultures started colliding within the company. At one point, the French executives accused the Swedes of not putting enough management power behind their decisions. At the same time, German and British managers were voicing similar complaints, saying that there was not enough hierarchy in the firm. The flat organizational structure that the founders were trying to establish throughout Europe encountered serious resistance in the other countries and even had a negative effect on the overall atmosphere in the firm. Furthermore, the Swedish culture caused confusion within the local satellites. While local managers believed that implementing the Swedish culture was a good idea and found it positive to be part of the decision-making process, they nonetheless had trouble abandoning their home culture. They repeatedly asked from more directives from the Swedish home office.

Boxman grew with the hype of the New Economy and went down when its bubble burst. Result has been experiencing difficulties itself, as more and more Internet-related companies have refocused on their home markets before expanding abroad. Nonetheless, the lessons learned are relevant for future international ventures. Entering foreign markets in Europe has necessitated extensive personal networks. Strong local management has been important to effectively combine the cultures of the founding team and the locals recruited in foreign countries. Entrepreneurship cultures vary from country to country. The executives of small companies going international are confronted with an ever-greater challenge to manage efficiently across borders. Owing to their head start and traditional international competence, Swedes may be more qualified to do so than some other nationals.

SUMMARY

The "new culture" has enabled Sweden to become a region of excellence in innovation. This atmosphere has attracted many global high-tech companies to the area. To leverage the full potential of this entrepreneurship revival, currently supported by a strong "fashion" to innovate, companies must understand the entrepreneurship culture of the region and train their employees to innovate across borders. Local management and personal networks play an important role for small companies seeking to expand in the global Innovation Economy, given the imperatives of speed to market and quickly attaining economies of scale. Even if hampered by the crash of the New Economy, Swedish entrepreneurs have been pioneers in this context and have progressed further along these lines than most of their European peers.

The speed of Sweden's transformation has been astounding. While Sweden's local innovations in mobile technologies have been exported all over the world, the country has retained its small-community atmosphere.

The economic and ideological crisis of the early 1990s presented itself as a window of opportunity for Sweden to initiate its path toward market-driven reforms, just in time for the mid-1990s worldwide boom in computing and telecommunications. Sweden's main asset throughout this development has been its intellectual capital. The excellent education of Sweden's population and the non-hierarchical culture at the Swedish workplace have enabled Sweden to develop faster than other European nations, and has made it the most important region in the world for mobile telecommunications today.

ENDNOTES

1. Stokab, *www.stokab.se*.
2. Teknikhöjden, *www.teknikhojden.se*.
3. Stockholm University, *www.su.se/english*.
4. CyberVote — An Innovative Cyber Voting System for Internet Terminals and Mobile Phones, *www.eucybervote.org*.

▶ *About the Author*

This chapter was co-authored by **Philip Heimann**. He studied management at ESCP-EAP European School of Management in Paris, Oxford, and Berlin, has worked for the consulting firm A.T. Kearney and is currently preparing his doctoral thesis on linking corporate and regional innovation systems. Philip currently resides in Berlin, Germany.

IV

GERMANY, THE UNITED KINGDOM, AND FRANCE

EUROPE'S INDUSTRIAL GIANTS ADAPTING TO THE GLOBAL INNOVATION ECONOMY

G ermany, the United Kingdom, and France are Europe's largest economies. Despite their geographical proximity (France and Germany share a border, while the U.K. is only a short train ride from France through the English Channel), and regardless of the European Union's efforts to homogenize its political and economic environment, the three countries are and will remain fundamentally different in culture, business environment, and government philosophy.

The following section portrays three regions, or locations, within these countries struggling to adapt to the global Innovation Economy in their own, distinctly different ways. Regardless of their differences, Munich, Cambridge, and Sophia Antipolis share the fact that the rapid rise of new ways of creating regional wealth around the world has forced them to learn a new culture of entrepreneurship and to build environments in which this new culture would be able to prosper. With their long traditions of large industrial economies, Germany, France, and the U.K. each face the challenge of forcing change into their existing economic and political structures. Regardless of considerable achievements, their economies still appear slow and cumbersome when compared with the dynamic drive of Silicon Valley, which has proven capable of constantly reinventing itself.

It is in these countries' struggles to adapt to business-culture norms such as openness and flexibility, and dismantling bureaucracy and hierarchy, that we can best see that attitudes in business are as important as capital investment in making a successful transition to the global Innovation Economy. The contrast with Ireland, for example, which achieved greater growth of foreign direct investment than their much larger industrialized neighbors, illustrates that competitive advantage is no longer based only on comparative size and resources.

The limited success at creating these environments in geographic pockets of their countries, however, proves once again that there is no magic formula for the creation of regional wealth in a global high-tech economy. The following chapters confirm that regions and companies cannot simply copy what has been successfully accomplished within another regional environment. While the global Innovation Economy may indeed imply global standards and global business cultures, each region's process of transformation to this model remains unique, necessitating unique approaches, initiatives, and policies to achieve successful results.

DIFFERENT ROLES OF GOVERNMENT WITH BUSINESS PARTNERSHIPS

The regions covered in this section each approach development differently. While a critical mass of large and diverse technology companies and state research institutions form the basis of Munich's high-tech environment, the environment in Cambridge has been created almost solely around its 700-year-old, world-class university. Sophia Antipolis, on the other hand, was created "from scratch" as a technology park amid the rolling hills of Southern France, which was well known for its tourism, but had no real intellectual or industrial heritage. While in France, the government has traditionally been "right in the middle," driving and channeling high-tech development, government policy in the Munich region has aimed to create initial sparks and then to leave development up to the forces of the market. In Cambridge, there is a clear rejection of the government by local high-tech entrepreneurs. The government here is expected merely to remove barriers and then to get out of the way of economic developments. As different as these approaches may be, the entrepreneurship cultures they are promoting all seem to point in a similar direction, encouraging individual initiative, creativity, the taking of risks, and an international and interdisciplinary exposure to enable groundbreaking new technology innovations.

10 MUNICH — THE HIDDEN CHAMPION

CREATING AN ENTREPRENEURIAL CULTURE WITH STATE GOVERNMENT IN PARTNERSHIP WITH BUSINESS

TRADITION AND DIVERSITY ARE THE KEY — GERMANY'S UNDENIED TECHNOLOGY CAPITAL

The city of Munich is the capital of the Free State of Bavaria, which is one of the 16 Länder (states) that make up the Federal Republic of Germany, the largest economy within the European Union. Germany has approximately 82 million inhabitants; after Berlin and Hamburg, Munich is Germany's third largest city, with a population of approximately 1.2 million. Since the 1950s, Bavaria and especially the Munich region have emerged as the most important high-tech region in Germany, competing with greater London on a European level, and with Silicon Valley, Boston, and Tel Aviv on a global level.

TABLE 10-1   Facts at a Glance — Munich

Population	1.2 million (Munich), 12.1 million (Bavaria), 82 million (Germany)
Political function	Capital of Germany's Free State of Bavaria
State government	Christian Social Union (CSU) Party
Minister president	Dr. Edmund Stoiber
Munich's region's ICT cluster age	Approximately 10 years
Munich region ICT companies	26,000
Employees in Munich region's ICT companies	350,000
Munich region media companies	11,425
Employees in Munich region's media companies	127,000
Students in Munich's higher educational institutions	80,000
Engineers, mathematicians, and other scientists in education	30,000
Foreigners as percentage of total employees	25%
Bavaria's GDP (1999)	Approximately $292 billion ($24,000 per capita)
Bavaria's investment in R&D	2.7% of GDP
Bavaria's FDI	Approximately $114 million (1998), $465 million (1999)
Foreign owned companies in Bavaria (including minority stakes)	1,709 (Revenues: $68 billion, 247,000 employ)
Bavarian unemployment	6.6% (Germany total: 10%)

Sources: www.invest-in-bavaria.de, www.stmwvt.bayern.de, Bayerische Staatskanzlei. Unless indicated, 2000 figures are cited. For European comparisons, see "Facts at a Glance — Sweden," on page 112.

In Bavaria, information and communications technology (ICT) is concentrated for the most part around the Munich and Nuremberg regions. More large technology companies have located within the Munich region than anywhere else in the world except for Silicon Valley. Traditional German technology companies such as Siemens, BMW, and MAN have attracted many smaller suppliers and partners to the area, and have increasingly been joined by large American high-tech companies such as 3Com, Cisco, Compaq, Intel, Lucent, Microsoft, Netscape, Oracle, and Sun. As of April 2000, 26,000 ICT companies were based in these two regions, employing over 350,000 individuals.[1] Currently, the most important Bavarian ICT and media industry sectors are:

- IT hardware, electronic components, and appliances
- Publishing and printing
- Data and IT services
- Marketing, market research, and journalism
- Audiovisual and multimedia
- Software

Of all the software companies present in Germany, 40% are located in Bavaria, as are 30% of all companies quoted on the Neuer Markt, the German equivalent of the Nasdaq. According to a study conducted by Bain & Company, 25% of all German Internet companies are based in Munich. Furthermore, Munich is home to the world headquarters of Allianz and Münchener Rück, making it one of the most important insurance locations in the world, and the second most important banking location in Germany. Leading even the greater London area, the Munich region boasts the highest venture capital density in Europe.

Regardless of its long technological heritage, Munich as a high-tech cluster only started developing in the 1990s and is thus younger than its global peers. According to Bain & Company, over 80% of the high-tech start-ups in Munich are less than five years old. Internet technologies make up the youngest sector in the region, while biotech and technology sectors are the oldest. Of Munich's high-tech companies, 50% employ 20 employees or less[2] (see Figure 10-1).

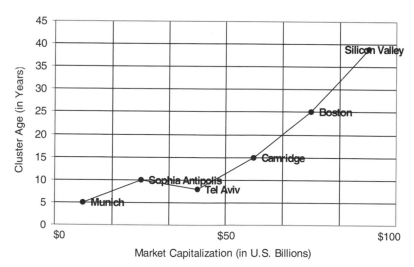

FIGURE 10-1 International age comparison of high-tech clusters. Source: Bain & Company, 2001.

FROM NEW MEDIA TO BIOTECHNOLOGY — A POWERHOUSE AT THE CROSSROADS OF EMERGING TECHNOLOGIES

The development of the Munich high-tech cluster has been supported by the region's history as Germany's most important media location. Within the greater Munich area, 127,000 employees are active in more than 11,425 media companies. Munich is considered to be the second most important publishing location in the world after New York. Thirty-six percent of all German radio and television providers are based in Munich, including the Disney Channel, MTV, RTL2, and Universal. Bavaria Film in Munich houses Europe's most important film facilities. The media activities of the region have attracted many high-tech companies dealing with digital and Internet- based media communications. A notable new media cluster in Munich is located around the town of Unterföhring, less than 30 minutes from the city center.

In addition, the Munich region has developed into one of Europe's most important biotechnology clusters. Martinsried, another town located just minutes from the city center, has become well known across Europe and even in Silicon Valley. Between 1991 and 2000, Martinsried went from having no biotech companies to having 50 of them within one square kilometer. On average, between 1997 and 1998, one new biotech company was founded every 14 days in the cluster. Ninety percent of these companies were spin-offs from the Munich-based Max Planck Society,[3] the Munich-based Center of Genetics, and Munich's university faculties for chemistry and biology. Today, Martinsried is considered to be the "Gene Valley" of Europe.

PROVIDING A LARGE POOL OF INTELLECTUAL CAPITAL — A LEADING UNIVERSITY AND RESEARCH TOWN

The Munich region's quality and the quantity of a highly skilled work force are considered its key success factor. Its higher educational institutions, which include the renowned Technical University of Munich,[4] currently educate some 30,000 engineers, mathematicians, and other scientists. When comparing Munich with the rest of Germany, as well as with other leading high-tech regions around the world, this number represents Germany's largest talent pool and the second largest in the world after Silicon Valley (see Figure 10-2). Furthermore, the prestigious research organizations of the Max Planck Institutes and the Fraunhofer-Gesellschaft[5] both operate their national headquarters in Munich.

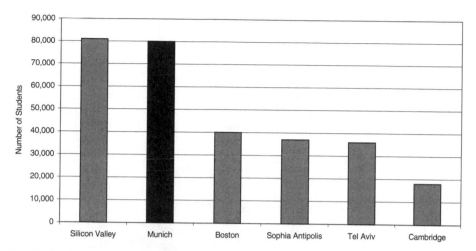

FIGURE 10-2   International comparison of regional talent pools: number of students.
Source: Bain & Company, 2001.

Bavaria currently has a capacity for 3,000 first-term students in software programming, which was recently increased from 2,500 by a government investment of approximately $30 million. This, together with the construction of a new building for the programming and mathematics departments of the Technical University on its research campus in Garching, close to Munich, indicates the dawn of an era of intensified research within these fields.

LINKING HIGHER EDUCATION VIA THE INTERNET — COOPERATION WITH REGIONAL EDUCATION SYSTEMS

In May 2000, the Bavarian government launched Virtuelle Hochschule Bayern (VMB),[6] a virtual university intended to include the best online courses offered by all Bavarian higher educational institutions on one central Web site. To launch the site, employees of Bavaria's universities worked as volunteers. It was not until August of 2000 that two full-time employees were recruited into the organization. Regardless of the technical difficulties during and after the launch, 504 students signed up for courses in the first term of operation, at a time when the organization still had no employees. For the second term, more than 1,055 first term students registered for 1,200 courses. Driven by strategic partnerships with industry players such as DaimlerChrysler and Siemens as well as with virtual university networks outside of Bavaria and Germany, Bavaria wishes to increase the competitiveness of its own universities while leveraging the intellectual capital of the region.

MUNICH'S UNLEVERAGED POTENTIAL — SYMPTOMS OF A YOUNG HIGH-TECH REGION

Given the large R&D potential within and around Munich, it is remarkable that many of the large American high-tech companies use the region merely as a base for their sales and marketing activities (see Figure 10-3). With the critical mass the cluster has achieved as well as its strategic geographic location, Munich is positioned to potentially become a major European high-tech hub. Still, even though most foreign high-tech companies have placed their German headquarters within the Munich region, they have located their European headquarters outside of Germany.

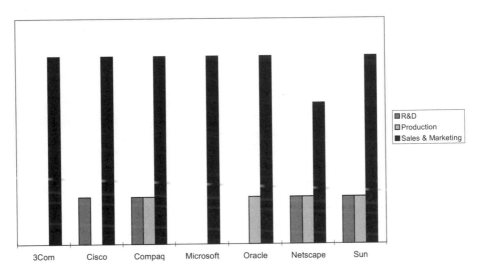

FIGURE 10-3   Employee functions in the Munich region. Source: Bain & Company, 2001.

This may be due to Munich being a newly emergent high-tech region and the fact that the successful development of such regions seems to be an accelerating process. Munich has not been covered by the international press with many high-tech success stories. This may be one of the reasons why companies have been slow to invest in R&D and production facilities in the region. In fact, from 1996 to 2000, Munich has received considerably less press coverage in *Red Herring* and the *Economist* than have Cambridge or Tel Aviv.[7]

The lack of local success stories has been measured by Bain & Company Inc., Germany, by comparing the market capitalization of locally based high-tech companies in Munich with those based in other leading high-tech regions around the world. The figures indicate that Munich is far behind, explaining the lack of global media coverage and indicating a lack of awareness of the region's potential.

Nonetheless, Munich is beginning to build awareness for itself as a magnet for global capital and high-tech knowledge workers. According to Dr. Lutz Weber, CEO of the biotech company Morphochem,[8] even though 25% of Munich's work force come from other countries, considered high for German standards, the expertise to internationalize its companies is still missing. Mr. Weber, who employs individuals from 17 countries, suggests that an important first step to global awareness of Munich has been the repatriation of German scientists, who had been successful in the United States. This brought a lot of international know-how back to the Munich region.

To transform Morphochem into a truly international company, Mr. Weber pioneered a concept foreign to Munich biotech companies at the time. In addition to local capital available in the Munich area, Morphochem sought capital in the U.S.

LUTZ WEBER

**Morphochem – Why a Munich biotech company
went to Silicon Valley to look for an investor**

As we prepared for Morphochem's second round of financing, we began speaking to a venture capitalist in San Francisco who was very experienced and had been one of the first investors in Genentech. But our German executives were apprehensive: "Do we even want to have this guy as a shareholder?" With a U.S. investor of his caliber on the board, we knew that Morphochem would need to begin operating with global-quality standards. We knew that the VC would never say, "This is a Bavarian company, so we have to be a little bit more careful." I immediately recognized that if I succeeded at winning the Californian as an investor, Morphochem would have more demanding, global-minded shareholders, which was exactly what the company needed.

It was the Californian venture firm's first investment in Germany and it has made them considerably more aware of the potential within the Munich region. Other Munich biotech companies have begun to follow our example and have increasingly started looking for capital abroad. Two days after you do something successful, it becomes a standard. This was a key moment for putting Munich's biotech companies on a tougher path toward global awareness and quality standards. ∎

In order to increase the international exposure and accessibility of Bavaria's high-tech regions, the Bavarian government recently founded goto-Bavaria,[9] a marketing and communications agency aimed at attracting high-tech investments to the area. gotoBavaria has since opened an office in Silicon Valley and Bangalore, India. In April 2001, gotoBavaria conducted a conference in Nuremberg, which was transmitted live to 200 U.S.-based investors whom they invited for breakfast at gotoBavaria's Silicon Valley office. Through a roundtable-type discussion, local executives, entrepreneurs, and politicians described the high-tech attractiveness of Bavaria from an international business perspective.

STATE GOVERNMENT INITIATIVE — THE BAYERNONLINE INFRASTRUCTURE INITIATIVE AND BAVARIA'S VIRTUAL MARKETPLACE

The Bavarian government recognizes that the potential of the Munich region is not fully utilized. For this reason, it is continually working to improve upon the environment needed for Bavaria's successful transition to a globally competitive information economy while increasing its attractiveness to foreign direct high-tech investment. Since 1994, numerous initiatives have promoted this transition, including BayernOnline and VHB, aimed at building a powerful information infrastructure while at the same time promoting the use of new technologies by society and businesses.

Once an infrastructure was in place and the adoption of new technologies was considered to have reached critical mass, the Bavarian government launched a virtual marketplace in order to accelerate the commercial and private applications of the Internet. Virtual Marketplace Bavaria (VMB)[10] was founded based on the belief that the Internet could generate many advantages for businesses, public institutions, and citizens, even though the dynamic and anarchic state of the Internet would make it difficult to attain the maximum leverage of benefit without first creating "law and order" in cyberspace. For this reason, the Bavarian government decided on a comprehensive approach to enabling the e-society and formulated several requirements for its online marketplace:

- VMB will aim to increase the utilization and the acceptance of the Internet among Bavarian citizens. Furthermore, it will aim to enable e-commerce, especially between small- and medium-sized companies in Bavaria's different regions.

- VMB will be useful to everyone from craftsmen to doctors to public servants, and by banks, insurance companies, and retail stores, while equally covering all work and leisure topics connected with daily life in Bavaria. The user will benefit from having a single Internet site to access services from public institutions, and at the same time will have access to well-structured commercial offerings. The offer is to be personalized so that each user may determine the content of the portal to fit his or her specific needs.
- Users will be able to post notices to which businesses in the region shall be able to respond, in an aim to facilitate the matching of supply and demand in the marketplace. The aim is to offer to buyers fast and comfortable price comparisons, while sellers benefit from increased information about their customers, enabling them, for example, to optimize stocks and production.

Instead of building the marketplace on its own, the Bavarian government organized a Europe-wide pitch for its construction in November 1999. By the end of January 2000, 14 valid entries were received. A consortium consisting of Siemens and SAP was finally awarded the grant, and by July 2000 the prototype of the marketplace was presented. Today, the VMB has a decentralized structure, with 20 regional marketplaces being held in place under the roof of the VMB. The Siemens/SAP consortium has the primary role of coordinating these marketplaces in a fashion that even though they remain decentralized, they appear united from the perspective of the user. Regardless of which regional portal the user enters, there will always be seamless access to the structured offer of all marketplaces. The consortium is furthermore responsible for the regional, national, and international marketing of the different marketplaces.

In summary, the market highlights indicate that Munich offers a favorable environment for the emergence of new technologies, such as new media and biotech, based on its strong infrastructure of higher education institutions and research centers, a critical mass of established technology and media-related companies, and a proactive government. Locals frequently claim that Munich's diversity and critical mass are its key success factors. However, the development of this innovation friendly environment did not occur by accident, and certainly not overnight.

Over the past 50 years, Bavaria has managed to transform itself from an agrarian state to one of Europe's leading technology clusters. The greater Munich region today is one of the wealthiest in Europe, boasting the highest quality of life in Germany. Bavaria and the greater Munich region have worked hard for many decades to attract technology-related business to the area. The aspiration to turn Munich into Germany's high-tech capital was formulated more than 40 years ago by the Christian Social Union (CSU) and

Franz Joseph Strauß, who was Bavaria's minister president from 1978–1988. Convincing Siemens to locate its main headquarters in Munich after World War II was one of Bavaria's first steps in an impressive process of regional wealth creation. The following sections illustrate the Bavarian government's high-tech initiatives, and the region's struggle to develop an entrepreneurship culture to fully leverage its far-reaching potential.

CREATING AN ENTREPRENEURSHIP CULTURE

Though it may be debatable to which degree an entrepreneurship culture can be created as opposed to it developing naturally, examples from Munich once again indicate that regions may possess large amounts of unleveraged entrepreneurial potential. However, this potential may be unleashed through measures such as business plan contests and the "importing" of an entrepreneurial culture by large corporations. When designing measures to support the creation of an entrepreneurship culture in a region however, be aware of "entrepreneurship killers" that may be inherent in the form of local culture or the political environment.

BUSINESS PLAN CONTESTS — AN INITIAL SPARK IGNITED FROM A McKINSEY STUDY

In 1996, only 2% of Munich region university students were willing to start a company. In the U.S. at the same time, the number was around 40%. In Germany, large and established companies remained the way to go for students after graduation. The initial spark that enabled Munich to create new regional wealth based on its substantial existing innovation potential was a study conducted by the management consultancy McKinsey & Company in 1996. The study indicated that creating an entrepreneurship culture would help to leverage the region's intellectual capital and to promote an economic structural renewal.

The McKinsey study found that one of the constraints on entrepreneurship in the Munich region was the German mindset. According to Dr. Frank W. Strathmann, managing director of GründerRegio M,[11] the organization responsible for promoting entrepreneurship at Munich's universities, this mindset can be described as follows: "I am an engineer, I have a small company, a secretary, and maybe one or two other employees and that's it. I don't need more and I don't want more," which is in clear contrast to the U.S.

"think big" attitude of trying to "think outside the box" and aggressively expanding product/service scope and expand markets, which is all entrepreneurial by nature.

Based on a model that had already been successfully implemented at MIT in the United States, McKinsey teamed up with Munich's universities, among others, to launch the Munich Business Plan Contest (Münchener Business Plan Wettbewerb),[12] a concept that was unique to the region at the time. Its initial aim was to increase the entrepreneurship quota at Munich's higher academic institutions. However, the contest eventually led to a paradigm shift in the entire region. It quickly became apparent that the entrepreneurial potential of Munich and its surroundings was just waiting to be released.

The MIT concept was aimed at contestants with serious business ideas and implementation capabilities. The traditional German lack of interest in "starting small and making it big," was addressed with another, more playful contest that borrowed the 1-Dollar Business concept from the University of Calgary (this approach assumes little or no available investment capital and forces creative marketing thinking to develop instantly profitable businesses), and renamed it to the more appropriate 5-Euro Business Contest.[13] Since the two concepts' successful implementation, they have been spread to universities throughout Bavaria and Germany. Dr. Strathmann provides his insight on how effective the Munich Business Plan Contest was.

FRANK W. STRATHMANN

Replicating foreign business plan concepts — The Munich Business Plan Contest

Even though people were already working to position Munich for the information age in the mid-1990s, the region at the time was characterized by a general lack of money and competencies in this respect. The initial feat of getting things off the ground was the biggest challenge. One possible solution was to create an entrepreneurship culture around the university-based business plan competitions that had already achieved considerable results in other countries.

Within this context, McKinsey played an instrumental role in transferring the implementation know-how for the contest from the United States to the Munich region while helping to win commercial sponsors for the project. During the first year of the contest's operations, its fundraising amounted to a total of approximately $500,000 donated by companies such as Allianz, BMW, Deutsche Bank, the Frankfurter Allgemeine Zeitung, and Microsoft. By 2001, this sum had risen to approximately $1.6 million.

The contest immediately achieved results that more than met its founders' initial expectations: 40 technology companies were launched in conjunction with the 1996–1997 contest alone, a result that proved how successfully knowledge and research results from universities could be integrated into the process of generating innovations in business. By 2000, the contest had created 103 new companies in the Munich region, employing 740 individuals. These companies were financed by a total of approximately $81 million, consisting of $55 million of venture capital, $20 million of government funds, and $6 million of business angel funds. The 1999–2000 contest generated a total of 483 entries by over 1,000 participants, of which 126 business plans made it to the final selection at the end of the third round. Once the success of the contest in the Munich region became apparent, it was implemented in Berlin as well. Today, numerous start-up contests operate all over Germany.

The Munich Business Plan Contest's concept is built on knowledge transfer, coaching, and team-building. Participation is open to anyone. The contest covers a period of several months, during which the business plan is developed in three stages, from a rough 10-page business plan draft to a fully detailed business plan capable of accompanying a team through the actual launch of its business.

Throughout the process, more than 100 coaches are available to the participants, providing them with one-on-one advice free of charge. Numerous crash-courses, lectures, cocktails, and a regular meeting accompany the process, enabling comprehensive networking. The contest's contact office is fully staffed, providing participants with comprehensive printed information and literature referrals.

The 5-Euro Business Contest

The contest invites students from Munich's universities to gather in small teams and to participate in four crash courses on the subjects of idea generation, project management, marketing, and legal/finance. With an initial investment of five Euro (approximately four U.S. dollars), the teams have five weeks to build a business, in the process of which they are continually coached. At the end of the five-week period, the students present their results to a jury of business people for the chance to win prizes valued at about $3,000. ■

Addressing students and scientists from diverse technology sectors, Munich's business plan contests have helped to spread a new entrepreneurship culture throughout the region and all of Germany. However, for such a culture to change the economic face of an entire region, strong initiative is required from additional players. For instance, large technology companies can help by coaching their employees about the imperatives of the global Innovation Economy. Our discussions with executives of Siemens indicate that the company is trying to import America's entrepreneurship culture to within its own four walls and to the Munich region.

LARGE COMPANIES REPLICATING SILICON VALLEY'S CROSS-FERTILIZATION

Anthony Maher, a former member of the board of Siemens Information and Communication Networks, and who was also in charge of Siemens' venture investments, believes that the technical universities in Munich and Bavaria are excellent. He explains that they generate many students with a great depth and substance of technical knowledge, and who have a strong wish to finally let all of their knowledge flow when they finish studying, having spent more time at university than students in the U.S., for example. However, in line with the general opinion on Munich's performance, Maher believes that these resources traditionally have not been leveraged to their full extent.

For Siemens,[14] working to instill a culture of entrepreneurship and innovation in the region has been a strategic aspiration, aimed at being able to capitalize upon the unexploited intellectual potential within its own four walls, but also outside of its corporate boundaries within the greater Munich region. Mr. Maher refers to the region's intellectual potential as "raw resources in the ground that just need to be picked up and polished" by giving them the space and to expand themselves. Whereas many traditional companies tend to "confine" the creative capacities of their employees, Siemens believes they need to be freed within a suitable environment. In attempting to create this kind of environment in Munich, however, Siemens found that the charisma and the spirit of Silicon Valley were missing and that entrepreneurial culture in the region was just at its beginning.

ANTHONY MAHER

Can large companies import an entrepreneurial culture into a region?

A company in a traditionally non-entrepreneurial region, seeking to create an entrepreneurship culture within its own walls first has to become a dedicated investor in small companies outside of its own corporate boundaries. These investments need to be made within and outside of its home region in order to enable a successful transfer of the required culture.

Siemens is headquartered in Munich, while many of the world's most entrepreneurial companies are based in the United States. For this reason, we began to invest in small U.S. companies to import the badly needed entrepreneurial culture to our headquarters in Munich, and then to spread this culture to the greater Munich region through local investments, spin-offs, and natural employee rotation.

When the high-tech investments in the U.S. were made, cross-cultural teams were built between these companies and each division of Siemens in Munich. Soon after, a rubbing off of cultures started taking place as both sides interacted and began helping each other. This rubbing off was necessary for people on the inside of Siemens to understand the outside entrepreneurial world, before attempting to develop it internally. Siemens' investments have not been limited to supporting entrepreneurial developments and fostering innovation within the company. After successfully learning from our U.S. investments, Siemens now actively promotes entrepreneurship and innovation within the entire Munich region, convinced that the culture surrounding the company is just as important as the culture within the company.

The increasing existence of small innovative companies around Siemens in Munich has contributed to making the region a magnet for innovation while enabling cross-pollenization between different technology sectors, all to the benefit of Siemens' global operations.

The role of youth and large companies as agents of change

Creating a culture for entrepreneurship within a region is a daunting task. However, I believe that starting with young people is one key to success, since the cultural differences between young people around the world are minimal. They have not had enough time to accumulate cultural baggage. Young people in Santa Clara and in Munich are not all that different if one applies motivational incentives, such as the perspective to acquire wealth and to achieve successful status.

In this sense, large local high-tech companies play an essential role in unleashing intellectual potential and in creating new regional wealth. They can help import new business cultures and can help spread these cultures, creating regional success stories along the way. Munich has not yet produced many global success stories and for this reason suffers from international underexposure. This in turn causes a general lack of understanding of how nice it is to live here and of what the young people here are doing and are willing to do. Siemens is playing an instrumental role at creating an environment that will foster the innovation and entrepreneurship necessary to enable the success stories that Munich will need to compete in the future. ■

While Siemens' efforts to import entrepreneurship have shown considerable results, the company has been struggling to deal with Germany's lack of a service culture and restrictive federal immigration laws. When compared with service-focused regions such as Ireland, Germany tends to be far more focused on engineering than developing user-friendly features or services for businesses and end-user consumers. These "entrepreneurship killers" are considered a serious disadvantage to the competitiveness of the Munich high-tech region.

"ENTREPRENEURSHIP KILLERS" — ARE GERMAN TRADITIONS BLOCKING THE RISE OF A NEW CULTURE?

Joe Kaeser, member of the board of Siemens Information and Communication Mobile, explains that the traditional lack of a service culture in Germany is a great risk for a company in the mobile phone business. Not being sufficiently able to recruit highly skilled workers from abroad creates a further regional disadvantage for ICM in the fast-moving mobile telecommunications markets.

JOE KAESER

Living with the entrepreneurial compromise — The missing service culture

Traditionally, many German technology companies have had little contact with the end-user consumer since most of their activities were business-to-business driven. The environment within these companies has been anything but entrepreneurial. In addition, German companies today still neglect competencies in sales and customer service. As a waiter in a German restaurant, you get tipped 10% anyway, so why try harder?

While service-driven jobs have traditionally been regarded as less prestigious in Germany than manufacturing and engineering jobs, the awareness of the need to change these circumstances has increased considerably. Technology companies like Siemens are becoming increasingly consumer focused, as the service sector is the fastest growing part of the German economy. Yet, Germans themselves consider the country to be a "service desert."

Changing attitudes is a slow and difficult process. Creating an entrepreneurial environment in Germany is still difficult, since entrepreneurship is not something that can be taught at university, but develops around freedom and creativity. To succeed at creating such an environment, Germans need to increase their sensitivity and acquire a deeper understanding of customer demands and of how these demands can be met. If a technology company wishes to shape customer demand and to build the standards for the future, it needs to be the first to meet the demands of the customer. If high-tech companies in the region do not learn to excel at understanding this, they risk ending up as "me-too's," playing catch-up in fast-paced, customer-driven markets in which others are calling the shots.

In an environment as dynamic as the mobile phone market, in which product life cycles range from 9 to 15 months at most, not hitting the "design window" by addressing the very latest customer demands can cause revenues to fall short by up to 50%. Mobile phones don't sell because of their features, but because people like their look and feel.

For this reason, Siemens has recently put together a cross-disciplinary team of engineers, market researchers, sales people, and production professionals to better understand what customers need and to learn more about how to better manage the business-to-consumer relationship. We still have a long way to go and I believe that the Munich region should attract more service-oriented technology companies to help accelerate the spreading of the missing culture.

The failed green card program

German national labor laws present a further constraint to entrepreneurship in the Munich region. Time is often lost as companies are forced to consider the unemployed people in their region for a job before being allowed to look for competence outside of Germany. In an effort to address the shortage of highly skilled workers in ICT and related sectors in the country, the national government offered 20,000 green cards to foreign individuals wishing to apply for high-tech jobs in Germany. However, the program did not get off to a good start. There was a lot of controversy surrounding the issue for months and when the law was finally passed, only a handful of foreigners applied.

It is not surprising that the turnout was so low. If you are the person in demand in a country such as India, for example, and you look to Silicon Valley, the message will be: "Please come to work here, this is what we can offer you . . . we want you to help us shape the future." Now, if the same person looks to Germany, what do they see? A bunch of people talking for who knows how many months about whether or not and under which circumstances foreigners could be employed and about which kind of tests they would need to undergo in order to even be allowed to apply. Where would you go? Before these highly skilled people from all over the world fill out huge stacks of paperwork in order to apply for a job in Germany, they will go to work in the U.S., if they have the chance. If Germany wants to attract highly skilled foreigners, it has to go out there and make them attractive offers. There is a global war for talent and this has not yet been understood by the German national government.

This doesn't mean that Siemens ICM has been complacent. The company has been doing what a lot of other companies have: If the people couldn't come to us, we went to them. This sort of logic will continue until national politicians have understood the implications of the shortage of highly skilled workers in the country. Certain corporate managers in Germany still believe that their employees should be happy to have a job. Well, there may be a few people that are happy to have a job, but in reality, it is a war for talent and if we are not careful, others will come and take away our best employees. ■

If improving Munich's reputation as a leading international high-tech region depends on the creation of international success stories, then a strong regional entrepreneurial culture is of central importance. In Munich, initiatives such as business plan contests have been effective at promoting entrepreneurial activities. However, they address a relatively small number of individuals. Comprehensive and lasting change can be further supported by large technology companies that actively promote an entrepreneurship culture inside their own walls and then enable it to spread to the region. The Munich example shows that such efforts may be inhibited by local cultural specificities or harmful national legislation. Nonetheless, Munich has been crowned the entrepreneurship capital of Germany. Leveraging its existing entrepreneurship culture has been facilitated by the region's excellent innovation infrastructure.

STATE GOVERNMENT IN PARTNERSHIP WITH BUSINESS

According to Bavarian State Minister Erwin Huber, Bavaria's successful development can be attributed in part to its political stability, resulting from over 40 years of consecutive rule of the Christian Social Union party. The aspiration to turn Bavaria into Germany's high-tech capital was formulated during the 1950s, when Bavaria was still a largely agricultural and impoverished state. Since then, long-term strategies for the region have been consistently implemented, and the Bavarian government has acted as the initial spark for many initiatives that today constitute key success factors of Bavaria's high-tech environment.

CONSISTENT STATE GOVERNMENT COMMITMENT TO DEVELOPING HIGH TECH — "LAPTOPS AND LEDERHOSEN"

Between 1994 and 2004, the Bavarian state will have invested approximately $1.5 billion alone into the development of its high-tech environment as a part of the state-wide High-Tech Offensive Bayern[15] initiative. After Germany's reunification in 1990, incentives offered by the Bavarian government convinced the two leading national research organizations, Max Planck Society and the Fraunhofer Institut, to refrain from moving their headquarters from Munich to Berlin, the new national capital. This is generally considered to have been a crucial move to ensure Bavaria's continued high-tech attractiveness. In terms of developing the environment for high tech and entrepreneurship in Bavaria, Mr. Huber explains that the government's key role has been to create a climate for innovation by giving important impulses that have led to regional development.

Bavaria was one of the few states in Germany that didn't use the funds generated by the privatization of its energy utilities to reduce its budget deficit. Instead, the money was reinvested into various high-tech clusters around Munich and throughout Bavaria. These government investments helped the high-tech region reach critical mass, eventually enabling it to attract new companies like a magnet.

The Bavarian government's approach to investing these funds has been quite entrepreneurial, and has helped Munich become the city with the highest venture capital density in the world after Silicon Valley. With a mission to invest in young Bavarian technology companies exclusively in partnership with locally based private venture capital companies, Bayern Kapital[16] was founded by the Bavarian government to promote venture financing in the region. Through Bayern Kapital, the Bavarian government has been investing in high-tech ventures, as long as its initial investment is matched by private venture capital funds. This has helped to reduce the private venture capitalists' risk exposure and has attracted large amounts of foreign capital to the region.

The Bavarian government has always been criticized for using public funds for risky venture investments, and indeed there may have been projects that weren't exactly worth the investment. However, Richard Roy, VP EMEA region corporate strategy, at Microsoft Germany[17] still feels that the government's innovative approach has been successful: "Where markets are developing, you need to follow the 80/20 rule." Mr. Roy furthermore explains that the investments that may not have been profitable in a strictly financial sense, have still initiated important multiplier effects that have benefited the entire region. Companies such as Microsoft, using Munich as a base for their German operations, seem content with the support received from the Bavarian state government, which has enabled an American company such as Microsoft to feel at home within the region.

PAMPERING THE "LIGHTHOUSE COMPANIES"

The increasing number of American high-tech companies that were locating their German headquarters in Munich implied new challenges for the Bavarian government's administrative environment. In order to leverage the region's full potential, the administration would need to be capable of accommodating emerging, fast-moving businesses, driven by the convergence of different and new technologies. By first attracting and then by retaining certain brand-name, or "lighthouse companies" as Microsoft's Mr. Roy refers to them, Munich has succeeded in attracting many more global players as well as a diverse array of supplying and partner companies. Taking on a very pro-business stance toward its lighthouse companies has been a key strategy of the Bavarian government. For example, the entrepreneurial freedom to place a headquarters practically anywhere a company wants to has been an important feature of "defanging the bureaucracy."

Mr. Roy explains that in 1998, Microsoft Germany decided that its facilities were inadequate to handle future expansion. The company decided to move to a new location custom-built especially for Microsoft and some of its partners. Even though the lot that Microsoft wished to move to was already designated commercial land, a considerable administrative process needed to be navigated, since some of it belonged to the municipality and some of it belonged to private investors. Permissions needed to be obtained, the land needed to be purchased, and an entire infrastructure of roads needed to be built in order to enable sufficient access to the property. With the help of the Bavarian government, the entire process was handled and the building completed in two-and-a-half years. According to Mr. Roy, this would have been absolutely impossible in many other German and European cities because of the bureaucratic complications that are usually required.

By clearing the way for the fast localization of office space around the city, Munich has encouraged the formation of several "cluster satellites" around the city's center. Today, these satellites, which were initialized by the Bavarian government, constitute a key advantage of the region.

BUILDING THE MUNICH "CLUSTER SATELLITE" MODEL — PROXIMITY MATTERS

The Bavarian model for regional planning has changed from building a little technology park for each city to building technology-oriented competency centers for different high-tech industries mainly around the city of Munich. Each is within an hour's drive of the other, but no more than 30 minutes from the city center. The idea was that if competency was bundled within a small area, innovation would take place more efficiently. The Bavarian government was convinced that there needed to be several different growth centers and that in each one of these, the key ingredients were incumbent players, university and other research activities, and effective start-up support. The aspiration was to create a unique symbiosis of old and new structures in the Munich region. This would derive its strength from a natural coexistence of lifestyle, technology, tradition, and progress, and foster cross-fertilization between businesses, education, research, and venture capital through the co-location of distinct high-tech industries in and around the city of Munich.

Initially, Munich's high-tech cluster satellite model was based on the decentralized structure of Munich's two universities, which are headquartered in the center of the city, with many of the departments and faculties located at different locations throughout and even outside of the city. An example is the small town of Garching, less than 30 minutes from the city's center. Here, the presence of the Max Planck Society and the Technical University's faculties for physics, chemistry, and engineering have recently also attracted the university's mathematics and software research faculties. The additional 3,000 students that are expected to begin studying in the town by the first half of 2002 will benefit from an excellent existing research environment, a newly completed $60 million building (a token of the state government's Software-Offensive Bayern),[18] and a newly installed technology start-up center.

Dr. Günther Ernstberger, managing director of the new media incubator Gründerzentrum für Neue Medien Unterföhring[19] (GZM), explains that placing Munich's high-tech clusters in the nearby suburbs has reaped substantial benefits. While easily accessible from the city center, these clusters are practically located in the countryside. This provides an attractive environment to many employees and takes some of the pressure off the housing shortage in the city's center. Unterföhring is another example of the state government's initiatives to build on existing industry structures, in this case media, by acting as the initial spark for the development of new high-tech clusters in the Munich region.

GÜNTHER ERNSTBERGER

New media at GZM Unterföhring

I consider the GZM to be a prime example of the private/public relationship that has been successfully driving the development of high tech in the Munich region. The GZM was originally conceived by the two Bavarian State Ministers Erwin Huber and Otto Wiesheu. They were convinced that the concept of an entrepreneurship center with incubation facilities pioneered in other high-tech sectors around Munich, would also work within the new media environment, especially if it was placed in Unterföhring, which had already been an important media cluster for several decades. The GZM was designed to complement Munich's strong existing media networks, while being considered a key investment into the future competitiveness of the media industry in the region. Today, more than 5,000 of the 10,000 jobs that exist in Unterföhring (population 8,000) are in media companies.

Critical to the success of the center has been the support from established media companies. The GZM was very well received by the established players from its inception, who saw the center as a chance to get closer to the cutting-edge developments that were going on in areas such as Internet services and content development, and were beginning to revolutionize existing media markets. The GZM today is sponsored by a large number of companies as well as the Bavarian government. The fact that these institutions assure a solid sum of finance is a key factor enabling the sustainability of the center. ■

The biotech cluster in Martinsried is another example of the Bavarian government's commitment to creating an entrepreneurial environment in the Munich region. While Unterföhring managed to develop out of its own dynamic, owing to the interest of established media businesses in the area, the Bavarian government practically built the infrastructure in Martinsried from scratch and then watched as more and more very promising biotech companies started to set up around the town.

While other German regions such as Berlin seem to be catching up to Munich as their governments invest large amounts of money into their technology start-ups, the growth of biotech companies in the Munich region indicates that state aid is important in the early stages of a company's development, but less so in later stages. As soon as companies start growing, the central question becomes, "Will the infrastructure of the region enable a start-up to become a real company?" This shows the limits of government support merely through funding. According to Dr. Weber of Morphochem, Munich remains Germany's leader in growth enabling infrastructure with a critical mass that includes experts from all scientific fields, an unmatched international openness, and an industrial diversity that is especially important for an interdisciplinary industry such as the biotech industry. This may be one of the reasons why Berlin has quite a few small biotech companies, but not many large ones.

LUTZ WEBER

Entrepreneurial infusion in Bavarian biotech — IZB Martinsried

Martinsried is a small town with a population of 5,000, located in the Bavarian countryside just outside of Munich. During the past few years, the state of Bavaria has invested more than $20 million into the Innovations- und Gründerzentrum Biotechnologie[20] (IZB), a biotech start-up center and incubator that today houses more than 20 companies.

The development of the cluster began in 1973 when this quiet country town, which consisted only of a few agricultural farms, became the new home to the biochemistry and neurobiology centers of the Max Planck Society. The new research campus was built five walking minutes away from a major Munich hospital and in 1983, the scene was complemented by the genetics center of Munich's Ludwig-Maximilians-University. Today, one of the key success factors of the cluster is the campuslike proximity of its key organizations, all within a few "bicycle minutes" from each other.

The nucleus of the cluster today are the company Bio^{M} [21] and its visionary founder, Prof. Horst Domdey, who is considered to be the pioneer of the cluster's success. Bio^{M} supports start-ups in the region by acting as a communications point between business and research, by providing access to networks, and by investing seed capital in collaboration with the Bavarian government's Bayern Kapital fund as well as with locally based venture capital companies. Bio^{M} invested in 29 of approximately 55 companies at IZB Martinsried and is financed by taking equity stakes in its clients' companies.

The success of Martinsried has caused a considerable repatriation of German scientists who had left the country for San Francisco or Boston, disappointed by Germany's bureaucratic and non-entrepreneurial environment. Coming back, they have brought the American spirit of uniting scientific and business mindsets, a new concept that could finally be realized in the intimate proximity inherent to the Martinsried cluster. ■

In between Munich's satellite clusters, smaller agglomerations of companies from specific high-tech sectors have formed "technology platforms" often close to large research institutions, which further enhance the efficiency of the region as a hub for innovation.

MUNICH'S SMALLER "TECHNOLOGY PLATFORMS"

In addition to Munich's considerable clusters for biotechnology, IT, new media, and nanotechnology, the Munich region also hosts smaller "technology platforms" that are being constructed in order to attract companies active in small industry segments from all over Bavaria and Germany to the region. One such technology platform is Merkator Park, which attempts to promote the convergence between navigation, telecommunications, and distance reconnaissance technologies. Merkator Park offers a platform to establish loose cooperations, exchange know-how, and work in an innovation center, all within the environment of the German air and space agency Deutsche Luft- und Raumfahrtsgesellschaft (DLR).[22] Even though Merkator covers only a small industry segment, it has been successful in attracting small companies active within this environment to the park in order to form close local networks. Without these networks, many of the small, highly specialized companies would have had serious problems leveraging their competencies as well as developing and commercializing their value proposition. A process of several years is deemed necessary for such a technology platform to reach critical mass, while on the whole, these types of platforms are considered to be an important competitive advantage for a region.

BUILDING INTERNATIONAL LIAISONS BETWEEN REGIONS

Within the context of the European Commission's PAXIS[23] (Pilot Action of Excellence on Innovative Start-ups) program, the PANEL (Pyrenean-Alpine Network of Entrepreneurial Liaisons) network links the cities of Barcelona, Milan, and Munich. The three cities are all technology and innovation leaders in their countries. They were selected to work together to foster the start-up of innovative high-tech companies within their respective regions.

The network's operation began in September 2000. For 18 months, the three regions communicated intensively in order to exchange information and knowledge as well as to develop successful initiatives on how to back and create new enterprises. The network expects to benefit from the transnational exchange of experiences, methodologies, and tools for the support of start-ups through, for example, setting up entrepreneurship seminars, contact bases, and various working groups. Jürgen Vogel, coordinator of the PANEL network (Pyrenean-Alpine Network of Entrepreneurial Liaisons between Barcelona, Milan, and Munich), explains that linking some of the most innovative regions in Europe is easier said than done.

JÜRGEN VOGEL

Linking entrepreneurship in Europe — The PANEL network within PAXIS

First of all, the regions had to be selected. Approximately 35 European regions applied to the PAXIS (Pilot Action of Excellency on Innovative Start-ups, which is supported by the Commission of the European Communities) program, of which 15 "regions of excellence" were eventually chosen according to strict competitiveness factors and grouped into four networks. The project is conceived to build long-term cooperation between the regions. The first phase is about identifying the potential lines of collaboration in innovative support. Central questions include: What are innovative measures in each of the regions? How can these innovations be applied within another region? Be it an idea, an incentive, or a process, what has been working and what has not? Which information should be made accessibe to and standardized in all regions? As an example, in each of the regions, incubation support mechanisms have been identified and some essential key economic players met to propose to help young companies to successfully launch.

As of October 2001, the PANEL network regions have succeeded in building up a directory of the collaboration potential and of what is inside their network. The next steps are to validate, to benchmark, and to find out what can be exchanged between the PANEL regions and also the other EU network regions, and how this exchange can be organized. For this purpose, it has proved very useful to have some key enablers from the different regions sit together regularly.

After the first year of preparations defining the assets, capabilities, and needs of the regions, PANEL is now beginning to enter into a phase of networking of successful initiatives. There is about $13.5 million of funding available from the Commission, including all four PAXIS networks as well as accompanying projects and measures. Spawned by the impetus of the action, and even though it is too early to judge the final results of this work in progress, the Commission has indicated its ongoing commitment by launching a follow-up program. This time the three PANEL regions of Barcelona, Milan, and Munich submitted a new proposal in collaboration with the city of Dublin. ■

Benny Ginman, director of governmental and educational affairs EMEA at Intel[24] in Munich, believes in the importance of the European Community's efforts to link its regions of excellence. He considers one of the advantages of the European Union as opposed to the United States to be its diversity of cultures, business environments, and approaches to solving business problems. However, to be able to benefit from this diversity, there needs to be a harmony to enable the fluid cooperation between regions. Mr. Ginman explains that in order to ensure its global competitiveness, the EU should not try to become a perfectionist system. Regulations should be limited as they could turn into invisible barriers and inhibit the compatibility between the EU and the U.S. for example.

SUMMARY

Munich's potent government-initiated innovation infrastructure, numerous initiatives to create an entrepreneurship culture, as well as its traditional technological diversity have enabled the region to gain critical mass in the global Innovation Economy. Whether Munich will eventually manage to better exploit its large intellectual potential, creating international success stories and ultimately attracting the best highly skilled workers from all over the world, may depend on how fast the new entrepreneurship culture takes hold and on the degree to which federal legislation supports the process of regional development.

ENDNOTES

1. *Bayerische Staatsregierung*, May 15, 2001.
2. Bain & Company Germany, Inc., "Hightech-Standorte im Weltvergleich — Erfolgskriterien und Herausforderungen für die Zukunft," 2001.

3. The Max Planck Society, *www.mpg.de/english*.
4. Technische Universität München, *www.tu-muenchen.de*.
5. Fraunhofer-Gesellschaft, *www.fraunhofer.de*.
6. Virtuelle Hochschule Bayern, *www.vhb.org*.
7. Based on information from Bain & Company Inc, Germany, 2001.
8. Morphochem — Small Molecule Therapeutics, *www.morphochem.de*.
9. gotoBavaria, *www.gotobavaria.org*.
10. Virtueller Marktplätz Bayern, *www.baynet.de*.
11. GründerRegio M, *www.gr-m.de*.
12. MBPW Münchener Business Plan Wettbewerb, *www.mbpw.de*.
13. 5-Euro Business — Ideen Kreativ und Erfolgreich Verwirklichen, *www.5-euro-business.de*.
14. Siemens, *www.siemens.com*.
15. *Bayerische Staatskanzlei, www.high-tech-offensive-bayern.de*.
16. Bayern Kapital, *www.bayernkapital.de*.
17. Microsoft Deutschland, *www.microsoft.de*.
18. Informations Platform Der Software — Offensive Bayern, *www.software-offensive-bayern.de*.
19. GZM Unterföhring — Multimedia Visionen, *www.gzm-unterfoehring.de*.
20. Innovations- und Gründerzentrum Biotechnologie IZB, Martinsried-Freising, *www.izb-martinsried.de/*.
21. Bio[M] AG — Munich BioTech Development, *www.bio-m.de*.
22. DLR, *www.dlr.de/DLR-Homepage*.
23. PAXIS, *www.cordis.lu/paxis*.
24. Intel, Munich, *www.intel.de*.

❯ About the Author

This chapter was co-authored by **Philip Heimann**. He studied management at ESCP-EAP European School of Management in Paris, Oxford, and Berlin, has worked for the consulting firm A.T. Kearney and is currently preparing his doctoral thesis on linking corporate and regional innovation systems. Philip currently resides in Berlin, Germany.

11 CAMBRIDGE — INCUBATOR FOR INNOVATION, "SMALL IS BEAUTIFUL"

WELCOME TO SILICON FEN, THE U.K.'S VERSION OF SILICON VALLEY

Greater Cambridge, with the city of Cambridge at its heart, sits within the wider region defined as the East of England. The East of England region is one of the fastest growing in the U.K. *Fortune, Newsweek,* and *Business Week* have identified the Greater Cambridge area as Europe's number one R&D location, and one of the most likely in Europe to challenge the U.S. region of Silicon Valley for high-technology–driven innovation. In the Cambridge area, a remarkable and vigorous process of new high-technology firm creation and spin-offs from Cambridge University and from other firms has been developing considerable momentum since the 1970s. Labeled by the Cambridge consultancy SQW[1] "The Cambridge Phenomenon," this process has completely transformed the region's economic structure, with the vice chancellor of Cambridge University even claiming that the Cambridge area represents "the British Equivalent of Silicon Valley" in 1996[2] — the name now adopted is Silicon Fen.

While elsewhere in Europe, many high-tech clusters have grown around large manufacturing companies (Ericsson in Stockholm, Siemens in Munich), the structure of Silicon Fen in Cambridge is more like California's Silicon Valley, although admittedly, it is much, much smaller. Cambridge has grown from the bottom up, in what locals call a grass roots dynamic into an entrepreneurial center that today is well plugged into a network of money and experience throughout Europe and America.

Cambridge is a small place populated for the most part with small companies. It does boast some large international names including Microsoft, Toshiba, and AT&T, but their activities are mainly confined to research and development. The cluster is furthermore characterized by its diversity and interdisciplinary nature, including biotechnology/pharmaceuticals, software/electronics, ICT, telecommunications, and Internet companies.

TABLE 11-1   Facts at a Glance — Cambridge

Population of Cambridgeshire (East of England)	730,000
Projected Cambridgeshire population growth	25% by 2021
Number of East of England ICT companies	Over 5,000
Number of East of England overseas-owned businesses	1,400
East of England pool of technologists	Approximately 90,000
East of England early output of IT graduates	Approximately 7,000
East of England average rate of economic growth 1993–1998	3.5%
East of England business expenditure on R&D as % of regional GDP	2.84%
East of England government expenditure on R&D as % of regional GDP	0.36%
Company investments in Cambridgeshire (5/2000 to 5/2001)	28 (40% growth over previous year)
Marketing by East of England Investment Agency (5/2000 to 5/2001)	Included 55 overseas company visits
East of England % of labor force in business R&D	1.22%
U.K. investment market share in Europe	26%

Sources: U.K government estimates; East of England Development Agency, eeda.org.uk.

THE INITIAL SPARK — CAMBRIDGE'S RISK-TAKING LOCAL HEROES

The story of Cambridge's high-tech development begins with an initial spark from certain key individuals who are referred to as "local heroes." These key individuals were pioneers, embodying the innovative and entre-preneurial spirit, that lies at the heart of today's Cambridge phenomenon. Developments were never formally planned by a central organization, nei-ther were there ever any long-term strategies aimed at building the competi-tiveness of the cluster. The local heroes were people with ideas that they were willing to put their money and/or "sweat equity" behind, with an opti-mistic confidence that things would work if they were given the chance. They undertook spontaneous initiatives that evolved within the framework of informal relationships, another key characteristic of Cambridge. "Nothing is impossible!" claims Dr. Phil O'Donovan, managing director and co-founder of Cambridge Silicon Radio.[3] This ease in dealing with uncertainty and risk still prevails in Cambridge today: local investors are used to taking risks and actually enjoy taking and managing them.

What remains important for Cambridge is not necessarily to achieve crit-ical mass, but rather to achieve critical commitment. There is a motivation and steadfastness of the people within the area to set things in motion and see them through. An analogy used by Peter Hewkin, managing director of the Cambridge Network,[4] is that of a group of guerrilla fighters, meeting in the South American jungle and winning a battle in a clearing, only to retreat and melt away into the forest without a trace. The individuals that undertook this sort of activism in Cambridge eventually became role models for the region, representing a "low-blame" culture if things went wrong and of a will-ingness to make quick decisions. Thus, the original source of entrepreneur-ship in Cambridge came from within its own network of entrepreneurial champions, not from the government, not from the university, and not from the major British technology companies.

THE CHANGE SUCCEEDING THE INITIAL SPARK — ENTREPRENEURSHIP OVER AND OVER

As the local heroes generated the awareness that a lot of high-tech poten-tial was waiting to be set free within the Cambridge region, various dynamics started picking up all over the place. The Cambridge model is made up of four fundamental drivers that have enabled the transition from an environment driven by sporadically acting local heroes to the development of a world-renowned and well-organized high-tech cluster. These drivers are:

- The University of Cambridge as a world-leading source of intellectual capital, and its increasing role promoting the transfer of technology
- The Cambridge consultancies as prime sources of high-tech spin-offs
- The lubricating function of innovation networks
- The role that the government plays, keeping well out of the high-tech environment

CAMBRIDGE UNIVERSITY — A LONG TRADITION OF KNOWLEDGE AND INNOVATION

Many in Cambridge University view its role as the place that produces ideas that change the world. The tradition of innovation and criticism, in the true sense of the word, has created an environment that has produced 76 Nobel Prizes, conveying to its pool of talented graduates the confidence required to try to make their ideas work and carry them out to the world. In sum, Cambridge University is fundamental in leveraging the intellectual capital in the region.

There are two fundamental motors that have driven the process of developing formal links and interchange between pure scientific research and market applications at Cambridge University. The first is the vice chancellor of the university, Professor Sir Alec Broers, who is considered to be a visionary in terms of how the university can play a role in enabling the growth of the region by linking with business throughout greater Cambridge. Sir Alec Broers believes that Cambridge has the capacity to become the center of Great Britain's competitive advantage in world markets.[5] He has taken an unprecedented role in linking the university with business by incorporating the marriage of the two cultures of science and of management in order to succeed at transferring technology to the commercial arena. His interactive style and strong leadership have altered the face of Cambridge and continue to be a key factor in the redefinition of the relationship between the university and the commercial sector, which has traditionally been restricted by a superiority complex described as "town and gown."

The second motor is the University of Cambridge Entrepreneurship Centre,[6] directed by Peter Hiscocks. The center's mission is to leverage what Hiscocks describes as "the still hugely underexploited potential of the university." With the slogan "Building Tomorrow's Business," the center's work echoes Sir Alec Broers' agenda of building an entrepreneurial culture within the university by training, developing, and supporting the people who will make new knowledge-based ventures successful. The center, founded in late 1999, hopes to act as an implementation tool for a process it calls "knowledge-based entrepreneurship," and so to exploit the university's most abundant resource. Supporting the center's mission is the liberal policy the university has toward intellectual property, allowing graduates to own the full rights of any innovation they develop.

THE CAMBRIDGE CONSULTANCIES — CREATORS OF HIGH-TECH SPIN-OFFS

The Cambridge-based consultancies have been instrumental in the creation of new businesses in the region. The birth of the first business technology consultancy was thus a fundamental seed of Cambridge's success, and was soon to become a special technology transfer mechanism, long before the beginnings of the University of Cambridge Entrepreneurship Centre. By recruiting the very best technical graduates of the university and exposing them to business thinking around the world, they were able to begin a tradition of incubation and spin-offs typical of the Cambridge phenomenon today. Initially these "midwives" of technology transfer began as pure-play consultancies, "high-octane environments" so to speak, that coincidentally and eventually perhaps inevitably gave birth to other technology-oriented consultancies and companies. Again, the organic dynamics that have driven the Cambridge model become apparent. As the potential of generating spin-offs dawned on the consultancies, they began to consciously develop the breeding of spin-offs, which has created a multiplier effect. Today, spun-off companies constitute the vast majority of the business community in Cambridge — a successful example being Cambridge Silicon Radio, which was spun out of the consultancy Arthur D. Little/Cambridge Consultants[7]. The spin-off culture has enlarged the set of local role models, creating an aura of success around developing an idea, gathering support, and then moving on to pursue it.

The central challenge to the Cambridge region seen by some today is the skills debate. A need for more marketing and administrative capabilities has been identified as necessary in order to complement the highly developed academic competencies already available. The University of Cambridge Entrepreneurship Centre aims to address this problem by offering training, development, and support in business skills in order to make new knowledge-based ventures successful.

THE CAMBRIDGE NETWORK — HERDING CATS? FORGET IT!

The nature of networking in Cambridge demonstrates its particular style. Instead of being directed by a formal infrastructure, networking in Cambridge is constituted by an informal game of personal contacts and familiar settings. Even the more formal structures that exist, namely the Cambridge Network, which consists of approximately 850 members, aims to support rather than to guide. The mission of the Cambridge Network is to "listen and to react accordingly," helping to create the right environmental settings and then to let people get on and do things on their own.

Cambridge can be described as a trust environment, this trust being built on a personal rather than institutional level, the impetus still coming from its grass roots. Cambridge's tiny size has undoubtedly helped in the generation of this culture. The Cambridge Network has not created networking, but it has moved it up a gear from the very informal meetings in those clearings of the South American jungle.

Individuals in Cambridge do not appreciate being told what to do. The entrepreneurial and confident spirit is considered to be enough of a driver in itself — hence the expression frequently encountered when asking about the possibilities of formalizing network relationships and interactions: "Don't try herding cats. It doesn't work." The Cambridge environment demonstrates that scientists can be highly individualistic, which is at the same time highly regarded as a key characteristic of quality. Cambridge has indeed had difficulties in getting people to cooperate. Trying to increase the levels of cooperation in the region has brought about the realization that the central prerequisite for such cooperation is a willingness to trust others. People here need to feel that they can trust somebody, working together with them because they want to, and not because some third party tries to make them. The resulting model is one of gentle persuasion into collaboration and cooperation. People in Cambridge are described to be increasingly more willing to come together and collaborate, and to see this collaboration in their own interests. It is a real bottom-up approach.

THE GOVERNMENT — KEEPING WELL OUT OF IT

The outline of the region described above already indicates that essentially, the role of the government (national and local) within the Cambridge model is very limited. There is an uneasiness with bureaucracy and government intervention in the region that dates back to the 17th century. Government intervention is seen as going against the trust-based grass roots model characterizing Cambridge and is thus viewed with suspicion. Professor Gordon Edge, managing director of the Generics Group,[8] emphasizes that the government has not provided any financial grants, and that their absence is a unique feature of the Cambridge phenomenon. The Cambridge high-tech community seems to believe that government intervention would stifle entrepreneurial innovation, since this should be a natural, not a constructed evolution. Furthermore, given the non-hierarchical and egalitarian nature of the cluster and its constituents, it is said that government would have a tough time trying to develop structures through which it could contribute any substantial benefits. Paul Auton, former chairman of Arthur D. Little/ Cambridge Consultants, suggests that if the government would like to play a role in Cambridge, then it should concentrate on removing impediments rather than taking a lead in economic development. While the government has, for the most part, stayed out of Cambridge, it still takes a keen interest. The local heroes keep in very close contact and have an influential access to key government officials, possibly more so than in other regions. They suggest that mobilizing key individuals in other regions may well be a successful tool to create constructive dialog between entrepreneurs and officials, and may help prevent destructive government intervention.

A major challenge to Cambridge is the issue of regional planning. Cambridge has experienced some tense interactions between local government and the business community when it has come to developing the area for physical growth. The physical infrastructure is poor, and if political problems continue to construct obstacles to growth, this could have serious effects on the future attractiveness of the cluster. Some are satisfied with the "small is beautiful" concept, which is true not only of Cambridge's physical size, but also of most of the companies that are based there. There are others who feel the need for the cluster to be able to grow and to attract big-name companies that, to date, are for the most part still absent from the Cambridge region.

CREATING AN ENTREPRENEURSHIP CULTURE

The Cambridge entrepreneurship culture is centered around the university and its long tradition of scientific innovations and international thought leadership. Until recently however, collaboration between the business and academic worlds was lacking, leaving many innovations' commercial potential underexploited. We will describe some of the key drivers that have enabled academic achievement to link with the business world to create new regional wealth for Cambridge and the surrounding county of Cambridgeshire.

BUILDING AN ENTREPRENEURIAL ENVIRONMENT AROUND A TRADITIONAL BREEDING GROUND FOR INNOVATION

During its 800-year history, the University of Cambridge has become a worldwide leader at the creation of intellectual capital — from Isaac Newton to Stephen Hawking, it has earned an unrivaled reputation for scientific achievement. The sheer quantity of scientific inventions originating from Cambridge is breathtaking, indicating the university's role as a global breeding ground for innovation.

The university's enormous intellectual potential has increasingly attracted businesses to the Cambridge region. These businesses have a natural interest in the creation of an entrepreneurial, market-focused application of what is "inside the university's heads." Peter Hiscocks of the University of Cambridge Entrepreneurship Centre comments that "most businesses today rely on the university for their intellectual capital, by collaborating with its departments for the recruitment of employees." Leading the pack at successfully creating an entrepreneurial environment that fits the Cambridge mindset, were the technology consultancies that increasingly began to settle here. Cambridge is a very intellectual environment. Many students eventually feel so at home that they take on positions within the university after graduation, often spending their entire lives in Cambridge, enjoying the quality of life and being surrounded by similarly gifted and intellectually driven individuals. The consultancies offered Cambridge graduates just that, plus a market orientation that promised interesting financial perspectives. They created an intellectually stimulating environment, within the direct vicinity of the preferred Cambridge environment, where Cambridge graduates would be surrounded by "their kind" and would be enriched by working together with top graduates recruited from other leading universities in the world.

Lindy Beveridge has been working together with the university in order to promote the entrepreneurship environment in the region. As author of *The Cambridge Entrepreneurs — In the Business of Technology*, she emphasizes the importance of the historical element to intellectual capital in Cambridge and the consequences this has had for the development of consultancy practices in the area.

LINDY BEVERIDGE

Innovation through criticism in the pure sense of the word

An important source of innovation in Cambridge is the study of science itself. This goes back to the 17th century and the local Puritan culture: the belief that one had to save one's soul by a long and arduous process, in which one was willing to be criticized by one's peers while living a sober, austere, and humble life. This is a quintessential part of the Cambridge culture that has never been lost. It gives people the right to ask any question at fundamental levels.

As opposed to certain cultures in other places, innovation in Cambridge is not an accident — it is part of the culture and the system, supporting and producing innovation at an intellectual level. It identifies interesting ideas, picks them up, and develops them. I believe that there are very few universities in the world that cultivate this kind of innovation, while I do not mean to imply that other universities cannot be successful at generating successful high-tech business. In general, universities aiming to create such a culture should try and establish centers of excellence in a relatively limited number of fields. Excellence is what I consider the whole global market in technology to be all about, it has to be there — this has to be the objective.

One of the first consultancies here was Cambridge Consultants, which mirrored this culture. Its founders had been students at the University of Cambridge and were happy to examine any new concept, to "throw it around and kick it to bits." This kind of criticism is a very crucial process for successful innovation. Once an idea has been tempered by this procedure, it has earned a kind of permission to look for the additional financial support needed for its realization. These procedures certainly happened at Cambridge Consultants, which is considered to be the grandfather of all consultancies in Cambridge.

In the meantime, the Cambridge technology consultancies have launched a large number of companies. Their special ability to nurture concepts from ideas to becoming independent businesses is based on a mindset that originates from the university and is referred to as the "research-group mindset." It describes groups of colleagues that roll out projects together — like-minded people who understand the environment and who actually want get together and work, relying on thorough support from their parent organization.

The research-group mindset furthermore implies a trust environment relating directly to individuals, without any intervening bureaucratic or hierarchical management structures. The way to accomplish one's goals in Cambridge is to become accepted within this trust environment. It is a question of becoming known and being referred by people. Personal network systems are the vehicle for this, not institutional or bureaucratic ones.

Cambridge Consultants were the first company willing to invest in a Cambridge start-up, which is considered to have been a key moment for the development of the of funding of early-stage companies in the region. ∎

As Cambridge graduates increasingly began setting up successful high-tech businesses in and around the city, the university's administration began to consider establishing links to the business world to enable a more efficient transfer of academic innovations.

CONTRIBUTIONS OF THE UNIVERSITY OF CAMBRIDGE ADMINISTRATION

The university's approach to the commercial application of research discoveries is designed to be open and non-bureaucratic. In February 1987, the General Board gave notice that the commercialization of inventions should provide a significant incentive to the individual inventor, as well as a financial benefit to the university and the corresponding university department. They therefore proposed that income received from commercial exploitation in the form of royalties, license fees, or other revenues, should be divided as follows, according to Table 11-2.

TABLE 11-2   Suggested Division of Income from Commercial Exploitation

NET INCOME	INVENTOR	DEPARTMENT	UNIVERSITY
First £10,000	90%	5%	5%
Next £20,000	70%	15%	15%
Next £20,000	50%	25%	25%
Excess over £50,000	33.3%	33.3%	33.3%

Source: "Commercial Exploitation of Inventions funded by Research Councils: Notice by the General Board, Cambridge University Reporter, March 18, 1987, www.challengefund.cam.ac.uk/docs/reporter.doc.

When entering into collaborative research programs with industry, companies are given access to the wide variety of skills and expertise available within the university and are assured of their right to use any intellectual property arising from their sponsored research for commercialization. Although the eventual publication of all research results is the norm, the university respects proprietary information and helps individuals and companies to protect new discoveries. The university's Corporate Liaison Office is an important tool supporting the transfer of technology as a portal to promote contacts between the university and industry, and to help academics find ways of commercially exploiting their research results. Leadership from the university's vice chancellor, Professor Sir Alec Broers, has furthermore played a central role in enabling commercial applications of intellectual capital. Lindy Beveridge underlines his importance next.

LINDY BEVERIDGE

The importance of leadership and the role of Sir Alec Broers at the university

In Cambridge, Sir Alec Broers is ubiquitous — he knows everyone by his or her first name and he turns up everywhere all the time. It is important to him to be involved with the business community, a behavior that is absolutely unprecedented in the history of Cambridge vice chancellors. Face-to-face meetings between the university and individuals from the business community occur considerably more frequently since Alec Broers became vice chancellor. Leading as a role model, he demonstrates the importance of such meetings by attending them himself all the time.

As a result of his personal background, Broers is able to communicate well within both the academic and the business environments, which is considered to be a key factor of his success. The university seems to be learning that Broers is unwilling to sit through baroque rituals of the past, wanting rather to deal with things in a much more direct style, adopting the perspective of business managers whenever it is needed.

What Broers personally demonstrates is a phenomenon that is increasingly proliferating throughout Cambridge — the meeting of different cultures. After his first five years in office, he is considered to have substantially altered the face of the city. He has shown leadership for example in tackling the planning issues around Cambridge, that were considered to be getting worse and worse, willing to tangle with local and central government, wafting in and out of the Cabinet Office. The president of Magdalene in Oxford complained to me that Cambridge was getting a lot more media and government attention than Oxford. I replied that this was all due to Alec Broers. If he wants to go and talk to members of the Cabinet, he does! He has a direct and interactive style with everyone within the government, business, and the university; which has been a real breath of fresh air. ■

IS CAMBRIDGE A LEADER? YES! BUT FAR BEHIND STANFORD

Hermann Hauser, one of the local heroes and founder of Amadeus Capital Partners,[9] mentions that while the University of Cambridge has undertaken considerable measures to promote technology transfer, there is a feeling that its potential is still underexploited. He illustrates this by citing that while Cambridge University has managed to create companies valued at a total of approximately $30 billion, Stanford University in California has given birth to companies valued at a total of $1.5 trillion.

Mr. Hauser attributes this to the more academic, less entrepreneurial environment in Cambridge. While he believes that there is a growing trend to move academically grown ideas into the commercial environment, he considers just getting to the bottom of things to be insufficient for success. The trend needs to be supported by various expertise such as venture capitalists, lawyers, marketing specialists, real estate, etc., of which some are still considerably lacking from the Cambridge region.

Mr. Hauser acknowledges the importance that local heroes played in the development of the entrepreneurial environment in Cambridge. Yet, he notes that their contributions to the development of the region were made possible by their strong personal affinity to Cambridge and by the fact that they had previously made enough money to act as business angels to the local community.

Regional ability to attract and retain very wealthy individuals is important for future growth. Providing attractive real estate, leisure, and educational facilities may increase the identification of ordinary people turned local heroes with a region to grow along with their success. Eventually, other heroes move to the region as well. In the end, the identification of Cambridge's local heroes with their region had its roots in the quality of life that they appreciate and wanted to see flourish in the future.

THE UNIVERSITY OF CAMBRIDGE ENTREPRENEURSHIP CENTRE: KNOWLEDGE-BASED ENTREPRENEURSHIP

The University of Cambridge Entrepreneurship Centre was established with funds from the U.K. government in the autumn of 1999. The center, which is currently seeking additional funding from the private sector, was established to develop the commercial potential of discoveries in the university. This was needed because of the poor linkages between the university and surrounding business and a lack of entrepreneurial culture within the university itself, ultimately resulting in too few spin-offs and start-ups.

The Centre's vision is to ensure that greater Cambridge becomes the leading region for knowledge-based entrepreneurship in Europe. While the objectives it has set for itself are:

- To build an entrepreneurial culture within the University of Cambridge
- To train, develop, and support the people necessary to make new knowledge-based ventures successful. The Centre wishes to make an impact on four levels:
  - ▶ University of Cambridge: identify, construct, and give support to enterprises based upon knowledge derived from the university

> East of England: provide support and counseling on entrepreneurship and the management of innovation to the business community in the region
> United Kingdom: contribute to national goals of economic growth, competitiveness and productivity
> Internationally: bring in aspiring entrepreneurs from other regions and participate in international collaboration, through which collaborators will be able to learn from each other

The Centre is active with three core areas:

1. Educational activities to inspire, build skills, and train their application through a course for graduate science and technology students called "Basics of Building a Business," a Web-based course on finance and technology ventures, a summer school, a lecture series, and business plan competitions.
2. Advice and mentoring of new ventures and entrepreneurs at early stages of development, including one-on-one advice clinics.
3. Research into best practices for the creation and development of world-class new business ventures and dissemination of the output of research as widely as possible. The Centre is working on a number of reports including a comparative study of differing approaches to supporting new technology ventures in Europe within the context of the Europe-wide PAXIS project, which is coordinated from Luxembourg.

Peter Hiscocks, the director of the Centre who comes from a business background and has started and run several companies on his own, uses the catch phrase "knowledge-based entrepreneurship" when describing what goes on inside the organization. Hiscocks sees his mission as changing the culture of the university, to encourage scientific academics to start thinking about business as well. He claims that the culture has to change in a way to make it possible and acceptable for professors to start their own businesses based on results of their research. Discouraged in the past, today professorial entrepreneurship is actively encouraged. It is now part of the university's strategy to act on its responsibility to exploit technological know-how in order to enable the creation of new business. In fact, Hiscocks describes Cambridge as having an entrepreneurial culture that is much more akin to the United States than to the rest of Europe. Cambridge has a mobile work force, an acceptance of failure, and a culture of "if you can do it, we like to see you become a success," whereas in certain European countries and other parts in England, the attitude is "oh, you made money, how horrible and dirty." In Cambridge, being successful and earning money are no longer shameful. So Cambridge is "a happening place" for innovation, making it attractive to many entrepreneurs.

A GENTLE PERSUASION TO COLLABORATE — ORGANIZING AND BUILDING THE CAMBRIDGE NETWORK

The Cambridge Network is a limited liability company that was jointly founded early in 1998 by 3i, Amadeus, Analysys, Arthur Andersen, N.W. Brown, and the University of Cambridge. All of them are shareholders and each takes a seat on the company's board. Professor Sir Alec Broers is its chairman. In March 2001, Dr. Peter Hewkin was appointed the Cambridge Network's CEO.

The network's focus is to encourage the exploitation of ideas and the birth of new ventures. Among others, it was the driving factor in the establishment of the University of Cambridge Entrepreneurship Centre, and has actively promoted the "Technologies of Tomorrow" campaign, which is designed to promote technology teaching at an early stage in the educational system.

The most important tool enabling the Cambridge Network to carry out this mission is its Web site at *www.cambridgenetwork.co.uk*, which gives general listings as well as detailed information about the activities of its members (company profile, products and services, news, job vacancies). In addition to this publicly available information, network members have access to special intranet pages, where they can exchange business advice on technology transfer. Network members are also encouraged to make suggestions to the management board in order to improve the effectiveness of the network. Via the Cambridge University Research Division, which acts as a transfer body within the Cambridge Network seeking to connect university research with outside businesses, a database covering collaborative research programs with industry and consultancies, the licensing of intellectual property, and the ongoing formation of start-up companies is provided.

Dr. David Cleevely, the managing director and founder of the consultancy Analysys,[10] is a leading authority on the digital economy who has worked with governments at a national and supranational level to create policy frameworks encouraging innovation and growth. He has advised the U.K. government on its "ecommerce@its.best.uk" report, and, most recently, contributed to government thinking on convergence and the Internet. Dr. Cleevely was also a key figure behind the development of the Cambridge Network. His explanation of the beginnings of the Network once again portray the Cambridge culture: The initial motivation for the local hero entrepreneurs who conceived and initially set up the network, was to give something back to their community by building a platform for business based on open standards.

DAVID CLEEVELY

The evolution of the Cambridge Network

It is said that the Cambridge Network is the most important thing that has happened in order to enable technological cooperation in the region. In 1997, there was a Cambridge University Local Links dinner, which Alec Broers, Herman Hauser, and I happened to attend. We started to talk about the fact that Cambridge wasn't marketing itself, after having spoken to some Malaysians who were packaging what their region had to sell and were making it sound really good. Herman Hauser at the time was already keen to invite some analysts from the U.S. to write about and publicize what was happening in Cambridge, so I decided to launch "Cambridge 2020: Meeting the Challenge of Growth."

In other regions across Europe, Munich for instance, the government would have done all of this by throwing lots of money at a marketing campaign or something similar. In Cambridge, on the other hand, it was being done because people sat around a table wanting to change something. Herman has a big sense of civic entrepreneurship about him. Later on during that same year, he called a meeting with about 30 people and the idea of marketing Cambridge came up again, this time within the context of a Web site. Herman came up with a logo and the idea of the Cambridge Network started developing. There were six founders, and all of us put in approximately $30,000 as a guarantee. When the local government asked us what they could do, we sent them away because we had already seen what they could do.

The support we have gotten from local industry has been phenomenal. Today, we can pull in more than 300 people into a Cambridge Network meeting. The Web site is the icon of the organization. It takes information from the members, and shares it with the members. The Cambridge Network itself hardly produces any of the information shown on the Web site and none of the information is commissioned. The whole thing is bound together by a structure that enables the sharing of the information in the network.

The six founders have put a lot of time and effort into the project, which has already started to help the Cambridge high-tech environment. For example, a small company recently wanted some money to hold a number of workshops, so the Cambridge Network gave them approximately $3,000, with no strings attached. For the same reason that the Internet is successful, we try to offer our members as many services as possible without charging for them, because the bigger the network is, the more use it is to everybody. Strategically, if you are confident that your network works, and you have hundreds of members, you can help anybody with anything they may need, because they will find that they prefer a sort of cooperation over an inflexible, strictly fee-driven model. ■

Adding new dimensions of entrepreneurship to Cambridge's existing innovation culture has necessitated an environment built around personal initiative and trust as opposed to third-party direction and bureaucracy. Structures that enable collaboration while respecting the individualistic character of Cambridge's scientists have been built. Once again, strong personal leadership, role models, and international success stories have proven fundamental to the successful development of entrepreneurship throughout the region.

Whereas the Bavarian government plays an important role supporting entrepreneurship in Munich, the Cambridge environment rejects government intervention almost entirely. Next we explore why Cambridge entrepreneurs are so skeptical of government aid, and which role they believe the government should play.

GOVERNMENT IN PARTNERSHIP WITH BUSINESS — THE ANTI MODEL

The nature of the Cambridge environment, in the cultural sense of the word, dictates a special relational dynamic regarding its interaction with government. Due to the general penchant for close, personal contact and the importance of mutual trust, there reigns a suspicion of intervention from the establishment. As Lindy Beveridge puts it, "This is a small, huddly community where everything happens on a face-to-face basis. Cambridge has a completely neurotic hatred and suspicion of bureaucracy in the high-tech community! They will not have anything to do with government organizations. This goes back to the 17th century; Cromwell was, after all, MP for Cambridge!" Professor Gordon Edge of The Generics Group further explains the Cambridge mindset.

GORDON EDGE

The government's role in getting things started? None.

As for the origins of the whole process, it was a kind of chain reaction. Outside of the university, there has never been any government money or any initiatives in this area. That marks it out as quite unique. You'll find that as you go around Cambridge, there is virtually no public sector activity, no defense activity, no European-type projects, practically none at all if you compare Cambridge with Sophia Antipolis, where there are a lot of EU projects. Such government intervention is a culture mismatch here.

Cambridge has always been very slow in terms of infrastructure. Many roads only have two lanes. The visions of the planners are very limited. We got involved in a planing battle with the Cambridge City and Cambridgeshire County Councils, as did the Wellcome Trust and the University Department of Animal Behaviour, but the city blocked all three applications. After three years and an appeal to the central government, we finally got permission to build according to our needs. The government appointed an inspector, who was independent and who came out with a very strong recommendation that we should be allowed to develop.

In general, whereas the government does express a great interest in what is going on, the question is, to what degree can it help us? People in Cambridge are very self-sufficient. They prefer doing it the hard way. They appreciate intellectual property, and generating cash flows, and not massive losses. It is not a culture of dependency. ■

CAMBRIDGE IN THE 21ST CENTURY

The commercial expansion of Cambridge has been a highly political issue since the 1950s. Many believed that the enlargement of the city and its infrastructure raised a considerable risk of reducing the quality of life in the area. Today, much of the local population still believes that the unique atmosphere found in Cambridge and the quality of life that it offers are being directly threatened by the high-tech sector's drive for growth.

As a result, planning officials have been restrictive and Cambridge is simply considered by many to be "full." Cambridge businesses today are confronted with some serious challenges connected with their successful development on the one hand and its limited space and infrastructure on the other, raising worries about the impact of their growth on the ease with which businesses can operate in the area. Some of these concerns are:

- House prices are going up, which leads to increased commuting and so congestion.
- Recruitment becomes more difficult because of acute competition for skilled staff in the city.
- The very character of the city becomes threatened and so entrepreneurs are deterred from moving there.

According to some of Cambridge's local heroes, the government is considered to have two key roles to play within this context:

1. Remove obstacles so that market mechanisms can function more efficiently.

2. Act as a catalyst, providing the impetus needed to get from pilot project to full-scale service.

Both of these are within the purview of central government, whereas local government only has a bearing on the second. Paul Auton, chairman of Arthur D. Little/Cambridge Consultants, affirms this.

PAUL AUTON

A constructive role for government: Remove impediments

If government wants to stimulate the formation and growth of new enterprises, it should concentrate on removing impediments rather than spending money on grants, soft loans, and providing advice. These latter might have been appropriate to development areas in Scotland, Wales, and northern England, but in Cambridge the limitation to growth is poor infrastructure. We do not lack entrepreneurial spirit, venture capital, or business advice, but we do suffer from poor transportation, lack of housing, and disjointed government — both national and local.

Government can help by putting resources into infrastructure, streamlining the planning system, and making the area as business friendly as Munich or Stockholm. Government should also invest more in universities and basic research. Finally they should remove tax disincentives. Changes to capital gains tax is welcome, but it is at the expense of great complexity and the National Insurance rules as applied to options is a disaster. ■

When governments aim to adapt their region's business environment to the imperatives of the global Innovation Economy, they need to understand that this environment needs to live up to standards of global competition. Transforming a slow-paced, and possibly regulated industrial region into a fast-paced, market-driven innovation region can be problematic for governments when implications of global technology, global competition, and other global market forces have not been fully considered. This becomes an issue especially for those regionally minded policy makers, who are traditionally used to looking inward at their region rather than positioning it within the context of global competition. *Questions of competing globally have often been dealt with by national policy makers, not regional ones.* In this context, the Cambridge model of limiting the government's role to removing impediments and letting market players drive the development of the region seems appropriate. However, the greater the extent of the change required for its transformation, the more difficult it will become for private business to drive the change for any given region. The example of Munich has shown us that the government was important to create certain initial sparks that lead to the development of innovation centers, high-tech clusters, and technology platforms. Bavarian State Minister Erwin Huber clearly stated that the role of his government was to merely create an environment in favor of innovation and entrepreneurship, but not to take the lead in the region's development. Benefiting from its world-class university and its "small is beautiful" orientation, Cambridge may indeed accomplish its transition to the global Innovation Economy without much government support. In other regions around the world the case may not be as simple.

ENDNOTES

1. "The Cambridge Phenomenon 1985," SQW Economic Development Consultants, *www.sqw.co.uk*.

2. University of Cambridge, *www.cam.ac.uk*.

3. Cambridge Silicon Radio, *www.cambridgesiliconradio.com/indexf4.htm*.

4. Cambridge Network, *www.cambridgenetwork.co.uk*.

5. Ablett, Broers, Cleevely et al., "Cambridge 2020: Meeting the Challenge of Growth," Analysys Publications, 1998.

6. University of Cambridge Entrepreneurship Centre, *www.cec.cam.ac.uk*.

7. Cambridge Consultants Limited, *www.camcon.co.uk*.

8. Generics Group, *www.generics.co.uk*.

9. Amadeus Capital Partners Limited, *www.amadeuscapital.com*.

10. *Analysys*, www.analysys.com.

❱ *About the Author*

This chapter was co-authored by **Philip Heimann**. He studied management at ESCP-EAP European School of Management in Paris, Oxford, and Berlin, has worked for the consulting firm A.T. Kearney and is currently preparing his doctoral thesis on linking corporate and regional innovation systems. Philip currently resides in Berlin, Germany.

CHAPTER

12 SOPHIA ANTIPOLIS — TECHNOLOGY PARK THE "FRENCH WAY"

FRANCE — A COMPETITIVE HIGH-TECH ENVIRONMENT

In the fast-paced world of global high-tech markets, France retains the legacy of a "joie de vivre" attitude and a cultural emphasis on fashion, art, and haute cuisine. However, the country has much to offer in terms of high tech as well. With 59 million inhabitants and a geographical location at the heart of the European Union, which is the world's largest trading area, France boasts the world's fourth-largest economy, as measured by GDP. Today, over 8,000 non-French firms operate in the country, attracted by its very high-quality high-tech labor force, excellent facilities in R&D and its fairly low wage levels. Wages in the hardware industry in France, for instance, are lower than those in Belgium, the U.K., and Germany.[1]

French engineering schools are recognized throughout the world for the quality of their graduates, and nearly 40% of all higher degrees awarded in France are in the fields of engineering and science — the highest percentage in Europe. High-tech intellectual capital in France is created by its 33 higher educational institutions specialized in IT, 25 specialized in electronics, and 19 specialized in telecommunications. French high-tech companies actively invest for future competitiveness by devoting more than 40% of total payroll costs to employee training. Despite the government's efforts to decentralize

French commerce starting in the 1980s, 60% of French engineers reside in the greater Paris area, while a further 11% live in the Rhône Alpes region.

France has more than 40 science parks and a wide range of top-level research facilities. The French government has traditionally attached a high priority to R&D. High-tech companies benefit from the state-run research through institutions such as CNRS (National Center for Scientific Research), INRIA (National Institute of Research in Computer Science and Automation), CNET (National Center for Telecommunications Studies), and others, which actively collaborate with companies and universities.

Among the science parks in France, Sophia Antipolis exemplifies the French vision toward its participation in the global Innovation Economy. Over the past 30 years, Sophia Antipolis has presented officials with a challenging struggle and success was not assured. Yet, in understanding the role of government in partnership with business in Sophia Antipolis, one can learn from an approach to the commercial development of science that is very different from what has been profiled in the Munich and Cambridge chapters.

SOPHIA ANTIPOLIS — A FRENCH HIGH-TECH VISION COME TRUE

In 1960, the French newspaper *Le Monde* published an article written by Senator Pierre Laffitte titled "Le Quartier Latin aux Champs," or "The Latin Quarter in the Fields." Partly inspired inspired by observations made while visiting the United States, Sweden, the U.K., and France, his theory was that creativity is born through the exchange between industrial, scientific, philosophical, and artistic minds. There is an ancient Roman and Greek legacy to integrating knowledge from multiple fields in the arts and sciences. Laffitte believed this mindset was required to enable an inspirational cross-fertilization severely lacking in France and many other European countries. In France, he saw an environment in which industry, universities, and research centers were scattered about randomly, and where individuals were increasingly taught to become specialists at the expense of having the perspectives of classic "all-rounders." It took Laffitte many years to realize his vision of a tri-polarity of research, academia, and industry. Today, this vision takes on the physical form of Sophia Antipolis, the science park in the south of France, less than half an hour from the Mediterranean Sea, and the southern suburbs of Paris, London, and Munich, which has become France's leading high-tech region.

TABLE 12-1   Facts at a Glance — Sophia Antipolis

Area	2,300 hectares (1/4 of the area of Paris), 2/3 of which are reserved as green space
Companies	1,300, 25% are involved in IT, providing 50% of the jobs
Employment	About 40,000
Students	5,000 in five universities and higher educational institutions
Research	4,000 public researchers in more than 50 institutions
Key activities	Information technology (especially databases and telecommunications), life sciences, material and energy sciences
International population	52% executive employees, 40% of which are foreign. 63 nationalities represented, 110 foreign-owned companies, representing 25% of the 25,000 jobs. Very dynamic foreign communities, many services for foreigners, many international schools
Infrastructure	Nice airport, 18 km from Sophia Antipolis, is the second-largest international airport in France, with 45 airlines serving 90 direct destinations worldwide including direct flights to New York
Environment	9 million tourists yearly at the Côte d'Azur, half of them of foreign origin

Sources: Côte d'Azur Development Agency Facts and Figures brochure; Côte d'Azur Development Agency's Web site, www.investincotedazur.com.

REALIZING THE VISION OF SOPHIA ANTIPOLIS

The Côte d'Azur is renowned as a tourist destination for its Mediterranean climate with hot summers and mild winters. The first international high-tech companies to move here were IBM and Texas Instruments. They located R&D centers in the area in the early 1960s, taking advantage of both the quiet, pleasant environment and an abundance of sunshine, which was considered conducive to research and innovation, and the convenience of nearby Nice airport.

The Côte d'Azur region has traditionally attracted many individuals who sought inspiration. It is a truly beautiful place with mountains, sea, and long stretches of coastline. Artists such as Monet, Renoir, Cézanne, Gaugin, Van

Gogh, Matisse, Picasso, Magnelli, Braque, as well as writers such as Hemingway, Fitzgerald, Huxley, Gide, Mansfield, and Lawrence, and modern day pop-stars such as Tina Turner and Elton John have all flocked to the region.

Intending to capitalize on the inspirational aura and international accessibility of the region, Pierre Laffitte initiated the Sophia Antipolis Foundation.[2] Toward the end of the 1960s, the Foundation bought 140 hectares of land using private funds. It was named Sophia Antipolis, and became Europe's largest technological park, located 9 kilometers north of Cannes, and dubbed "the California of Europe." The name Sophia Antipolis was chosen by Pierre Laffitte. Sophia coming from the Greek word for wisdom, and Antipolis coming from Antibes, the name of the nearest town. Local authorities were invited to join in the 1970s and governement help began in 1976.

Originally, only a few companies and institutions settled in the park. Its growth was constant in percentage (30% per year) from the beginning. During the 1980s, up to 185 companies per year located in Sophia Antipolis. The high-tech park developed its image and its brand, and as it started reaching a critical threshold of participants, it was able to draw more and more companies, research centers, and educational institutions to the area. Of course, with the current economic downturn, the growth is down to about a 10% annual increase.

Initially, the different players from industry, research, and education had the habit of working separately, almost in isolation from each other. The Foundation team developed academic, business, engineering and artistic events every week over a period of years, in order to change the sociological and cultural habits. Recently, Sophia Antipolis has seen numerous initiatives and projects, which, by linking different players and creating synergies from their expertise, have helped to lead the way toward a more substantial cross-fertilization. Nonetheless, a vital ingredient of Pierre Laffitte's vision of inspiration and creativity is still partly missing from Sophia Antipolis: the integration of art, the humanities, and philosophy, which he regards as critical in order to create a full picture of human knowledge. Steps have been taken in the right direction, but Laffitte himself is not yet satisfied. But in the fields of innovation, and modern economic spirit, success is complete.

Following Laffitte's vision, two-thirds of the park's area was to remain as green space, none of the buildings were allowed to be constructed taller than the hills that directly surrounded them, and no fences or walls were allowed. He believes that mushroom collectors ought be able to wander about freely and without restrictions between the company buildings, collecting mushrooms and enjoying the nature as if the park had never been built. Laffitte opposed the construction of any residential buildings on the park's ground, as he intended for employees to live in the surrounding villages and towns in order to avoid the development of "engineers' ghettos." Today, Laffitte's plan is to avoid too big an expansion of the park's original outlines. As an answer to the demands for growth, he proposes constructing high-tech satellites, small Sophia Antipolis villages within the close vicinity, and thus convenient for networking and easily connectable by modern telecommunications broadband networks.

Office and accommodation space is scarce in Sophia, and the surrounding infrastructure of roads has reached its capacity. Nonetheless, the area continues to attract new high-tech business, causing the Sophia Antipolis region to be second only to Paris in terms of job creation and business growth in France. When considerable layoffs by the foreign companies in Sophia occurred due to the economic slump of the early 1990s, it was noted that the population of foreign business professionals in the area nonetheless remained constant. It became apparent that the region was a place that people liked to move to and stay in, so they were willing to look for new jobs in the region rather than to move elsewhere.[3] The area offers a comprehensive infrastructure for foreign employees, including international schools, country clubs, and other international organizations; in short, the infrastructure needed to attract and retain an international community. Sophia's population consists of 63 different nationalities.

PIERRE LAFFITTE

The Latin quarter in the fields — Building a high-tech metropolis from scratch

Cross-fertilization is difficult to construct. It requires a lot of commitment and an organization that takes charge. In Sophia for instance, we have organized a breakfast once a month for the past 30 years where we discuss topics of general interest. The myth of Sophia has probably helped its successful development. This myth has attracted risk-takers from all over the place.

I believe that the people who originally came were attracted by the quality of life and the new concept. After a certain time, the corporate managers realized that the productivity, the number of publications, and even the number of patents created in Sophia Antipolis were somewhere around 20% to 30% higher than in comparable regions and certainly a lot higher in relative terms than in the Paris region. People needed to become aware of this because relative advantage is not something that you can "see." Cross-fertilization and conviviality — sources of creativity — are not written on a wall in red paint — they are in the air.

The concept of Sophia Antipolis was not originally part of the French business culture. In the beginning, we attracted the large technology companies and went step-by-step from there.

What is cross-fertilization?

Cross-fertilization occurs when a solid state physicist, a specialist in chemical aromas, and a butcher meet and try to find a solution to some problem. Sophia is still lacking the butcher, or at least the butchers in the area don't have the required state of mind. Sophia doesn't have a suitable city center that is required for this to happen. Nonetheless, there is a lot of networking going on. Just recently, I set up a Franco-Indian club so that the Indians in the region would have a better opportunity to meet and so they would feel more at home. Soon we will create a Nordic Sophia club! This is an important factor for cross-fertilization. As soon as they feel at home, they will start to exchange ideas and thoughts between the different companies that they work in.

I think that every region must think hard in order to exploit each and every possibility for networking and to have a lot of networking events. Many people ask me, "How are you organized? There are so many clubs and associations in Sophia, can't you just regroup them all under one umbrella organization?" I tell the people that this would contradict what we are actually trying to achieve, which is spontaneity, diversity, and organic developments.

Indeed, the development of Sophia took 30 years. However, when we celebrated our 20th birthday 10 years ago, we invited many Americans who were amazed at how we managed to attract so many companies to an area that had practically been a "desert" before. Surely, I was an optimist when I estimated that Sophia would have 20,000 people 20 years after its foundation. However, 30 years after its foundation, it is near to 40,000.

I do not think we should grow much further because this would provoke certain bottlenecks such as constant traffic jams that would compromise the actual reason why everyone is here: the quality of life. We will naturally grow a little bit, but in terms of real growth, we will have to build satellites around the core of Sophia and employ teleworking technologies to link the individual players.

Of course, we would like to double the number of people that currently work in Sophia, but 100,000 jobs implies a city of 300,000 citizens. A city of 100,000 engineering jobs would imply a population of nearly one million. Urban concentration will not be necessary if we employ teleworking technologies. Otherwise, the key competitive advantage, namely the higher productivity through reduced stress, will be lost.

Getting people to properly use these technologies requires a period of training and an adjustment of management practice. As a result, millions of kilometers worth of car pollution could be spared, companies would have lower turnover rates, less days would be lost due to employee illnesses, the satisfaction at the workplace would be higher, and everyone would benefit. In a recent experiment, the efficiency of face-to-face contact between colleagues at work actually increased dramatically when they only met at the office for one day a week and worked apart for the rest of the week.

Anyway, I am convinced that cross-fertilization works better with hundreds than with thousands of people in one place. I am convinced of the fact that the huge First Tuesday events in Paris are less efficient than the smaller start-up club events that we have in Sophia. Here, the people know each other, there is a greater feeling of proximity. I think there is a critical mass of people that should not be exceeded in order to optimize cross-fertilization.

A marker in one hand and a cup of coffee in the other

Of course, physical distance matters. The R&D center of a big company in the United States hired MIT to conduct a study for them to find out how the level of contact between people was affected by their distance from each other at work. The first thing the study found was that the level of contact was highest when the people were sitting right opposite each other in the same room. How surprising! However, the study interestingly also found that the distance between individuals increased incredibly when people were sitting on a different floor. The results corresponded to being 300 meters away from each other. This distance could be reduced if there was visual contact between the different floors. The distance again increased considerably if people were located in different buildings even if they were located right next to each other. This corresponded to a distance of approximately one kilometer!

The company responded to the study by constructing a building with two floors and a stairway that allowed visual contact between them. Also, they placed a coffee machine on one of the floors with a blackboard right next to it. It worked! Soon, engineers from the different floors could be seen discussing problems with a marker in one hand and a cup of coffee in the other!

In the beginning, I forbade companies in the park to have their own cafeterias. This rule was adopted, and now you have groups of people from different companies in exchange over lunch, even if they have their own cafeteria! Also, I systematically insisted that groups of students visit the park in order to show them that there are no physical barriers, that one can freely walk around among the companies, and that there is nothing mysterious about it. Concerning the new interdisciplinary campus they are currently building in Sophia, I predict that even though the planners conceived it for increasing proximity, the different university departments will still be confined to their own buildings, which is a mistake. Twenty years ago in Chinese universities, students and professors were permitted to enter only their own faculty's library. They were banned from all the rest. The spirit in France is still a little bit like this.

Innovation occurs when people are anti-conformist, when they think differently. I tried to locate language and arts faculties within the park, but I failed. Those that did give it a shot returned to Paris after a couple of months because they felt Sophia was too far away from where the distribution of government funds was decided and too distant from the best students. We tried to convince the University of Nice to locate an R&D center of the arts in Sophia, but we have not yet succeeded. The concept is still too new. The university is on the way with a new usage laboratory for telecom services. It is in its own interests to do this. The phenomenal potential of a center of multimedia development, for instance, is connected with artistic, humanistic, and scientific studies working together.

It is not too late for other regions to try and start their own innovations park but they should take care not to copy. One has to take into account the characteristics of each environment, which are essential for innovation, even if innovation is generally based on an open spirit and on frequent exchange between cultures and disciplines. Many events need to be hosted that invite people from other countries and regions to attend. The role of the coordinating organization should be to motivate those that wish to change something to do so. They should help the people to accomplish things rather than doing everything for them. ∎

Senator Laffitte's vision was far ahead of its time when it was first formulated in the 1970s. Today, companies, research and academic institutions, as well as regional politicians still need to be convinced of the importance of entrepreneurship. Those who have understood the implications of the global Innovation Economy are working hard to create an entrepreneurship culture in the park, as our next section indicates.

CREATING AN ENTREPRENEURSHIP CULTURE: HIGH-TECH START-UP AND SPIN-OFF CREATION IN SOPHIA ANTIPOLIS

In the beginning, the development of Sophia Antipolis was driven mainly by the large, multinational companies that used the region as a base to conduct research and development. These companies were able to transfer their research results to create commercial applications simply by extracting them from Sophia and then commercializing them through their global corporate infrastructures. Such an infrastructure, however, has been largely missing for research carried out by Sophia-based national research institutes and the ideas coming from individual entrepreneurs. In brief, the commercial potential of the science park was grossly underutilized. In order to bridge the gap between research and its commercialization, academic institutions in Sophia Antipolis have increasingly been attempting to include a broad mix of commercial, marketing, and management skills into their traditionally science-based curricula. The initiatives and projects of two educational establishments, CERAM and Institut EURECOM, both based in Sophia Antipolis, illustrate attempts to successfully transfer local technologies through cooperation between research, education, and industry in an interdisciplinary context.

Michel Bernasconi is professor of management and head of the High-Tech Entrepreneurship Chair at CERAM Sophia Antipolis, a leading management school belonging to the Nice Côte d'Azur Chamber of Commerce. The school has an international orientation, with students representing over 60 different nationalities.[4] Having been active in the fields of technology transfer and start-up creation for more than 15 years, Bernasconi spent a sabbatical leave in Silicon Valley from 1992 to 1993, examining its methods of transferring technology, by interviewing the French entrepreneurs in the area. In 1999, Bernasconi set up the High-Tech Entrepreneurship Chair at CERAM with the objectives of studying the mechanisms of creating and developing young high-tech companies in France and the worldwide, in order to develop an entrepreneurial spirit among the students at his university.[5]

His efforts include getting the attention of the international community of venture capital companies by regularly participating at an international VC summit in the region, so that the VCs will consider Sophia Antipolis start-ups for their portfolios.

MICHEL BERNASCONI

Providing the key ingredients for technology transfer

While most large companies employing CERAM students have an excellent understanding of their markets and their commercialization strategy, high-tech entrepreneurs with a technical or engineering background usually do not even know who their potential customers are or whether a market actually exists for their product or idea. Such entrepreneurs need commercial partners able to understand their technology to the point that they can actually invent the commercial problem and solve it at the same time. This implies that CERAM students, educated with the perspective of working on the transfer of technology, need to have a broad-based understanding of technology and markets in order to complement a scientist's very specific knowledge in one field of science.

Therefore, "interdisciplinarity" is the key word. This presents a huge challenge to our business school, as it requires us to bridge the considerable gap between science and business.

There is no magic recipe for turning technology into market share, but I have however been able to acquire an understanding of the essential ingredients: First, an entrepreneurial culture and spirit are needed. In order for such a culture to be created, scientists need to see success stories that have originated from within their own environment. They can then follow the example and feel encouraged to become entrepreneurs themselves with their own ideas. Second, there is a great need for information in the form of newspapers or mini-conferences, for example. The information needs to come from "within the system" and fulfill the task of explaining to anyone interested how this system works and which issues need to be addressed in order to build a company. Third, a key point for enabling technology transfer is the creation of clubs, associations, and networking.

Nonetheless, even if all of these ingredients are present within a given region, true technology transfer cannot begin until the scientists are complemented by good marketing people and managers who have a track record in the field. In Sophia, these people are far more valuable than any developer, they are a key element of the strategy. The final key success factor is funding, the need for venture capital.

Attracting investors through an International Venture Capital Summit

Since the region of Sophia Antipolis had no industrial tradition, with tourism as the only significant economic activity, there was a problem in attracting sufficient venture capital to finance emerging start-ups. The region is still in the building phase as far as venture capital is concerned. The situation has, however, been improved considerably by the decision to attract venture capitalists through the region's own International Venture Capital Summit.[6]

The summit, while being open to VC companies from all over the world, invites a specific and different country every year to discuss the dynamics of venture capital markets while meeting with Sophia-based start-ups in search of finance. The first guest country was Canada, the second one the United Kingdom, the third one Israel, and the fourth one Germany. Organized by CERAM, the fifth summit took place in December 2001. As a result of the initiative, there has been a strong increase of venture capital flowing into Sophia Antipolis. Remarkably enough, nearly 50% of the venture capital firms investing in Sophia today are foreign, with money principally being attracted from the U.S., Singapore, the U.K., Germany, and other countries from all around the world.[7]

The Summit has also helped Sophia Antipolis to create a strong global brand, dramatically improving its international awareness. Whereas the name Grenoble, belonging to another leading French technology region, is equally associated with the city of Grenoble (the region as well as its technology), the Sophia Antipolis brand is exclusively associated with the technological science park and its unique focus on cross-fertilization, giving the companies located within the park a very positive image. ■

HIGHER EDUCATION HAND-IN-HAND WITH INDUSTRY IN SOPHIA ANTIPOLIS

Ulrich Finger is director of Institut EURECOM,[8] a leading engineering school and a research center specializing in communications and networking with an emphasis on corporate, mobile, and multimedia communications. Institut EURECOM was jointly founded by the Swiss Federal Institute of Technology in Lausanne and the Ecole Supérieure des Télécommunications in Paris. The school is administered by a staff of academic and corporate professionals including individuals from the companies Ascom, Swisscom, Bouygues, France Telecom, Thales, Motorola, Hitachi Europe Ltd., Texas Instruments, STMicroelectronics, and Cegetel. The founding schools were joined by the Politecnico di Torino in 1995, and the Helsinki University of Technology in January 2001. From the outset, Institut EURECOM was intended as a prototype for tomorrow's advanced training requirements. When the institute admitted its first students in 1992, it immediately won acclaim within the international scientific community.

Ulrich Finger stresses the importance of a close relationship with industry players, and of promoting interdisciplinarity and extracurricular activities in order to educate students in a way that keeps up with the rapid pace of developments in the telecommunications sector.

ULRICH FINGER

Entrepreneurial environments need to be international

Since telecommunications in of itself is international, there is a need for students who are experienced in working in international teams and overcoming cultural and language barriers. Nationality is something you are born with, but culture is something you learn. Seventy percent of the professors at EURECOM are foreign, and 60% of the lessons are held in English. The cultural mix intensifies the development of imagination. A further, very important factor for this development is sunshine and a pleasant and inspiring environment, both of which are present in Sophia Antipolis. These were two major motives for the joint venture between the two schools of French and Swiss nationalities to locate in Sophia Antipolis.

An extremely fast-moving discipline such as telecommunications does not fit with the traditional style of teaching. A rapidly adaptable and continuously evolving curriculum is therefore a necessity. As a private university with one-third of its finance and control originating from its industrial partners, the industry largely determines Institut EURECOM's curriculum, making sure it is always in step with the latest developments in the industry. The mutually beneficial partnership with industry allows for a practical and highly applicative education centered around company projects, internships, and other forms of cross-border collaboration.

Its financial situation enables the Institute to hire first-class professors from the international market and to pay them higher wages than those paid in state-run academia. In return, EURECOM expects its professors to keep up with the pace of technological advancements, and to experiment and adapt to the applicative side of research. Unlike within a traditional university environment, EURECOM professors are evaluated on the successful application of theory, in addition to the papers they publish. Many of the school's professors are actively involved in local start-ups.

I am also aware of the need to integrate different disciplines in order to enable innovation through cross-fertilization. In early 2004, a large new interdisciplinary campus (STIC — Le Campus des Sciences et Technologies de l'Information et de la Communication de Sophia Antipolis/Nice) will open in Sophia Antipolis, bringing together different higher educational and research establishments as well as some of the entrepreneurship clubs and associations of Sophia Antipolis. Creating a "little Stanford" in the south of France is a revolutionary concept for traditional French academia, as it puts less of an emphasis on purely academic facilities, while focusing on creating a pleasant, light-filled environment conducive to an exchange of ideas, creativity, and innovation, and allowing everyone to have a broader perspective. Students and teachers of different disciplines alike will have an opportunity to interact over lunch in the marketplace and enjoy themselves on the campus' new athletic fields. The concept corresponds to the original vision of Senator Pierre Laffitte and is expected to play an important role in enabling and facilitating technology transfer in Sophia Antipolis in the near future. ■

THE PEOPLE FACTOR — HOW SOPHIA ANTIPOLIS ENSURES A SUPPLY OF HIGHLY SKILLED EMPLOYEES

The importance of quality of life in attracting highly skilled workers to a region can be demonstrated through an example put forward by Philippe Servetti, marketing director of Côte d'Azur Développement (CAD), the semi-public body responsible for promoting the area to international companies. Mr. Servetti proudly tells the story of a company that created two R&D centers simultaneously in Sophia Antipolis and in Munich. Recruitment campaigns for both locations were instantaneously run in national and international newspapers. While Sophia Antipolis received 900 applications, Munich only received 30. It is thus no surprise that the slogans "high-tech, high-life," "where business and people flourish," "Côte d'Azur, creativity in action," and "Sophia Antipolis, intelligent by nature" have been used for the promotion of the Côte d'Azur by the CAD.

Nonetheless, whereas retaining highly skilled personnel once they have come to the region has not been a challenge, attracting them to come has become a pressing issue. According to Christian Poujardieu, director of IBM in La Gaude, close to Sophia Antipolis, companies seeking to employ engineers were short of 1,000 to 1,400 graduates last year. The educational institutions of Sophia, which hold 5,000 students[9] at any given time, have been unable to satisfy the demand for qualified graduates. In order to address this shortage, the Telecom Valley association has gathered numerous Sophia Antipolis players to unite and jointly collaborate with local educational establishments as well as the local government.

Jacques Gros, president of the Telecom Valley association from 1999 to 2001 and director of IBM's e-business Solutions Center in La Gaude, believes in the need for networking and co-opetition between Sophia-based businesses in order to address the skill shortage in the area as a critical success factor for the future.

JACQUES GROS

Telecom Valley — Co-opetition and networking, e-recruitment, and m-tourism

Telecom Valley is a nonprofit, business-driven association, which was set up in 1991 by Alcatel Space, Compaq, France Telecom, IBM, Texas Instruments, and ETSI, in order to confront the issue of skills shortage in the Sophia Antipolis region. Born out of a shared need for competencies and skills, this association unites competitors in an example of co-opetition and networking that transcends the conventional competitive borders between businesses. Today, the association consists of approximately 70 members, including high-tech companies, educational and research establishments, and the local chamber of commerce.

The association identifies critical issues for the region's success and proposes solutions, which it then presents to local government or realizes through its own projects. One of the first actions of Telecom Valley has been to work together with the local universities and government to create a diploma in telecommunications. Another major project was the conceptualization of the STIC campus that is described above. Other initiatives include an annual competition on innovation in order to promote technological developments in the region, as well as the attempt to attract microelectronics schools to Sophia Antipolis. Furthermore, the association's Education and Recruitment Commission was the first in Europe to set up an e-recruitment service with Web cams on the Internet. Hiring member companies placed their job offers on the Internet, while students from selected engineering and commerce schools throughout the whole of France placed their CVs on the pages of the site. Matches were made and interviews conducted through Web cams. This initiative increased the number of hits on the Telecom Valley Web site per month[10] from 4,000 in October of 2000 to 14,000 in May of 2001.

Linking telecom to tourism

Aiming to develop major economic perspectives for the region, Telecom Valley has recently launched a project called "m-tourism," which stands for mobile tourism. The project intends to convince local government of the potential that new technologies hold even for the established tourism industry within the region. It is believed that this perspective will improve the standing that Sophia's high-tech companies have with local authorities, which are often critical of high-tech's real benefit to the region. The e-tourism project will build a bridge between the Telecom Valley mobile e-business and mobile technology centers and the region's traditional and politically powerful tourism industry.

The aim is to enable hotels and other tourist-driven businesses to personalize their product offering and to add value to their services by offering specifically targeted information, distributed via mobile technology. Telecom Valley now organizes a yearly conference on m-tourism in Nice; at its first conference in 2001, 525 people attended, and that number is expected to double for several years to come.

Hence, not only does Telecom Valley raise the awareness of the region throughout the world, it also helps to bridge the huge canyon between the local politicians and high tech. The slow process of establishing a constructive dialog between industry, regional politicians, mayors, universities, the chambers of commerce, etc. in the region and actually creating change, presents a considerable contradiction to the incredibly fast-moving world of high tech. The key to success in such an arduous process is to take things one step at a time, and to make sure that one project that is undertaken is successfully brought to a close and implemented before proceeding to the next one. A lot of trust and understanding needs to be built in the process. Achieving only one success story will broaden people's minds and prove the benefits of the high-tech industry within the region.

A major restriction to the association is the fact that all projects are undertaken by employees on a voluntary basis, in addition to their regular jobs. Meetings take place on the evenings or weekends, outside of normal working hours. Although this leads to very effective work, I consider that the appointment of some dedicated, full-time, paid project managers might increase the scope and effectiveness of the association. So far, however, a first attempt to set the association up as a profit-making company was abandoned, since its actions would have created competition between the association and some of its members. ■

Sophia Antipolis demonstrates the importance of a multi-disciplinary approach as a key ingredient of cross-fertilization and entrepreneurship. Creating an entrepreneurship environment from scratch requires many years of development and careful planning. In the case of Sophia Antipolis, large companies came first, and worked mainly in isolation. Later on, they were joined by national research institutions and then by educational faculties. Not until 30 years after its foundation did the park begin to develop the modern networking structures that have become the norm in high-tech regions such as Silicon Valley in the U.S. We next discuss how French national interests once claimed a monopoly on entrepreneurship, and describe a perspective on possible future state monopolies in the information economy.

ENTREPRENEURSHIP FOR THE NATION!

Early on, it was considered important by French national government that its research institutions should be actively promoting the transfer of research results. Scientists were encouraged to innovate and develop new technologies to benefit the economic and political position of the French nation within a global context. Examples for this activity in Sophia Antipolis include the research institute INRIA[11] (Institut National de Recherche en Informatique et en Automatique, or the French National Institute for Research in Computer Science and Control).

Gérard Giraudon is director of INRIA's Development and Industrial Relations Department. As a national research institution, INRIA has been a pioneer in technology transfer and spin-off creation, demonstrating the interest that the French government has taken in the field. Mr. Giraudon explains that the French phenomenon of entrepreneurship is indeed very much driven by the motivation to contribute to the international competitive position of the French nation.

GÉRARD GIRAUDON

INRIA — Rallying in support of entrepreneurship in France

In the beginning, the only way to convince the government to support the development of an entrepreneurial environment was to prove to them that this environment would benefit them directly. Also, since the population in the Sophia Antipolis region wasn't convinced of hosting high tech, let alone having high-tech entrepreneurship in the region, it took some time until the first financial investments were directed away from the traditional engineering schools and into Sophia. The money eventually came, since it was apparent that without students on the site, the business park would not be able to succeed. Therefore, the arrival of academic research institutions such as INRIA was vital for the future success of Sophia Antipolis. Finally in 1983, INRIA was established, at a time when Sophia was still nascent, in line with Senator Laffitte's vision for innovation and advanced research through synergy between education, research, and industry.

However, before this synergy could begin to take place, the barriers of convention had to be broken. In 1980, Jacques-Louis Lions, a famous mathematician who was the director of INRIA at the time, decided to structure INRIA into different focus areas with project teams in order to enable the eventual commercialization of certain technologies. To gather support for his entrepreneurial innovation initiative, he considered that applied mathematics was a strategic issue for France and thus built a consultancy tool for the French industrial companies. For this purpose, an independent company named Simulog was created as a subsidiary of INRIA with the explicit aim of serving the state through this new technology. From this time on, INRIA was seen as an institute willing to work for the state, for the common good of the country. This proved to be a small revolution within research institutions at the time; the spirit of creating companies didn't exist and was, in fact, frowned upon by other academics. Therefore, the idea of an institute maintaining a high level of research and at the same time an industrial aim, was something that was practically unheard of.

I believe that the only reason this industrial aim fell barely within acceptable limits was that the company was created purely to benefit the French nation. Lions' Simulog initiative did not follow any type of business development model. It was purely directed toward serving the state as a tool to warrant the independence of the French nation against the implicit threat of U.S. domination. Lions had no personal interest in creating this company, other than the interest of seeing his research implemented.

Obviously, this model for entrepreneurship was in stark contrast to the traditional U.S. model, where new businesses are created as individual businesses aiming for shareholder value, personal achievement, and wealth, which reflects a much more individualist culture. The spirit of serving the nation is still present in INRIA today.

Within this context, the role model effect that developed when Lions decided it was all right to start a company is considered to have been of critical importance. In addition, since INRIA's employees were employees of the state, I cultivated the "elastic effect," under which anyone who tried to start a business but failed could return to his or her original job with the institute at any time. Especially in a transitional period in which individuals might be unsure about the risks of starting a company, this factor was an important contributor to the center's spin-off creation success. The opportunity was thus made interesting in terms of both human experience and financial gain, while the leap of leaving the secure environment of the public institution even with the awareness of the risk of failure could be supported.

Today in France, even in the private sector, the case of someone having attempted to create a business by taking a risk is generally seen as a positive thing. People learn by making mistakes. This outlook is a new development in the French culture. I believe more in company creation by "seniors" aged 40 to 45 with serious scientific backgrounds. When trying to assemble teams for a company launch, you need to address younger people and older people using a different language, since their motivations are usually different. Young people often have their own network. They have just finished school and have friends from different fields. Older scientists usually have a different type of network. Therefore, integrating different age groups in a start-up company creates a dynamic and interesting environment. ■

THE FUTURE OF EUROPE'S INDUSTRIAL GIANTS

In the race of the regions to develop the critical mass of successful high-tech activities needed to compete on a global scale, companies and governments alike must take into account the existing strengths and opportunities of their regions. Building on what already exists may prove more fruitful than trying to create something entirely new. The time factor should not be neglected in this context. Sophia Antipolis took 30 years to develop (with much acclaim), Munich has been a technology capital for close to 50 years, and Cambridge has been a worldwide leader in science for hundreds of years.

Whether the European industrial giants Germany, the U.K. and France will ever catch up to Silicon Valley remains to be seen. In any case, they each like to claim that they are serious competitors of their U.S. role model. Germany, the U.K., and France have each undertaken considerable measures to plug into the Innovation Economy. Entrepreneurship cultures are increasingly taking hold, and governments are repositioning to enable their economies to compete in the 21st century.

ENDNOTES

1. Institute National de la Statistique et des Etudes EconomiquesInstitut National de la Statistique et des Etudes Economiq (INSEE), *www.insee.fr*.

2. Fondation Sophia Antipolis, *www.sophia-antipolis.org*.

3. Material taken from the author's interview with Michel Bernasconi, CERAM.

4. CERAM Sophia Antipolis, *www.ceram.edu*.

5. CERAM Sophia Antipolis, High-Tech Entrepreneurship Chair, *www.ceram.edu/v1/site_fr/esc/chaire-entr.htm*.

6. See International Venture Capital Summit at *www.ivcs.org* for further information.

7. For further information and figures see "Le monde entier investit dans les start-up de Sophia Antipolis," May 14, 2001, a study (in French) on venture capital by Michel Bernasconi and Franck Moreau, *www.ceram.edu/site_fr/chaires/dynamis.htm*.

8. EURECOM Sophia Antipolis, *www.eurecom.fr*.

9. "Sophia Antipolis- the Right Place to Invest," leaflet published by SAEM Sophia Antipolis Côte d'Azur.

10. Telecom Valley, *www.telecom-valley.fr*.

11. INRIA, *www.inria.fr*.

▶ *About the Author*

This chapter was co-authored by **Philip Heimann**. He studied management at ESCP-EAP European School of Management in Paris, Oxford, and Berlin, has worked for the consulting firm A.T. Kearney and is currently preparing his doctoral thesis on linking corporate and regional innovation systems. Philip currently resides in Berlin, Germany.

HIGH-TECH
ISLANDS OF
TAIWAN AND ISRAEL

At first blush, it seems odd to group Taiwan and Israel together. They have different races, religions, and histories, and are on opposite ends of the farthest geographic limits of Asia.

Yet, in the Innovation Economy, Taiwan and Israel are kindred lands and spirits. Both have:

- Defied circumstances of history and achieved physical survival and economic prosperity despite great adversity. They are in perpetual danger from larger, cumbersome enemies (mainland China for Taiwan and the Arab societies for Israel).

- Created through wars in the mid-20th century. Because each society was developed through immigration in the last half of the 20th century, they do not have entrenched long-standing "sunset" industries to hold them back. Each is welcoming to change and innovation to a remarkable degree.

- Learned to be nimble, flexible, and courageous in the face of hostility. They have a special relationship for their very survival with the United States on a military basis, and special ties economically through their transnational Diaspora communities.

- Excelled at conducting business with an American edge, linking to the high-tech industries of U.S. multinational companies. While each country has its distinctive personality and character, they easily integrate into multilocation company strategies. Both economies are externally focused, seeking to transcend their limited internal national markets.

- Depended upon and have leveraged Diaspora social and professional linkages of engineers and venture capitalists who create wealth at home and in American high-tech communities where their compatriots live and work. Their extended Diaspora communities provide a great advantage to these countries in the development of start-ups as well as in the sharing of best practices and techniques. To a large degree, both Taiwan and Israel have become world-class high-tech regions because they have benefited from joint knowledge sharing and enterprise creating with these Diaspora communities.

- Developed societies that are entrepreneurial and free wheeling. They share a spirit of "anything goes" and constant innovation to stay ahead of the technology curve.

- Derived from ancient religions and peoples, who venerate knowledge and education. Neither have significant natural resources, but look to their human knowledge capital as the source of their well-being. Both have utilized their university systems as engines for societal and economic benefit to ensure that regional wealth will continue to be created by tapping into their great reservoir of human intelligence and ingenuity.

13 TAIWAN
TECHNOLOGY
PARKS AND NGOs

T aiwan is a great example of a region dedicated to the enhancement of the quality of life for its citizens through participation in the Innovation Economy. It is a very strong high-tech market. While it lacks land and natural resources, it more than makes up for these inhibiting factors with some terrific strengths in its societal culture: hard work, propensity to save, entrepreneurial orientation, and the capacity to engage in risk-taking activities.

Taiwan attracts great venture capital streams to its industries, so there is plenty of ready capital for both infrastructure investment and business development. It has a highly educated population and an international perspective, which makes it easy for foreigners to work and establish business relationships. It has a great supply of high-tech management professionals who have many years of experience in manufacturing.

There is close collaboration between high-tech companies and universities. Universities integrate their curriculum into the high-tech industry through the relationship of the schools with high-tech parks. Most educated Taiwanese are well-versed in English and they use English-version textbooks in colleges and universities. The science-based knowledge and education system is a good fit with technology and problem-solving innovation.

Taiwan has a strong work ethic and its highly skilled, quality-driven work force is a major competitive advantage. This region has focused step-by-step to develop a high-tech industry as a national priority. The tax and incentive system from the government is highly favorable for the kind of capital investment, profit, and legal regulations necessary to enable high tech to thrive. The Taiwan government supports but does not try to directly control investment decisions in the high-tech economy as Singapore and mainland China do.

Taiwan has very close interaction with Silicon Valley and is a good example of a completing region. It has not tried to replicate Silicon Valley, but rather link into it with a great deal of joint research and development, business creation, and manufacturing activity.

Taiwan has transformed itself from a low-cost manufacturing hub to a high value-added manufacturing center for the worldwide Innovation Economy. It is the preeminent region of the world for integrated chip (IC) manufacturing. The Taiwan foundries are manufacturing specialists who are subcontracted by the major semiconductor companies. These foundries, such as $5 billion Taiwan Semiconductor Manufacturing Company (TSMC), focus purely on manufacturing, slashing costs through economy of scale. Through aggressive investment, research and development, and the advantage of the experience curve in manufacturing, Taiwan has developed chip-making technologies on par with Japan, and at a lower cost. So, many firms worldwide design and sell chips without having to build factories because they outsource the manufacturing to Taiwan.

TABLE 13-1   Facts at a Glance — Taiwan

Population	22,369,000
Gross national savings rate in 1999	20%
GNP growth rate in 1999	5%
Government funding of all R&D investment in 1999	38%
Increase in per capita GNP from 1993 ($10,954) to 2000 ($14,188)	30%
Unemployment rate in 2000	3%
Post high school education institutions in 2000	150 with 1.1 million students
Percent of GNP by sector in 2000	Manufacturing 26%, and service 65%
Number of companies operating in Hsinchu Park in 2000	287
Percent of sales by integrated circuits in tech park in 2000	61%
Number of employees in Hsinchu Park	102,000
Average age of employees in Hsinchu Park in 2000	31 with 16% having post-bachelors degrees

Sources: Government of Taiwan Council for Economic Planning and Development; Hsinchu Science-based Industrial Park administration.

When the information technology markets in the U.S. and Europe have a downturn, Taiwan is especially hard hit. Taiwan also faces a special challenge in its relationship with mainland China. There is an emerging partnership between the two adversaries in the mutual development of manufacturing capabilities. Much of the lower-end manufacturing that depends on cheap wages and lower working conditions have moved from Taiwan to China. Taiwan is now faced with similar problems as Ireland in that the cheap labor, land, and differential tax advantages are largely gone. So now the Taiwanese have to be very aggressive in maintaining their advantage as a magnet for investment and manufacturing.

By upgrading Taiwan's technology and investment and making its industry distinct from mainland China, the Taiwan government hopes to avoid the trap of de-industrialization. So, they would like to position Taiwan as a global center for high value-added manufacturing.

The Economic Development Advisory Council (a government industry partnership)[1] has identified six areas of support systems to achieve this objective:

- Creative research and development
- Cargo storage and transshipment centers
- Venture capital investment mechanisms
- Supply-chain management networks
- High-tech industry capital accumulation systems
- Value-added financial service systems

One of the jewels in the crown of Taiwan's success is the Hsinchu Science-based Industrial Park (HSIP), which is a great example of public/private and university partnership making wealth for the region. Since it opened in 1980, the Taiwan government has invested almost $800 million in the Park's infrastructure and administration. HSIP is a great example of a home-grown park with international linkages for companies in the Park as well as international companies into Taiwan.

Hsinchu Science-based Industrial Park (HSIP)

Hsinchu Science-based Industrial Park is located 70 kilometers from Taipei and is the hub of technology industry in Taiwan. The combined sales of companies within the Park is $30 billion (2000), making it one of the most successful technology parks in the world. The six sectors concentrated in the

HSIP are integrated circuits, computers and peripherals, telecommunications, optoelectronics, precision machinery, and biotechnology.

TABLE 13-2   HSIP Industries in 2000

INDUSTRY	COMPANIES	EMPLOYEES	SALES ($ MILLION)	GROWTH (%)
IC	116	61,288	18,496	67
Computers/peripherals	49	16,064	6,815	8
Telecommunications	50	7,334	1,628	28
Optoelectronics	44	16,167	2,595	61
Precision machinery	12	1,351	233	55
Biotechnology	18	636	36	75
Total	289	102,840	29,803	46

Source: HSIP administration, April 2001.

HSIP is envisioned to be a self-sustaining society, containing industrial, residential, and recreational areas. Besides the standard plants built by the government and the factories built by the companies in the Park, a clinic, a post office, a customhouse, banks, warehouses, and truck depots are all located in the Park.

The Park administration is operated under the auspices of the National Science Council, which is a Taiwan government agency.

UNIVERSITIES ARE INTEGRATED INTO THE PARK

The Park is located close to both National Tsing Hua University and National Chiao Tung University. National Tsing Hua University is a multidisciplinary university, including six colleges, 8,021 students, and 509 professors. Meanwhile, National Chiao Tung University has five colleges, 9,188 students, and 554 professors. Both facilities provide the Park's companies with excellent human resources as well as strong support for professional training.

As of the end of 2000, the Park employed 102,840 people, approximately 62% of whom had at least a college degree. Meanwhile, the average age of the employees was 31. Returned expatriates, mostly from the U.S. accounted for 4,108 people. Historically, expatriates have played a critical role in the Park's activities, owing to the technologies and business concepts they brought back, which were further developed to promote the development of high-tech industries in Taiwan.

The Park's integration of universities, research institutes, and diversified high-tech companies makes it the Asian version of Silicon Valley in the United States. Dr. James Lee is director general of HSIP. He shares his perspective on how the role of government has evolved and the relationship with universities in HSIP.

JAMES LEE

The evolution of the government's role in HSIP

HSIP was developed by the government to provide a better environment for investors with improved infrastructure and facilities, such as streamlined administrative procedures and convenient bank loans. The government was acting as the guide to point out the main direction to go for industries in the private sector in the early stage of the development of the science park. Initially, the government set the rules of the game in this science park through legislation to ensure a fair game for all participants interested in high tech in the future. The government was also promoting some privileges and incentives to encourage those daring pioneers to march into the unknown frontier. As an added sweetener, the government tried to build up the business connections for local forerunners with major international financing groups to open up the local economy to the worldwide theater. Currently, the government is acting merely as the administrator of the science park because the fervency for high-tech investment has become prevalent in Taiwan.

Economic downturn greatly affects HSIP, but rebound will be felt quicker as well

Taiwan is experiencing an economic downturn recently mainly because of the slowdown in 2001 of the worldwide economy after years of overheating. Taiwan's high-tech industry is highly related to the market in North America. The 9/11 tragedy worsened the global economy with 50% decline (in the quarter from October to December 2001) to Hsinchu Science-based Industrial Park. However, Taiwan's high-tech products have been moving up in the hierarchy ladder from downstream assembly to upstream materials and components over the decade (65% of worldwide notebook PCs and more than 80% of flatbed scanners are from Taiwan, including name brands like Sony, Toshiba, IBM, Compaq, HP, Dell, Hitachi, Sharp, and Epson). This move-up narrows the time lag between the modulation of local economy and that of North America. The IC foundry industry in HSIP is especially closely associated with major clients such as AMD, Cyrix, S3, Xilinx, Altera, Infineon, etc., thus being able to forecast the rebound sooner. Major industries (IC, PCs and peripherals, telecommunications, optoelectronics, precision machinery, biotechnology) in HSIP are climbing uphill at slow speed with confident paces since the third quarter of 2001. An expected recovery of the U.S. economy will boost the rebound of local high-tech industry with greater momentum.

HSIP is expatriate friendly, and they add great value to our industries

The infrastructure and the environment of HSIP were developed to be amicable to "expatriates" (those college graduates who went to North America for post-graduate degrees and stayed there many years). We seek to recall them to come back for their own ventures. They bring great value by introducing the international business protocol along with their managerial experience from those global giants like AT&T, IBM, HP, and Xerox. This improves the internationalization of local business practice. The IPO (initial public offering) of Park companies at local stock exchanges encourages entrepreneurship and also modernized local approaches to the manufacturing sector from traditional labor-intensive manufacturing. The streamlined administrative efficiency of HSIP is vital to attract high-tech investment. The joint effort between the academics and the research institute is also vital to the success of local IC industry. There are 35 spin-offs based upon technologies from ITRI (Industrial Technology Research Institute) in HSIP to form the clustering effect in IC industry.

The universities are our partners

The site of HSIP was intentionally chosen to be near the two major national universities (Tsing-Hwa University and Chiao-Tung University) for their talent resource. Today, those university graduates have become the natural source of supply of engineers and management. Sixteen Park companies were founded based on the ideas originated from incubators for new companies on both campuses. Founders and entrepreneurs share their experience in the classroom to remind those young minds that the real world is somewhat different from the theories in the textbook. Intensive programs leading to professional certificates were also taught by professors or senior officers of Park companies on campus for those students or workers with career ambition. Talent tournaments are offered by companies and held on campus to seek the fittest. Professors get projects closer to the real world from Park companies with grants to sustain further interests. ■

RESEARCH AND DEVELOPMENT IS A HIGH PRIORITY

One benchmark of a region's commitment to quality and focus on moving up the value chain in innovation technology is the level of investment in research and development. The HSIP companies collectively show a great commitment to R&D. This high level of investment is all the more admirable given the cutthroat price competition Taiwanese companies engage in to attract manufacturing contracts.

In addition to government grants, The Park's companies spent $1.2 billion on R&D in 1999, representing about 6% of sales revenue for the year. The figure compares favorably with only 1% investment in R&D from the Taiwan manufacturing industry in general. The IC industry accounts for $882 million in R&D investment, representing 71% of total HSIP R&D investment. The Science Park has over 10,000 researchers, which makes it one of the most innovation intensive as well as fast-growing revenue parks in the world.[2]

To get some perspective from an insider in the IC industry in HSIP, we sought out a leading company in the Park and chose Winbond Electronics Corporation. Winbond Electronics is the largest brand-name IC supplier in the Taiwan IC industry. Its focus is in process technology, worldwide marketing networks, and wafer processing. Established in 1987 in HSIP, Winbond's areas of expertise include R&D, design, process, manufacturing, marketing, and customer service, focusing on digital consumer, multimedia, communication, non-flash memory, and computer logic ICs as well as SRAM and DRAM products. It has 4,000 employees in the U.S., Hong Kong, Singapore, Europe, and Japan with over $1.4 billion in sales. It is a fast-growing company, almost tripling sales volume between 1995 and 2000.

Mike Liu, public relations manager for Winbond Electronics, provides his perspective on HSIP and the reasons for success for high-tech companies in Taiwan.

MIKE LIU

**Agility, flexibility, and communication are
essential for manufacturing with MNCs**

We had already moved from mass production in Taiwan to worldwide resource leverage in multinational subsidiaries. We have to be flexible and agile in decision making and information sharing. Communication plays an important role as a connection of multinational subsidiaries for the companies of the HSIP. The internal network system eases the flow of information to every office, which speeds up the workflow considerably. This enhances our capability to quickly respond to the rapidly changing environment and make quick decisions to adopt the competitive marketplace.

Multilocation use of technology makes this business possible

We have about 200 people doing R&D and sales functions at Winbond America. Via our intranet, we use the same platform to discuss the design of IC board, which allows us to interact simultaneously. The communication channels through videoconference, and our company mirror site helps our employees share updated information easily and speed up the product life cycle. The virtual company communication channels are the key for multinational corporations in the HSIP to leverage resources worldwide and maintain the competence. ∎

While homegrown companies, such as Winbond, have achieved great success in HSIP, multinational companies have also thrived in Taiwan and greatly appreciate the concentration of experience, talent, innovation, and expertise in the Park.

The success of Taiwan's industrial development took a long time and was affected by both internal societal factors as well as external influences from Japan and the United States. To get that perspective and the reasons for HSIP success we sought the opinion of Alexander Huang, regional director of Greater China, Microsoft Taiwan.

ALEXANDER HUANG

Historical success factors of HSIP

There are three important reasons for the success of HSIP:

1. Timing
2. Government support to create the environment
3. Human resources

First, the HSIP was developed at a relatively competitive time, when the semiconductor industry was not yet popular. With the four competitive capabilities (land, know-how, capital, and quality), the HSIP already started to develop its own style of foundry wafers about 20 years ago. This early timing of forming the right process has given the HSIP a perfect background to earn competitive advantage globally.

Second, the government has highly supported the development of the HSIP and created the environment that attracted Taiwanese Americans with high-tech knowledge back from the United States. The government has provided many programs, such as tax incentives and cheap land, to encourage the high-tech investment in Taiwan. The factor of government support has played an important role in transforming the HSIP from the labor-intensive 1970s, to the capital-intensive 1980s, to the knowledge-intensive 2000s.

Third, since the 1990s, the historical relationship between Taiwan and Japan, and the Japanese style of management influenced HSIP to focus on quality manufacturing as a priority, which is one of the competitive advantages of countries in Southeast Asia. This has built up many high-quality workers with strong know-how. The Taiwanese hard-working culture and high civilization are critical factors in making HSIP a success worldwide. The father of high tech in Taiwan, Lee Kuo-Din, had continually contributed to the blueprint of HSIP and built the vision for the Taiwan high-tech industry.

Through the foundation and interaction with United States, Taiwan has accumulated a strong capability to allocate capital and gain knowledge as a basis to develop its unique position in the high-tech industry.

Competency success factors for a science industry-based park

According to the HSIP experience, there are four basic factors to make a science industry-based park successful:

1. R&D
2. Finance
3. Manufacturing
4. Marketing intelligence

First, the companies in the park should focus on R&D in order to develop high-quality products. The more quality we focused upon, the higher cost advantage we gained. Customers are willing to pay more to get higher quality. As long as the standard of quality increases, we have more customers and then gain cost advantage. This principle has been the first rule in the Taiwan high-tech industry. From the OEM (original equipment manufacturing) to the C&D (copy and development) and to the ODM (original design manufacturing), Taiwan has devoted time and money in R&D to develop high quality products. This gives Taiwan companies experiences that confirm quality is the most important thing and that R&D is the fundamental to increase quality standards to attract customers.

Second, capital allocation, such as venture capital and IPO, provide a foundation. This is an important key to helping companies to emphasize R&D as a tool to increase quality standards.

Third, the structure of the industry is an important factor in determining whether it is appropriate to develop that certain industry in a science-based park. The most important competitive advantage in the Taiwan high-tech IC industry is that we are "vertically disintegrated." We have independent IC designing companies, manufacturing companies, assembly companies, and testing companies. Together, they provide a complete spectrum to fill the orders from IBM and other main corporations. We can get every component needed to assemble computers in a very short time. It takes only few hours to ship components to clients. This proximity certainly gives an advantage to speed the process of manufacturing, and definitely increases the efficiency of our services.

Fourth, to maintain the competitiveness, we leverage our capital and human resources worldwide to understand what our customers need. This helps us to work 24 hours a day, to stay agile in the changing marketplace.

Information integration and wireless communication make the multilocation business model work

Companies should realize the importance of information integration and wireless communication inside the company to speed up the flow of information and communication in this multilocation model today. We communicate in different formats, such as PDA, laptop, and mobile phone. Toward the purpose of communication anywhere and anytime, we need to establish our IT infrastructure and boost up wireless services.

A notification agency will provide the available information and sense the location (mobile phone or PDA) with different formats. This is a machine-to-machine information exchange. For example, a person has a trip to Hawaii. But he is stuck in the airport because the flight is delayed two hours. The notification agency will receive a signal from the airport network and automatically send a notice to the Hawaiian hotel and car rental company to postpone the reservation. He doesn't need to worry about whether the hotel and car rental reservation would be cancelled because the notification agency has already done the machine-to-machine communication. This is the future of IT infrastructure. We need lots of human resources and database agents to work toward this purpose.

The future development of HSIP and the transformation of corporations should consider R&D, finance, manufacturing, marketing, and IT infrastructure to be a whole. Utilization of IT integration to leverage resources, knowledge, and R&D is an important key to maintain global competitiveness. This will help a company or a park to communicate and interact closely in a multilocation marketplace. ■

The government, industry, and university partnership in HSIP demonstrates how congruent and focused the Taiwan region is. Another societal strength, derived from the Chinese culture, is an extraordinary cohesiveness and ability to work in formal and informal groups. Taiwanese venture capitalists, engineers, entrepreneurs, and other sectors have many non-government organizations (NGOs) that enable them to work together in Taiwan as well as link internationally to a Chinese high-tech Diaspora.

In addition to Chinese formal and informal networks, Taiwanese are well represented in global industrywide networks. The Taiwan region has utilized these NGOs very well for their own development. To help better understand how NGOs play a significant role along with government, corporations, and universities, we focus on SEMI Taiwan.

FOCUS ON BUSINESS ASSOCIATION SEMI TAIWAN

SEMI (Semiconductor Equipment and Materials International) is the largest business association for the semiconductor industry, with a worldwide membership of 2,600 companies. It is best known for its trade shows, which are highlight events for the semiconductor industry.

SEMI Taiwan opened its office in Hsinchu in January 1996. The SEMI Taiwan office sponsors the inaugural SEMICON Taiwan exhibition usually held in September at the Taipei World Trade Center. SEMICON Taiwan is primarily a local show, however it draws attendees from most of Southeast Asia and other parts of the world and is now the world's fourth-largest industry exposition.

The worldwide semiconductor industry is a $142 billion market. Taiwan's semiconductor revenue is about $14 billion or 10% of worldwide sales. The semiconductor capital expenditure for 1999 in Taiwan was $5.5 billion, representing over 20% of worldwide expenditures.[3] This verifies the enormous commitment to invest in capital plant and equipment in Taiwan.

Semiconductors are a vital sector to the Innovation Economy. Taiwan is a dominant player in the global information technology industry, with major market share in the manufacturing of PCs and peripherals.

George Lin, president of SEMI in the Southeast Asia region, is responsible for operations of both the Taiwan and Singapore offices. He discusses the reasons for the extraordinary success of Taiwan in the semiconductor industry, the role trade associations play, and the reasons why the Chinese culture is particularly well suited to the Innovation Economy.

GEORGE LIN

Reversing the "made in Taiwan" stigma

Government support of high-technology manufacturing and development has clearly played an important role in the rapid growth of Taiwan's industry, especially in the development of the semiconductor foundries, a business model with its roots in Taiwan. But perhaps just as important has been a dedication to building and providing world-class manufacturing capabilities. For many years, "made in Taiwan" was a negative label, with many consumers seeing Taiwanese-manufactured goods as cheap and inferior. To overcome this, Taiwanese companies placed a significant amount of emphasis on quality and continual improvement, the same way that Japanese companies did in overcoming their own image problem of the 1960s. As Japan was able to turn its industries into models of quality and advanced technology, Taiwan too was able to prove that its companies were capable of producing electronics and other high-value products of extraordinary quality.

Taiwan and semiconductor industry are well suited to each other

The development of a full-spectrum technology industrial economy, from materials providers up to electronic systems manufacturing, has put in place a technology infrastructure that is well suited to semiconductor manufacturing. The real key to the successful development of a semiconductor industry is having the supply, support, transportation, and other infrastructure elements in place that enable lower production costs and increased productivity. The basic elements grew quickly with the development of all the different technology industries, and as semiconductor equipment and materials suppliers recognized the tremendous growth opportunities in Taiwan, their expansion and presence in Taiwan enabled the industry's development to accelerate even more.

Technology parks have made a big difference for Taiwan

The technology parks are an important and integral part of the high tech development in Taiwan. HSIP, for example, has contributed a great deal in the world of high tech; it has the longest history and occupies the largest area in Taiwan. In recent years, another park has been developed in Tainan, a southern city on the island. It will have the newest facilities and convincing scale in all respects. Taiwan semiconductor industry would not have been this successful, had it not been for the parks advantage. Its location, infrastructure, financial, and logistics all account for the noted success of the industry.

Business associations have an important role to play in linking Taiwan to the world

The role of an association is primarily to aid its members in expanding business opportunities, so for any industry, participation with and support of industry associations is important. For a global association such as SEMI, this is even more true as we enable growth and development of business opportunities around the world. By having a presence in Taiwan, SEMI is able to address the needs of the local industry, and by having offices, events, and services worldwide, we enable Taiwanese companies to extend their reach beyond their shores to every market where there is significant semiconductor manufacturing activity. Likewise, through our presence in Taiwan and through our industry events and trade shows, we bring the global industry to Taiwan, enabling our members from around the world to establish relationships with Taiwanese companies.

Taiwan works well with multilocation companies through Taiwan transnationals

Of course, the miracle of Taiwan's high-tech advancement did not happen just overnight. It has had its difficulties, frustrations, and obstacles over years. Isn't it true about what they say, "Success breeds success." There are a few products such as scanners, monitors, notebooks, and computer peripherals that captured the eyes of the world, largely through the pioneering efforts of those who had studied in the United States and came back in early 1980s to make an impression.

Homecoming often is a sense of feeling and calling of those whose roots are in Taiwan. As such, working on mulitple locations, multiple environments, and even multiple mindsets can easily become a second nature for the individuals involved. We should not overlook the fact that most of these engineers and companies have the Chinese and English language advantage that sets them apart from others.

There is something special about the Chinese culture

The Chinese culture is a great advantage in the high-tech industries, for these reasons:

- Willingness to contribute seems to be an in-born nature. What else can one be more proud of than to do what one feels a sense of repayment of what one owes in life? This is not patriotism per se; rather, the opportunity is right for the Chinese to stand tall after being suppressed for generations.

- There is a Chinese saying, "No matter how tall a tree grows, when it comes time for the leaves to fall, they all return to the roots." This kind of mentality, consciously or unconsciously, is in every Chinese mind. The output of such a mentality goes without saying.

- Politics aside, one can work well in all localities. China is picking up very quickly to provide opportunities for those willing to work in high tech; much more so today than in previous years. As a contrast, science and high-tech people outside China have enjoyed the freedom of working in a totally free environment, which is easily taken for granted. They enjoy the opportunity of being creative and are eager to contribute to the new economy, where one can aspire to a greater society, country, and a race on this earth. ■

Taiwan seems to always be in the forefront of change, and its people are able to make regional wealth whatever happens in the external world. It is often cited as one of the best examples of a developing country that took its economic fate into its own hands; they focused on a unique role in the world economy, leveraging the intelligence, diligence, and pluckiness of its people for their common good.

ENDNOTES

1. Republic of China on Taiwan Government Information Office, *www.gio.gov.tw*.

2. HSIP administration, April 2001.

3. SEMI Taiwan, *www.semi.org*, January 2002.

14 TAIWAN'S FINANCIAL CAPITALIZATION

THE CHINESE NETWORKING CULTURE EXTENDS TO CHINA AND BEYOND

TAIWAN'S MIRACLE

With a land area one-tenth of that of California, Taiwan manufactures:

- 80% of the world's PC motherboards
- 80% of the world's graphics chips
- 70% of the world's notebooks
- 65% of the world's microchips
- 91% of the world's scanners

Not too bad for an island with a population of mere 22 million. Yet, if asked to name any brands originating from Taiwan, most people would not be able to name too many. This is because most of the Taiwanese companies are OEMs (original equipment manufacturers). These companies most likely manufacture notebook computers from IC (integrated circuit), PCB (printed circuit board), or power supplies and casings, but the brand name on top of the casing is likely to be Dell, HP, or Compaq.

THE ENTREPRENEURIAL CHINESE

Ironically, the social status of the businessman is not high in Chinese society: Shi (scholar), long (farmer), kong (worker), shan (businessman) —

the businessman used to be regarded as the lowest trade in ancient Chinese society. For many commoners, the most effective way to rise to prominence before the 1911 revolution, which overthrew the Qing Dynasty, was through imperial examinations. Once a scholar passed the imperial examinations, he would be appointed as an officer in the imperial court. With position and power, the money would then start to come.

Toward the end of the 19th century, however, the Middle Kingdom experienced extreme instability. The invasion of the country by the Western powers in the 19th century, Japan at the beginning of the 20th century, and the subsequent civil wars have caused much hardship to the civilians. Many Chinese fled the country to avoid war and famine. Millions settled down in Southeast Asia. As strangers in a foreign land with no political and social backing, the only source of security for them was money. Due to language problems and other issues, many Chinese had a hard time getting good employment from the natives or the local governments. Therefore, they chose to set up their own businesses. Today, ethnic Chinese, who comprise 6.5% of the population in Southeast Asia, control the bulk of listed companies in the region's stock markets — more than 80% in Thailand and Singapore, 60% in Malaysia, about 50% in the Philippines, and 70% in Indonesia.

THE PARANOID TAIWANESE

For the Chinese in Taiwan, the story is a little different. A large number of mainlanders, about 2 million in total, fled to the island after the Communist victory in 1949, comprising 25% of the island's population of 8 million. Many of these mainlanders were government officials or worked with the government. They brought financial capital and management expertise and set up business enterprises on the island.

The Taiwanese are still very entrepreneurial: one company for every 18 people, which is probably one of the highest company-per-capita densities in the world. There is a Chinese expression that captures this entrepreneurial spirit, "People would rather be the head of a cock than the tail of a bull." The motivation for such strong entrepreneurial spirit is similar to the Chinese Diaspora in Southeast Asia. Since the retreat of the Kuomintang to the island, the Chinese Communists have been trying their best to reunify the island as part of greater China. As a result, Taiwanese tend to feel psychologically insecure; their only source of security is money, which provides portability and options. When they have made enough money, they will acquire the citizenship of another country, preferably the U.S. or Canada, or in some desperate cases, Latin American or African states.

The following story demonstrates how widespread the phenomenon of dual citizenship is. Recently there was a controversy over the dual nationality of Ms. Hsiao Bi Khim, one of Taiwan President Chen Shui Bian's interpreters. Apparently, Ms. Hsiao held a foreign passport. The opposition legislators were questioning the loyalty of the interpreter. They argued that if the interpreter had pledged loyalty to a country other than Taiwan, she should not have been appointed as the president's interpreter, a position that allows access to most of the nation's classified information.

CLUSTER OF TALENTS FOR HIGHLY SKILLED ENGINEERING AND RESEARCH FUELS INVESTMENT

The country's 75 universities and research institutions educate more than 8,000 engineers annually. In Taiwan, engineers generally enjoy high social status and as a result, the best students choose to study engineering.

There are many research institutions, mostly set up by the government, universities, or sponsored by local conglomerates. Among them, the most prominent research institution is The Industrial Technology Research Institute (ITRI). Over time, ITRI became a great source of talented people. Since its establishment in 1973, over 13,000 employees have graduated from the portals of ITRI, 76% of whom joined private industries, especially the semiconductor industries. In fact, many successful managers such as Morris Chang (chairman, Taiwan Semiconductor Manufacturing Corporation) and Robert Tsao (chairman, United Microelectronics Corporation) in the semiconductor industries originated from ITRI.

Many successful companies spin off from ITRI. Following the transfer of seven-micron CMOS IC processing and design technology from RCA (Radio Corporation of America), ITRI established the foundations of Taiwan's semiconductor industry. Fueled by continuous technology transfers, spin-off IC companies such as UMC, TSMC, TMC, and VISC attracted over $3.6 billion in investments in IC wafer manufacturing. Numerous IC design and testing companies were also established. With total production value of $8.6 billion in 1998, Taiwan is the fourth-largest IC supplier in the world.[1]

ITRI has been instrumental to the success of Taiwan's economy. As a government sponsored institution, it pioneers into high-risk industries that most private enterprises would avoid. It is also an incubator to nurture engineers and scientists for the various industries in Taiwan. It was so successful that many countries in the region have established similar research institutions to fuel the growth of new technology and entrepreneurship. One example is the Kent Ridge Digital Labs in Singapore.

DISCIPLINE KILLS CREATIVITY, BUT . . .

A unique work force characteristic in Taiwan is its high degree of discipline. Owing to the Chinese Confucian influence, Taiwanese are in general very disciplined. While discipline may kill creativity and innovation, it is conducive to a high degree of precision and repeatability. These are particularly important worker capabilities for successful manufacturing.

Mr. Shen Jung Chin has worked with ITRI as a researcher for many years. His research interest was in the development of semiconductor industries in Taiwan.

SHEN JUNG CHIN

Tightening of nuts and bolts

There are many reasons why Taiwan succeeds in IC manufacturing. One of the crucial factors is the nature of discipline in the work force. In a manufacturing environment, engineers need to be highly disciplined. As a result, the best engineers in the U.S. and many parts of the developed world will never want to work in manufacturing environments. However, in Taiwan, the best engineering graduates opt to work for large IC manufacturing companies such as UMC and TSMC. The disciplined environment is not something unfamiliar to Taiwanese engineers.

To illustrate how discipline can be crucial to the yield of IC and other manufacturing processes, I offer this example:

Semiconductor equipment requires regular maintenance. This involves dismantling and reassembling of parts. In the reassembling of a part, if there are four bolts and nuts to be tightened so as to secure the part (Figure 14-1), a certain sequence should be followed: tighten nut a and nut c slightly, followed by nut b and nut d. After that, tighten nut a and nut c further, followed by nut b and nut d. This process is repeated a few times until all the nuts are completely tightened. It is tedious. But by doing so, one can increase the yield rate significantly. The engineers must have such discipline in order to achieve high yield rates all the time. ■

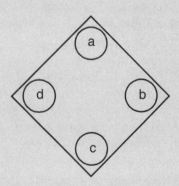

FIGURE 14-1 Discipline required in manufacturing process

Such is the high degree of discipline required. It is not surprising that shortly after adopting the technology from RCA, Taiwan's IC yield rates were higher than the U.S. average in the late 1970s.[2] Today, Taiwanese IC yield rates remains one of the highest in the world.

REWARD AND INCENTIVE — THE TAIWANESE WAY

Taiwan fixed wage is generally 40% lower than those of Singapore and 60% lower than those of Hong Kong. However, depending on the exchange rate between Singapore dollar and New Taiwan Dollar, the cost of living in Taipei and Hsinchu can be higher than that of Singapore. Until very recently, stock options were not allowed in Taiwan. Therefore, employers had to offer something more to motivate the employees, as explained through the stock shares program detailed below.

CASE STUDY:
HOW COMPANY STOCK OPTIONS WORK

A stock option gives its owner the right to buy stock at a specified exercise or striking price on or after a specified exercise date. It is common for American companies to give incentives to their top executives to raise the share prices of the companies by offering them stock options.

By offering stock options, it is hoped to align the goal of the executives to that of the shareholders: to increase shareholders' value. To illustrate how it works, look at the following example:

The share price of Company A is $10 per share on December 31, Year X. An executive of Company A is awarded on that day stock options to buy 10,000 shares of Company A at $12 per share on December 31, Year (X + 2). If on December 31, Year (X + 2), the share price of Company A is $20, the stock options will bring $80,000 (10,000 shares × ($20 – $12)) profits to the executive. However, if the share price of Company A is equal to or below $12, the stock options will be worth nothing to the executive. Therefore, it is in the executive's interest to increase the share price of Company A (as opposed to buying corporate jets or building new luxury offices) as much as possible.

Taiwanese employers keep their employees motivated by offering them company shares. Many companies set aside 15% to 20% of the shares for the employees (this excludes the percentage of shares owned by directors).

If a company is doing well in one particular year, instead of paying cash bonuses, the company might issue free bonus shares to the employees and its shareholders. The par value of these new shares is always NT$10 each. If the company decides to issue 10 million shares, it will transfer NT$100 million (NT$10 par value per share × 10 million new shares) from the retained earnings account of the balance sheet to the paid-up capital account. By doing so, the company will be able to keep the precious cash within the company and yet keep the employees and shareholders happy. This scheme is extremely successful. At the peak of the capital market, it is not unusual for employees of successful companies such as UMC and TSMC to receive shares equivalent to two to four times their annual wages.

This bonus share scheme has an important by-product — a vibrant capital market with the second-highest liquidity in the world.

FINANCING CAPITAL — BOTH FOR FUNDING AND EXIT

Taiwan's stock market has one of the highest liquidity in the world. The average monthly liquidity (transaction volume ÷ average total market value) is about 30%. The presence of international institutional investors is insignificant. The retail players control the market. It provides excellent revenues for listed companies to raise funds (by right issues) and exits for venture capitalists.

However, in the start-up world, funding is not always readily available.

CAPITALIZATION OF START-UPS

Except for the semiconductor and a few other blessed industries, most start-up companies in Taiwan lack funding. Up until the mid-1990s, most of Taiwan's banks were state owned. These banks are mostly risk-averse and SMEs (small and medium enterprises), so they generally have difficulty borrowing money from the banks. In fact, even Taiwan's listed companies have such difficulties and as a result they have one of the lowest debt-to-equity ratios in Asia: about 30%. What this implies is that most companies have to borrow money within their own network (often friends, relatives of the owners, or even loan sharks) and be operating cash-flow positive. This somehow crafts the uniqueness of Taiwanese companies: *flexibility*. The following case shows how adaptable successful Taiwanese companies can be.

CASE STUDY:
UNITED MICROELECTRONICS CORPORATION

United Microelectronics Corporation (UMC) is the second-largest fab in the world. Its growth, however, has not been smooth sailing. Within its relatively short span of 20 years of existence, it has changed its overall strategies and product offerings many times. When it was first established in 1979, it manufactured ICs for digital watches. Today, the company does not design its own ICs, but manufactures ICs for its customers according to their designs. Its evolution demonstrates the flexibility typical of many Taiwanese companies.

In 1982, the U.S. government opened its market for telephone equipment, hence stimulating the growth of the telephone manufacturing industry in Asia. UMC was fast to capture the opportunity, planning for the production of telephone ICs long before the market liberalization took place. The company formed strategic partnerships with leading telephone manufacturers in Taiwan, Hong Kong, and South Korea. The strategic partnership covered telephone equipment specifications, product development, technical support, and priority of supply of products. Such partnerships not only secured orders from these partners but also guided the company's product roadmaps. The partnership was very successful with its tone/pulse switchable IC, capturing huge market share. In 1983, among the top 500 enterprises in Taiwan, UMC ranked number one in terms of revenue growth and number two in terms of profit growth.

In 1983, however, the telephone IC market collapsed due to overstocking and price wars among telephone manufacturers, leading to market consolidation. As a result, many telephone manufacturers in the region cancelled their orders. Immediately, UMC was hit badly; its monthly revenue dropped 60% in one year. In the second half of 1984, however, the company's sales doubled, thanks to its swift switch into the fast-growing markets for music, calculator, and digital watch ICs.

On the technology front, UMC worked closely with external institutions, including:

- Transfer of CMOS ROM and cache memory technology from Elite and Integrated Silicon in 1989
- Transfer of EPROM technology from Brigh in 1990
- Transfer of BiCMOS technology in 1991 from ITRI
- Codevelopment of 486 CPU with MSI in 1991
- Codevelopment of RISC 80 MHz SPAC microprocessor with ITRI in 1993

Since UMC had acquired a wide range of semiconductor technologies, it was ready to go into SRAM production when SRAM prices escalated at the beginning of the 1990s. However, the high profit margin of SRAM attracted many newcomers, including Korean giants such as Samsung. Commoditization and oversupply of SRAM led to a sharp price decline. In 1995, UMC decided to reduce its dependence on SRAM. Before the collapse of SRAM prices in mid-1996, UMC had successfully reduced its involvement in SRAM from 50% to 10% of its revenue.

During the same period of the 1990s, the company was also active in CPUs, PC chipsets, and telecommunications ICs. With too much diversification, however, UMC's management resources were spread too thin. Some of the product range faced stiff challenges from Intel:

- UMC's CPU business faced litigation from Intel
- Its chipset business encountered direct competition from Intel

To resolve it, UMC had to make the tough decision to either terminate or spin off those businesses.

By 1997, UMC had shed most of its product lines, leaving only IC contract manufacturing as its main business. The company has huge success in terms of growth and profitability as illustrated in the Table 14-1.

TABLE 14-1 UMC Revenue and Net Income Growth

	REVENUE (U.S.$ MILLION)	EBIDTA	NET INCOME	NET INCOME (% OF REVENUE)
1993	310	121	74	24
1994	469	249	197	42
1995	746	448	407	55
1996	684	290	232	34
1997	760	231	295	39
1998	558	158	133	24
1999	882	343	318	36
2000	3,091	N/A	1,494	48

Source: UMC Annual Reports.

At the same time, many of UMC's spin-offs such as Mediatek and UniMicron are faring very well as independent entities in the Taiwan capital market. Mediatek's market capitalization ranged between U.S.$1.97 billion to U.S.$5.57 billion in 2001 while that of UniMicron ranged between U.S.$250 million to U.S.$756 million.

Such is typical of Taiwanese companies. Driven by the need to survive, Taiwanese companies constantly struggle to generate cash to sustain their operations. As a result, we can see that most of the start-up companies in the earlier period did not engage in R&D activities as much as their counterparts in Israel or the U.S. They preferred to invest in manufacturing facilities, doing subcontracting work for other companies and generating precious cash right from the beginning of the company's existence. It is only during the past five years, when venture capital funding has been more readily available, that Taiwanese start-ups have been able to allocate more into R&D.

As for the Taiwanese semiconductor industry, the government was the venture capitalist that started it all.

Professor Wu Se Hwa is dean and professor of the Department of Business Administration, National Cheng-Chi University. His research interest is in technology and asset competitiveness analysis, technology strategy, and knowledge management. Professor Wu spent many years studying the growth of the semiconductor industries in Taiwan.

WU SE HWA

The economic advantage of Taiwan's semiconductor industries

Threatened by Japanese semiconductor companies' growing market share in the 1960s, U.S. semiconductor companies decided to outsource certain parts of the semiconductor manufacturing processes, such as IC packaging and testing, to the developing countries, so as to lower the total cost of IC manufacturing. For example, from 1969 to 1973, Texas Instruments and RCA established IC packaging companies in Taiwan.

In the early 1970s, Taiwan was forced to withdraw from the United Nations. Many realized that to survive, Taiwan had to develop itself. To support the economy, the government decided to focus upon the semiconductor industries. As the amount of capital investment involved was huge, the government decided to lead the charge.

An advisory council, the TAC (Technical Advisory Council) was established. Its members constituted mainly Taiwanese engineers working in the U.S. After studying different strategies to develop semiconductor industries, TAC recommended buying technology from RCA. After much negotiation, RCA transferred its seven-inch IC technology to Taiwan for a consideration of U.S.$3 million. The technology transfer included IC design, fabrication, packaging, and testing, and other tacit details such as logistics, accounting, and production management.

In 1977, a research plant was established. It had a capacity of 4,000 three-inch wafers per week. Its first product was an IC used in the manufacturing of digital watches. Within four months after commencement, the plant's yield rate was at 81%, exceeding that of RCA (80%). By September 1978, the research plant had produced more than 1 million digital-watch ICs, and the plant was profitable. Subsequently, the plant successfully designed and manufactured ICs for toys, telephones, and memory chips.

However, such success did not bring much joy. Because of the short life cycle of the semiconductor manufacturing, a lot of money had to be invested to upgrade the research plant and the government was not willing to continuously finance such capital requirements. Furthermore, the semiconductor engineers trained in the research plant were very mobile. They could have easily moved on to join foreign companies and hence defeat the plan of establishing Taiwan's own semiconductor industries. Therefore, the government decided to spin off the research plant as an independent company, and that company became UMC.

From its humble beginning of producing simple consumer electronics ICs, UMC is today the second-largest foundry in the world, with market capitalization of U.S.$20 billion. At the same time, Taiwan has become the fourth-largest semiconductor producing region in the world. ■

GOVERNMENT'S ROLE IN DEVELOPING THE PRIVATE SECTOR

Taiwanese government's success in grooming IC manufacturing industries is remarkable. Today, Taiwan's IC production is the fourth-largest in the world and the world's two largest IC fabs, TSMC an UMC, are in Taiwan. At the same time, the success in IC manufacturing has fueled the growth of other industries. Fabless IC design industry, where Taiwan is number two in the world, is one of them.

In the case of IC manufacturing, the Taiwanese government's direct involvement in kicking off the industry was crucial. Due to the capital-intensive nature of the IC manufacturing industry, many private investors did not want to invest in the industry, even when plants set up by ITRI were having yield rates better than those of their U.S. counterparts. It would be hard to imagine that any private entities would have wanted to invest in IC manufacturing in the late 1960s.

Hong Kong's capital market did not have the versatility of government financing, and its manufacturing industry took a different route, as explained below.

CASE STUDY:
DIFFERING GOVERNMENT CAPITAL ROUTES —
CONTRAST HONG KONG AND TAIWAN

The versatility of Hong Kong is similar to that of Taiwan. Mr. Lee Ka Shing, the richest man in Hong Kong, started his multibillion-dollar business enterprises from a small, humble plastic flower manufacturing plant. Subsequently, the tycoon made his fortune in the real estate boom in Hong Kong. Today, Mr. Lee's flagship company, Hutchison Whampoa, is an active player in property development, port operations, retail, manufacturing, telecommunications, and energy infrastructure development. In fact, in the 1960s and 1970s, Hong Kong companies demonstrated similar flexibility and versatility. Once it was one of the largest exporters of electronics, toys, and garments. However, ever since China opened up to the world in the late 1970s, Hong Kong's business community has seized the opportunity and moved most of the manufacturing activities into China to tap the country's low-cost labor. Manufacturing activities have virtually disappeared from the former British colony. Taiwan, on the other hand, is still prosperous with manufacturing activities today (although some of the labor-intensive industries have been relocated into China).

The main difference is that in Hong Kong, the British colonial government at the time chose not to interfere with the economic activities of the colony (as a matter of fact, for many years, Hong Kong was considered the freest economy in the world). Without the government's lead into the risky high-tech industries, the business community instead channelled its capital into the lucrative property and equity markets for quick profits.

THE EVOLVING ROLE OF GOVERNMENT INVESTMENT

However, the beauty of the whole episode was not how the Taiwanese government got involved at the beginning, but rather how the government withdrew from the industry when the industry reached its competitive maturity. In many countries, the governments are involved in spearheading new industries. In certain industries such as defense or education services, the governments' involvements are out of strategic considerations. In other industries, the governments' involvements are out of economic and financial interests. If the government supports certain companies in order to nurture a particular industry, the government must learn when and how to reduce its involvement over the time and allow these companies to compete freely in the domestic market. Overinvolvement of the government in an industry may not make it efficient. The government-linked companies may succeed at the national level because of their link to the government. However, at the regional and international levels, those companies may not be able to compete efficiently because they no longer enjoy the privileges (such as priority to government contracts, etc.) they are used to in their own countries. *Only companies that have emerged from domestic competition will have a good chance of success at the international market.* Government's involvement in an industry may distort the competitive ground necessary for the natural selection process; hence, there is no guarantee that the best will emerge as victors.

The capital market seems to endorse such views. For Chinese companies listed as H shares in Hong Kong, investors are willing to pay a premium for successful private companies over successful state-owned enterprises. Many institutional investors believe that private enterprises (instead of state-owned enterprises) are going to drive of growth of China for the next few years.

PROFESSIONAL MONEY VS. SOCIAL-NETWORK MONEY

For many other start-up companies, it is extremely difficult to borrow money from banks. Its peculiar political situation means that Taiwan is not a member of many international organizations, including the IMF (International Monetary Fund). As an entity, it has to rely on itself. This may be why Taiwan's foreign reserves are the third highest, about U.S.$110 billion in total, after Japan and China, while its foreign debts are one of the lowest in the world. So, the Taiwan government's monetary policies have been fiscally conservative.

Therefore, for inspired start-up companies, most have to turn to the owners' or the managers' social networks for capital. Such a social network is flexible and trust-based. There is hardly any due diligence involved, and the process of raising money can be quite fast. Even now, when Taiwan has developed its own VC (venture capital) industry, it is not unusual for investments to be made based on trust and relationship. Investment decisions can be made over a phone call or golf game by senior fund managers. Subsequently, junior analysts are instructed to write investment reports to justify the decisions. Often an investment process from deal origination to closure can be as short as one week. Typically, a foreign firm may take three months to make a decision for the same investment.

The advantages of social-network funding are its speed and timeliness. The disadvantages are its size and the issue of reciprocity: If you lend me $5 today, I am obliged to lend you $5 or am obliged to buy products from you in the future. This may not be the most efficient way of resources allocation. If such reciprocity happens at a personal level, only the persons involved are affected. However, if the owner of a listed company lends the company's money to support his or her friend's start-up out of such reciprocity, this may destroy the value of the listed company and is irresponsible to other shareholders.

The traditional intimate relationship between local VC firms and the industries, gives the local VC firms a strong understanding of the Taiwanese start-ups. Hence, local VC firms are more aggressive on equity pricing. Many foreign VC firms find it difficult to compete with the local VC firms for speed and valuations.

The importance of social-network funding is certain. It offers a small start-up company a chance of survival. Without such funding, many of the successful companies of today would not have survived. However, successful start-ups must be able to graduate from social-network funding to funding from professional institutions, so they may leap forward to the next stage of development. In many cases, VC firms are closely related to conglomerates and financial institutions, which will be able to help start-ups with resources, networking, and even purchase orders. This is especially so in Taiwan where 61% of the venture funding comes from corporations, compared with 15% in the U.S.

THE TAIWAN/CHINA RELATIONSHIP

The Taiwan/China relationship can serve as a model for developed and developing countries' economic relationships despite political difficulties.

Very few people in Taiwan will deny that China has a lot of influence on the island, be it positive or negative. It is a love-hate relationship. On one hand, the island has its Chinese heritage and is proud of its association with the long history of China. On the other hand, Taiwanese feel bullied and threatened by its giant neighbor in the international political front.

Kuomintang is the political party that supposedly aims to recapture the mainland China from the Communist rule and the Democratic Progress Party (DPP) is the political party without such ambition. One would expect China to be friendlier to DPP. However, the reality is exactly the opposite. China prefers Kuomintang to be the ruling party. In its awkward effort to sabotage DPP in the year 2000 presidential election, China's political leaders gave stern warnings to the Taiwanese not to vote for DPP candidate Chen Shui Bian. The end result was that Chen Shui Bian won the election. Many would agree that the biggest help Chen Shui Bian secured during the campaign was from the leaders of mainland China.

Politically, the two places couldn't be farther apart. Economically, they are tightly integrated. Taiwan is the largest investor in mainland China and hundreds of thousands of Taiwanese live in China. Many of them are in fact members of the Communist Party.

As recently as 1999, Taiwanese companies were not allowed to invest in China. Nor are Taiwanese below a certain age allowed to travel to China. Under the policy of "jie ji yong ren" (which means that "my dear friends, as the cross-strait situations are unusual and dangerous, you have to exercise patience and control in any interaction with the mainland Chinese") of ex-President Lee Teng Hui, Taiwanese are told not to have anything to do with the mainland Chinese. Over the years, however, many have circumvented the policy by investing in China through holding companies in Hong Kong.

ECONOMIC BENEFIT MATTERS MORE THAN POLITICS

Taiwanese companies have no choice but to set up manufacturing plants in China. Most of the time, the drivers for such move are either their customers or their competitors.

Most Taiwanese companies engage in contract manufacturing. Very often, before awarding purchasing contracts to them, their customers will ask the Taiwanese companies if they have plants in China. The reason is simple. These customers know that in 5 years' time, Taiwan will not be competitive compared with China. By selecting manufacturing partners with facilities in China, they do not have to worry about cost issues and can afford to work with the Taiwanese manufacturing for quite some time. After all, it is very costly to switch manufacturer partners.

In other cases, Taiwanese companies move into China because their customers go there. These customers will need support in China and therefore they have to move along with the customers.

Having manufacturing facilities in China is definitely a competitive advantage that many will not want to miss.

TAIWANESE BRANDS COULD STAND TALL IN CHINA

Besides low-cost labor, China also offers lucrative markets. For many years, Taiwanese manufacturers have been obscured by manufacturing products for others. They have been successful, but being an OEM is a hard job. They take the least attractive role in the supply chain and are rewarded with margins as low as 2% to 5%. Why not establish their own brands? The Taiwanese companies have tried but have not been very successful in most parts of the world.

However, China offers Taiwan a unique opportunity. With identical cultural heritage, the Taiwanese will have an advantage over the Western companies in understanding the market trends in China. The mainland Chinese watch Taiwanese movies, listen to Taiwanese singers, and read Taiwanese books. All these will make the Chinese receptive to Taiwanese brands. In fact, some Taiwanese brands are already very prominent in China. Brands such as Yong He Soya Bean and Kang Shi Fu (in the food industry) are household names in China. Therefore, the China market offers a unique opportunity for Taiwanese companies to establish their own brands and earn a higher profit margin.

However, whether such dreams can become reality will very much depend on the development of the cross-strait relationship and the political games in Taiwan.

As you have seen, Taiwan has learned to become a world-leading region by focusing on the strengths and talents of its people and very intelligent government support to initiate leadership in the IC semiconductor industries. Financing both from social networking and Taiwanese corporations have made a critical difference for Taiwanese manufacturers as they continue to service the world as well as expand into China to maintain their cost competitive advantage.

ENDNOTES

1. The Industrial Technology Research Institute, *www.itri.org.tw*.

2. Material gathered from article by Shen Jung Chin and Wu Se Hwa, appearing in Chinese in the *Taiwanese Industry Research Book*, 1999.

▶ *About the Author*

This chapter was authored by **Li Chun**, vice president of OTTO Capital Partners. Mr. Chun has more than nine years of working experience including heading a European private equity investment firm in Asia; management consulting with Gemini Consulting; and project management with Mobil Asia Pacific. He has an MBA from INSEAD, and a BEng (Electrical Engineering, Honors) from the National University of Singapore.

15 ISRAEL'S MILITARY TECHNOLOGY

THE TRANSFER TO CIVILIAN APPLICATIONS AND UNIVERSITIES AS INCUBATORS

Israel's image today is that of a country in constant political turmoil, with an economy that is isolated from its direct geographical environment and with a focus on technology, industry, and defense superceding agriculture. Very few specialists know the characteristics of Israeli high-tech companies and their respective strategies, which are often established in conflicting circumstances.

What is the reality of Israel's high-tech economy? What is the country's real advantage in technology? Which are the most interesting examples that should be mentioned? Are the most creative sectors linked to the country's socioeconomic state or to other geopolitical factors? These are the questions that need answers to understand the phenomenon of tech creation in Israel.

To get a complete understanding of Israel's high-tech development, we have to look at the different weaknesses of the "Israeli High-Tech Island," such as the relatively small size of start-ups, a marked lack in marketing management, the high salaries of Israeli engineers (about 10% to 15% higher than in California), and the financial burden of Nasdaq introduction.[1]

The most problematic feature of the Israeli high-tech model appears to be the "American temptation," or more precisely, the acquisition of successful Israeli start-ups by leading American high-tech firms. For instance, Cisco acquired the Israeli start-up Class Data System for $50 million, and Sun Gard made a purchase of Oshap Group (a financial software developer) for $210 million. Similarly, AOL bought Mirabilis for $287 million.

This American acquisition wave may be explained by a lack of Israeli development strategy and ambition. It has been suggested that the government should pay much more attention to supporting successful companies, to keep them in Israel. This country has all the technological know-how but needs marketing expertise to develop real multinational muscle, instead of just developing talent and technology for others.[2]

TABLE 15-1 Facts at a Glance — Israel

GDP	$99.5 billion in 2000
Per-capita GDP	$16,950, places it 21st among 200 countries in the world
R&D contribution to GDP	2.2%, from over 1,000 R&D-based companies, 80% are less than 10 years old
R&D industry	9 of every 1,000 workers, ranked 1st worldwide for R&D investment
Land area	290 miles in length and 85 miles in width at its widest point
Population	≈ 6 million
Geography	Located in the Middle East, along the eastern coastline of the Mediterranean Sea, bordered by Lebanon, Syria, Jordan, and Egypt, at the junction of three continents: Europe, Asia and Africa
Religion	80% Jewish
Education	More than 60% of the working population has an educational level equal or superior to high school, out of which more than 25% are graduates and more than 12% hold post-graduate degrees. Ranked 6th worldwide in science and education (1999)
High-tech industry	100,000 employees, in 2,000 high-tech firms and 2,000 start-ups
Number of scientists and engineers	145 per 10,000 employees, ranked 4th in terms of availability of skills and 4th in terms of basic research
Growth rate of electronics industry	10% per year
Entrepreneurship	Israel was ranked 6th (1999), ranked 5th worldwide with regards to its creation of firms
PC penetration	One-third of Israeli homes have computers, ranked 5th in terms of Internet usage

Sources: "Tableau de bord de l'économie Israélienne," in Revue Française de Coopération Economique avec Israël, June, July, August 2000, No. 173, pp. 26–27; Stephane Garelli, The World Competitiveness Yearbook 1999, IMD, 1999.

In this chapter, we present and analyze the key characteristics of the Israeli model, focusing our approach on the lessons that can be learned from Israeli high-tech companies and from their business experience.

A GROUND FOR TECHNOLOGY CREATION

Israel represents the second most intensive high-tech concentration in the world after California. The country has a technologically advanced market economy and it has been targeting high-technology niches in international markets such as medical scanning equipment.

Today, Israel is in the midst of an important and promising period in the fields of high-tech industry and information technology. Within just a few years, Israel's technological industry has penetrated world markets and has become a research and development center eyed by firms dealing in high-tech products and software for communications, medicine, and engineering around the world. The thousands of university graduates who immigrated from the former Soviet Union during the 1990s were among the prime catalysts that propelled this industry to today's level.

Since then, Israel has been considered one of the best hopes in the high-tech industry, allowing the country entrance into the circle of the industrialized countries.[3]

With 100 companies having equities negotiated on the U.S. financial markets — NYSE, Nasdaq, and AMEX — Israel comes just after Canada in terms of its foreign presence on Wall Street.[4] In Israel, approximately 100,000 people work in the high-tech industry, one-third of them being highly paid, while in the rest of the economy the wages are stagnant.

The high-tech industry has been one of the most important engines of Israel's economic growth during the past 10 years.

R&D AND HIGH TECH: FUNDAMENTAL COMPONENTS OF THE ISRAELI SYSTEM

Despite its size, Israel has gained a good reputation in R&D and academic research (determined by the number of scientific publications per capita, Israel publishes about 1% of the world's scientific papers[5]).

The country has over 1,000 R&D-based industries, including many small new start-ups and software houses which, already in 1994, accounted for over half of Israel's $15 billion in exports. The key to Israel's situation in the high-tech sector is its highly trained population; in 1993, some 20% of the employed industrial (manufacturing) work force had college degrees. The figure is even higher when the software sector is included. In fact, about nine in every 1,000 Israeli workers (all sectors) are engaged in R&D. This rises to 30 per 1,000 within the manufacturing industries. This well-trained work force triggered the entry of multinational companies to Israel.

The rapidly growing high-tech industry has the potential to grow at an even faster rate. In terms of productivity per employee, Israeli high tech still has a long way to go compared with international standards. Although output per employee in the industry is $160,000 per year, some other countries boast an output of upward of $250,000 per employee per year.

ISRAEL.COM: KEY CHARACTERISTICS OF ISRAEL'S HIGH-TECH INDUSTRY

Why has Israel, a small country with a relatively young population of six million inhabitants, emerged as a dynamic force in high technology? For many experts and specialists in Israel, the success of this country in the high-tech field is mainly due to the influences of the Israeli Defence Forces, the country's military industries, its military intelligence units, its research institutes, and its universities. The success of the UAV is one such example that is linked to the Israeli model of development.

CASE STUDY:
UNMANNED AIR VEHICLES — UAVs

Originally, the idea behind developing UAVs, also called drones, was to cut the loss of pilots to a minimum in the event of war, and to track enemy territory. Currently, drones are used for reconnaisance purposes, but major technological advancements are required before they can be used for combat purposes (mainly because these are rapidly changing situations in which human intelligence is more efficient than computers).

The main world producers of UAVs are Teledyne Ryan Aeronautical and Northrop Grumman in the U.S., Target Technologies and Aérospatiale in Europe, I.A.I. in Israel, Kentron in Africa, and Fuji Heavy Industries in Asia.

An analysis of the industry reveals the following key elements of Israeli strategy:

■ Succeeding at all costs in the long term by using technological inno-vation as a priority and establishing technological partnerships with foreign industrialists in order to make the best of technological know-how.

■ Assimilating all technology and know-how without becoming victims of the "not invented here" syndrome; Israeli industrialists and scien-tists have no difficulty in integrating foreign know-how in their prod-uct development and are capable of using reverse engineering in a quasi-scientific manner (dismantling competitors' products to rebuild them).

■ Using economic and technological intelligence as a management tool: given the highly competitive nature of the industry, Israelis are closely watching and analyzing the operational strategies of other players in the market in order to compete.

■ Turning toward civilian or military authorities for direct or indirect support (R&D financing, testing orders, tax exemptions, free trade zones, etc.). These authorities, working on tight research budgets, usually scatter orders across at least 20 companies thriving around the market leader, Israel Aircraft Industries (IAI).

An increasingly keen and organized competition

According to experts, the world market for UAVs should jump from rev-enues of almost $2.3 billion in 1998 to more than $4.31 billion in 2004. Once technological and regulatory issues are overcome to the satisfac-tion of the potential market, revenues should increase dramatically. Moreover, the market is forecast to become increasingly competitive, which will reduce the number of participants.

The increasing maturity of technology in the UAV industry would lead to a reduction in the number of manufacturers, which currently range in size from market leaders such as IAI Malat Division and larger manu-facturers such as Lockheed Martin to smaller national companies.

It is also important to note that the Israelis start with new markets. Thus, Singapore Technologies has signed a $14 million contract with Israel's Emit Aviation Consultancy for the new Blue Horizon UAV and is set to develop its own larger, more powerful variant called Firefly. Israeli drones also find applications in new fields, such as mine detec-tion and radar jamming.

It can be argued that Israel's major competitor in terms of entrepreneur-ship, creativity, hunger for innovation, love for change, and danger is Silicon Valley. On the other hand, many nations surpass Israel in terms of technol-ogy, management, marketing, and production.

The entrepreneurial class is highly educated, multilingual, and nonpoliticized. Their origins are European and North American. They have little contact with Orthodox Jews or Arabs and have a youthful, outward looking, and flexible approach combined with a desire for growth and change and willingness to take risks that is specific to their culture.

Through its rich and turbulent history, the country's confidence has strengthened until today its economic success is built on firm foundations. Israel has managed to create and develop an economic model with its own characteristics and strengths.

The discussion above identified the main components of this model and the key success factors that have directly or indirectly enabled the emergence of what is today one of the most dynamic and interesting areas in the industrial world. The next section will discuss the role of entrepreneurship in the succes of Israel's high-tech model.

A CULTURE OF ENTREPRENEURSHIP

The highly energetic entrepreneurial spirit is a crucial characteristic of the Israeli mindset. This is illustrated by the number of start-ups that are being created every year in the country, and is a quality one can find in a large number of Israeli people, many of whom forged vital contacts while serving in Israel's army.

Another source of this entrepreneurial spirit might be the vital need to manage in a country with very few raw materials, which necessitated creating intellectual value to survive against worldwide competition. The country does not have a choice: a lack of raw materials and a limited domestic market are factors pushing companies to export sophisticated products.

This entrepreneurship might also be due to the constant political turmoil that has characterized Israel all through its history. In particular, many Israelis have the capacity to react very fast and to adapt their lifestyle according to the evolution of their environment. If we take the example of tourism, which at the beginning of 2001 almost disappeared owing to the political tension between Israelis and Palestinians, it is amazing to see how people who depended upon this sector managed to change their professional and business orientation. Many of these people are now adopting a proactive attitude and are creating new businesses and opportunities.

It is also amazing to see how active youngsters are in regard to start-up creation. Mirabilis ICQ for example, which was created by Vardi (age 28), Visiger (age 26), and Goldfinger (age 27), has become an inspiring model that has been followed by many other young Israelis.

CASE STUDY:
MIRABILIS

Four young Israelis founded Mirabilis in Tel Aviv, with the aim of developing new ways of communicating on the Internet. They designed an instant mail software, ICQ (read: I seek you), which enabled users to know instantly if the people they communicated with most were on line.

The founders all had a passion for computers and the Internet. Their conclusion was simple: the Internet was fascinating for an increasing number of people but, in most cases, users surfed without communicating with each other. What was missing was a way of directly linking users. The founders of Mirabilis thus decided to create a new communication technology capable of simultaneously interconnecting millions of users through the same network.

Mirabilis did not generate any revenue as freeware (except through sales of ASPs to enterprises). However, soon after its launch, millions of copies of the software had been downloaded, of which 60% went into regular use. This community of millions of subscribers constituted an extraordinary capital (to be used later for electronic advertising). This success did not escape the attention of AOL, which bought Mirabilis for $287 million in 1998.

Mirabilis is one example of how the Israeli economy has lived through a fantastic revolution. In the 1960s, 70% of Israeli exports were oranges and agricultural goods. Today, high-tech products make up two-thirds of the exports and agricultural produce comprise less than 3%.

It can be said that the greatest export from Israel during the last few years is neither diamonds nor oranges but entire companies, usually to the United States.[6]

HIGH EMPHASIS ON EDUCATION AND SCIENCE

One of Israel's biggest advantages has been its high level of education: 60% of the active population is educated up to high school level, a phenomenon that has been boosted by the arrival of an impressive number of researchers from the former Soviet Union. While Israel does not possess any natural resources (no petrol, no gas, and insufficient water resources), this country is distinguished by very skilled human resources with very high levels of education and qualification.

Education in Israel is understood to be a precious legacy. Following the tradition of past generations, it continues to carry a fundamental value in Israel's society and is recognized as the key to its future. Education is notably considered a fundamental component of the Jewish religion.

The availability of high-quality universities and compulsory military service explain this highly qualified work force.[7] Israel's universities and research institutions, such as the Technion (Israel Institute of Technology) and the Weizmann Institute, are world-class. In addition, military service in National Defense Forces is compulsory in Israel. This service provides young people with technical and practical experience by insisting on group work in fields such as technology.

Most new start-ups are created by young men who became friends and used to work together during their military service in R&D laboratories and elite army units. In the framework of partnership between the Technion and new start-ups, managers are very often retired soldiers who left the army at 42 years of age. Belonging to the scientific and technological elite of the nation, they are usually willing to meet the challenge of managing a new start-up with a modest salary, because they still receive their military wage. Thus, the Israeli military service and the very prominent role of military defense in Israeli society is a crucial catalyst for high-tech development.

ISRAELI UNIVERSITIES SUPPORT INDUSTRY

Universities play an active role in the economic develoment of Israel. Professor Michel Revel, from the Weizmann Institute of Science, gives his perspective on the link between the academic world and Industry. Prof. Revel is a member and rapporteur in the UNESCO International Bioethics Committee, chairman of the Bioethics Advisory Committee of the Israel National Academy of Science, president of the board of the World Association for Medical Law, and chairman of the National Biotechnology Committee for Israel.

MICHEL REVEL

Israeli universities are working in close collaboration with industry and facilitating the develoment of focused research centers

The impact of the academic world on Israeli life is very strong. The Israeli public recognizes the role of the university and of the academic world in the survival of the state of Israel. From the foundation of Israel there was early recognition of the importance of academic science. Actually the universities started before the country existed.

The link between the university and industry is very close and allows flexibility. A professor of the Weizmann Institute is free to work in a company one day a week. There is great freedom to work for industry, and to spend a decent amount of time working on private activities.

What is more, there is a very intimate relationship between the academic world and the state. The state has located industrial parks around universities, making it possible to easily go from university to industry.

In the biotechnology field for example, we created national centers for the relevant technologies in genomics, proteomics, transgenic animals, transgenic plants, bioinformatics, and in high-throughput screening. All these centers were created with the help of the Israeli government. They serve both the university and industry. Industry pays for the service and these national centers make the technology available to the research community.

This close interaction between Israeli universities and the industrial world is a key characteristic of the Israeli model. ■

TECHNOLOGY AND RESEARCH ARE KEY ASSETS OF THE ISRAELI MODEL

Israeli leaders have always readily embraced new technologies and developments, viewing technology as the driving force behind innovation and a foundation upon which to build a strong economy. Israel's technological success can be mainly attributed to the presence of some 50,000 high-quality engineers and scientists. Close to 10% are involved in industrial research and development. Every year, thousands of graduates from seven Israeli universities are joining them and also building relationships with graduates of Harvard and MIT.[8] The direct consequence of this success is that more than 150 foreign firms have invested in R&D in Israel and more and more Israeli companies are being quoted on foreign stock exchanges, particularly on the NYSE.

By 1990, Israeli companies had filed hundreds of patents in the United States. Israel is ranked as the fifteenth most important country from this point of view. The number of patents filed by Israeli universities is one of the signs of the strong synergies between industry and academia in Israel. Universities are the most significant technology patent holders in Israel as well as abroad, and their participation on this level exceeds most higher education systems in other countries. Due to high R&D spending, Israeli universities register twice as many patents as their American counterparts and nine times more than Canadian universities.

Israel's advanced skill base is also reflected in the high proportion of scientific publications per inhabitants. Relative to the size of the labor force, Israel has by far the largest number of publishing authors in the natural sciences, engineering, agriculture, and medicine. Israel is rated among the top 20 countries for technology publications in the world.[9]

THE FOSTERING AND FACILITATING ROLE OF THE ISRAELI GOVERNMENT

Israel is also characterized by strong state support for the R&D sector in general, and for start-up creation. A unique Israeli phenomenon is the office of the chief scientist at the Ministry of Industry and Trade, which distributes grants totalling nearly $400 million to various R&D projects. The projects that succeed are expected to pay royalties to the chief scientist's office for a number of years.

Through the Scientific Office in the Industry and Trade Ministry, the Israeli government fosters high-tech development by granting substantial financial support to high-tech companies. Companies may obtain financial support of 30% to 60% of their gross expenses, which may be refunded through royalties. During the last few years, the Scientific Office has financed more than 1,000 projects per year with a budget of $400 million, and subsidized more than 200 seed companies located in 26 technological incubators spread all over the country. Therefore, thanks to this proactive government policy, Israel is in the first rank worldwide for R&D investment as a percentage of GDP (during the last few years, an average of 2.5% of GDP).[10]

TECHNOLOGY INCUBATORS: AN ASSET FOR NEW ISRAELI COMPANIES

In the belief that the country's economic future is largely dependent on the success of its technological industry, the government launched a technological incubator program in 1991. This program enables any entrepreneur with an innovative technological idea to turn the idea into a product. The incubator program is applied in all parts of the country, under the guidance and with the support of the Office of the Chief Scientist of the Ministry of Industry and Trade.

Technological entrepreneurship incubators are supportive frameworks that enable start-up entrepreneurs — whether they are residents, returning residents, or immigrants — to take innovative technological ideas into the preliminary stages of development, turn them into commercial products for export, and establish factories for this purpose in Israel.

Through the technological incubators, the government provides entrepreneurs with physical premises, financial resources, tools, professional guidance, and administrative assistance so that, during their stay in the incubator, they may turn their abstract ideas into products of proven feasibility, novelty, advantage, and necessity in the international marketplace.

Because the state provides most of the budget during a project's incubator phase, it holds the management of the incubator responsible for the sound and efficient professional operation of each project in the incubator, including budget management and commercialization of the product being developed.

The rationale here is that, in order to keep good ideas from failing, the state, practically speaking, assumes the risks in the incubator program that commercial investors are loath to take, by funding the riskiest stage of their development.

Today, with around 24 incubators operating all over Israel, with over 750 projects launched, more than 63% have completed the incubator program. And 60% of these continue as independent companies. With a total of $233 million invested in 217 projects by the capital market and industry, 52% are at the sales stage. More than $76 million of products have been sold, of which $65 million were in exports. In addition, the "graduate" companies now employ over 1,780 people. Thus we can see that, from a pan-Israeli perspective, the Israeli incubator systems could be considered a success story.[11]

CASE STUDY:
THE WEIZMANN INSTITUTE OF SCIENCE
AND THE ITEK INCUBATOR

Incubators have played an important role in the development of Israel's new economy, with initiatives undertaken by the government but also by public entities or universities. Among them is the Weizmann Institute of Science, Israel's multidisciplinary center devoted to research and teaching in the natural sciences.

Located on a 1.2-square km campus in the town of Rehovot, 22 km south of Tel Aviv and 42 km west of Jerusalem, the Weizmann Institute employs 1,600 scientists, technicians, and research students. It operates on an annual budget of some $176 million and manages more than 250 research groups across the spectrum of contemporary science. The Institute comprises five faculties: biology, biochemistry, chemistry, physics and mathematics, and computer science, as well as the Feinberg Graduate School.

Within the Israeli R&D environment the Weizmann Institute plays an important role. The Institute is involved in almost all the scientific activities in hard science in Israel. It was the first in Israel to introduce cancer research; helped and supported the creation of the first science park, Kiryat Weizmann; and was the first to create a commercial arm to promote exploitation of Institute research. Furthermore, the Institute has extensively contributed to the Israeli economy and society in the fields of creating new drugs, agriculture, research, and education.

The Institute is the third oldest among the six universities in Israel that are engaged in research in hard sciences. It is looked upon as a model inside Israel in relation to technology transfer and enjoys national and international reknown in R&D.

In addition, the Weizmann Institute was the first academic institution in Israel to create a technology transfer organization to promote the commercialisation of its research: Yeda Research and Development Co. Ltd. Founded in 1959, Yeda's mission is to transfer technology from the Institute to the world marketplace by locating venture capital to create the necessary start-up companies. Today, it employs 11 people, of which five are professionals: a director who is an experienced businessman, a scientist, a lawyer, a patent attorney, and an accountant.

Yeda participates in start-up companies based on projects initiating Institute research. Six such ventures were set up in 1998–1999: two each in the fields of life sciences, chemistry, and electronics. By September 1998, 19 start-ups were established as a direct result of Institute research; in 14 of these Yeda was an active partner. Yeda realized that it was unlikely that any of the companies would show profits overnight, but if they showed the patience, they would probably thrive in the long term.[12]

In 1997 Yeda made an agreement with PAMOT, a venture capital fund. PAMOT now has the right of first option on all Yeda's projects. They are obliged to create a start-up but cannot deal with licensing so they cannot compete with Yeda. However PAMOT can create a "virtual company" within the institute and check the application of the technology to the market. So far they have established six new companies.

By associating with a venture capital fund, Yeda solved a problem faced by many research inistitues: how to attract pre-seed funds. Furthermore, Yeda does not demand up-front payment from start-up companies, as they would do in a licensing operation; this is done to ease the financial burden on the start-ups.

Another important creation from the Weizmann Institute is ITEK, the Incubator for Technological Entrepreneurship Kiryat Weizmann, which started operating in August 1991 and hosts 11 high-tech incubator firms. Another nine have already left and operate independently. An analysis of this incubator shows the characteristic key success factors of a major Israeli incubator:

- Substantial financial support provided to the start-ups.
- Incubator administrators play an active role in each project for the entire duration. Yerushalmi, the head of the ITEK incubator, is personally involved in each of the start-ups, therefore contributing to a permanent link between the incubator activity and the companies emerging from it.
- Consultancy as a complete set of services is concretely and easily available for the start-ups.
- Responsibility is expected of the incubator managers vis-à-vis the state, who must show proof that the incubator operates as a normal commercial company, although it is a nonprofit organization. This guarantees both professionalism and credibility of the incubator's involvement.
- Scientists can work undisturbed during the two years authorized for start-ups.
- A small but very active and dynamic steering committee (five people, volunteers) with minimum bureaucracy.
- Focus in a few subjects (product creation, high tech, company creation etc.).
- Measurement methods, measuring success by the amount of money raised from investors.

THE DYNAMIC TSAHAL CULTURE

The Israeli army contributes to Israeli innovation through team spirit inherited from work pools in the army and exhaustive teaching in cutting-edge technology to form a new generation of high-tech entrepreneurs.

One might consider Tsahal an R&D catalyst. The military service being compulsory (three years for men and two years for women), it provides the most talented with an unparalleled technical and practical experience. Organized in small and swift units, the Israeli army influences Israeli managers by conferring upon them a commando-like mentality, which is strongly reflected in the country's industry. This culture of moving fast, handling innovative projects, and prompt improvisation perfectly suits today's net economy requirements.

The most prominent figures of Tsahal's R&D labs are mythical units called Talpiot, MAMRAM, or 8-200. They find their early roots in the creation of the Israeli state and the need to decipher the enemy's codes or break into defense systems. Today, they are synonymous with first-class investments, and considered among the best technology recipients by Japanese and American investors.

The competition for these special units of Tsahal is fierce. Top high-school students compete in UNIX operating systems, C++ programming, and advanced mathematics and languages, to live the ultimate experience of entering these highly esteemed corps. However difficult may be the six-year formation in inhospitable camps lost in the scorching Judean desert or in Tel Aviv cubicles, they believe they will soon be high-tech millionaires as they have watched others succeed in this way before them.

Indeed, the unit encourages creativity by obliging young officers to quickly respond to impossible challenges. The unique efficiency of these units stems from their permanent obligation to react to actual threats that have to be dealt with immediately to save lives. The result is a rather informal, but extremely competent team of "entrepreneurs in uniform," rehearsing their future venture. The other compelling advantage of service is the networks and comradeship created among individuals of the same age sharing interests and backgrounds, and rapidly becoming friends. These solid connections are still very visible in large companies such as Compugen, AudioCodes, Sapiens, or NICE Systems, where many meetings resemble a pleasant alumni reunion.

TRANSFERRING TECHNOLOGY FROM THE MILITARY MARKET TO THE CIVIL MARKET

In the mid-1980s, confronted by a post Cold War's fading demand for weapons and triple-digit inflation, the Israeli army began downsizing and restructuring its forces by adopting a technology-intensive strategy. This transformation, alleviated by an exceptional relief of regional hostilities in the 1990s, aimed at a faster reaction to terror and isolated skirmishes.

Israel's defense benefitted its inborn peculiar structural split between large government firms (Israel Aircraft Industries, IAI), large private businesses (Tadiran), and dedicated small- and medium-size companies. In 1984, the Israeli Ministry of Defense began promoting the conversion to commercial product lines, adopted the R&D Encouragement Law, and increased spending on higher education. The initiative was a success, and companies such as IAI and Rafael launched commercial spin-offs, which rapidly outperformed certain defense production units.

Some civil firms such as Elbit Systems, ELISRA, and Rafael have successfully marketed high technologies that were first developed for military applications. The achievements are especially noticeable in the space sector (IAI, Elop, Elbit), telecommunications (Gilat Satellites, ECI telecom, Tadiran, Comverse, LocatioNet), and security (CheckPoint, RadGuard, Tarzana).

More surprising is the incursion of military technology in the medical sector. Rafael (acronym for Israel Weapons Development Authority) created a dedicated structure for military technology transfer called RDC, which bestows the permission to convert military knowledge in exchange for shares. Galil Medical, a spin-off of Rafael, specializes in minimally invasive surgical equipment and develops interfaces between different imaging devices. Galil Medical now sells in North America and Europe, and supplies first-class customers such as the University Hospital of Harvard.

Elbit Systems specializes in military and aviation goods and has already launched commercial companies in telecommunication and aerospace. They have recently introduced MediGuard, a start-up that will develop minimally invasive navigation systems based on military expertise in optical fiber and routing technologies. MediGuard will improve surgical operation by offering 3D imaging for catheterization, endoscopies, and heart surgery, without any use of x-rays.

The case of Check Point Software, illustrates the factors that have made such military technology transfers successful. Check Point was created in a small apartment by Gil Shwed, Shlomo Kramer and Marius Nacht. The founders have more or less the same profiles: they were below 30 years of age and they met in the Israeli army, where they became familiar with information security systems.

CASE STUDY:
CHECK POINT

The three founders were quick to recognize the potential of the Internet and network systems to provide companies with exposure to the outside environment, but also saw that this exposure left companies vulnerable to internal and external threats. They saw that companies would need security systems more and more.

Starting the company was not easy. At the end of 1993 Nacht went to the U.S. to try to sell the initial security software product of the young firm. He had no marketing or sales background and was using his car as an office.

But, success came in 1994 in Las Vegas, where Check Point won the first prize of NetWorld, the prestigious Internet trade show. In 1994, the company's revenues were $24,000. Today, Check Point has more than 450 employees and two main offices (in Redwood City, California, and Ramat-Gan in Israel) and the firm controls 40% of the world market for firewalls (more than 60% in Europe). According to the International Data Corporation, a market research firm specializing in high tech, this market has shown an annual growth of 27% through 2001.

The initial funding for Check Point came through venture capital. In 1993, an Israeli company, BRM Technologies, invested $300,000 and in June 1996, Check Point went public on the Nasdaq and is now capitalized between $11 and $20 billion. After the IPO, Check Point produced three millionaires: Mr. Gil Shwed and his two partners, who each owned 10% of the company.[13]

The success of Check Point is characteristic of the Israeli high-tech sector, as it was created by three army friends who had worked together as computer-savvy draftees in military intelligence agencies. For them, being identified as Israeli in the security trade is an advantage, and even the name "Check Point" has military connotations. When they left the army they had a clear idea of what a commercial software product could be. Gil Shwed is considered a role model in Israel today, as his example allows other young Israeli companies to believe they may prosper internationally with Israeli technology and management, even when remaining Israeli. Check Point arrived at these heights after just four years on the market.

The range of products deriving from Israeli military blueprints stretches from unmanned planes for firefighting to voice recognition in telemedicine.

The downsizing of Israel's defense industry has led thousands of skilled personnel to the civilian marketplace, while lessening the country's dependency on military production.

There is in fact a strong link between the Israeli Ministry of Defense and industry. Schlomo Dror, spokesman of the Israeli Ministry of Defense, commander of a tank battalion, and security officer in the MoD mission of the Israeli Embassy in Paris, expresses his view on the relationship between military and industrial sectors.

SCHLOMO DROR

Reciprocal cooperation between the army and private companies is a key characteristic of the Israeli model

The relationship between industry and the military in Israel is very different from other countries. In Israel, this relationship is so tight that sometimes, when you are visiting a company and you meet someone, you don't know if they are working for the Israeli Ministry of Defense or industry. Comverse (ex-Efrat) is an example of one company where you meet a lot of people coming from the Israeli intelligence units, especially computing. There is complete permeability between the civilian and military spheres. It is a kind of osmosis, going both ways.

In typical systems, such as U.S. industry, when you build a plane, you have to plan for R&D and prototypes to test it afterwards and if the army performs these tests, it will take a very long time, and large amounts of money. When you want to launch a project in Israel you develop everything together with the army if you need its assistance. For example, if Elbit is designing a new engine, they can trust the army for the testing as soon as the prototyping is finished.

The army is sharing its world-class equipment with private companies. If a private high-tech company needs equipment, they can come to the Army and work on its computers. Army and industry often work together on diverse projects. For instance, when we have an innovative idea but lack the human resources to follow through with it, we ask industry who would be the best to do it and launch common R&D. We can go to Elisra for an electrical system, tell them what we want and discuss the opportunities.

Working in the same field and from the same units

Let me give you an example. If we are working in a very specialized area of research and we know that the best engineer for developing the project left the army three or four years ago and works for a high-tech firm, we contract with the given company for a limited period of time and hire this engineer for the mission. Reciprocal cooperation is important, because we need skills that have now left for the private sector, and the high-tech companies need our assistance and equipment for their development. And what we end up with is a product that fits the market and supports the Israeli economy.

In other countries, the cooperation with government institutions, especially defense, is very restricted, and the deals are never as unquestionable and guaranteed as with the Israeli Ministry of Defense. For example, the *milouim* is very important in our lives. It is an annual reserve duty for all Israeli males that gathers the members of a unit for 4 weeks every year. During this time, I meet my comrades with whom I was in the army and university 27 years ago. We served three or five years and then people scattered in various fields around the world, but at least three times a year we are united again. This kind of friendship that unites Israeli comrades is very unique and serves as a life-long networking resource.

This unique relationship is persistent especially in certain units (tankers, paratroopers, commando, and intelligence) and fields (computing, security). When two Israelis meet, usually the first question is, "Where did you serve in the army?" This helps create links and common references.

On the other hand, you can understand the difficulties faced by persons who didn't serve, and the suspicions aroused. People tend to think that they suffer some disease or that they are too individualistic and that they didn't want to give something to the society. When you want to hire people, you want people dedicated to the company, not people working for themselves.

Still, if you ask me if I like this system, I would answer that I'd rather have less good friends and live in a country in peace. Here it's not really a normal life. Of course the relationship developed around the army is very important, but I'd rather not be scared for my children, and not see them go to the front during their military service. That service lasts three years . . . and this is a very long time. ■

SUMMARY

Despite its size and its limited natural resources, Israel has developed a strong economy through education, research, entrepreneurship and technology. Although the strength of Israel's military is a double-edged sword for its society, the defense industry has been a key factor in the fast-paced growth and success of high tech in this country. The Israeli government's support of technology incubators through the universities and the fluid flow of resources between the military and industry bode well for the continued growth of the high-tech industry in Israel.

ENDNOTES

1. "Israel, terre promise des entreprises françaises," in *Revue Française de Coopération Economique avec Israël*, June, July, August 2000, No. 173, p. 31.

2. William A. Orme Jr., "New Israel: Land of Milk and Money," *The Jerusalem Post* and the *New York Times*, April 16, 2000.

3. Guy Rolnik, "Another Country," *Ha'Aretz Economic Supplement*, December 31, 1999.

4. D. Bourra, "Israel: The Promise land of High-Tech," Chamber of Commerce France – Israel, No. 173, p.7.

5. *Science in Israel: A practical guide*. Israel Ministry of Science, 1996, 1997.

6. Guy Rolnik, "Another Country," *Ha'Aretz Economic Supplement*, December 31, 1999.

7. "L'industrie israélienne des télécommunications," in *Revue Française de Coopération Economique avec Israël*, June, July, August 2000, No. 173, p. 17.

8. Phillipe LeFournier "L'Expansion," October 19, 1989.

9.–10. Revue de la Chambre de Commerce France – Israel, Premier semestre 2001, No. 176.

11. *Technological Incubators in Israel*. Ministry of Industry and Trade, Office of the Chief Scientist, July 1999.

12. *Annual Report 1998*. Weizmann Institute of Science, p. 29.

13. William A. Orme Jr., "New Israel: Land of Milk and Money," *The Jerusalem Post* and the *New York Times*, April 16, 2000.

16 IMMIGRATION TO ISRAEL, VENTURE FUNDING, AND ENTREPRENEURSHIP

CHAPTER

EX-SOVIET UNION RUSSIAN IMMIGRATION IN THE SCIENTIFIC DEVELOPMENT OF THE COUNTRY

Due to political events in the former USSR, almost one million Jews have migrated to Israel since the beginning of the 1990s, comprising one-sixth of the total population.

Jewish immigrants from the former Soviet Union (commonly referred to in Israel as Russians) represent a major advantage for the country's future. Initially this great influx increased unemployment, intensified housing problems, and strained the government budget. At the same time however, the immigrants brought to the economy scientific and professional expertise of substantial value. Many skilled and experienced people, including 60 to 70 international-level scientists, have been fully integrated into the Israeli economy. Israel continues to actively recruit renowned scientists.

The Ministry of Science and Technology has also allocated a special budget for subsidies to research centers situated in the peripheral areas of the country, away from the large coastal population centers near Haifa and Tel Aviv. However, it is the Ministry of Commerce and Industry's initiative to create technology incubators that is the most remarkable of all Israeli efforts in this area. In 1993, with a budget of $50 million, the ministry approved 148 projects (of which 79 were proposed by immigrants) to be carried out in 24 technopoles for creating and developing future products. These 24 centers already employ 650 researchers, of which 513 are recent immigrants. These incubators are indicative of the integration efforts aimed at helping the former Soviet scientists to develop the Israeli economy through innovation.

THE AMERICAN CONNECTION

A very close relationship exists between American companies and Jewish American industrialists investing in Israel. There has been a U.S. presence in Israel for at least three decades. Two high-tech giants — IBM and Motorola — established local subsidiaries for sales and technical support in the 1960s. Over time the local plants evolved into full research and development facilities. Motorola took the process one step further and established one of its largest manufacturing facilities in Arad, near the Dead Sea. During the late 1970s Intel Corporation began operations in Israel. Today, Intel's activities range from R&D in Haifa to wafer manufacturing in Jerusalem (designated Fab 8), and a new plant under construction in Kiryat Gat (designated Fab 18).

The American government is a major factor in the Israeli economy. Roughly half of the Israeli government's external debt is owed to the U.S., which is its major source of economic and military aid. Three billion dollars have been given annually to Israel since the Yom Kippur War of 1973, and other substantial help and funds have been regularly provided to the country. These funds have been particularly useful for the building and developing of Israeli industry.

NON-U.S. FOREIGN INVESTMENT IN ISRAEL

Israeli high-tech companies benefit from international know-how and professional experience from Europe as well.

Foreign industrialists and companies like Volkswagen, Hoescht, Henkel, Samsung, Daewoo, Fujitsu, Nestlé, Volvo, Nokia, and Carlsberg have started understanding the potential of the country. The net amount of foreign investments in Israel in 1995 reached a record $2 billion. More than 150 foreign companies have invested in R&D in Israel and the country has signed binational industrial cooperation agreements in R&D, with countries including the United States, Canada, France, the Netherlands, Spain, and Hungary. Israel also has free trade agreements with Europe and the United States.

DEVELOPMENT OF THE
VENTURE CAPITAL SECTOR

A dynamic venture capital sector has emerged in Israel since the mid-1990s. The country is now the third-largest regional venture capital recipient in the world: in November 1999, for instance, some $276 million was invested, with only California and Massachusetts exceeding this amount.

This sector has increased from only one company with $34 million of investment funds in 1994, to 70 investment companies with more than 50 funds relevant to high-tech industries. Moreover, since the beginning of the 1990s, the Israeli venture-capital industry has invested around $2 billion, of which $800 million was earmarked for high-tech companies.

Many of the investors include major companies from North America, Western Europe, and the Far East looking to profit from Israel's unique capabilities in communications, computer software, medical equipment, and biotechnology. The list of foreign investors ranges from leading investment banks like Hambrecht & Quist and Goldman Sachs in the U.S., George Soros' Quantum, and Converse Technologies, and major worldwide business corporations like France Telecom, Germany's Siemens and Daimler Benz, and Japan's Kyocera. The U.S. aircraft manufacturer Boeing also recently invested in an Israeli venture capital fund — its first such investment anywhere in the world.[1]

One unique aspect of Israeli venture capital is that the government initiated this most capitalistic of endeavors. Yigal Erlich, a former chief scientist at the Ministry of Industry and Trade, set up the government-owned Yozma Management and Investment Fund, which raised some $200 million in the first wave of venture capital investment. Yozma, still headed by Mr. Erlich, has since been privatized.

In Israel, the venture capital assumption — that only a small percentage of these start-ups will actually succeed but that the profits from these companies will be enough to make the investment worthwhile — has paid handsome dividends, with the average fund earning 40% to 50% in annual returns during the high-tech market expansion of the late 1990s.

THE NETWORKING CULTURE

The Israeli culture is in many aspects very close to the Silicon Valley culture of young and dynamic people working and playing together. These past few years have been characterized by the development of many "serial creators," who have become the new go-getting superstars of commerce such as those who created Mirabilis and Check Point.

The unique Israeli spin is that these creators are not only animated by the spirit of the economy, but they also have developed a strong capacity to network, which forms the basis of the Israeli model. These networks, which include business partners and competitors, and also their families, schools, the Jewish Diaspora, and Israel's American links, are omnipresent in the daily life of these managers. The networks are maintained and strengthened every day through any exchange and communication opportunity that might appear. Not surprisingly, Israel is one of the countries with the largest number of mobile phones per inhabitant.

Some government efforts have been made to set up formal networking, mainly initiated by the Ministry of Industry and Trade. In particular, a magnet program that resembled an R&D network was initiated to convert military technology into civilian applications.[2] Scientists from the Institutes take part in a few Magnet programs. Today the magnet program is not limited to the conversion of military technology.

ACCEPTANCE OF TECHNOLOGY IN THE HOME

Israel has firmly established itself as the most computerized country in the Middle East; it even surpasses some Western European nations. In 1997, more than 250,000 PCs were sold in Israel with a population of 6 million, compared with 102,000 sold in Egypt with a population of 60 million, and just under 300,000 sold in Turkey with a population of 65 million.

Israel also leads the Middle East with the highest penetration rate of PCs in private homes. There is a personal computer in nearly one out of two households, a ratio similar to that of the United States, Canada, and a very few European and Far Eastern countries. In recent years, the education system has purchased tens of thousands of computers for use by students, from kindergarten through university age.

Compared with other so-called high-tech tigers, such as South Korea, Singapore, and Taiwan, Israel is unique in that it is a true high-tech country, with a highly developed domestic market for computing and telecommunications. Israel is also a quick adopter of advanced technologies. Local expenditure on information technology is estimated at $2.4 billion in 1997, with a steady annual growth rate of 12% to 15% compared with worldwide expenditure on information technology totalling about $700 billion, with a five-year compound annual growth rate of about 10%.

CONSEQUENCES OF THE HIGH-TECH EVOLUTION ON THE ISRAELI SOCIETY AND ECONOMY

The values of the traditional Israeli economy (collectives, hierarchy, social security, political support) appear to have been diminished in response to market forces, particularly American market forces.[3] A new elite has appeared in Israel, composed of high-tech entrepreneurs, employees, investors, and executives, and this has brought about a social revolution.

It can be argued that all those changes have influenced Israeli culture, but the high-tech sector is concentrated in a 30-km area around Tel Aviv called Kiriat Atidim, and in a small area of Haifa. These enclaves have one of the highest GNP per capita in the world and its population is fully Americanized: working between Kiriat Atidim and the U.S. can be seamless.

For many Israelis these changes are reshaping not only the economic landscape but also the whole of Israeli society. The digital divide is producing economic schisms in a society that was once proudly egalitarian. Most of the wealth is going to a small percentage of the population. Around 100,000 people work in high-tech in Israel and a one-third of them are highly paid, while in the rest of the economy the wages are stagnant and with the economic downturn, the unemployment rate in Israel is hovering at 10%.

SOME IMPORTANT WEAKNESSES ARE STILL THREATENING THE ISRAELI MODEL

Despite of the clear strengths that have been developed by the Israeli system, some weaknesses remain.

First is the country's dependency on the international high-tech economy. Drastic economic changes, like those that affected the Nasdaq in 2000 and 2001, have hit Israel particularly hard. In addition, the small size of most of these companies makes it particularly difficult for them to weather strong economical and financial pressures. In past years, many Israeli high-tech companies had no other choice but to be acquired by bigger ones, notably from the United States.

The country's geographical isolation and small domestic market make it totally dependent on its export market and company partners. The direct consequence of this is that Israeli companies are particularly sensitive to foreign economic or political movements, or to the financial situation of a major foreign client or partner.

THE ISRAEL MODEL IS STILL STRONG

Despite these short-term reversals, Israel benefits from a leadership position in high tech, thanks to initiatives and governmental incentive measures inspired both by volunteerism and pragmatism: a high proportion of GDP dedicated to civil R&D; creation of numerous start-ups by young scientists; synergy between universities, research institutes, and start-ups; the establishment of investment funds ($100 million) in order to attract foreign investment the establishment of technological incubators; and, lastly, emphasis on technological niches such as database protection systems, management of computer networks, Internet traffic management, biotechnology, and ophthalmology.

Figures 16-1 and 16-2 illustrate the key components of the Israel model.

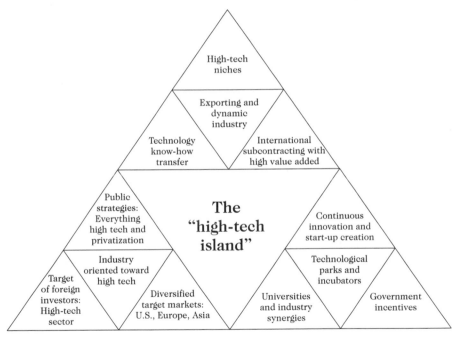

FIGURE 16-1 The "high-tech island."

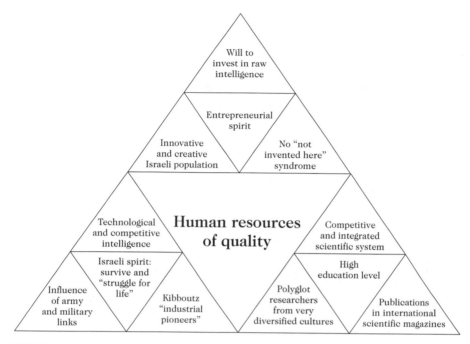

FIGURE 16-2   Human resources of quality.

ISRAELI ENTREPRENEURS AND VENTURE CAPITALISTS

We sought out an Israeli venture capitalist, Edouard Cukierman, as well as an Israeli start-up founder, Marc Arbitbol, who each provide an insider perspective on the dynamics of the Israeli venture capital and start-up company market model.

Cukierman & Co. Investment House is an investment banking company dedicated to providing strategic counsel and assistance to Israeli growth companies in their efforts to draw upon European capital markets through private placements (PP) and initial public offerings (IPOs).

Created in 1999, Catalyst is a development capital fund of Cukierman that invests primarily in Israeli and Israeli-related high-technology companies prior to IPO or other exit. Edouard Cukierman, is the chairman of Cukierman & Co. Investment House Ltd., and CEO of Catalyst Fund. He provides his perspective on venture funding in Israel.

EDOUARD CUKIERMAN

Venture capital criteria for funding Israeli start-ups

I think one major characteristic is the absolute obligation, for most Israeli companies, to develop the business internationally at a very early stage.

Take the example of OTI, in which the Venture Capital Fund Astra invested in 1995 and managed until 2000. OTI is a technology leader in the field of contactless smart cards, for which there was a very limited local market in Israel. It was therefore necessary for this company to start their marketing efforts abroad, which was a major challenge for this company to overcome very early in its development. In the smart card field in particular most players of the first generation of technologies were French, and OTI found it very hard to penetrate these organizations. At that time, these companies essentially worked only with French technologies.

OTI, therefore, started to establish partnership alliances with German and Asian companies, which, together with the U.S. companies, were starting to compete in the smart card market with second-generation technologies. The success of the first activities initiated by OTI made it possible to take the company public in the Neuer Markt in Germany.

From a general point of view, Israeli companies are often obliged to compete with leading technologies and leading players worldwide. In addition, these companies do not have access to the markets in which their products are sold, as they are not physically present. The consequence is that they need additional resources, notably in terms of marketing and distribution, which they do not usually have.

The solution chosen by many companies — like OTI — is to operate with market-driven players with which they establish partnership agreements. Israeli companies therefore provide technology solutions, while foreign partners market the products. This was the case with another Israeli company, Vcon, which we accompanied as their investment banker during their IPO on the French Nouveau Marché (equivalent to the U.S. Nasdaq). The company established OEM agreements with players like Siemens, Philips, Sony, and others, which initially realized 100% of its sales before Vcon was able to market their product using their own brand name. And it was only a few years later that Vcon started opening subsidiaries worldwide and setting up its own sales force.

Strengths of Israeli high-tech companies

Entrepreneurship culture is a key asset of Israeli companies. The experience provided by the army, notably, gives Israeli people the ability to take and manage risk.

Another asset is technology expertise. Israelis are very technology driven. Their education, in particular, provides a very practical training to engineers: early in their education they have to choose specific applications on which they will work until they graduate.

I do not think however that this approach necessarily has to be imitated. Asian companies, for example, are more focused on manufacturing whereas European companies may be more focused on market distribution, and it works. You have to focus on your strengths and leverage them.

In the Israeli system, the technology sector benefitted from the active support of the government. The Israeli state co-invested with private funds in many start-ups, operating indirectly with the launching of incubation programs, the development of industrial parks, etc.

Israel faces special difficulties

Of course Israel's political situation has some impact on the business arena, as it might sometimes affect the perception of foreign companies which could be more reluctant to invest or develop their activities with an Israeli company.

The biggest constraint however is linked to the Nasdaq crash of 2000 and 2001, which strongly affects high-technology companies. As a consequence, many small-to medium-sized Israeli companies — that is, the majority — will have a more difficult time finding funds, and this is precisely where they need to develop.

Israeli companies have two main options to surmount these hurdles: to restructure and reorganize or to be bought by or merge with bigger players. ∎

ENTREPRENEURIAL PERSPECTIVE: VISIONIX

Visionix Ltd. is an Israeli high-tech company that develops and manufactures optical lens inspection equipment. Founded in 1994, the company is considered a world leader and its technology can be found in over 30 countries around the world. With offices and R&D facilities in Israel and the United States, Visionix has succeeded in building a wide customer base of leading companies in the fields of optics, construction, and aeronautics.

Until now, the ophthalmic lens and mold analysis measurement process was conducted by a one-point-at-a-time lensmeter. This provided limited information on only one small portion of the optic element. The technology developed by Visionix enabled quick and simultaneous measurements of all of the optical parameters of an entire lens, contact lens, or mold. Within seconds, lens manufacturers and laboratories are now able to obtain a comprehensive and accurate picture of the lens' sphere, cylinder, axis, and prism, while users are ensured an instantaneous and accurate examination of the entire optical element.

This technology, developed by a team of Israeli and international experts, quickly proved to be an "eye-opener" for the electro-optic and ophthalmic industry. By applying this user-friendly technology to their routine, lens manufacturers and labs found they were able to obtain a real-time, comprehensive, and accurate picture of all of the optical parameters of an entire lens within seconds. Recently, Visionix was able to apply the above technology in the development of a lensmeter for the ophthalmologist, optometrist, and optician.

On February 1, 2000, Visionix completed a successful IPO at the German Neuer Markt (New Market).[4]

Marc Abitbol, founder, chairman of the board and CEO of Visionix, discusses the context in which his company developed a worldwide presence from a base in one of Israel's high-tech regions.

MARC ABITBOL

Immigrant innovators are encouraged by government support

At the beginning of the 1990s, a significant migration of Russian Jews converged on Israel. More than a million reached the country, representing nearly 20% of the Israeli population. Both from an economic and social perspective it was necessary for the Israeli state to build an infrastructure that would enable Israel to thrive despite this influx of immigrants.

The Israeli state therefore decided to launch a series of programs to facilitate and foster the emergence of technological areas within Israel. This program particularly focused on providing incubation facilities to high-tech start-ups. Between 1994 and 1996, Visionix developed in this context. During these years the company grew within the Jerusalem College technology incubator, which was key to our success as we started with a team with no experience in running a company and developing a business. One of the founders had a sales background while the other came from a technical background. In the incubator, we were coached and taught how to manage a company, to build a budget, to be international, to understand the global challenges we were facing, to build up the team, etc. In addition, this active support enabled us to reduce the time between the idea and its implementation on the market. After two years we became totally different people with the capacity to launch our company.

Today Visionix is located in an industrial park that includes many other start-ups. This industrial park does not provide particular support to these companies, but it does provide a suitable environment to develop high-tech activities.

Technological superiority is one key to success for start-ups

As for many Israeli companies, the first asset we developed was our technology. Providing technological innovation was the condition of success to penetrate the market. This is necessary when you are a small company and you want to compete with giant international firms in the same field. Visionix has, therefore, developed a unique technology for lens measurement, which enabled us to strongly position ourselves.

The second component is people. You can't start a company without highly moti-vated and talented people. The quality of the team is a key issue, not only in man-agement, but also in marketing, research and development, and in the administrative side. It was also very important to have a good marketing manager, someone able to "feel" the market and to guide the R&D people in a positive direc-tion. Developing strong marketing leadership was fundamental, and at Visionix we managed to have customers before we had a product. This is particularly crucial for an Israeli company as we are far from the market, which is mainly located in Europe and in the United States. This is in fact a major key success factor of many Israeli companies that are forced to go outside the country to sell their products.

IPO in Europe is a good option

We chose to have our IPO on the European market rather than on the Nasdaq, since Europe is leading the optical technology market. France, and especially Ger-many, take the lead with regards to optical technologies. In addition, 60% of our business was done in Europe, and our industrial clients are European, so Visionix chose to go public on the Neuer Markt to be close to its strong European customer base. We felt confident that our core technology and current applications for opti-cal diagnostic equipment would be well appreciated by leaders in the optics indus-try. Through the IPO we strive to increase our brand awareness within the European market, which sets standards throughout the optical world.

We have also concluded an important agreement with the French Essilore, which is number one worldwide in ophthalmic lens manufacture. We collaborated with this company in 1998 to produce a new diagnostic device for opticians and optom-etrists, which has been distributed all over Europe since 1999. We also have a retail distribution agreement with Marco in the U.S.

Israel as a "high-tech island"?

Around 98% of our sales are for export, although there is nothing in the Middle East. Major high-tech products could not find markets in that area. This has nega-tive and positive impacts.

The negative impact is that it is more difficult for us to sell across the world. The positive impact is that it forced us at a very early stage to look outside Israel. We have to think globally, and therefore the drawback of being isolated from the mar-ket became an advantage that forced us to become a global company. ∎

SUMMARY

Israel currently endures a difficult political and economic situation. It has suffered from the same economic setbacks as other linked Innovation Economy regions, such as Ireland and Taiwan, caused by the dot-com melt-down, the recession of 2001, and the aftereffects of the September 11 terrorist attacks. In addition, Israel is hurt by ongoing terrorist activity, which has taken its toll on foreign confidence in its short-term attractiveness. However, Israel is still perceived as an R&D hotbed of innovation. The fundamentals of military transfer of technology to civilian application, well-run university incubators for start-ups, a huge Russian Jewish immigrant cadre of engineers and scientists, vibrant venture capital, and entrepreneurial champions are all in place for its continued integration as a world leading region for the Innovation Economy.

ENDNOTES

1. Based on material published in the local Jerusalem newspaper *Kol Ha'ir*, August 30, 1996.

2. "Vekstein D. Defence conversion, technology policy and R&D networks in the innovation system of Israel." *Technovation*, Vol. 19, October 1999.

3. Guy Rolnik, "Another Country," *Ha'Aretz Economic Supplement*, December 31, 1999.

4. The Neuer Markt is the market segment for high-growth companies of the Deutsche Boerse AG. As of September 2000, 318 companies were traded on the Neuer Markt.

VI

India: The Best Hope for Bridging the Digital Divide

Perhaps no other country in the world has staked as much hope and relative financial resources on the Innovation Economy as India. The government has made great strides to open markets and create a globally competitive economy. The institutes of higher education have set an excellent standard for universities as a great national resource for research and economic development. Indian software engineers and programmers have succeeded as equal members of multinational teams. Indian entrepreneurs have created many successful start-ups in India, Silicon Valley, and other regions. Indians throughout the world's most important technology companies have risen to the highest levels of management. Indian venture capitalists and successful NRIs (non-resident Indians) have taken major roles in helping to transform the Indian economy from a marginal third-world country barely able to feed its teeming population to a fast-growing economic powerhouse of great promise.

In this section, we explore each of these factors to help understand the Indian model for adaptation to the Innovation Economy.

17 INDIA'S IT SECTOR AND GOVERNMENT INITIATIVES IN EDUCATION

The Indian IT sector developed out of a much-needed government emphasis on economic reforms. Spurred by the economic crisis of 1991, the Indian government took widespread action to liberalize and open the economy to major foreign investments. This shift began with the election of Rajiv Gandhi, whose administration was the first to recognize the potential of the Indian IT industry for the nation's economic development, and continues under the current administration of Prime Minister Atal Bihari Vajpayee in 2002.

In the interim, the Indian IT industry has shown remarkable growth, especially in the area of software exports. Today, the service-based sector of the IT industry has made significant progress, gradually shifting from the low value-added IT tasks of writing applications for foreign software to creating their own. The low costs of offshore development have been a key factor in India's presence in the global IT service industry. India's competitive base however consists of an increasingly large set of English-speaking, technically skilled professionals, motivated and inspired by India's recent success in the software sector.

Our focus on the Indian Institute of Technology as an example of India's leading technical universities showcases the ability of a developing nation like India to mobilize its existing strengths to combat its weaknesses. For example, the degree of competitiveness and cost-effectiveness of India's engineering and computer science graduates is a strong incentive for multinational companies (MNCs) to invest in India despite its infrastructure hurdles.

A large cluster of educational institutes and IT MNC investments, combined with ideal living conditions, have created the IT cluster of Bangalore, where the majority of Indian and MNC IT software companies are located.

DEVELOPING NATION STATUS

While the rest of the countries profiled in this book are in the top 25 nations for competitiveness, India represents the developing world with a competitiveness ranking of 41 in the 2001 World Competitiveness Overall Scoreboard (see Table 17-1).

TABLE 17-1   India Compared with Other Developed Countries by Competitiveness Ranking

	INDIA	U.S.	IRELAND	SWEDEN	GERMANY	ISRAEL	TAIWAN	U.K.	FRANCE
Rank	41	1	7	8	12	16	18	19	25
Score	40.4	100	79.2	77.9	74.0	67.9	64.8	64.8	59.6

Source: Stephane Garelli, The World Competitiveness Yearbook 2001, IMD, 2001.

With the problems of poverty and underdeveloped infrastructure, the status of "developing nation" can bring with it the advantage of a thirst for prosperity based in deep-rooted values of hard work and reverence for knowledge, a particularly valuable characteristic for the Indian people in the global Innovation Economy.

TABLE 17-2   Facts at a Glance — India

POLITICAL SYSTEM	
Official name	Republic of India
Government	Democratic, parliamentary (executive, legislative, and judiciary branches)
Political system	Republic with federal structure (25 states and 7 union territories)

TABLE 17-2   Facts at a Glance — India (Continued)

GEOGRAPHIES	
Land area	3.29 million sq km
Languages	Multilingual, Hindi spoken by largest percentage (38%) and English the preferred business language
International airports	New Delhi, Mumbai, Chennai, Calcutta, and Thiruvananthapuram
GDP ranking	India ranked 4th globally in 2000 with $1,797,746 million
GDP per capita	136th in 2000 with $1,773 million

INDIAN IT INDUSTRY	
1999–2000 revenues	$8.67 billion
1999–2000 growth rate	50% (relative to revenues of $6.05 billion, 1998–1999)
1995–2000 compounded annual growth rate	42.4% (double the rate of most developed countries)
1999–2000 IT spending (% of GDP)	1.68%
2008 projected IT spending	3% of GDP

IT SECTORS	
1999–2000 software contribution to total IT revenues	Over 65%
1999–2000 IT employment	Over 200,000 workers
1999–2000 software growth rate	53% (revenues at $5,053 million)
Annual manufacturing growth rate	30% to 35% over past decade
1999–2000 peripherals growth rate	38% (revenues at $462 million)
1999–2000 IT training growth rate	37% (revenues at $400 million)
PC penetration	5 PCs per 1,000 people (as of December 31, 2000)
Internet subscribers	5.5 million (as of December 31, 2000)

POVERTY ESTIMATES	
People living below poverty line	350–400 million (75% of these in rural areas)

Sources: Census of India 2001, www.censusindia.net; NASSCOM, www.nasscom.org/ it_industry/indic_statistics.asp; "India — A Country Study," The Library of Congress, lcweb2.loc.gov/frd/cs/intoc.html.

1991 INDIAN ECONOMIC LIBERALIZATION

After gaining independence from the British in 1947, the Indian government adopted a protectionist policy of strict control over the economy that left no room for innovative ventures. A mere 55 years later, the rest of the world is watching in marvel as India has transformed its closed-door model of self-sustenance into an economy fostering rapid developments and entrepreneurial endeavors in the technology sectors.

Shifts in the Indian economy began after the election of Rajiv Gandhi in 1984, when India's protectionist policies gave way to a new focus on opening up the economy for emerging IT and software-related industries. Soon after Gandhi took office, the government began to liberalize the computer and software industries and, in 1986, Texas Instruments received permission to establish a 100% foreign-owned subsidiary in India. This led to the influx of numerous MNC investments in India, with over 2000[1] global IT companies involved in the Indian IT industry today.

India's economic crisis began in 1991, when it faced a foreign debt emergency that made international loans for the country less available. The World Bank recommended significant economic reforms in India, which the government followed with a mass liberalization of the economy to open up the Indian market. These liberalization efforts included a complete overhaul of foreign investment regulations, a simplification of existing tax policies and the introduction of significant new tax incentives in key sectors in need of development, such as building infrastructure. This led to the entry of MNCs that began to invest in specific innovative regions in India that comprise vibrant centers of IT development today.

Some of the key MNCs investing in India include IBM, whose Global Services in Bangalore include a 10-year outsourcing project for applications development, enhancement, and maintenance; Sun Microsystems, which has identified India as one of its top five locations, with the potential to create in excess of $1 billion over the next five years, and plans to expand its Indian working force from 400 to 4,000 in this period; and Intel, which has committed a $25 million investment and plans to expand its engineering staff by 50%.[2]

The investments brought in by these large MNCs are creating urban conglomerates of concentrated high-tech activities in India. In addition to the task of generating wealth within their own localities, these IT clusters have the added responsibility of fostering wealth in surrounding second- and third-tier regions, such as Mysore and Mangalore around Bangalore. In a developing nation like India, these regions have the potential to not only strengthen their distinct clusters, but also to diffuse wealth in specialized zones nearby that lack the negative burdens of their high-tech counterparts, like high costs of living, pollution, traffic congestion, and overpopulation.

The Indian economy is also currently benefiting from policy reforms made in the 1980s that opened up opportunities for a software export industry based on "body shopping" (migration of programmers to client sites) in the U.S. This growth in the IT industry has branded India as an important destination for large investments from MNCs that are seeking to outsource their software needs. NASSCOM (India's National Association of Software and Services Companies) is the unified voice lobbying collectively — and effectively — to promote the Indian IT industry both in India and abroad. Founded in 1988 with 38 members, by 1999 its 464 members represented 95% of Indian software industry revenues.[3] NASSCOM estimates that offshore outsourcing by MNCs will grow 23% during 2002, as companies rapidly seek to establish a presence in the Indian software export industry.[4] A significant chunk of India's software export revenues, 15%,[5] stems from accounts with MNCs. Thus, India is aggressively seeking to develop its competitive edge in this industry.

Under the new liberalization measures of the economy in 1991, India has become attractive for direct foreign investment. Since this process of economic reforms began, tax rates are on par with those of developed nations and shifts toward favorable economic policies, combined with an awakening of government support, are establishing India as a competitive destination for international companies expanding their global IT operations. While the country is catching up on much-needed developments in infrastructure and government policies necessary to support a thriving high-technology industry, specific IT clusters like Bangalore are leading the way with examples of conducive interactions between government, industry, and educational bodies for the sustainable growth of IT in India.

INDIA — DESTINATION FOR GLOBAL IT SOFTWARE OPERATIONS

Rapid technological developments have contributed significantly to the growth of the IT industry, and India is now emerging as an important destination for global IT business. The growth of the computer industry spawned vibrant software and hardware industries as well as the rapid adoption of the Internet in India. Both the government and private sectors have emerged as major end-users of computer systems and software, and thousands of local Internet cafes are mushrooming all over India. The Internet and technology has not only become a trend, but is quickly acknowledged by most Indians as the wave of the future for both the nation's success and their own.

Indian software companies are concentrated most in the areas of banking, financial services, insurance, manufacturing, the Internet, and e-commerce. The IT area of enabled teleworking services (call centers, medical and legal transcriptions, data and map digitization, CAD, management of large databases, Web content creation and animation) is the latest software sector to attract large interest and investment in India. This sector currently employs 25,000 people and is expected to explode over the next decade to create an estimated one million jobs.[6]

In 2000, Internet home connections in India were estimated to be about 1.6 million, while the total number of users was at about 4.8 million. Internet users[7] were in the age group of 19–34, of which 80% were male. Basic estimates[8] indicate that the Internet user spends about 10 hours per week on the Internet, earns over Rs. 6,000 (or $125) per month, and is most likely to use the Internet for accessing e-mail. Current demographics indicate that less than 5% ever buy anything online.

Despite the 2001 economic slowdown, the IT industry has continued to grow at an annual rate of about 50%. Joel Ruet, coordinator of economics at the Centre de Sciences Humaines in New Delhi, is author of a comprehensive analysis on the Indian high-tech sector.[9] His areas of expertise are in the fields of reform of the public sector in developing countries and integration of informal sectors in the global economy. Dr. Ruet discusses his thoughts on the implications of the economic slowdown of 2001 on the Indian IT sector.

JOEL RUET

Effects of the economic slowdown on the Indian IT industry

Despite the negative effects of the current economic recession in the U.S. on the Indian IT industry, the long-term expectation for the global IT industry is that it will continue to grow. The immediate result of this slowdown is probably a much needed shakeout of the companies in this industry. Only the most competitive and the most viable are likely to emerge out of this phase of the economy. But the IT needs of global companies will continue to grow, and thus firms will continue to invest in information systems, which in turn will continue to generate services.

This is great news for the Indian IT industry, which is largely service-centric. Multinationals are likely to turn to India's low cost differential during these tough times in order to cut costs and to increase their return on IT investments. This can be a great opportunity for Indian companies to enter new markets through this second wave of IT investments. ■

COMPETITIVE CHALLENGE FOR INDIA'S SOFTWARE INDUSTRY: MOVING UP THE IT VALUE CHAIN

Indian companies placed themselves on the high-tech map as providers of low-cost software development in the mid-1990s by offering price-competitive, high-quality software development. This in turn attracted a multitude of MNCs that quickly set up remote development centers or contracted work to local firms.

The Indian software industry began with onsite staffing services at clients' overseas locations. From this low end of the value chain of IT services, the industry is steadily becoming more sophisticated. By 1999, up to 40% of high-tech exports were in offshore services or packaged products. While Indian software companies before 2000 relied mostly on contracts to fix Y2K glitches, these companies are now slowly beginning to move up the value chain to write software for e-commerce, wireless applications, embedded software, and customer relation management (CRM).

However, despite India's success in the IT industry, it is still a low-cost service provider. According to the K.B. Chandrasekhar Committee Report[10] on VC (venture capital) in India, it is time for India to take a stronger position in the high-tech value chain. As outlined by this report, the sequence of steps is information, knowledge, ideas, innovation, product development, and marketing. India is still at the knowledge level in this chain.

IT IN BANGALORE: THE INDUS VALLEY, INDIA'S SILICON STATE

One of the most important factors for the success of Bangalore as the pre-eminent region for high-tech development in India is the positive, open attitude of its people. Bangalorites have a long tradition of receptivity to ideas. Kailash Joshi, president of TiE, Silicon Valley, has characterized this region as having "cosmopolitan soil." This attitude positions the region for success in the globally linked innovation economy.

As the capital of the southern state of Karnataka, Bangalore benefits from early developments in infrastructure and strong government support for future growth in facilities. The establishment of the Indian Institute of Science (IISc), India's most prestigious research institute, was also key in drawing investment to the region. Also important was the setting up of the Indian software technology parks in 1991. In 1997 the government of Karnataka became the first state government to announce its own IT policy, and in 1999 the Indian Institute of Information Technology (IIIT) in Bangalore was established.

Bangalore has long been likened to the Silicon Valley in California for its attraction of entrepreneurial enterprises and innovation. Its historical emphasis on engineering and defense industry work, combined with the pleasant climate and high quality of life, has made it a magnet for skilled entrepreneurs seeking to make a fortune in the IT industry. In 1984, when the Indian government gave Texas Instruments (TI) the right to establish a 100% self-controlled offshore center in India, TI chose Bangalore as its site. Since then, MNCs have been flocking to this region.

The conglomeration of large global corporations like TI, Siemens, Phillips, Lucent Technologies, Motorola, Cisco Systems, Ericcson, Sony, Oracle, and Sun Microsystems has been another critical factor in the influx of investments in this region. In fact, these MNCs and successful Indian software companies like Wipro and Infosys have made considerable cooperative investments with leading local universities like the IISc and the IIIT in Bangalore. IISc itself has evolved from 10 joint projects with the industry sector in the last three years, to over 80 in the last year.[11]

The literacy rate in Bangalore is relatively high (80.5%) compared with the national rate (52%). The state government's IT policy has resulted in fairly strong connectivity (155,000 telephone connections, 10,000 Internet connections, and 11,500 e-mail connections in the year 2000[12]), which is well appreciated by the IT firms that have established base in Bangalore.

The 25 engineering colleges around the city provide a consistent surplus of talent. The IT sector is the biggest industry in Bangalore, with 32% of India's software production based there.[13] Besides the illustrious science and technology institutes, the Indian Institute of Management (IIM) and National Institute of Advanced Studies (NIAS) are also based in this city.

The concentration of these educational institutes, IT firms, and skilled talent in this region combine to make Bangalore the most technologically advanced of the high-tech regions in India. Strong government support in the form of legislative and infrastructure commitments serves to create a secure environment, as the government is building better roads and an international airport. At the same time, its existing educational systems are being enhanced by the development of learning centers and competitive R&D facilities.

INTERNATIONAL TECH PARK, BANGALORE: THE ONE-STOP IT SOLUTION

The International Tech Park of Bangalore is located about 20 km outside of Bangalore, and represents about 55% of the government's investment in the region. A joint venture between the investment section of one of India's largest corporations, the Tata Group, a consortium of Singapore companies led by Ascendas Land International Pte. Ltd., and the Karnataka Industrial Areas Development Board, the aim of this park is to create a "one-stop solution"[14] environment for the high-tech needs of knowledge-based MNCs in India. The park already accommodates major international conglomerates in IT-related services like telecommunications, R&D, financial services, biotechnology, and electronics. Despite the recent slowdown of the economy, Bangalore is gearing up to extend its commitments to current and future occupants. The following table shows the dramatic growth of the number of companies and the volume of exports over the ten years of development since 1992.

TABLE 17-3　Software Industry Growth and High-Tech Exports from Bangalore

Year	Number of Companies	Exports in $ Millions
1992	29	0
1993	53	0
1994	79	3
1995	125	42
1996	163	100
1997	207	202
1998	267	368
1999	782	692
2000	812	995

Sources: Olivier Bomsel and Joël Ruet, "Digital India: Report on the Indian IT Industry," Centre d'Économie Industrielle, Ecole Nationale Supérieure des Mines de Paris, www.cerna.ensmp.fr/Documents/DigitalIndia-MainFindings.pdf; STPI (Software Technology Parks of India).

THE QUALITY MOVEMENT: INDIA'S COMPETITIVE ADVANTAGE

India has fundamental advantages in competing for IT investments because of its combination of a skilled and English-speaking work force willing to work at internationally competitive wages, a reliable communications network in the major cities, and an ideal time zone placement for 24-hour, 7 days a week production. Some of the key success factors placing India in a leading slot for software developments compared with other nations include:

■ **Reputation for quality** — India's tremendous pool of highly skilled intellectual capital in the fields of technology and engineering are a critical asset. As of October 2001, India had 32 companies at Software Engineering Institute (SEI) Capability Maturity Model (CMM) Level 5 (highest) assessment, whereas there are only about 58 organizations in the world to have acquired such standards of excellence.[15]

■ **Competitive costs** — According to NASSCOM, the cost advantage of developing services in India ranges from 30% to 80% lower than those in the U.S. or Europe.

■ **English fluency** — Besides India's ease with technology and engineering, its preference for the English language for business practices serves to facilitate communication. The country's pool of English-speaking scientific and technical personnel is the second largest in the world (after the U.S.), and thus a key business consideration for investments.

■ **Expertise** — A track record of success in the IT industry has created a significant presence for India on the global IT front. Software exports by large MNCs in India grew by a sharp 30% in 2000 as more companies diversified and expanded their Indian operations. Government investments in education during the 1960s also played a significant role in producing India's pool of highly skilled engineers and programmers.

■ **Enormous talent pool** — India's vast output of engineering students is a tremendous resource in staffing the global needs for technically skilled manpower. The Indian venture capital (VC) industry has grown in recognition that supporting this enormous talent pool will be an important prerequisite for the growth of an innovative and entrepreneurial economy in the country.

■ **Time zone placement** — The 12-hour time difference between Indian Standard Time and Pacific Standard Time in the U.S. provides a convenient way to maintain the 24/7 service standard of most MNCs; service centers in the U.S. are thus able to send in their day's work to India for continuing work so that significant progress is made overnight.

■ **Vendor sophistication** — More than 285 Indian IT software and services firms were quality accredited by 2001,[16] and the emerging number of vendors operating under international standards of excellence across a wide gamut of IT software and service areas are a key source of future strength for India's performance in the IT industry.

■ **Transnational support from the Indian Diaspora** — India's vast network of professionals abroad, commonly referred to as non-resident Indians (NRIs), are a key advantage for Indian companies within the nation. The reputation of these entrepreneurs, built on their widespread success across a variety of business enterprises — often in key managerial positions of prominent global companies — has laid the groundwork for the intellectual potential within India. This community of immigrants, once considered India's loss in terms of it's intellectual "brain drain," are now acknowledged to be a vast resource in terms of their access to capital, business expertise, key networks, and emotional commitment to the homeland.

■ **The ethic of hard work** — The ability and drive to work beyond the "call of duty" is an important aspect of the Indian mentality that serves to distinguish the Indian work force. This drive to top every expectation is a natural result of the degree of competition that Indians face in each aspect of life — from getting into the best schools and universities to competing with millions of other talented and driven Indians for jobs, promotions, and future success.

■ **Supportive government IT policies** — Against the backdrop of unprecedented central government mobilization in the IT sector, state government initiatives are also becoming increasingly competitive. For example, the government of Karnataka created incentives for the IT industry by postponing its levy of a 4% sales tax, while the central government in New Delhi has already approved the online payment of specific transactions.

GOVERNMENT INITIATIVES IN EDUCATION

The government of India has recognized the link between the creation of wealth in IT clusters and certain "enabling" characteristics that encourage this wealth creation. In order to create as conducive an environment for attracting IT investments as possible, the government is actively putting these "enabling factors" in place. One of the most critical of these is the development of India's educational institutes, particularly those specializing in the expertise of technology and engineering.

INDIAN EDUCATIONAL SYSTEMS

The Indian educational curriculum is characteristically rigorous — students are aware early on of the competitive prerequisites for receiving a quality education, and strive to enter the most prestigious institutes and streams of emphasis such as mathematics and science. There is great social value derived from being a leading student from a top science or technology-based institute.

With the recent success of Indians in the domestic and international IT industry, the new trend in education — supported firmly by parents — is in the fields of engineering and computer sciences. As a result, the current generation of students in India graduating from both government and private universities are prepared early for their participation in this industry.

India is estimated to have over 4 million technical workers graduating from more than 1,832 educational institutions and polytechnics that train over 67,785 computer software professionals every year.[17] Graduates from outstanding institutes such as the IITs, the IISc, the recently established IIITs, and Regional Engineering Colleges (RECs) are in high demand for an industry seeking disciplined and highly skilled talent with current technical expertise. These educational facilities combine to create the second-largest English-speaking technical work force in the world. In addition, an annual output of over 200,000 engineering graduates combined from public and private colleges, and specialized technical and computer diploma courses, along with about 40,000 management graduates from institutes like the Indian Institutes of Management (IIMs) create a quality and quantity advantage in human resource that gives India a major competitive edge in the IT sector. Indeed, India is the "motherlode" for knowledge-skilled human resources in the worldwide quest for the treasures derived from intellectual capital.

In India's vision of developing a large cadre of knowledge workers from its educational institutes, the Indian government has thus demonstrated its greatest achievement in support of making regional wealth in the Innovation Economy. The government has also further committed to stepping up both the number and quality of computer and technical training facilities in the country in order to capitalize on this extraordinary human resource, with goals of tripling or at least doubling the number of engineering students that emerge from India.

IIT BRAND EQUITY AND NETWORKS OF EXCELLENCE

One of the most well-known systems of technical education of international caliber is the IIT. Spurred by the decision of Sir Jogendra Singh, member of the Viceroy's Executive Council at the Department of Education, Health, and Agriculture, to set up institutes of higher technical education for post-war industrial development in India, the first Indian Institute of Technology was set up in 1950 in the region of Kharakpur. Over the past five decades, five more IITs have been modelled after the resounding success of Kharakpur, each of them a beacon of success in their particular area of expertise. Alumni of these institutes have created an extensive network of high-powered management of MNCs all over the world.

Dr. Shyam Sethi is a visiting professor at the IIT in Delhi, with a vast background in the IIT system of education; he graduated from IIT Kharakpur, and got both his Masters and post-graduate degrees from the IIT. He talks to us about the qualitative advantage of the IITs in producing the world's most talented pool of engineers and programmers, and important lessons from the successful and failed practices of this system of education.

SHYAM SETHI

The IIT stamp of quality: Crème de la crème

IIT has strong brand equity based on its indisputable reputation as the producer of the best brains in engineering and technology. One of the main reasons for this is the competitive entrance examination where really only the "crème de la crème" get in. Out of the 115,000 that appeared for the JEE entrance exam in 2001, only about 3,000 were accepted. This ensures that the caliber of students is exceptionally high.

Another thing maintaining this level of quality is what we call the midcourse correction system at IIT, which consistently evaluates IIT's system of education. One of the biggest concerns for the IIT system is how it can continue to maintain its position as India's pre-eminent institute of technological education and research development.

To address this issue IIT is considering ways to both accommodate more students and to maintain its characteristic level of qualitative output. Boundaries between disciplines are becoming increasingly blurred with the convergence and cross-fertilization of ideas. And IIT is struggling to accommodate an appropriate curriculum that covers new developments in reasonable depth.

The process of redefining the curriculum[18] on a continuous basis requires the active involvement of industry leaders who can ensure that the material equally covers the core essentials of their fields and relevant emerging trends.

Trends in the education curriculum at IIT: Meeting the quality challenge

The IITs are taking many steps to maintain this highly recognized level of quality. One of the newest trends is the incorporation of management as a subject. For example, Delhi has it own business school of management and now its graduates are not only India's top engineers, but also have a strong background in management. The Indian Institute of Management (IIM), in comparison, has a largely management focus.

I think that another important reason for IIT's reputation is the prestigious network associated with the school. A large number of Indians in very senior positions promote the creation of wealth through their vast informal networks. The basic premise is that if you've done IIT, you're good.

IIT — A legacy of education

The students who graduate from the IIT recognize the legacy of this education. Successful alumni are giving back to their alma mater both financially and in terms of time and effort. For example, Vinod Gupta is one of the most successful Indians in the U.S. (founder of American Business Information, with a turnover of $250 million, employing over 1,800 people). After graduating from the IIT in Kharagpur he has committed $8 million to the Vinod Gupta School of Business Administration at IIT, Kharagpur, and one of the goals of this school is to have a computer in every room in the hostel. With 4,000 to 5,000 students, this is a tremendous commitment that requires more than just a financial grant. Emotional commitment and drive are critical elements in the success of NRI relationships with their alumni. In addition, the government plays its part by facilitating the funding of education at the Indian Institutes of Technology, making any kind of corporate sponsorship totally tax deductible.

The Indian government has realized that the production sector is not that viable anymore. There is an overwhelming consensus that IT must be promoted — everyone knows the importance of the knowledge economy in India. And the advantage for Indians is that wherever they are, they feel Indian, they maintain their sense of traditions, their heritage, drive and humbleness.

Lessons for other institutes of higher education from IIT's successes and failures

There are some important lessons from the IIT commitment to becoming one of the most eminent engineering institutes in the world:

- *Maintain an exceptionally high standard of education:* Educational institutes must never compromise on the quality of the intake of their students, and this can be maintained through a rigorous entrance examination system.

- *Maintain autonomy and independence:* It is important for the IITs to remain autonomous institutes with no political or outside influence, so that they can continue to update the curriculum independently, with input from industry experts. The faculty and facilities at the IITs are the best possible in the academic field in India.

- *Be self-renewing through continuous assessment of educational facilities and curriculum:* This has been a proven and successful system for the IITs, where the same teacher teaches and examines. Depending on the intellectual capacity of the students, the teacher can thus improve the standard to any level that the students can take.

On the negative side, the laboratories at IIT have unfortunately not been fully updated to keep pace with time as compared with Europe or the U.S. Also, students go for subjects where they can maximize the immediate gains. Careers for academic technology challenges are thus avoided, resulting in the failure of long term R&D gain.

IIT system of education: A successful experiment

The system of education at IIT is a wonderful experiment of free India; it has provided a very even playing field for aspiring and deserving students from every nook and cranny of this great country. Our role is to continue to carry out this vision. ■

Thus, major technical and scientific institutes of higher education like the IITs are an enormous asset for the growth of regional wealth creation in India. The competitive advantage provided by India's tremendous pool of highly skilled workers available at relatively low costs is one that Indians in this industry have understood and used for the purpose of getting their foot in the door in the IT sector. India's maintenance of the exceptionally high standard of these institutes, combined with planned efforts to double or triple this intellectual capital without compromising on their "brand equity," will be key markers of future success. For Indians, this is one way that the country's overpopulation is an advantage — there is a tremendous amount of talent to choose from. An additional benefit is that the competitive spirit created by this environment requires a dedicated drive and ambition for each individual to stand out and succeed.

The Indian experience demonstrates that a nation's investment in its people through an excellent educational system is easily reimbursed by the students' lifetime capital value. Not only do Indians take pride in each other's successes, but also the opportunities for wealth creation for both the individual and the nation are tremendous. The success of graduates from the IITs both abroad and at home proves that given the right environmental factors, India could excel far beyond anyone's expectations.

A COMING SHORTAGE OF TECH WORKERS?

The task at hand for India's educational institutes is now to both match the demand for computer science and engineering graduates of the future, and to train the existing talent pool to keep up with the ever-changing technological developments. While prestigious institutes like the IITs provide the crème de la crème of the Indian technological work force, facilities like India's RECs provide a large bulk of the technical expertise to power the IT innovation needs of the future. Based on NASSCOM projections of the India IT work force, there is an expected growth of three times the number of experts needed from 2002 to 2008 (see Table 17-4).

TABLE 17-4 NASSCOM Projections on the Requirement of IT Work Force in India

YEAR	IT WORK FORCE
2001	90,000
2002	115,000
2003	150,000
2004	195,000
2005	250,000
2006	300,000
2007	340,000
2008	370,000

Source: NASSCOM, www.nasscom.org/it_industry/indic_statistics.asp.

Here, India's strength lies in its overall output of engineers, combined with the rigorous selection process for student acceptance into the IITs. The average intake of all IITs combined as of October 1, 2001, was a total of 6,469 students, as compared with that of all degree, diploma, and master's in computer applications approved RECs (a total of 3,086 institutes) with a combined intake of 529,671 students per year.[19]

TABLE 17-5   Number of Technical Institutes and Annual Intake of Students per Institute

INSTITUTE TYPE	NUMBER OF INSTITUTES	ANNUAL INTAKE OF STUDENTS
IITs	6	6,469
RECs (degree engineering)	1058	271,719
RECs (diploma engineering)	1231	220,947
RECs (masters in computer applications)	797	37,005

SUMMARY

The Indian government has focused its efforts to lift India's development in the high-technology sector utilizing the inherent strengths of the country. A hard-earned reputation for quality and expertise based on India's enormous talent pool, combined with competitive cost advantages, has allowed India to excel in the IT service-based industry. The Indian ethic of dedicated hard work is a societal asset that corporate managers of large MNCs value greatly. It also counter-balances the risks of establishing development sites in a region that is notorious for insufficient infrastructure and bureaucratic roadblocks. Indians have established their reputation for dedicated diligence through both their performance in the Indian IT industry and their compatriots in high-level management and engineering positions all around the world.

India has the combined support of government leadership in education and an actively involved worldwide Diaspora that invests and develops financial and intellectual capital back and forth. It can now focus both on the future growth of its software industry and the potential impact this industry can have to transform the Indian economy to progress into the status of "developed nation."

ENDNOTES

1.–7.   Department of Information Technology, *itfriend.mit.gov.in/*.

8.   Bangalorenet, *www.bangalorenet.com/internetindia/index.htm*.

9.   *Digital India: Report on the Indian IT Industry*, Centre de Sciences Humaines, 2001.

10.   Report of KB Chandrasekhar Committee on Venture Capital, Securities and Exchange Board of India, *www.sebi.gov.in/report/venture/venrep1.html*.

11.–13. *Digital India: Report on the Indian IT Industry*, Centre de Sciences Humaines, 2001.

14. International Tech Park, Bangalore, *www.intltechpark.com/*.

15.–16. Indian IT Industry — Statistics 2001, NASSCOM, *www.nasscom.org/it_industry/indic_statistics.asp*.

17. Embassy of India, *www.indianembassy.org/indiainfo/india_it.htm*.

18. "Spreading the Light of Education Programme," part of India's Golden Jubilee Celebration, which celebrates India's 50th year of independence.

19. Government of India, Department of Education, *www.education.nic.in*.

▶ About the Author

This chapter was co-authored by **Arti Kuthiala**. With a bachelor's in applied psychology from Delhi University in India, she has worked for the United States Chamber of Commerce and the San Francisco Global Trade Council. Arti is currently pursuing a master's degree in business administration at San Francisco State University, where she is also collaborating on numerous projects with the Ohrenschall Center for Entrepreneurship.

18 TRANSNATIONAL LINKS IN VENTURE CAPITAL FOR THE PUBLIC GOOD — AN ADVANTAGE IN NETWORKING

I ndians both overseas and in India are making innovative spin-offs work for the betterment of the country's poorest. India's newly developed venture capital (VC) industry and fast-paced IT developments make up the networks that are opening doors both for business and for the people of India.

THE PROBLEM OF INFRASTRUCTURE: SOFTWARE TECHNOLOGY PARKS PROVIDE ISLANDS OF RELIABILITY

One of the biggest roadblocks to a real development of the Indian IT industry is the dearth of supporting infrastructure. The government recognized that Software Technology Parks of India[1] (STPIs) were an important prerequisite for MNC investments in the country, creating wealth through offshore software development and production. Such facilities had previously been unreliable and difficult to access, creating one of the biggest disincentives for MNCs to invest extensively. In 1991, the unreliable and inadequate state of India's basic power, electricity, and connectivity infrastructure resulted in key government initiatives to develop the STPIs.

The STPIs were created as autonomous organizations under the Department of Electronics, which is responsible for the direction and development of India's technology park schemes. Thirteen parks have already been installed in diverse cities such as Bangalore, Hyderabad, Chennai, and New Delhi, running at full strength with a highly sophisticated infrastructure. The parks provide multinational IT companies with the power and fiber-optic networking to operate their outsourcing needs. Specific advantages include 100% foreign equity, no import duties on capital goods, duty-free imports of hardware and software within the STPI units, zero corporate income tax until 2010, exemption from excise duty for domestic purchases of capital goods, reimbursement of central sales tax, and overseas investments up to $100 million.

Demand for office space is expected to exceed 66 million square feet over the next five years, while the estimated availability is only 22.5 million square feet. This large gap between supply and demand for stable infrastructure is creating a market for technology parks in India, fostering regional wealth in the form of jobs and corporate investments.

Thus, despite the poor infrastructure of a developing nation like India, countries can still provide islands of reliable facilities for the developmental needs of MNC investments. Building off of these initial investments in the surrounding region, the potential for future wealth creation is enormous.

ADDRESSING CORRUPTION: THINGS ARE BEGINNING TO CHANGE

Abhijit Halder, consul of community affairs of the Indian Consulate in San Francisco, talks about the challenges that both the Indian Diaspora and government face in combating corruption to meet the needs of the IT industry. He stresses the critical role of Indian champions leading the way to success in the knowledge economy.

ABHIJIT HALDER

Strong emotional ties to the homeland despite corruption and red tape

When it comes to investing in India or looking at India as a prospective place to expand their business, most Indian Americans are hesitant because they fear having to face the bureaucratic system, the uncertainty about support and logistics, corruption, and apprehensions about the family of an individual being able to adjust to the new environment. This has held back the entry of non-resident Indians (NRIs) into the Indian market and economy.

But there remains a feeling of patriotism among NRIs, who respond to sad occasions — a cyclone, an earthquake, or a war. The same force, enthusiasm, and energy needs to be directed toward nation building, or at least the building of certain progressive sectors like IT in which Indians abroad have earned a name.

Dealing with corruption: Fear through public exposure

The only way to curb corruption and red tape is by spilling the beans and exposing it to the public. For example we had the TEHELKA scandal in which the army was accused of doing deals by taking major cuts, and the recent case regarding the importing of coffins for Indian soldiers at prices far higher than the actual cost. Public scandals like these usually create a fear among people, so they may hesitate to act.

Moreover, there has been a very proactive intelligence and investigative establishment at work. They conduct surprise raids and even reward people for providing information about anyone indulging in corruption, so that appropriate action can be taken against them. Things in India are beginning to change.

The importance of leadership champions in successful government action

Despite the Indian government's recent progress in the IT industry, one important thing to remember is that the government is good at announcing policies, but poor at implementing them. One of the key factors that will make a difference in our government's ability to remove corruption and implement policies is the presence of leaders who make important promises — and keep them. And we have such a person in Pramod Mahajan (minister, information technology, communications, and parliamentary affairs). He has been delivering what he has promised, and this credibility increases the success of any program that is implemented.

Powerful and influential leaders are needed to take on important issues and programs. If you look at those states in India that have been successful in implementing IT related programs, they all have a leading personality. The state of Andhra Pradesh has been doing well because of Chief Minister Naidu and now Karnataka is trying to catch up because of the support and backing of the chief minister there. These are the champions who make a difference. ∎

India's political leaders are thus showing the entrepreneurial characteristics needed for proactive initiatives[2] in developing their particular region. The state of Andhra Pradesh[3] is a leading example of how a region with almost no infrastructure or key enabling factors in place can mold itself into an attractive destination for MNCs like Microsoft and Oracle, which have invested considerably in the state capital of Hyderabad. The entrepreneurial spirit of Andhra Pradesh's chief minister, Chandrababu Naidu, has been key in drawing national attention to the importance of regional developments of IT clusters in India.

IT DEVELOPMENT THROUGH POLITICAL ENTREPRENEURSHIP

The state of Karnataka is another example of political leadership in the technology sector. The state government announced India's first state IT policy in 1997, which was an important catalyst for the growth of the IT industry in this region containing the Indus Valley of Bangalore.

In addition, the government recently announced its Millennium IT Policy called Mahithi[4] to keep up with the changing needs of the IT industry. Striving to utilize the key strengths of the IT sector, this policy aims to address gender, poverty, and unemployment issues through the use of e-governance in developing a more proactive and responsive government. Mahithi offers important incentives in the areas of land costs, registration fees, and regulations for large corporations. It has been instrumental in establishing the Indian Institute of Information Technology in Bangalore with world standard infrastructure, sponsored by companies like Sun Microsystems, IBM, Microsoft, and Oracle. In an effort to bridge the digital divide, the government has invested significant efforts in providing a transparent and responsive interaction to take IT to the common Indian in Karnataka.

State governments can pioneer some of the most innovative policy moves to boost the IT sector. India's central government has followed suit with the creation of independent decision bodies that have the autonomy to carry out major IT initiatives and make direct changes in critical regulatory measures. Probably the most successful example of this is the National Task Force on Information Technology and Software Development, created at the impetus of the prime minister to address India's future growth needs in the IT and software industries. Pulling together influential "heroes" from a vast cross section of the society — industry, non-government organizations (NGOs) and educational bodies — this task force convened to make 108 recommendations for immediate steps that the government needed to take to boost the Indian IT industry. The results of this report and subsequent progress on the recommendations are placed on the Web site of the Ministry of Information Technology[5], with complete information regarding which specific tasks have been implemented, which are in progress, and which have been rejected.

The active participation of this diverse task force resulted in a highly ambitious IT Action Plan. This plan is based on a clear understanding of the barriers to building the needed infrastructure to develop the Indian IT sector. The action plan defines several targets to break down these barriers including the elimination of environmental constraints, the promotion of the nascent VC industry in India, the penetration of IT for all by the year 2008, and a dedicated campaign for universal computer literacy for the masses.

This amazing shift in government procedures from bureaucratic red tape to that of open action is a resounding example of the Indian government's attempts to create the right environment for IT growth in India. Soliciting input from leading representatives of society thus becomes an important first step in achieving a fuller picture of the potential for IT, as well as structural and regulatory barriers that need to be addressed. In addition, support for these kinds of initiatives often needs to come from the topmost leader in the nation for a true mobilization of the sector.

R. M. Abhyankar, special secretary in the Ministry of External Affairs of the government of India, discusses some of the ambitious government initiatives for ensuring the success of the knowledge economy in India. He talks about the work needed to remove barriers to a widespread implementation of IT in India, and the importance of transnational flows of knowledge.

R. M. ABHYANKAR

Government focus: Ensure the Indian potential

As the consul general of India in the Silicon Valley during the IT boom, we dealt hands-on with the Indian government's ambitious targets in the IT industry to ensure that the Indian potential is not lost like it was during the industrial revolution. The government-established National IT Task Force sought to identify areas of key legislation and financial infrastructure, as well as to ease the synergy between the Indian software industry and successful Indians in Silicon Valley, like those represented by the IndUS Entrepreneurs (TiE).

There is an increasing flow of resources, ideas, and people in *both* directions, which is key. And we can expect this trend to continue, because many in the Indian software industry are trying to get IT-enabled services back to India due to the time difference and cost-savings differential. There are three levels at which this operates. First, there is the crème de la crème, where graduates from India's topmost technical universities like the IITs are setting up companies and leading entrepreneurship across both nations. Then we have Indian computer programmers with differing levels of expertise on limited visas. Finally, there are service sectors like call centers.

Wealth creation in India: Intellectual property is portable wealth

India's dramatic increase of software exports was due in large part to input from leading Indian entrepreneurs on government, telecommunications, and IT committees regarding needed policy changes. To capitalize on these links, we facilitated key connections between high-level government, policy, finance and industry representatives by early 2000, while well-attended events in India like TiE VC seminars emphasized the potential for synergy.

Very little of the wealth created by Indians in Silicon Valley has flowed back to India. Yet, there are new sources of wealth being created in India. There is an upsurge of financial resources due to the momentum created for the Indian software industry by companies like Infosys, Wipro, and Tata, which are hiring people for contracts with multinational companies and creating new applications and software.

A different form of wealth being created is in the form of intellectual property, which is equally important in the long term. This is done more in the U.S., because that is where the cutting-edge technology lies with opportunities to test different innovations. This experience is improving the whole outlook for the overall Indian economy. People are thinking of ways to further develop the Internet to serve the needs of mainstream industry. There is a different basis for entrepreneurship today as compared with the past colonial mercantile system, both because of the non–location-specific nature of the Internet, and because the actual resource used is brainpower. These factors are creating a new system of global linkages between economic partners.

Evolving Indian values and dangers of innovation in a knowledge economy

The experiences of Indians in the Silicon Valley are changing the values of people in India in terms of expectations about services, infrastructure, government, speed, and flexibility. Indians are beginning to expect the same hassle-free delivery, which is not always possible there. But this is good because they are pushing people to meet these demands, creating rewards for changing the old ways. People setting up companies in India are creating a new kind of system with contemporary requirements for employees and management. Indian society has changed tremendously due to the introduction of consumerism after the liberalization of the economy in 1991, and it is important to remember that these changes predate the effects of the technology industry in India.

The government also has to be extremely sensitive to the fact that rising expectations quickly lead to disillusionment if the expectations are not met. At the social level, access to the Internet can negatively affect social norms, for example with pornographic sites. In fact, with regards to cyber laws, India was one of the first countries to accept online documents legally. At the same time, a key concern at the government level is the dangers of cyber-terrorism. India is again one of first countries to have laws against cyber-crimes.

Government initiatives: Innovative IT applications for the masses

India is aggressively addressing bandwidth shortages, which are a huge constraint in meeting IT targets like our expectations of the Indian software exports reaching $50 billion by 2010. Many regions are being developed with fiber optic infrastructure, because we have a great awareness of the need for connectivity in India to become globally competitive. The government is making a conscious effort to use the existing and potential technology of the IT industry to achieve developmental initiatives in education, health, business, and trade, aiming to make things easier.

At the same time our government is also exploring innovative applications of the Indian IT market like better availability of farm prices for agriculture and small businesses. India is already experimenting with e-governance, online education, and major initiatives to get IT to the masses, all of which require key legal resolutions.

However, it is imperative for India to find a viable way for IT to improve the lives of everyone in India. If not, the IT industry will remain insulated, creating wealth for some Indians, but not creating the widespread impact desired. While there are many examples of the potential applications of IT for the good of the common Indian, the most important initiative is the use of the Internet to spread education to the masses.

We need legislation as a framework for growth, but we also need to make sure it does not inhibit entrepreneurship. So what we need is regulation, not control. In fact, a single regulator is preferable for all IT-related issues to truly ensure fair business practices. The question then remains, how do we remove or alleviate existing laws affecting the IT sector without diluting their initial purpose? ■

From the government perspective, the influx of technology needs to be carefully harnessed so that the Indian potential is fully developed within the knowledge economy. While a majority of the wealth created by Indians in the Silicon Valley remained there, a different form of wealth is accessible across transnational boundaries — intellectual capital. The cutting-edge expertise and knowledge acquired by the NRI population in Silicon Valley is a vast asset for future developments of the Indian software industry, especially in its move up the value chain of higher value-added services. We shall now examine the effects of increasing transnational connections on the dangers of a digital divide in India.

THE THREAT OF A DIGITAL DIVIDE IN A PORTABLE CULTURE

With the increase of transnational connections, Indian society is taking on an increasingly global outlook. The concept of globalization and its effects on India are of key concern to the Indian nation. While the exposure to global practices has led to better expectations in terms of productivity, the events of September 11 have fatefully highlighted the fact that the inevitable process of globalization can also have severely negative implications for certain regions in the new Innovation Economy. There is a clear connection between the events on September 11 and the power of globalization in either creating a bridge or a wall between rich and poor nations. As a result, there is now a renewed focus on the dangers of the cyber-world of the future.

In this interview, Christophe Jaffrelot, director of the Centre d'Etudes et de Recherches Internationals (CERI) in France, and Kiran Karnik, president of the National Association of Software and Services Companies (NASS-COM), discuss the effects of globalization on India and their grave concerns over cultural homogenization and the digital divide.

CHRISTOPHE JAFFRELOT AND KIRAN KARNIK

Christophe Jaffrelot
The Indian flavor of globalization — The "McMaharajah"

Globalization is at the center of great controversy in these times. In fact we must realize that globalization is not a global policy; it is a state of affairs, a trend driven by technology and communications. India is part of the developing world, so it has a very distinct position on globalization. The important question is how India *lives* globalization.

The number of Indians abroad has drastically increased; there are something like 42,000 Indian students in the U.S., and about 30% of Silicon Valley is Indian. This has led to major social changes. For example, the concept of McDonald's in India is a radical shift, and perspectives on these changes can be positive or negative. In India we've seen an increase in Hindu protectionism that is not in favor of global-ization, because there are fears of Americanizing the Indian culture. But even McDonald's is offering vegetarian burgers, and one of its most popular items is named the Maharajah (King) Burger. So the culture remains Indian, there is a bal-anced development, because India has shown that it can translate globalization into Indian terms.

Kiran Karnik
Government initiatives in bridging the digital divide

In light of India's potential in the global Innovation Economy, it is very important to look at where the technology is going. Our background of socialism inevitably leads to concerns regarding technology; can it be a tool for oppressors to control the poor? There are strong and legitimate concerns about the creation of a digital divide between those who have access and power versus those who do not. But the power of the Internet can be used to do exactly the opposite. We need to look at the positive potential of the Internet and examine how technology can be used to deal with India's most basic problems. For example, there is increasing exposure to satellite TV and the Internet in India today; can these be used to bypass literacy gaps? These uses range from experiments in e-government, to cutting down cor-ruption, to improving education and health. The IT industry in India is very new and very young, and there is tremendous potential in what can be done with it.

The media tends to drive in the fears of homogenization, or cultural imperialism, but it's true that Indians don't homogenize easily. The resulting backlash does have both positive and negative aspects. On the positive side, compared with the medium of satellite TV, the Internet allows for a many-to-many scenario, which opens up the potential for development. But on the negative side, we have intense protectionism and the possibility of "portals" acting as gate-keepers to consolidate with commercial interests. So we may be moving from a state government to a commercial government, and one possibility for countering this is through technology, the production of low-cost computers with Indian languages to localize its effect.

The member of parliament of Pondicherry, Shri M.O.H. Farook, has taken one district and provided 500,000 people access to the Internet. Regions in the state of Himachal Pradesh are often cut off for six months because of snowfall, and recently the local health center was connected to the All India Institute of Medical Sciences in New Delhi to provide continuous medical advice. So the government is already successfully building bridges across the digital divide. India's next challenge is, how do we replicate these successes? ■

The innovation era of intense flows, driven by new technologies, will clearly have tremendous social consequences, especially for developing nations. For countries like India where cultural traditions are sacred, there are great fears that the Internet will Americanize the Indian way of life. However fears of such homogenization may be unwarranted; as Mr. Jaffrelot points out, Indians tend to hold on to their cultural identity very strongly and are adept at "Indian-izing" their world wherever they go. This is epitomized by the lives of Indians in Silicon Valley, who have created pockets of India in American cities like San Jose and Fremont.

We have seen in this section the Indian government's commitment — both at central and state levels — to building an IT infrastructure upon which to grow its economy. Now we shall see how industry, education, and NGO sectors are contributing to society by innovative applications of the very technology that has made them successful in the global Innovation Economy, thus replicating the bridges across the digital divide, as suggested by Mr. Karnik.

SOCIAL ENTREPRENEURSHIP: INNOVATIVE APPLICATIONS OF TECHNOLOGY

Philanthropic efforts of the past in India are being surpassed today by less ambitious, but far more precisely defined efforts of successful industry corporations and non-governmental entrepreneurs. The tremendous potential for technological applications in a developing country like India is thus leading to very distinct humanitarian efforts by large and successful corporations.

India's most successful software firms like Infosys and Wipro have created individual funds for delivering the right amount of difference to the right beneficiaries. While the Azim Premji Foundation for Wipro emphasizes universal elementary education, the Infosys Foundation focuses more on diversified areas such as healthcare and education.

These charitable efforts have brought a result-oriented corporate discipline to the art of giving by demanding direct and measurable returns on investments. There is a multipronged effort to address the digital divide both across sectors and across the uses of technology. Due to the lack of widespread implementation of technology, there is a great potential for the use of existing technologies for wealth creation demonstrated by the Digital Equalizer[6] (DE) project, where centers provide disadvantaged children with digital access to educational content.

THE DIGITAL EQUALIZER (DE) CENTERS: DIRECT CREATION OF REGIONAL WEALTH

Inaugurated by Kumar Malavalli, trustee of the American India Foundation[7] (AIF) and Kailash Joshi, president of the Silicon Valley chapter of TiE,[8] two revolutionary centers of digital access for underprivileged children were opened in Karnataka on August 14, 2001.

Conceptualized specifically as a means to address the vast digital divide in India, the DE centers directly target the uneven distribution of educational opportunities in India. Each center provides digital access to disadvantaged children in grades nine to 12 through computers, Internet access, and prescribed educational content.

The impact of each center is calculated by the expected increases in regional wealth creation. At the rate of India's per capita income growth, the maximum lifetime earnings of the average child without digital access is estimated to be $30,000. The exposure to computers at these centers increases the confidence, skill set, and drive of each student and is expected to at least double their lifetime earning to $60,000.

Thus, the simple use of computers and Internet access — facilities that the western world takes for granted and that are, in fact, becoming increasingly popular in large urban conglomerates in India as well — can provide a real opportunity to create wealth. While the DE project is an example of creative implementations of existing and widely used technologies, many viable concepts are emerging from innovative applications of educational R&D, such as the Simputer.[9]

SIMPLE, INEXPENSIVE, MULTILINGUAL COMPUTER: THE "SIMPUTER"

This device was created to match the needs of local Indian conditions. Its most distinguishing factor is that it is based entirely on free software and thus sells at a market price of $200.

For the average Indian, however, this device is still beyond affordability. This problem is addressed through the Simputer's smart card feature, which enables it to be shared by communities such as village schools and panchayats (village systems of democratic self-governance). Local representatives like shopkeepers and schoolteachers can thus loan the device to individuals in the community for specific periods of time, much like library books.

In addition, its voice feedback system ensures that illiteracy is no longer a barrier to computer exposure. Potential uses for this device include Internet access, large volume data collection, and providing critical information to farmers on important agricultural issues, as well as innovative uses devised by the user, further applying the creative implications of "pure" technologies.

Fledgling innovations bridging the digital divide through innovative uses of technology are laying the groundwork for India's reach to provide the stated goal of IT to the masses. A supportive financial infrastructure for the development of technological innovations could well make the difference for India's shift from the status of a developing to developed nation. In the next segment, we take a look at how India's budding VC industry is one of the fastest-growing sectors of the Indian economy.

VENTURE CAPITAL AND TRANSNATIONAL LINKS

The VC industry has been gaining increasing interest worldwide for its ability to foster and sustain innovation and entrepreneurship. In India, the concept of risk capital is relatively new, as the liberalization of the economy in 1991 was the single most important factor in opening up the way for foreign and private venture capitalists.

As you saw in chapter 17, India's software industry is one of the fastest-growing sectors in the economy. The characteristically high-risk, high-gain nature of this industry makes VC funding an extremely suitable form of financing. Software ventures also need strong management support and guidance, and VC funding provides this critical asset for the growth of Indian software industries.

HISTORICAL PERSPECTIVE OF THE INDIAN VC INDUSTRY

At present, the Indian VC industry is in a state of rapid development. Built on a foundation of small- and medium-sized enterprises and a strong public equity market, the progressive successes of NRIs and domestic Indian software firms have combined to push for much needed government initiatives to facilitate the development of a nascent, but promising VC industry.

The Indian VC industry outlook seems gloomy in the short term, as many investments have been based on Internet projects that have dried up considerably since the dot-com bust. However, NASSCOM still maintains its projections for India becoming one of the top five locations for the creation of technology ventures in the world, confident that with the right groundwork, the necessary VC funds will flow into the country.

While the beginning of the VC industry in India was spurred by economic reforms in 1991, the second phase of VC growth began with the release of Securities and Exchange Board of India (SEBI) guidelines in 1996. These guidelines for domestic and overseas funds freed the industry from many inhibiting governmental barriers in investing, and led to the increase of competition with the entry of numerous foreign funds. The resulting access to capital and international industry standards created the beginning of a more institutionalized VC industry in India.

Because general lending conditions in India have been expensive, private methods of self-financing have been the most common means of starting a business. However, VC in India has expanded since 1998 with the operations of large global banks and corporate and VC funds, both Indian and American.

CHRONOLOGY OF THE GROWTH OF THE INDIAN VC INDUSTRY

- **Phase 1: Post Independence (1947–1984)** — Among other reasons, closed-economy government policies led to the emigration of India's most brilliant engineers and scientists to seek opportunities overseas beginning in the 1950s. Originally claimed as India's brain drain, they are now being increasingly recognized as a source of information, advice, and capital gains for India's VC industry needs.

- **Phase 2: The Gandhi Legacy (1984–1991)** — The election of Rajiv Gandhi in 1984 paved the way for regulatory reforms needed to develop a domestic VC industry. The Ministry of Finance issued the first set of guidelines in 1988 to legalize VC operations in India and the Industrial Credit and Investment Corporation of India (TDICI) became the first firm to identify itself as a VC operation.[10] In 1991 the Indian government made widespread policy changes to loosen investment regulations.

- **Phase 3: The Current Scenario (1995–2002)** — In 1995 the availability of risk capital under Indian management drastically increased after Draper International's decision to become the first major MNC to invest in India, combined with a relative decline in the part played by multilateral development agencies and government financial institutes.[11] These changes were followed by the release of SEBI's first guidelines for VC registration and investments in India, which further intensified investments from overseas and domestic sources.

There has been a notable increase in both domestic and foreign VC investments since the 1991 economic reforms. While only eight domestic VC funds were registered with the SEBI in 1996–1998, with the addition of 20 new VC funds in 2000, over 30 additional funds were registered in 2000–2001. Total VC investment[12] in the first three quarters of 2000 was $79.9 billion, an astounding 137% increase over the corresponding period in 1999. Of these investments, technology firms received about 75%.

In 1999 the government made additional reforms after viewing a decade of NRI and domestic IT successes in high-tech industries, and in January 2000, SEBI came out with a committee report on VC with specific recommendations, some of which were adopted by the Ministry of Finance as early as June of that year.

INDIAN SUCCESS FACTORS FOR A VIBRANT INDIAN VC INDUSTRY

Some of the preconditions of the Indian environment that led to the development of the VC industry were a sophisticated stock market that could manage public stock offerings,[13] fast-growing high-tech industries, the interest of NRIs familiar with Silicon Valley VC operations and skills, and a pool of skilled engineers in India to generate the creation of wealth.

Several additional success factors continue to draw both domestic and foreign investment in IT. The country has a huge number of small business enterprises unveiling a truly entrepreneurial spirit, a strong public equity market, substantial capital resources, comparatively low wages relative to more developed countries, and a rapidly growing domestic software industry. In line with the unprecedented mobilization in the IT industry, the Indian government has acknowledged the importance of a strong Indian VC industry to sustain innovation and entrepreneurship, and is now trying to catch up to the needed simplification of regulations. In addition, India's vast output of highly skilled manpower is an important prerequisite for the growth of an innovative and entrepreneurial economy and development of a VC industry in India.

THE MICROLAND GROUP

One of the most successful examples of an Indian VC firm is the Microland Group,[14] which provides end-to-end technology services solutions to a global customer base. Comprising a diverse network of entities, Microland employs over 900 professionals across its offices in India, Asia-Pacific, and the U.S. The firm has investments from J.P. Morgan Partners, the Industrial Credit and Investment Corporation of India (ICICI) Ventures, and General Electric Capital, among many other renowned strategic investors. The company currently has five offices in the U.S., with headquarters in San Jose. Local presence has been essential for Microland in seeking businesses from U.S. companies.

Pradeep Kar, founder, chairman and managing director of the Microland Group, is a member of the Chief Minister's Task Force on IT in Karnataka, and a charter member of the TiE chapter in Bangalore. He divides his time between Silicon Valley and India, and here he discusses the important role that VC plays in the development of the software industry in India.

PRADEEP KAR

Challenges and opportunities of transnational businesses

India has the potential to be the global provider of all remote services using its vast pool of educated manpower, cost competitiveness, and use of English in business and education. The Indian industry is estimated to grow from its present size of $6.5 billion to $85 billion in 2008, employing over 1.5 million new professionals, including 800 telecom services among all support and customer transaction services.

The challenges lie in convincing a larger number of MNC customers of the benefit of outsourcing work to India and in providing assurance that it will be done on time and to the expected quality standards.

Wealth creation through VC investments: Silicon Valley compared with India

The model of VC investing is very similar across the Silicon Valley and India. When a company is being conceived, the founders seek to raise monies from U.S. VC companies with a presence in India as well as from VCs based in the U.S. who are open to investing in Indian companies.

Investment money today is global. Hence, you can easily see the correlation of the Nasdaq with the Bombay stock exchange and other Asian exchanges. Exit options for investors in Indian companies are through public offerings in the Indian exchanges or the issue of American depository receipts in the U.S. exchanges.

Role of venture capitalists in India

An important role VCs play is finding CEOs who are entrepreneurs and who can share their passion and vision. Indian CEOs do not spend adequate time and focus in hiring their teams. I define and share the vision, hire top-notch management teams, set the expectations, plans, and milestones clearly, and institute a clearly defined review process. Subsequent to that, we work together with the company management team to help raise the next round of capital.

Two examples of companies we funded that have been successful are indya.com, a large portal that was recently acquired for cash by News Corporation, and planetasia.com, a leading Internet middleware software company.

Government role in the high-tech economy

The Indian federal and state governments have realized that India's future is in the knowledge economy. These sectors create large numbers of jobs, earn foreign exchange, and foster education.

Hence, for the first time the federal government and most state governments have ministers of information technology, including a secretary of information technology, whose role it is to focus on creating an enabling environment through policies, infrastructure and, to some extent, subsidies for the growth of this industry.

Government allocation of VC funding is not a very useful or important role. However, creating policies that encourage VC investments in India and helping VC companies easily set up shop are initiatives that can make a positive difference. ∎

Thus, despite the recent spurt of changes in its financial and regulatory framework, India is still far from an ideal environment for the development of a vibrant VC industry. Many crucial barriers stand in the way of a self-sustaining industry able to spur the growth of truly innovative ideas for the development of the Indian economy.

BARRIERS IN THE CURRENT VC INDUSTRY

The legacy of publicly regulated institutional advances and a tightly controlled economy has been difficult for India to shrug off. Despite government initiatives to clear up regulatory impediments, India's bureaucratic business and "risk-averse financial systems" combine to create strong institutional barriers for funding innovation. Creative funding resources are also hindered by the corrupt reputation of the bureaucracy. Despite the committed reform and deregulation attempts of the Indian government, excessive regulations still continue to frustrate the development of VC in India.

Corporate laws remain inflexible in terms of risk sharing, control, and exit arrangements between financers and private firm management. And "even in 2001 the Indian rupee was non-convertible," hampering VC inflows from offshore and requiring approvals from multiple agencies.[15] Three separate bodies continue to standardize the industry with their own regulations: SEBI, the Ministry of Finance, and the Central Board of Direct Taxes (CBDT) regulate domestic VC funds, while foreign firms have two additional regulatory controls: the Foreign Investment Promotion Board (FIPB) and the Reserve Bank of India (RBI).[16]

Jyoti Gupta, who is currently a professor of finance at the ESCP-EAP European Business School of Management in Paris, discusses India's historical problems of corruption and the potential for wealth creation through Indian networking.

JYOTI GUPTA

Bribery is another name for political lobbying in developing countries

The concept of bribery in India is diminishing with weakening government control and increasing liberalization; thus the chances for bribery in this environment also lessen. But first, let's think of the term "bribery." In developed countries bribery is sanctified into the system of political lobbying; it is a transparent way in which people openly give money and politicians publicly take up causes because of this money.

This does not exist in developing countries, where it's considered illegal to give cash. In India, because the administration is so bureaucratic, you have to give money to make decisions, and this is corruption. The Indian government has had to accept that it has to change, and it is moving in that direction. One of the biggest reasons for this is the immense freedom of press that we have, where the press can get away even with calling the prime minister a fool. The Indian press took up the cause of exposing bribery by bringing out cases systematically. Now the politicians are terrified to do something illegal. Only then can the law follow.

Indian networking practices link innovation with VC investments

NRIs are also a successful force in the development of the Indian VC industry. There is a difference in the way Indians network from other ethnic groups. For example the VC industry in Silicon Valley is derived from the existing industry and surrounding prestigious institutes. In India we had the eminent educational facilities but the infrastructure wasn't conducive for the industry, and initial cash was not there. This cash came from the Indians abroad. This is one of the most distinguishing characteristics of Indian networking. ■

With two important elements in place — NRIs equipped with international expertise on VC operations and talented Indians beginning to venture into the fields of entrepreneurship and innovation — the special art of Indian networking has become a critical leveraging point for the development of India's VC industry. In a field where knowing the right people at the right time makes all the difference in terms of appropriate funding and support, the vast Indian network of entrepreneurs are a breeding ground for natural links between ideas and finance.

THE TRANSNATIONAL ASPECT OF THE VC INDUSTRY: NRI INVESTMENTS

Despite great nationwide concern about the so-called brain drain of the 1950s–1970s, most Indians who left their country maintained significant ties with family, friends, and classmates from India. In turn, the impressive successes of the Indian Diaspora led the government to seek ways to maintain their involvement in India, resulting in active solicitation of their thoughts, needs, and concerns about their native land.

INDIAN NETWORKING PRACTICES

Rafiq Dossani is a consulting professor and a senior research scholar at the Asia/Pacific Research Center, (A/PARC)[17] at Stanford University, which is responsible for developing and directing the South Asia Initiative. He serves as an advisor to SEBI on VC reforms, and is on the advisory boards of two VC companies, Garage.com and East Gate Capital. Previously, Dr. Dossani worked for the Robert Fleming Investment Banking group, first as CEO of its Indian operations and later as head of its San Francisco operations.

A key representative of the transnational authorities working between Silicon Valley and India, Dr. Dossani exerts important influence on venture funding as well as government finance policies in India. In our interview, he discusses key lessons from the initiatives of NRIs and the Indian government in the Indian VC industry, effects of the economic slowdown on this industry, and the leveraging value of Indian networking practices.

RAFIQ DOSSANI

Lessons from NRI and government initiatives

NRI initiatives in the Indian VC industry took the form of both investments and support for policy reform, but it was the Indian government that initiated policy reform. Both outcomes offer lessons. First, getting the environment right is difficult because of the tangle of laws that affect VC, none of which can easily be changed without affecting other aspects of company law and governance. It is thus easier to create a specific set of rules for VC. Second, good thinking in a relatively new domain like VC policy cannot be done only by government or local industry; it requires global input on best practices as seen by practitioners and scholars. It is also of little use to look at best practices in most countries because the starting points are so different; for example the U.S. does not have very much legislation or civil law regarding VC laws, because the environment did not call for it.

Those who left India found better opportunities outside. If the opportunities in India had not improved since the 1991 Indian economic reforms, I doubt if the emotional/financial commitment to India by NRIs would have manifested in the results that we see today.

The 2001–2002 economic slowdown has led the Indian VC industry to a major downturn, just like in the U.S., but for different reasons. Their investments have mostly been in small and medium enterprises (SMEs), offering software services rather than tech product firms. While business for the industry is still growing, SMEs in India have lost considerable market share.

Leveraging Indian networking practices

Indian corporate leaders have an advantage because of their strong networks of ready-made and dedicated teams that will stay together long enough to create value, and VCs in Silicon Valley recognize this as an asset.

In fact many of the popular views about Indian immigrants in Silicon Valley ring true: they are highly educated, entrepreneurial, and derive important benefits from their networks. In a recent study[18] that we conducted, 80% of Indians worked in firms founded between 1996 and 2001, while 43% currently work in firms with less than 100 employees.

Both formal and informal networks allow Indians to increase the benefits that they can derive from a growth area like Silicon Valley. These benefits are often in the form of better jobs and access to capital or technology, leading perhaps to higher levels of innovation and entrepreneurship.

Generally, informal networks such as current and former colleagues, friends, and alumni are much more important sources of information, capital, and jobs than professional networks. Professional, immigrant, and alumni associations ranked third in our study below business media and business colleagues as sources of technology, business, and employment information, and fourth below family/ friends, business colleagues, and alumni as sources of funding for start-ups. Of the Indians surveyed, 89% worked in firms founded by someone from their region of birth, suggesting that informal networks provided employment connections as well.

Drained brains can circulate back to the homeland

NRIs do look toward their countries of birth as places to return to, subject to appropriate conditions like professional opportunities. Half the respondents indicated an interest in returning to live and work in India, with a greater preference among younger participants. Professional opportunities, culture and lifestyle, and a desire to help their countries of origin were all important deciding factors. ∎

SUMMARY

India has the beginning of a VC industry in place with interested investors, a large pool of talent entrenched in a history of local entrepreneurship, and increasing government commitment for building the infrastructure to support it. In addition, Indian successes in the domestic and Silicon Valley markets have created the necessary spirit and excitement needed to mobilize a vested interest in this industry. What India needs now is the risk capital and managerial guidance to take its VC industry to the next level.

Besides the growth of domestic VC capital, an estimated $10 billion is expected in the form of foreign investments. This wealth would then lead to sustainable employment generation of approximately three million jobs in the skilled sector over the next five years. Spin-off effects from this employment can create a position of rapid economic growth and a position of strength for India in the Innovation Economy.

The VC industry in India can be an important catalyst for India's success in the knowledge Innovation Economy by making much-needed risk capital and managerial expertise available for early stage funding. The broad role of VC as opposed to other forms of funding provides not only much needed finance for Indian funds, but also the hands-on managerial expertise and support for entrepreneurial development.

ENDNOTES

1. Software Technology Parks of India, *www.stph.net*.

2. "A Regulatory Regime That Regulates the Least," Andhrapradesh.com, *www.andhrapradesh.com/*.

3. Andhrapradesh.com, *www.andhrapradesh.com/*.

4. *Mahithi* means *information* in Karnataka's regional language of Kannada.

5. The active participation of this task force resulted in a highly ambitious IT Action Plan (*www.mit.gov.in/atrnt.htm*) based in a clear understanding of the barriers to building the needed infrastructure for developing the Indian IT sector. The Action Plan defines several targets to break down these barriers including the elimination of environmental constraints, the promotion of the nascent VC industry in India, the penetration of IT for all by 2008, and a dedicated campaign for universal computer literacy for the masses.

6. Olivier Bomsel and Joël Ruet, "Digital India: Report on the Indian IT Industry," Centre d'Économie Industrielle, Ecole Nationale Supérieure des Mines de Paris, *www.cerna.ensmp.fr/Documents/DigitalIndia-MainFindings.pdf*.

7. American India Foundation, *www.aifoundation.org/*.

8. The IndUS Entrepreneurs, *www.tie.org/*.

9. Simputer, *www.simputer.org/*.

10.–11. Rafiq Dossani and Martin Kenney, "Creating an Environment for Venture Capital in India," World Development, V.30, No. 2, pp. 227–253, 2002.

12. NASSCOM, *www.nasscom.org*.

13. Rafiq Dossani and Martin Kenney, "Creating an Environment for Venture Capital in India," World Development, V.30, No. 2, pp. 227–253, 2002.

14. Microland, *www.microlandgroup.com*.

15.–16. Rafiq Dossani and Martin Kenney, "Creating an Environment for Venture Capital in India," World Development, V.30, No. 2, pp. 227–253, 2002.

17. Asia/Pacific Research Center (A/PARC), *aparc.stanford.edu*.

18. Rafiq Dossani, "Chinese and Indian Engineers and Their Networks in Silicon Valley," Working Paper, Asia/Pacific Research Center, March 2002, Stanford University.

▶ *About the Author*

This chapter was co-authored by **Arti Kuthiala**. With a bachelor's in applied psychology from Delhi University in India, she has worked for the United States Chamber of Commerce and the San Francisco Global Trade Council. Arti is currently pursuing a master's degree in business administration at San Francisco State University, where she is also collaborating on numerous projects with the Ohrenschall Center for Entrepreneurship.

19 ENDNOTE

W e began this inquiry with the idea that if we spoke with renowned theorists and successful entrepreneurial champions in the Innovation Economy across diverse geographic regions in the sectors of government, education, venture capital, non-government organizations, multinational corporations, and start-ups, we could learn from their collective insight and practical wisdom how to be successful in a new era.

At the conclusion of our efforts, we have been both humbled and gratified to have had the opportunity to speak to and learn from so many people who freely shared their experience and advice so others could benefit. We have tried to present their experience, insights, and recommendations as faithfully as we could.

From their collective conversations and our research into the regions they work from, here are several broad themes that we have gleaned:

■ **Attitude drives accomplishment** — Reverence for knowledge, openness to new ideas, flexibility to adapt, and capacity to work with people from other cultures are all assets for regional wealth creation. In countries such as Ireland this attitude is deeply rooted in the culture and it is rewarding them. In countries such as Germany, where the cultures have not been as open and entrepreneurial, there is a growing recognition that a societal attitudinal change is necessary.

■ **Education and investment in people is a clear priority for governments** — Education, tied to skills demanded of knowledge workers, is now an economic engine for regional development. Major universities and regional technical colleges connected with research institutes and technology parks have worked in countries as varied as India, Sweden, Ireland, and Taiwan. Government efforts to expand research budgets for basic science in small countries such as Ireland and Israel demonstrate the recognition that to develop intellectual capital government must provide the research infrastructure, just as they do the transportation infrastructure, to keep competitive.

■ **A convergence of societal institutions must work together for a region to succeed** — The delineations between government, NGOs, educational institutions, and industry are now permeable. As initiatives develop, each sector collaborates so the region can succeed. Efforts such as those we highlighted in the Smart Permit system in Silicon Valley and the initiatives in e-government and shared telecom infrastructure in Stockholm are examples of these kinds of collaborations.

■ **Entrepreneurial risk must be rewarded and encouraged for individuals** — Entrepreneurs drive innovation. Regions that have encouraged this risk-taking, such as Taiwan, have an advantage. In regions such as Cambridge, England there is a growing recognition that incentives must be initiated to encourage risk-taking. In countries such as France it is beginning to take hold against long held biases against business and risk.

■ **There is an evolution to regional success and working up the value chain** — Economically disadvantaged regions enter the Innovation Economy as low-cost manufacturing and service centers. With consistent and comprehensive focus by all societal institutions, these regions work their way up the value chain for higher level skills and integration into the multinational companies that are driving the Innovation Economy. Ireland, India, and Taiwan have each demonstrated this move up the value chain. In the case of Taiwan, its ability to integrate mainland China into its industrial complex could be a great model for regional integration.

■ **Successful regions have staked out important distinctive competencies that they can excel in, rather than try and replicate those of Silicon Valley** — Regional emphasis seems to have evolved with intentional leveraging of societal advantages. Ireland as a multinational corporate service center for software for Europe; Sweden as a world center for mobile telecommunications; Israel for military applications and transfer of technology for civilian purposes; India as the source for engineers and programmers for software and international job sharing; and Taiwan as the center for semiconductor foundry manufacturing, are all examples of this phenomenon. These regions are not totally defined by these competencies, but certainly have excelled in these areas for competitive advantage.

■ **Technological innovation is viewed as a liberating and emancipating factor for regions and people who have a self-image as oppressed or disadvantaged** — Perhaps most surprising is the sentiment expressed by Irish, Israeli, Taiwanese, and Indian entrepreneurial champions across all professional disciplines about how proud they are of their societies for creating regional wealth and providing their people with economic opportunities. These changes have meant that permanent emmigration is no longer the only option for their brightest and most ambitious people.

In this Innovation Economy, transnational Diasporas are not a "brain drain," but a "brain gain" as knowledge, wealth, and business opportunities are created in multiple regions. Venture capitalists and private equity investors have an important role in these regions' development.

In Conclusion

For much of the world, poverty, ignorance, and societal dysfunction has led many to despair, anger and fanaticism as the only way to attain human dignity. Perhaps the promise of *Creating Regional Wealth in the Innovation Economy* will provide another way for the benefit of all.

DIALOGUE ACROSS THE ATLANTIC: LESTER THUROW AND JACQUES ATTALI

To gain broader perspectives on the Innovation Economy, we asked two internationally renowned economic theorists to provide their views in a dialogue. Lester Thurow, an American, and Jacques Attali, who is French, each provide world views, which are complementary in how they interpret the economic and political trends that have both changed and have yet to shape our world.

Lester C. Thurow is the Lemelson Professor of Management and Economics at the Massachusetts Institute of Technology. He also directs the Technion Institute of Management in Haifa, Israel. Professor Thurow has authored several leading books including *Building Wealth: The New Rules for Individuals, Companies, and Nations in a Knowledge-Based Economy; The Future of Capitalism: How Today's Economic Forces Shape Tomorrow's World;* and *Head to Head: The Coming Economic Battle Among Japan, Europe, and America.*

Jacques Attali is a leading French commentator on social and economic affairs. He was adviser to the president of the French Republic from 1981 until 1991, president of the European Bank for Reconstruction and Development from 1991 to 1993, and, since 1993, has been a member of the Council of State in France. He is the author of many books, among them *L'anti-économique, Economie de L'Apocalypse, Verbatim* (a three-volume diary of his experiences as an adviser to President Mitterrand), and *Millennium: Winners and Losers in the Coming World Order.*

THE THIRD INDUSTRIAL REVOLUTION AND THE NEW MIDDLE AGES

Thurow ■ We are in the middle of the third industrial revolution, shifting from an industrial economy to a knowledge-based economy. For the first time in history, human knowledge has great economic value. In the past, the richest person in the world owned natural resources such as land or oil. Now, Bill Gates is the richest person in the world and what does he really own? He controls a knowledge process. This fundamentally changes economic development. It addresses the topic of this book, *Creating Regional Wealth in the Innovation Economy*. How do regions get intellectual growth nodes started and thriving?

Regions can have many of the ingredients, but no one of them can guarantee success. For example, in the U.S. there are lots of good universities, but there are none of these Silicon Valley or Boston Route 128 complexes around them. Nobody is going to replicate Silicon Valley; even Route 128 is not exactly like Silicon Valley.

> *For the first time in history, human knowledge has great economic value.*

One interesting test for a region is whether after a downturn it is capable and versatile enough to pop back up again. Some regions may make a wrong bet on technology and they may have difficulty re-emerging. It may be focused differently than it was before. Resilience is something you want to take a look at.

Attali ■ We are in a New Middle Ages. Middle Ages were not an end, but a beginning of a new world. People began to become free of feudal societies and empires. They became interested in cities, finding new ways of connecting through the printing press. That destroyed and fragmented the empires, giving more power to the cities. This also gave birth to the capacity of critiques by people and scholars. It is what is happening today. With the fragmentation of the large empires, such as the former Soviet Union, there is the emergence of new nations. New technologies can be seen as the equivalent of the printing press, creating more networks and fewer pyramids, and opening to a lot of potential futures.

LIMITS OF FRANCE AND EUROPE IN THE THIRD INDUSTRIAL REVOLUTION

Attali ■ France is the leading nation in the world in tourism. It is difficult to be the first nation of the world in everything. France will not be first in technology, because networking is essential to success. France is a nation of centralization; it is an old nation. So, it will be difficult for France to lead.

There are two reasons for a nation to be linked to new technologies:

- To be decentralized
- To have a nomadic culture or nomadic mentality; flexible mobility

The U.S. is a nation of nomads because of its origin; people are coming from everywhere. The culture of America is a culture of movement as well as a culture of decentralization.

France is a nation of peasants, sedentary — and our culture is far from being linked to the new technologies. The only way for France to lead is to go through another route. To use the nation and the state as a door-opener for new technologies. For instance, if we could lead a large international program for e-government. The future of France in new technologies is linked to its capacity to develop e-government (Internet-based, online access and interaction with government for all its functions with business and individual citizens), but we are not there yet.

But France must be considered within the context of the European Union. Europe has a tremendous potential for jointly developing leadership in specific areas such as telecommunications and mobile phones. We have a huge potential if we can create what has been missing in Europe, which is the relationship between university research and industry.

> *The future of France in new technologies is linked to its capacity to develop e-government.*

Thurow ■ The United States had an advantage in the 1990s relative to Europe because we had a greater flexibility to fire people. In the prosperous years, when the economy was booming, big profitable American companies were still laying off between 600–800,000 employees a year. If you develop a new, efficient technology breakthrough then you have to be able to reduce the number of people working, otherwise why invent the technology? Closing down the old is even more important than opening up the new. If you cannot close down the old, then the new won't emerge.

Attali ■ These are two different problems. We are not too slow to close down. Unfortunately, we have been able to close down enough so that we have a large unemployment problem. It is true that we are very slow in creating new companies and people are not receiving enough incentives to create new companies, to do their own business. It is important to create a climate that encourages the creation of new start-ups; we have to do more than we are doing now.

RAPID GROWTH OF LARGE COMPANIES

Thurow ■ Europe's problem is not lack of entrepreneurs. The real problem is that it is difficult to rapidly grow a successful start-up into a world-class company. Take the 10 biggest companies in the U.S. Six of them were founded since 1960. If you take the 10 biggest companies in Europe, none of them were founded after 1960. You can argue that Nokia is a new company, because it changed to reinvent itself from a wood products company to an electronics company. But it is an exception.

> *We should not make an apology for not having "shooting star" companies.*

Attali ■ The birth of companies is good in most of Europe. If the company is Seibel, which had very rapid growth, then that is good. But if it is a company with rapid growth like Enron in Texas (a company that rose quickly through hedging derivatives in the energy industry and then fell rapidly, wiping out pensions and retirements for many Enron employees and other individual shareholders), then maybe we should be more cautious. We should not make an apology for not having "shooting star" companies.

The emergence of new large companies among the top group may be good, if the new companies are strong. The other side of the coin is to say that the other former young companies are dead. The life expectancy of companies in America is shorter than the life expectancy of companies in Europe. This is not good. The fact that companies are new and short-lived is not proof of quality.

There will be two kinds of companies in the future that we can characterize as either theatres or circuses. In the theatre, people are together for only one mission: to make a movie or a play. That company exists just long enough for the production. In the circus, such as a long-lasting company like Ringling Bros. and Barnum & Bailey, the shows and products are changing every year, but the circus continues to exist. A healthy economy is full of circuses, not theatres.

INDIVIDUAL CHANGE AGENTS ARE RESPONSIBLE FOR INNOVATION, NOT INSTITUTIONS

Thurow ■ Institutions always have vested interests. Big companies may invent a new technology and then not be able to use it. For example, the cellular telephone was invented by AT&T, which owned the copper wire system. They thought the cellular telephones had no future. Revolutionary changes blow up institutions and so the institutions resist them. Someone starting from ground zero has a better chance to innovate.

The key thing to being an entrepreneur and having an entrepreneurial environment in business, government, and NGOs is the willingness to tolerate failure. In the U.S., in venture capital supported companies, nine out of 10 companies will go out of business within five years. Since the probability of failure is about 90%, you have to have a fall-back position. The individual should feel confident he can get another job or he can get financing to start another business in a different area. The best, most successful entrepreneurs, are most likely to succeed on their third try — because they learned something in the first two failures.

If you are in an institution, failure has bad personal consequences. And that is why most institutions have difficulty innovating. A venture capitalist will fund somebody who fails more than once. Historically, big institutions have shown that they will not trust somebody who has failed more than once.

American universities are very tolerant of professors going off and trying to start businesses. They might fail, and then come back to being a professor. Or they may run a successful business and still be part of the university. A great example is Dr. Amar Bose of Bose Corp. (one of the top selling premium sound systems companies), who also teaches acoustics at MIT. In many places that is just not allowed.

Attali ■ We have many entrepreneurs in France who belong to a decentralized new elite. This new elite is made up of leaders of growing and mature start-ups, venture funds, and city government. There are now mayors and heads of regional entities who are taking risks and encouraging their universities to create new companies. The new local elites will create something out of the blue, like a New Middle Ages.

The bureaucracies can only create the conditions for the non-bureaucrats to create the companies. I initiated the Eureka project in 1985. This program provides a match for the university and industry. If you have a joint program between a research center and a company, we in the bureaucracy will fund this program. If you take risks, we will take risks with you. Eureka has been at the source of genome mapping.

The only field where the bureaucracy may not take initiative is with e-governments, because this can transform government, and bureaucrats may not want to give up power.

CRM (customer relationship management) is a dictatorship of the consumer, which transforms drastically the organization of business. Instead of customer relationship management, we need citizen relationship management, where citizens through the new technologies could direct what they want, to find out about their rights or financing for their rights, and to be informed rapidly. Then a huge transformation would happen.

GLOBALIZATION: WHAT DOES IT MEAN, AND IS IT A BLESSING FOR THE WORLD?

Attali ■ We have to distinguish if globalization is Americanization. The answer to that is to be more parochial. For example, in France we protect our cinema industry, and it has continued to thrive. The Germans, British, and Italians did not protect their film industries and they are dead.

But the protection cannot be to close the borders. The answer there is not less globalization, but more globalization. We have seen that closing of national borders is not an answer. But rather for us, to create Europe as an entity is the answer. In this way we not only create a single European market. Europe would be a sample of a case where globalization, if it is only linked to a market, is creating anarchy.

> *You can have globalization if it is not only globalization of the market, but globalization of the institutions.*

You can have globalization if it is not only globalization of the market, but globalization of the institutions. Markets never exist without a state. Markets need institutional mechanisms for rules under law: property rights and protection. There are two kinds of places in the world where you have free markets without institutions. The first is the world itself. The second is Somalia: A free market without a government. Somalia becomes a metaphor for the world if globalization is not going to be tamed by institutions.

Thurow ■ In globalization there is job sharing, which is egalitarian. For the first time, through the Internet, people from different regions can work on a technology project together. For example, in chip design this is an advantage not because of cost, but because you can work on a project nonstop and get a speed to market advantage. Most high-tech companies will say that speed is more important than cost. Wages have gone up remarkably fast in places like Taiwan and Bangalore. So the wage differential gap has narrowed.

One of the reasons that some people are concerned about globalization is that there is the emergence of high-tech global citizens, who can move from country to country all within the same company. The tech clusters of the world are linked. Taiwan is part of Silicon Valley. They do contract manufacturing based on the technology developed in the U.S. Bangalore writes software for the wealthy industrial world. When it started it was low-level software, now it is more sophisticated. Look at Ireland! Basically, Ireland is a good place in Europe for off-shore manufacturing. Most of the development is not from Irish companies; it is from international companies locating operations in Ireland.

But remember, a capitalist is a coward. In the U.S. Navy, the brave captain is supposed to go down with his ship. But a CEO or a venture capitalist wants to get out of a business before it fails. Physical insecurity can hinder economic development. Israel is an example. It has an advantage in that its high-tech firms are connected to the U.S., and so they can get the capitalization and scale of a large international company through their U.S. counterparts.

One thing to be tested is whether the venture capitalists (most of whom are not Israelis), who are financing Israeli operations, will demand that the people and operations be moved from that environment, if physical insecurity remains unresolved.

THE ROLE OF TECHNOLOGY IN REVOLUTIONIZING EDUCATION

Thurow ■ The great promise for the revolution in education is in primary and secondary school levels in the developing world. A place like Thailand cannot wait the 75 years needed to train teachers, build classrooms, and focus the resources required to give everyone a basic education. You need to use electronic systems combined with teaching assistants to speed up the process of educating people.

The second place is in the business firms. How do you train people in Otis Elevator Company to be able to fix all makes of elevators all over the world? Give them a laptop. Then mechanics can have on-location assistance if they have to repair an elevator that is 100 years old. In business, most on-the-job training will be done in a virtual classroom.

In universities, it is more complex. If you would like to provide for student creativity, then there will be the need for "rubbing elbows." Distance learning cannot completely substitute for those relationships. At MIT, we run a master's program in systems design and management. At the beginning, it was completely done electronically. What we do now is bring the students in for three weeks in the semester. We found that the electronic interaction with the professor was pretty good. But the students would not interact online with each other. Once they met each other physically, then they would be more comfortable to interact online. So the future for university electronic education will probably be some mixed mode of electronic and classroom learning. The big problem at this time for university electronic education is that nobody has figured out how you pay for it. In the U.S., people are not willing to pay high tuition for electronic education.

THE PROMISE OF TECHNOLOGY TO SERVE THE GREATER PUBLIC GOOD AND CHANGE NEEDED IN LIGHT OF THE SEPTEMBER 11 TERRORIST ATTACK

Attali ■ There is an enormous capacity of mankind to forget. I would not say to forgive. I hope that we may be in a position to forget if there are no other incidents of mass destruction and we can look at September 11 as a past nightmare.

But if we forget, we might not take the right lessons. My forecast is that people will forget and go back to normal life. This is the most probable outcome of everything, and it is silly. But we live in a world where "the show must go on."

The main lesson is that you cannot win the war against violence if you don't try to win the war against poverty. Our enemy is not Islam. Our enemy is poverty. No one can win that war alone.

I am involved in a large project to use the new technologies to speed up the process of the poor to create their own jobs. We have created an NGO based in Paris, that uses an Internet platform to assist in the development of microfinance institutions, which are banks helping the very poor to finance their own businesses and create jobs. This is *climatefinance.org*.

What the net can do is plug in the very poor to access finance, training, and institutions so they can participate in the world economy.

GOVERNMENTS CAN HELP MAKE REGIONAL WEALTH IN THE INNOVATION ECONOMY: A DIALOGUE BETWEEN KAILASH JOSHI AND DAVIDI GILO

To conclude our quest for perspectives from entrepreneurial champions, we present a dialogue between leaders in the Innovation Economy, whom you may recall from Chapters 1 and 2.

Kailash Joshi is from India, and is the Silicon Valley president of TiE (The IndUS Entrepreneurs), a multinational NGO, with 30 chapters and 10,000 members, dedicated to entrepreneurial advancement. He started his career on the research faculty of Cornell University in New York and had a distinguished career with IBM that spanned 23 years. He was the general manager of IBM Lexington, which is now Lexmark. Now retired, he devotes his time to TIE, which he helped found in 1992.

Davidi Gilo is from Israel and founded DSP Communications, which pioneered software development for the answering machine and other communications devices. He sold that company to Intel in 1999. In recent years he has been part of a high-tech international consortium advising the Israeli government on government policy on technology.

While both reside in Silicon Valley, each has maintained close interest in and contact with his native country's government to help them be more competitive in the global economy. They provide their perspectives in the hope that governments around the world, and the institutions in their countries, will work to make regional wealth increase everywhere.

In their dialogue, they discuss several areas that are essential for developing world governments to address if they want to be competitive in a free market environment: tax structures, employee stock options, company stock buy-backs, opening up telecommunications, company privatization, and the need to eliminate corruption and special interest protection.

GOVERNMENT POLICY MUST BE A PART OF CREATING REGIONAL COMPETITIVENESS

Joshi ■ The biggest hurdle for entrepreneurship, other than money, is protective government policy. This is particularly true of countries like India where they have had very socialistic, bureaucratic, and slow government processes, very similar to Israel, and have been very protective of the local industry.

At TiE, our interest in entrepreneurship is rooted in the Silicon Valley culture: freewheeling, risk taking, and finding new ways to do things.

Along with the Silicon Valley culture, we build upon the very strong cultural heritage of India. It is the guru-chela /teacher-disciple tradition of how all arts, music, and even religion was taught in India. Generation after generation, knowledge was passed that way. The teacher imparts knowledge and experience, but the student also stimulates the process with the currency of questions as well as the new realities. TiE combines these two traditions.

India is opening up its market. At this stage, they are probably 60% open in relation to where they need to be. The rules have been relaxed and the bureaucratic process simplified. In the last five years, the government has become very receptive to outside ideas. Prior to that, its attitude toward those of us who were successful in high tech and wanted to help was, "We know what is best for our people and the country. Don't come here and give us this unsound advice. You do your own things; you left this country, come and visit us but don't bother us with your ideas."

Significant changes have occurred. The end of the Cold War may have had something to do with opening minds. In addition, the significant human flow back and forth, between the U.S. and India, and the explosion in international TV channels have helped Indians see the possibilities for themselves.

I have seen a sea change in the attitude and receptivity of the government relative to changes in areas such as tax structure, duty rates, venture capital, telecommunication policies, and privatization. Very positive changes are taking place in India.

Several Indian companies have now been listed on the Nasdaq, or issued ADRs (American depository receipt) on the New York Stock Exchange. Such listings will probably double in 2002, despite the global economic slowdown. So the U.S.

and Indian financial markets are getting cemented together. This is the most effective way of strengthening the relationship between two countries. This also increases the two-way flow of people between them.

HOW TIE CAN WORK BEST TO BE A CHANGE AGENT FOR INDIAN GOVERNMENT POLICIES

Joshi ■ At TiE we found that official committees on policy matters do not seem to work; they are more fanfare than content. The most effective way we have found to change government policy is to host conferences on various topics and issues at Stanford University. Each year we host an India Economic Policy Conference. Last year, it was on financial markets and privatization. In prior years, the topics were telecommunications policy and venture and tax structure, particularly in relation to venture capital.

Next year, we may focus on the federal-state relationship in India. This will get us in to the geopolitical issues, because part of India's problems also stem from the fact that the Indian states often feel they do not enjoy sufficient autonomy.

In these conferences, we typically invite world-class speakers. For example, last year's invitees included former Clinton administration Treasury Secretary Larry Sommers, former Reagan administration Secretary of State George Schultz, and several faculty members from the business school at Stanford. The Indian invitees included the finance minister and other high-level government decision makers as well as economists, journalists, and entrepreneurs. These are the people who affect policy changes. The decision-makers go home from these conferences well armed with facts and figures that allow them to persuade their colleagues in parliamentary debates and other venues.

Each year so far, the outcome of the conference has been instrumental in helping with some concrete changes in Indian economic policies.

Government officials need the backup information and rationale to protect the bureaucracy and the politicians. For example, how they might deal with the flak for shutting down public-sector companies or the reaction of the traditionally protected domestic companies. The prevailing perspective is that you cannot shut down factories since they employ thousands of people, even though they have lost money consistently for the last 30 years. Well, this makes for heated debates within the government and among the public.

The sensible analysis tells us that we need to deal with these problems separately. You cannot sustain a nonprofitable venture that uses public funds and has no hope of turnaround. Nor can you have high unemployment rates, because that destabilizes the nation. The answer invariably revolves around encouraging the private sector to go after new business and entrepreneurial opportunities. Government needs to get out of the way.

Gilo ■ The issue of privatization is a big one in Israel. The government directly or indirectly still employs one-third of the labor force.

Joshi ■ In India, the numbers are significantly higher, because the government is still making bread and steel.

Gilo ■ It's really amazing to hear the similarities of the two countries. What I found effective in Israel is that every couple of years, we deal with one of the issues. For the past few years, we have been fighting with the government on tax structure or tax payment of venture capital. The regulations were structured to make it unattractive, especially for a foreign venture value fund, to invest in Israel, since they already have to pay taxes in their home country. The Israeli government officials think, "Why should we give up the taxes?" The answer is because they invest in the U.S., they pay taxes in the U.S. They don't pay taxes in Israel. I'm sure in India, it's the same kind of situation.

We have to convince government officials of the benefits of having additional capital coming into the country, generating jobs and stimulating the economy. So what if taxes go out? You get those funds back in a different way. That kind of thing is difficult to change in Israel. In fact, there were significant venture capital firms who decided not to come to Israel.

In the mid 1980s, Israel was not structured for stock options at all. Every time you got stock options you got the tax hit on the day you got the option. The poor employees never had any money to pay taxes; they were

> *The answer revolves around encouraging the private sector to go after new business and entrepreneurial opportunities.*

penalized for getting the stock option. It took many years to get the government to change the stock options regulations. We approached individual bureaucrats, patiently working through different organizations within the high-tech industry and chambers of commerce. And finally we got those changes through.

Once we got these changes through, the Israeli government became smarter. They just looked at what had been done here in Silicon Valley and adopted it. The initial response was, "We got revenues from tax money. Why shouldn't we get it for stock options?" Not knowing and understanding unique technology markets, governments have to make these changes to be competitive.

Joshi ■ The concept of stock options didn't exist in India until 1997. These were first introduced when Indian companies such as Infosys (a major Indian software company) first listed on the Nasdaq in the U.S. Since knowledge workers move back and forth between the two countries, the Indian high-tech workers were saying, "Wait a minute, we do what the U.S. workers do, but they get much higher salaries and have options on the company's stock. So, at the urging of the global companies, the government had to adopt stock options in a hurry.

Gilo ■ In Israel, it started with people like me. I was based in the United States for more than 20 years. I gave stock options to the U.S. employees, because here you have no choice if you want to be competitive. And I felt very strange because most of our employees were in Israel. The technology was in Israel, and the U.S. staff was mostly management, marketing, and sales positions. How can most of the people who make the greatest contribution, the innovations and the technology, not get stock options, while over here, every secretary had stock options? It didn't seem fair.

I fought to change it. And we did fund it before stock options were in effect in Israel; we did phantom plans with all kinds of mechanisms. We could write a whole book on how we can circumvent the tax issues presented by stock options, until we have stock options to give to people.

In Israel, the Day's Calendar Is Changed by Somebody Else

Gilo ■ When Ariel Sharon won the Israel election for prime minister in 2001, one of his focal points was the economy. He has a strong background based on economics having served as Israel's finance minister, minister of industrial development, and housing minister. He was mindful of needed economic changes. But there are days when he wakes up in the morning and suddenly there is an attack on a bus and 10 people have been killed. His day is changed and the economic policies become less urgent. You and I have more control of our daily calendar than he does.

We prepared a report with a significant list of changes. I believe Sharon was honestly committed to doing something about it. But the mindset of everybody in Israel is now on security for daily life, not paying attention to the economy.

On the Issues of Opening Up Telecommunications

Joshi ■ The telecom monopoly of the government was the most glaring example of the socialistic policies of the Indian government. After waiting for years for a telephone hook up, the Indian consumer was given very poor quality service at exorbitant costs. Some of the common problems of India and Israel come from their common past, rooted in the British colonial system. When economic policies do change, the results are impressive. The changes in venture tax laws have led to significant increases in venture capital activities in India. The employee productivity among Indian high-tech companies is comparable to the U.S., and stock options have something to do with this. Open telecom is already showing improvements in the quality and cost of service to the Indian consumer that would have been unimaginable only a few years ago.

Gilo ■ In Israel the cable, steel, and big telephone companies are all government owned. Really, there's no second carrier. Cellular is the only area in telecom that is open.

Joshi ■ In India, one very interesting thing happened. The government could not regulate cable TV. So, the imaginative small entrepreneurs decided to provide this service to their own neighborhoods. Around their own satellite dish, they pulled the cables and wired the neighborhood without any government approvals. For a nominal monthly charge the consumers enjoy some 60 channels, and about 50 million households are connected with the world. The government scratched its head and could not come up with any existing laws that prohibited this phenomenon. Well, these cable signals are quite like sunshine and they thought they could regulate sunshine, but couldn't. So you have this flourishing cottage industry. Now we hear the same entrepreneurs want to do something similar for household telephony. I would love for it to happen. After all, no one can regulate sunshine!

Gilo ■ When you look at high-tech business in India today, is there any focal point that through government intervention/assistance you have concentrated upon? Has your focus moved, for example to software development versus telecommunications or semiconductors, or is it all over the place?

Joshi ■ The role of government in India is a very interesting story. In 1963 India had a massive problem in not being able to feed itself. So the government got out of the way and gave the farmers freedom, facilities, and tax incentives to grow and India today not only feeds its one billion citizens, but also outproduces the U.S. in agriculture, dairy, poultry, etc. It also has the largest reserve of food grains. This is truly an impressive story of supportive government actions.

Next comes the example of India's successful software industry. Here, the government did not quite know what it was and how to deal with it. They gave the industry export tax incentives in days when India was faced with a foreign exchange crisis. But, by and large, the government has stayed out and the results are there to see. Contrast this with the performance of the Indian hardware industry and there is not much to write home about. The governments had ridiculous requirements of domestic content in each product and import duty rates were sometimes several hundred percent. This led to inferior, expensive, and often outdated products, with very limited product options available to Indian consumers. The domestic hardware manufacturers had no incentive to be competitive under these protections.

Now, things have changed for hardware too. The automobile, television, and personal computer industries are great examples of the positive changes taking place in the Indian hardware manufacturing sector. Virtually every world-class manufacturer is now engaged there and some are finding India an attractive source of exports, such as the Mercedes cars being shipped from India to neighboring countries.

There are governmental bodies for long-term policy making, but the private industry associations are playing an increasingly effective role in shaping new policy changes in India.

DO NOT TRY TO REPLICATE SILICON VALLEY — SILICON VALLEY AS WE KNEW IT DOES NOT EXIST ANYMORE

Gilo ■ Any region or company thinking they can recreate Silicon Valley as a self-contained region is wrong. Even here in Silicon Valley, the Silicon Valley we knew does not exist any more. We are in a global technology market. That means today Hewlett-Packard manufactures in India, they may manufacture in Ireland, and they may do R&D or some product development in Israel. And they have huge resources, incredible marketing, strongly promote their brand name, and have stood for quality for many years.

Joshi ■ I think that's where the governments might be in the dark. Free markets are ultimately the drivers of the world's economy and the determinants of individual company or industry sector success. The global free market, for example, is going to decide whether the Israeli security software is the best or not, and if the Brazilians can come up with better software in this area, then the industry in a few years will shift to Brazil. No government can alter that reality. So, Ireland or any other region can dream all they want about being the next semiconductor hub. The reality is that they will have to outperform the Taiwanese and the Koreans who have become the masters of this sector. By the way, I think there will be only one Silicon Valley in our lifetime. You need that kind of ambience, spirit, infrastructure, risk capital, very supportive government framework, and, above all, the diversity of ideas. That is what Silicon Valley represents. And it has been in the making for over 50 years.

> *Any region or company thinking they can recreate Silicon Valley as a self-contained region is wrong.*

What is more likely is the emergence of global centers of excellence stemming from the core competency of a region and the associated economics. Local factors and global economics will determine which region does what best. If you can grow apples better than others, why use the land for growing almonds?

IS THERE A NET GAIN OR BRAIN DRAIN?

Joshi ■ I have some very strong feelings on the subject of so-called brain drain. A government that believes that it controls the destiny of its people will fail and will be finally rejected by its people. When a government dictates who does what business, who gets what salary, who gets stock options, and who can go where, it has made the country non-competitive. Only the people in business and the entrepreneurs can establish the position of their nation in the world markets. Enlightened governments provide the policy framework and infrastructure to maximize the potential of their citizens.

In India, after independence in 1947, with its socioeconomic policies, the government strongly instilled the feelings of *maibap*, (*mai* means mother, *bap* means father). Government became maibap and people looked at it as the provider and protector. This also related to the preceding British system where the king held the power and gave a little of it to the people. Contrast this with the U.S., where people held the power and gave some of it to the government.

So when there was talk of brain drain in India during the '70s and '80s, the government had the view of its people as national property. Their departure from India for pursuit of personal goals was described as brain drain.

On the other hand countries of Europe and Israel did not look at their people the same way. Free flow of people became an accepted part of these societies, as it was seen as a positive aspect of becoming competitive. Therefore, it seems to me that flow of people between free countries leads to economic ties, which can more than compensate for any net immigration. This is more so today where one can create economic value around the world without large investments.

Specifically speaking, the immigration from India to the U.S. has created hundreds of new companies, thousands of new jobs around the world and joint ventures in India. Furthermore, the immigrants are assisting the educational and training institutions there in significant ways. Much of this would not have happened if they had stayed behind, because the environment was not conducive for such economic activities.

Gilo ■ In Israel, it's a bit different because of the political or the military situation of people who serve a month in the reserves every year. Also the population is small. People sometimes do not understand Israel and how it can keep up with the situation. There are other factors that prompt people to leave the country, not just economic or government restriction on business. In general, I think it's the same way. If you look at the overall, even I am looking at my own experience of coming here, without taking anything out from Israel, no wealth, nothing, and over the last 15 years, I employed thousands of people in Israel and gave them stock options. When I sold DSP to Intel, the Israeli government made a few $100 million in taxes, revenues collected from stock options.

You have cases of those who have been very successful, go back to Israel and become venture capitalists. So the venture capital community in Israel became sophisticated very quickly by having Israel move, develop and learn from the experience of the U.S. market. All those exchanges are very important.

People who live in Israel were very derogatory about those who left. In the last five to seven years it has changed. You needn't defend yourself about why you are not in Israel, I think because of globalization and the connections between professionals. For a long time, you had to say, right now I'm in Silicon Valley, *but* I'll come back to Israel. Now you can say wherever you are, you don't need to defend yourself. You don't need the *but* anymore.

Joshi ■ The beauty in the knowledge economy is that even if you don't go back there, you may send a small division of the company to create jobs and markets. So, I am convinced that if the movement between people is between two democracies that also are free markets, then the broad question of brain drain should not arise.

To be sure though, brain drain is a real phenomenon and happens when people either leave for oppressive reasons or have no interest in the land of their origin, such as the Jews leaving the Soviet Union during the Communist regime.

THE RESPONSIBILITIES OF THE HIGH-TECH INDUSTRIES AND THE REGIONS THAT ARE MAKING WEALTH TO THE REST OF THE WORLD

Gilo ■ When I look at globalization, the governments, and the free markets, there is no balance today, obviously between people that have and people that have not. And part of the issue we are facing in Afghanistan is not just the religious phenomenon in some soil. People are frustrated because they don't have the basic needs of life; and with the communication today, everyone sees everything on CNN everyday. Before, the ability of the people in poor regions to see or understand what the wealthy nations had was very remote. Now everybody sees everything and where cooperation between industries, governments, and countries has to take place is really looking at those issues, because we can't continue with the way we lead our life like that.

There are a lot of issues to globalization that are not easy to deal with, such as the environment, employment, and distribution of wealth, that we have to be much more concerned about. Especially those of us who can bring new resources and approaches to how to do it, not in the bureaucratic way, and not in the big government way, but still deal with those issues.

Joshi ■ I fully agree with these concerns. The biggest challenge of globalization is indeed the responsibility of the "haves" in a nation toward the global "have nots." You can't just stay cocooned in the U.S. The shocking and tragic events of September 11 clearly brought home the message that care must be extended to the have nots everywhere in some fashion.

Gilo ■ Maybe some of the things in the high-tech arena that people are doing in industry can be applied to world problems. So, the emergence of the philanthropic foundations of the people who make a lot of money, through NGOs, play a significant role in third world countries. Look at Bill Gates, for example. He gave huge amounts of money to fight AIDS and distribute medicines to third world nations (through the Bill and Melinda Gates Foundation). But we have to deal with it and our governments have to deal with it. We can't just be takers. We have to be givers as well.

HUMAN RESOURCES MANAGEMENT IN THE INNOVATION ECONOMY: SELF-MANAGED LIVING SYSTEMS

By Thierry Picq, Professor at E.M. LYON

To thrive, high-tech companies must excel at the management of human capital: human resources systems and practices. These systems, like their technology counterparts, have to be highly innovative and, at times, unorthodox to satisfy the demands of this unique business environment. It is evident that this population of autonomous, techno-literate, mobile, and entrepreneurial knowledge workers cannot be satisfied by classic human resource management (HRM) systems based on an industrial context for dominantly worker populations with little education who are looking for stability and security. Traditional approaches seem to be ill adapted to knowledge workers, who are in a position to set the HR agenda.

THE HUMAN CONTEXT OF IE COMPANIES

Companies operating within successful IE regions share some common attributes. They are highly adaptive, flexible, self-renewing, and emphasize learning. They are also fragile and sometimes irrational. In these companies experimentation is the norm, local solutions predominate, participation and individual contributions are encouraged, and there are fewer levels of management. Employees of high-tech companies don't believe in top-down approaches and have the capacity to self-organize without any externally imposed plan or direction. They build communities of practices (virtual or not), self-managed teams, and networks of relationships. Change is the organizing force in these companies, not a problematic intrusion. And leaders emerge from the need of the moment. High-tech companies are in some ways self-managed living systems.

AN EMPHASIS ON KNOWLEDGE WORKERS AND KNOWLEDGE-BASED COMPANIES

Grassroots companies in the IE are different from the more traditional industrial ones according to four main dimensions: the nature of the task they perform, the nature of the asset they provide, the nature of the work force, and the nature of the value creation process itself. Thinking in the IE is shaped by computer technology. The average number of computers per home (including non–high-tech workers) in Silicon Valley is 1.7. One-third of Israeli homes have a computer. And 65% of the Finnish population is online.

THE NATURE OF THE TASK

Knowledge-intensive tasks have to deal with problem solving and non-standardized operations where creativity is needed. Intellectual processes are emphasized to transform information, as opposed to labor-intensive or capital-intensive operations, to transform raw materials.

THE NATURE OF THE ASSET

Knowledge-intensive companies mostly rely on individual intelligence and are less dependent on material assets. What is critical is in the minds of employees. For these companies, market value far outstrips conventional assets and rests instead on intellectual capital.

These domains have their rules and one must be admitted into the right networks. This admission depends on personal reputation, competence, and the respect of local customs. You have to be a recognized professional and know how to give as much information as you receive. In these environments, it is assumed that a person is worth what his projects are worth. Professionals who work in Silicon Valley don't have relationships, but references. In regions of strong immigration, nationality networks can also play a role in situations where the risk of isolation exists.

Executives move from high-tech companies into venture capital, professionals teach in the universities, and R&D labs are the grassroots for future entrepreneurs. Many faculty members are also advisors, consultants, and board members. Venture capitalists are often involved in the management of start-ups. At Stanford business school half of the students are directly or indirectly involved in a venture project. The famous institution has incubated numerous successful technologies and companies, among them Silicon Graphics, Sun Microsystems, and Yahoo.

THE NATURE OF THE WORK FORCE

The workers of the IE have abandoned the idea of a job for life within one organization. They are looking for an employer of choice who will enable them to develop, to meet challenges, and to work with brilliant people on exciting projects — all while earning a lot of money.

A significant proportion of the personnel in knowledge-based firms have advanced education (engineers, Ph.D., MS) and a high degree of professionalism through experience. They posses complex, domain-specific expertise that does not readily transfer to other unrelated activities. Workplace demographics have also shifted significantly with the addition of a younger generation that has learned self-reliance. They have a direct style, act as independent problem-solvers, are attracted to a risk-laden environment, and are willing to be more mobile and impulsive regarding career opportunities.

Employees appear far more loyal to innovation than to their employers. Coupled with the absence of a stigma for changing jobs regularly, this attitude often results in rapid turnover of employees.

THE NATURE OF THE VALUE CREATION PROCESS

In knowledge-intensive companies, the added value is created directly by individuals, based upon their expertise, creativity, energy, and talent, rather than associated with the organization's routines, organized work processes, size, or volume factors. Innovation or even anti-conformist behavior is highly regarded. The HP commercial shown worldwide depicting a child inventing his own toy, with the voiceover *"He could work for us!"* was a perfect example of how highly independent thinking is valued.

Hierarchics lose meaning in this context. Many executives (notably in HR) don't have titles on their business cards, where only their name is printed. When they are asked why, they reply in the following way: *"If I don't have a title on my business card, it's because my function is not a lasting one. Today, I have an added value for the company as vice president of HR. Tomorrow, I may be most valuable as a simple collaborator, in a project team."*

In addition, proximity within a small and well-defined geographic location enables formal and informal networking and a rapid transmission of information, knowledge, ideas, resources, and technology. This phenomenon is sometimes called the "Internet paradox," to underline the importance of physical location in a virtual medium.[1]

Finally, the IE has been characterized by unequalled growth over a very short period. From 1995 to 2000, more than 300,000 jobs were created in Silicon Valley. Almost one-third of all the world's venture capital went to feed its frenzied appetite for development. Nearly 10 new firms were incorporated every day. Even with the financial downturn of 2001–2002, it seems that high-tech activities will contribute to the long-term economic growth.

A MODEL FOR HRM IN THE IE

Four core principles are important to HRM in the IE: developing human capital through individual talents; developing social capital through communities of practices and networks; developing agility, learning capabilities, and readiness for innovation; and developing new leadership skills.

DEVELOPING INDIVIDUAL TALENTS FOR KNOWLEDGE-INTENSIVE ORGANIZATIONS

The challenge human resources managers face is how to get the best talent and make the most of individual resources, competencies and skills.

The basic tenets of human resources, defining the work to be done and the parameters under which the work will be done and setting pay scales based on measurable and defined criteria, have not changed in this IE, but new kinds of employee/company relationships have emerged, as follows.

- **Work style** — Employees perform project-based work and must learn to be self-reliant and self-sufficient.
- **Contingency relationships** — Companies adjust their human resources on short notice according to their needs. In environments where the social legislation is less restrictive (as in the U.S.) some companies go as far as to adapt their recruitment to the phases of a project.
- **Individualized relationships** — Roles, salaries, and career possibilities are determined by individual talents and performance more than by industry negotiations that set general pay and classifications systems.
- **Contractual relationships** — the organization's day-to-day life is structured around short-term and project-based relationships.

In a context of qualified work force shortages, intense competition to attract top talent, and high employee turnover, the traditional competence-based approach has limited efficacy. High-tech companies face three critical issues over time: attracting more talented employees, developing their skills, and allowing them to grow as the company grows to retain the best performers. Therefore, new approaches must be invented in recruitment, training, and retention.

Inventing New Recruitment Processes

Buying individual knowledge on the open market still remains the basic solution to rapidly increasing a firm's intellectual capital. In a competitive climate of low unemployment, firms need to create an employee value proposition or brand that distinguishes them among the potential employee market.

In addition, new recruitment approaches must be developed. The hiring decision is more and more disconnected from available jobs or assignments. High-tech firms generate contacts, watch for the best on an ongoing basis, and try to hire them and then fit them to a job. For example, some companies are paying employees referral bonuses (as much as $3,000) for recommending a qualified worker. Cisco Systems recruits 50% to 60% of its new hires through referrals from its Friends Program. For HR managers, outside networks can represent fertile sources for finding talent and understanding the dynamics of the job marketplace.

Finding the Right Retention Package

Once people are hired, organizations must retain them. The average job tenure in Silicon Valley is 2 years,[2] compared with 3.5 years in high-tech start-ups in other places in the United States or 6.5 years for the mining industry.[3] In knowledge-based industries, losing talent is no longer an HR issue; it's a business issue. A company with 50,000 employees and an annual 6% turnover rate incurs replacement costs approaching $18 million a year.

There is no silver bullet that will retain skilled employees. It takes a package including such amenities as equitable pay, rewards and recognition, training and development, cutting-edge technology, interesting projects, and on-site services such as childcare, shopping centers, and laundry facilities. In addition, each company has its distinctive and more visible favorite tool: stock options for Cisco, continuous training for Hewlett-Packard, intellect challenge for Genentech, teamwork at Quantum, a friendly atmosphere and fun at Peoplesoft, etc. Some of these companies view this tool to be so important that they have created a vice president for retention.

Evolving from Training to Learning Processes

Developing a resilient and adaptive work force requires new training methods. One of the current practices is to encourage a "self-reliance" approach in employees' professional development. High-tech companies are interested in the idea of self-reliance because they hope that employees will adapt more quickly to change and commit to creating a learning environment at every level of the organization. IBM calls its program Career Fitness Service, using the fitness analogy to suggest that career development should be viewed as something you do continuously to keep in shape professionally.

Traditional training has to be redefined for the high-tech context. Learning time must be provided at the right moment, when needed. People want to be convinced that it is useful, especially in learning non-technical skills. Therefore, training should focus on end results and place learners in control. To accomplish this, training methods are evolving toward action learning (using role play, simulation learning, just-in-time training, and in-the-moment coaching) with more flexibility in the choice of locations, times, and media.

FOSTERING SOLIDARITY, COOPERATION, AND CROSS-FERTILIZATION AMONG INDIVIDUALS: SOCIAL CAPITAL

Social capital is another key asset in knowledge-based companies. Sharing the same culture and shared values builds a sense of community. At HP for example, the "HP way" and its "rules of the garage" promotes each employee as a member of an extended family. This culture can be witnessed through a company's expressed mission, or vision statement, such as 3Com's "to transform the way people live, work, communicate and learn thanks to information technologies." A company's culture is also based on myths, former projects, outstanding innovations, and extraordinary personalities that become role models for all employees. Culture replaces structure as an organizational principle and values are used both to explain and guide action.

HR plays an important role in encouraging common values, informal networks, and communities within a company, allowing the company to develop its social capital and collective intelligence. In high tech, the most used organizational form is modular projects that keep the responsibility at the level of small and relatively autonomous small groups.

DEVELOPING AGILITY: IN SEARCH OF "FAST HR"

High-tech industry executives call for a flexible and fast HR that delivers instant services to line managers, finds alternative options to expensive and time-consuming training classes, and replaces complex job descriptions with flexible roles. The HR function must be prepared to quickly adjust everything for which it is responsible. Complex information management systems allow people to create, link, and share information from a variety of media such as text, graphics, audio, video and image, across time zones and distance both from within and outside the organization.

DEVELOPING NEW LEADERSHIP SKILLS: A NEW MANAGEMENT MODEL FOR THE IE

Leadership is important to the development of knowledge-based companies because it helps build a cohesive vision for the flexible and unbounded companies of the IE as well as cohesive work units. The conception of leadership itself is changing in the IE. New expectations, roles, and skills are emerging, far from the traditional management approach of command and control.

MANAGING IS LIKE GARDENING

A commonly used analogy in the U.S. when speaking of this change, is gardening management. Like a gardener, who cannot control the elements (rain, sun, drought), the manager must cope with a number of external hazards. All the manager and the gardener can do is imagine their garden in a near future and to do their best in order to make it happen (sow seeds, water just enough, protect specific plants, leave others to develop themselves, weed, turn over the soil, cut and trim where necessary, add peat, etc.). The gardener (like the manager) has to nurture an environment that will allow the garden (or his project and objectives) to grow as planned, so that the seeds (and the teams he is in charge of) develop and give their best.

Rather than representing perfection, the multi-skilled manager, the "new" manager-gardener, quite simply reflects a different way of managing, neither good nor bad in itself, but better adapted to more complex and transversal situations, where hierarchical authority does not work as well as uniting and motivating.

So, knowledge-based companies are using new approaches to help leaders grow. Employees are developed through a combination of formal external education, in-house training, career-pathing systems, succession planning, team projects, on-the-job experience, and mentoring. This process is more than a series of isolated events. Continuous on-the-job activities replace the traditional program approach, which was composed mostly of discrete training events.

New leaders are no longer identified through the traditional great performers model. Now the process is as important as the result, and some basic leadership skills such as risk taking, relationship building, leading change, and having an entrepreneurial mindset must be taken into account. Companies are beginning to track innovations back to the source to identify the people who played key roles and who seem willing and capable of challenging the status quo.

SUMMARY

The HR model for the IE is not ideal. Skill-based management may better recognize human intelligence, but it can also mean the end of people protection mechanisms and evaluation systems that are more brutal. Furthermore, the reality of high technology is often formed out of professional contexts where the pressure is very high, where the competition is always very tough and where working hours are endless. The terms *burn-out* and *work/life balance* frequently crop up in the analyses,[4] and raise the question about what happens to those who are not top talents. Although building strong company culture has been instrumental in the success of some companies, it may also increase pressure and social control, putting employees at risk of being irrevocably excluded by their peers if they do not respect the behavioral norms of the community. Similarly, the inherent flexibility and pace of change in the high-tech world can be difficult for some. Finally, gardener management can be nothing but a manipulation in a world where profits and keeping the shareholders happy are the only real indicators of success.

In short, the regions that are going to develop will be those who offer the best infrastructures in terms of training, quality of life, and network dynamics. The companies of the future will be those who best know how to develop their human and social capital. And successful individuals will be those who constantly learn and take risks to invent new models.

ENDNOTES

1. Joint Venture: Silicon Valley Network, *www.jointventure.org*.
2. Paul Mackun, "Silicon Valley and Route 128: Two Faces of the American Technopolis," *www.internetvalley.com/archives/mirrors/sv&128.html*.
3. U.S. Labor Statistics Office, 2000, *stats.bls.gob/news.release/tenure.nr0.htm*.
4. For example, the weekly working hours of high-tech firms employees are on average 30% above the standard in the U.S.

▶ *About the Author*

This appendix was written by **Thierry Picq**, professor of human resources management at E.M. LYON, a leading French business school. Thierry teaches both students (master's in management and MBA) and executives in the fields of organizational behavior, team management, and project management. He was previously a consultant in the largest French consultancy company, Bossard/Gemini Consulting, where he carried out many projects in organizational change and management development for large French and international companies.

INDEX

8 reasons why you should read the Financial Times for 4 weeks RISK-FREE!

To help you stay current with significant
developments in the world economy ...
and to assist you to make informed business
decisions — the Financial Times brings you:

① Fast, meaningful overviews of international affairs ... plus daily
briefings on major world news.

② Perceptive coverage of economic, business, financial and political
developments with special focus on emerging markets.

③ More international business news than any other publication.

④ Sophisticated financial analysis and commentary on world market
activity plus stock quotes from over 30 countries.

⑤ Reports on international companies and a section on global investing.

⑥ Specialized pages on management, marketing, advertising and
technological innovations from all parts of the world.

⑦ Highly valued single-topic special reports (over 200 annually)
on countries, industries, investment opportunities, technology and more.

⑧ The Saturday Weekend FT section — a globetrotter's guide to
leisure-time activities around the world: the arts, fine dining, travel,
sports and more.

FT FINANCIAL TIMES
World business newspaper

The *Financial Times* delivers a world of business news.

Use the Risk-Free Trial Voucher below!

To stay ahead in today's business world you need to be well-informed on a daily basis. And not just on the national level. You need a news source that closely monitors the entire world of business, and then delivers it in a concise, quick-read format.

With the *Financial Times* you get the major stories from every region of the world. Reports found nowhere else. You get business, management, politics, economics, technology and more.

Now you can try the *Financial Times* for 4 weeks, absolutely risk free. And better yet, if you wish to continue receiving the *Financial Times* you'll get great savings off the regular subscription rate. Just use the voucher below.